Women in American History

Series Editors
Mari Jo Buhle
Jacquelyn D. Hall
Anne Firor Scott

A list of books in the series appears at the end of this volume.

CIVIL WARS

CIVIL WARS

Women and the Crisis of Southern Nationalism

GEORGE C. RABLE

UNIVERSITY OF ILLINOIS PRESS
Urbana and Chicago

Illini Books edition, 1991
© 1989 by the Board of Trustees of the University of Illinois
Manufactured in the United States of America
P 5 4 3

This book is printed on acid-free paper

Library of Congress Cataloging-in-Publication Data

Rable, George C.
  Civil Wars : women and the crisis of Southern nationalism / George
C. Rable.
        p.   cm.
  Bibliography: p.
  ISBN 0-252-06212-4
  1. United States—History—Civil War, 1861–1865—Women.
2. Confederate States of America—History. 3. Women—Southern
States—History—19th century. I. Title.
E628.R3 1989
973.7′15′042—dc19   88-23242
                                                                   CIP

For Kay, Anne, and Katie

and

To the memories of
John D. Unruh, Jr.
and
T. Harry Williams

Contents

Preface

THIS BOOK IS ABOUT THE SOUTH, about women, and about the Confederacy. Putting three such apparently disparate subjects together may still strike some readers as odd. Anyone familiar with mainstream Southern history knows how short a shrift has been given women in both the scholarly and popular literature. So too Confederate studies— long dominated by historians whose primary interests lay in military and political history—have been largely untouched by the sources, methods, and questions of the new social history.

The time has come for a work of original research and synthesis that tries to make appropriate connections among these areas of inquiry. Complicated questions about the relationship of gender, class, race, and regional identity led me to examine the roles and status of white women in a society based on a racial, class, and sexual hierarchy. How did white women of various classes assimilate, adjust to, embrace, change, or rebel against their society's definitions of woman's place? To what extent did the Civil War undermine their social identity, their view of themselves, their world?

The war itself brought many of these questions into sharper focus. Historians long have argued that war often causes unintended social changes, especially for women, who are suddenly expected to do many tasks normally reserved to men. Indeed the Lost Cause celebrations of Confederate women along with the early historical treatments of their tribulations celebrated heroic womanhood on a grand scale. But for historians who have been more interested in women than in the Confederacy, the war presents many interpretative difficulties. Although Anne Firor Scott has argued that the Civil War undermined the Southern patriarchy and opened important doors of opportunity (at least for some upper-class women) and although Suzanne Lebsock and Jean Friedman have entered qualified dissents, historians have not given much attention to the war itself. In most work in nineteenth-century Southern women's history, the war has been either something to be hurried through in order to consider more important topics or simply an epilogue to the story of women in the antebellum South. But for many white women, the Civil War was central to their lives, and for this reason alone, wartime experiences deserve more careful scrutiny.

During this great crisis of Southern nationalism, women as well as men had to decide where their loyalties lay. But for women, these decisions were more problematic. Historians have often emphasized women's expressions of discontent with life in the South, especially discontent with slavery. But in so diligently searching out dissenters—and in a few cases trying to turn them into not only abolitionists but also closet feminists—these scholars have largely ignored women who buttressed as well as suffered from the status quo.

The war therefore sheds considerable light on the responses of women to a conservative (in some ways, a reactionary) social order. To view Southern women as either seething with discontent or mindlessly mouthing the truisms of their society is to ignore their painful and often deeply ambivalent roles as social actors—actors who might occasionally criticize but who also could bolster their society's basic and often unspoken assumptions. Indeed the old image of die-hard female Confederates contains its own inverted combination of myth and insight. By the end of the war, many women wavered in their support for the Southern cause, but they seldom questioned the racial, class, and sexual dogmas of their society. White women shared certain experiences common to their sex but also functioned as members of a supposedly superior race as well as members of particular economic and social classes. The clashes among planters, yeomen, and poor whites—which the war had intensified—along with the poverty pervading much of the Confederate and postwar South, made racial and social distinctions seem even more important to women who had come of age in an environment steeped in a hierarchical tradition, a tradition that many women hoped to see restored.

In a sense, then, the war became a two-front conflict: a battle against the Yankees and at the same time a bitter, certainly an internal, and in many ways a cultural contest. And even though women could not vote, they were part of the political culture and helped both to sustain and to undermine Confederate economic and military policies. By absorbing and reinforcing traditional definitions of male and female honor, many white women helped their families, communities, and the South itself survive without abandoning the past. This fundamental conservatism, often based more on habit than on ideology, at the same time proved to be more flexible than anyone might have expected.

The themes of this study are broad ones, yet the reader should be warned of certain limits because it is often as helpful to define what a book is not as to define what it is. Although I have been influenced by both the substance and methods of the new social history, I have used quantification sparingly and generally have relied on traditional literary sources. This obviously brings an elite bias into my examination of the Southern economic and social structure, but for the war years, at least, direct statements from both yeoman and poor white women are relatively plentiful.

The quality of this evidence varies widely over the years covered by this study. Voluminous wartime correspondence between husbands and wives offers useful details on many aspects of Southern marriages. Likewise the letters sent to Confederate and state officials provide intimate glimpses into the daily lives of married and single women alike. Indeed scholars have relied too long on collections of family papers while ignoring the voluminous materials in public archives. But for Reconstruction and after, the available sources become thinner in both quantity and quality. There are few comments, for example, about the problems of restoring the day-to-day intimacy of marriage after the war. By the same token there is good information on widows seeking financial relief or trying to earn a living by teaching school, but these women seldom left behind diaries or letters that revealed the dimensions, character, and meaning of widowhood.

I had intended to include material on both black and white women in this book, but that would have lengthened considerably an already bulky manuscript. Given the recent work of Deborah Gray White and Jacqueline Jones, which ably treats many of the important questions about black women, I have chosen to maintain the focus on how women of the ruling race (though from varying economic classes) helped sustain the Southern social order. In making this decision, I have obviously forgone some interpretative opportunities and opened up others. Some readers may not be comfortable with this trade-off, and I certainly believe that a carefully balanced study of the relationships between black and white women, sensitive to the nuances of race, class, religion, social status, geography, and change over time, is long overdue.

By dealing with the entire Confederate South and by stretching the story back into the antebellum period and forward into Reconstruction, and even a bit beyond, I have also given up the advantages of a more restricted study of a single state, city, or county. Indeed much of the best recent work in women's history has carefully treated women's communities and what often have been called "female networks" in ways that the breadth of this study precluded. I am convinced that historians need to examine microscopically both the "interior" and social lives of Southern women, especially in small towns and the Southern country-side. Abundant census and local records suggest that much remains to be done by casting one's net deeply.

Casting a wide net brings its own rewards. Often overwhelmed by the cacophony of women's voices heard from Virginia to Texas, I have not grown tired of listening to them and have tried to make sense out of what sometimes sounded like a din, often like a chorus in a Greek tragedy, at still other times like a simple solo of joy or lamentation. Whether speaking about their daily round of activities, their views on public issues, their spiritual pilgrimages, or the dramatic events that shattered so many lives, Southern white women offered many penetrating observations about themselves, their families, the South, and the Confederacy.

Acknowledgments

THE MOST CASUAL PERUSAL OF THE NOTES will show how much this book depends on the unpublished diaries, letters, and official documents scattered in depositories from Washington, D.C., to Texas. On several research trips, I have been welcomed by librarians and archivists eager to share their treasures and assist in many other ways. For going beyond the call of duty in helpfulness and friendliness the staffs at the following institutions deserve special commendation: Manuscripts Department, William R. Perkins Library, Duke University; Southern Historical Collection, University of North Carolina; Alabama Department of Archives and History; Special Collections Department, Robert W. Woodruff Library, Emory University; Georgia Department of Archives and History; Special Collections, University of Georgia Library; and Department of Archives and Manuscripts, Louisiana State University. Renee Cruikshank and Jill Prichard of Anderson University responded promptly, creatively, and cheerfully to my many interlibrary loan requests.

Much of this research could not have been completed without generous financial support from several sources. A National Endowment for the Humanities summer seminar at the University of Virginia in 1982 allowed me to conduct brief research forays into Washington and Richmond. More important, I was able to work with William H. Harbaugh, who ever since has been a constant source of help and encouragement. Grants from the American Philosophical Society and the American Association for State and Local History supported completion of most of the manuscript research. A generous summer research grant from the

Indiana Committee for the Humanities gave me time to organize the material and begin writing. Anderson University provided a sabbatical leave during which I composed most of the first draft.

The number of students, colleagues, and friends who helped this project along is embarrassingly large. Douglas Brice, a former student, generously volunteered to search Confederate payroll records in the National Archives. Margaret and Dwight Agner kindly welcomed me into their home during a research jaunt to Athens, Georgia. My good friend Joseph G. ("Chip") Dawson III not only shared some helpful comments on the Union blockade but over the years has been a steady source of encouragement and good cheer. Another close friend, Will Greene, supplied me with several important documents and no small amount of diversion. Although he feigns indifference to anything a mere *historian* might do, my friend and colleague Doug Nelson has followed the progress (or lack of progress) of this project from the beginning and has patiently listened to my frequent laments. I will always be grateful to another friend and colleague, Glenn Nichols, for dragging me into the age of word processing, all the while showing great patience and good humor in answering all my neophyte questions, but I don't think I can ever forgive him for also introducing me to that unending source of frustration known in the awful jargon of the 1980s as database management. William J. Cooper, Jr., a former teacher and now valued friend, read some early chapters of this work and made his usual sharp and useful suggestions; over the years Bill has always supported me and my work in countless ways. Likewise Randy Roberts read the manuscript, made some helpful general suggestions, and provided excellent advice on questions concerning publication. Herbert H. Hyde copy-edited the manuscript with great care and made many improvements.

There are five people who were indispensable in every sense of that overworked word. My good friend Thomas E. Schott waded through chapter after chapter with his sharp eye for nonsense and bad style; Tommy's pointed criticisms improved every paragraph. From the beginning Lawrence J. Malley, Editor-in-Chief of the University of Illinois Press, has been enthusiastic about this project; Larry's encouragement and sound editorial judgment have been invaluable throughout the long transition from first draft to book. Anne Firor Scott read a bulky and rough early draft of the book and provided a wonderful critique that forced me to rethink the shape and thrust of the entire project. On matters of both interpretation and emphasis, her advice has been superb.

Jacquelyn Dowd Hall provided equally fine suggestions on straightening out interpretative snarls and likewise helped reorient the focus and direction of the arguments. I am happy to say that my wife, Kay, did no typing of the manuscript and was also spared from working on the index, though she cheerfully accompanied me on two early research trips, and I did persuade her to help read proofs. To mention spouses last is a long and not especially wise convention in publishing acknowledgments. But last does not mean least because without Kay's assistance, support, and love, I doubt that I could write history—or do much of anything else for that matter.

CHAPTER 1

Tradition, Change, and Uneasy Accommodation

AT EIGHTY-NINE, MYRTIE LONG CANDLER looked back on a long life in central Georgia and vividly recalled the security of an antebellum childhood. "Safety," she wrote, "was the keynote of my life. My world was intrinsic and self-sufficient. Pa would always be its benevolent ruler; Ma its gracious spirit of beauty; my brothers bulwarks of strength and fascinating personalities. The servants would always be my friends who could smooth every path for me. . . . My world could never change."[1] A planter's daughter had naturally seen life in the Old South as a cozy experience. Yet the very security which she then felt and which many other women—whether in plantation families or among their yeoman and poor white neighbors—so highly valued, was also fragile. By the end of the 1850s, this well-established social system faced its greatest challenge.

Southern historians have often stressed the patriarchal character of Southern society with special emphasis on its rigid definition of sex roles. But if patriarchy means male dominance over women and children—a set of beliefs and practices that cuts across many centuries and civilizations—then such a description is merely a truism.[2] The historian's interest should go further to examine the forms of patriarchy or the particular mechanisms through which female subordination was maintained in the South. And even here the notion of Southern distinctiveness often proves illusory—especially when changes in property and divorce law, to cite only two examples, took place in the South as well as in the supposedly more progressive Northeast.

What, then, makes the status and roles of women in the Southern states worthy of close study? As Gerda Lerner has remarked, women have often collaborated with men in maintaining their own subordinate position, and nowhere in the nineteenth-century United States was this truer than in the eleven states that would make up the Confederate States of America. Historians have often dwelt on women's expressions of discontent or even looked for the origins of a modern feminism in commonplace complaints; less attention has been paid to the ways in which women—both actively and passively—buttressed the existing social order (including slavery).

To be sure, some of this support was shaky and depended on maintaining the polite fiction of class unity. Despite common bonds of race, the willingness of yeomen, much less poor white women, to sustain an economy based on slavery and to embrace a hierarchical social order had distinct limits—limits that would become painfully apparent during the Civil War. By the same token, though the extent of dissatisfaction among upper-class women has been exaggerated, often based on a superficial reading of Mary Boykin Chesnut's "diary," female opinion was not monolithic. After all, even had they been so inclined, Southern women generally lacked both the power and the opportunity to challenge their society's cherished assumptions about proper female roles.

So although women did not uniformly embrace the value system of the Old South, they did much more to uphold than to undermine it. Nor should such support be surprising. To the extent that women managed to survive and even create their own culture in a male-dominated society, they remained wary of change. By the same token, if women could ignore, alleviate, or shield themselves from the harsher and most exploitive elements of male-female relations, they seemingly had little to gain and much to lose by adopting any radical ideology that threatened the domestic status quo. Although rigidly defined sex roles were by no means confined to the South during the antebellum decades, Southerners of both sexes reveled in the notion that they had somehow been able to quarantine their homes, churches, and schools from the forces of modernity that threatened to destroy traditional values. Women who had grown up in a society that exalted their reproductive functions naturally found much to praise in Southern attempts to protect the sacred roles of wife and mother from the infectious isms that seemed to have had such a destructive effect in the Northern states.[3] Along with Myrtie Candler, many Southern women preferred to operate in their own well-defined sphere than to compete with men in public life. Better to serve as guardians of the home and the humane values that supposedly flourished there than to enter an evil world that showed little respect for female virtue.[4] If many women preferred having more security and less independence, they did so realizing just how vulnerable women could be in a harshly competitive economic and social order. Indeed much of the force of both the intellectual and the more popular Southern critique of Northern capitalism rested on the notion that unbridled competition and a breakdown of traditional sexual roles would ultimately destroy the home, thereby claiming many female victims.

1

To limn the general relationship between Southern white women and Southern society is one thing; to uncover the details of how women fit into this complex social order and how Southern social assumptions shaped their attitudes toward themselves, their families, and the society as a whole is much more difficult. Any historian trying to reconstruct the lives of Southern white women works on a vast jigsaw puzzle with most of the pieces missing. Few women bothered to record their experiences, much less analyze them. Scribbling hurriedly in her diary in Brazoria, Texas, Rebecca Pilsbury recognized the problem of historical anonymity: "Another day has passed of little incident but of such are the lives of every-day people and they are perhaps the most important class in the community, they quietly, and unostentatiously pass through the journey of life, performing little duties and pass to their long home but little missed." Death closed out lives lived in obscurity, but "doubtless there is not a heart that beats but longs to be remembered after death, yet not one in a thousand are thought of by any but their bosom friends."[5] However much they may have longed for historical immortality, most could not escape historical oblivion.

Travel accounts and other contemporary sources supplement the surviving diaries and family papers but too often describe Southern women as static, ideal types unaffected by change. Yet a bafflingly intricate Southern social order that has too often been described simply as a reactionary anachronism contained some surprising ambiguities and inconsistencies. Despite being hedged about by numerous cultural, social, and economic restrictions (and taboos), upper class and even yeoman and poor white women shaped their own lives in important ways. Even in the minds of conservative Southern intellectuals, women occupied a precariously balanced social position: domestic duties were vital to their families and society but should not reduce them to drudges. This delicate combination of sometimes competing and contradictory characteristics formed the basis of an ideal definition of womanhood that seemed to especially flourish in the South. Daniel R. Hundley, a cautious and perceptive observer, described Southern women as the "model women of the age in which we live." Contrasting them to the gossipers who lounged about hotels or the "flippant butterflies of fashion," Hundley celebrated ladies who were "simple and unaffected in . . . manners, pure in speech . . . in soul, and ever blessed with inborn grace and gentleness of spirit lovely to look upon." Shunning the "twaddle and senseless disputes" about the rights of women, these self-effacing and mild ladies exerted their quiet influence in the home. As mothers, Southern women were "pure, peaceable, gentle, long-suffering and godly— which they never can be, if permitted or inclined to enter the lists and compete with selfish and lustful man for the prizes of place and public emolument." They embodied these virtues, Hundley believed, because family ties in the South were stronger than in the North.[6] This romantic portrayal ignored the tensions and uncertainties of women's roles in the South and sometimes seemed more caricature than description but at the same time accurately summed up the expectation that women would early on learn and eventually internalize their assigned social roles.

Yet contemporary analyses of Southern womanhood are sometimes hard to interpret, in part because of their amorphous and shifting character. Attitudes toward women were in a state of flux—and not only in the reform-minded North. The most conservative Southerners denied that their society in any way restricted women's advancement and asserted that the condition of women had improved remarkably since the days of barbarism and feudalism. Christianity, claimed Martha Lumpkin, had ended the degradation of women that had characterized heathen society. And even in the South there was considerable discussion about improving educational opportunities for women. Although evangelical Southerners (and some of their Northern brethren as well) remained skeptical about human progress, few denied that women were making ever more important contributions to civilized life. Virginia Cary, the author of an important advice book for young women, celebrated an "age of intellectual improvement" that would "penetrate the night of ignorance in which custom and prejudice had enveloped the female mind." The elevation of women occurred because men no longer opposed the development of female intellect and character, and Cary predicted the continuation of this cooperative spirit.[7] Thus women's sphere of activity might appear increasingly elastic, if not ill-defined, even among a tradition-bound people.

The Southern defense of hearth and home contained many ambiguities and contradictions. As the winds of doctrine shifted, it became difficult even in the South to form and preserve clear, coherent ideas about women and their roles. Were women to be socially polished belles or hardworking farmwives? Were they to acquire intellectual sophistication or cultivate simple domestic skills? In romantic novels and in some of the religious literature, the virtuous woman proved her character by submitting to masculine authority and by remaining socially passive. Even the well-educated polemicist Louisa S. McCord suggested that women were "made for duty, not for fame." At the same time, the Southern agricultural press praised the sturdy farmwife who relied on her own good judgment to run her household, tend the garden and livestock, and in many other ways contribute to Southern economic life.[8]

Notions of gentility competed with those of utility, making the ideology fragmented and inconsistent. Southern thinkers—with the partial exception of George Fitzhugh—poured too much intellectual energy into the defense of slavery to define women's status carefully or to link such a definition to a larger apologia for their own social order.[9] Daily experience battered and reshaped the social practices so lovingly outlined in the advice literature. Social customs for the most part rested on unspoken assumptions that hardly needed elaborate analysis but at the same time gave women some surprising options within a rigidly defined sphere. If a real-life example of the mythical Southern belle was hard to find, the myth of Southern womanhood was equally elusive in the Old South.

2

Much of this ideological uncertainty rested on a defective analysis of class. Contemporary commentators and later historians mistakenly tried to define Southern womanhood by referring to the genteel ideals of plantation mistresses and their counterparts in the fashionable society of towns and cities. To assume that such examples apply to yeoman and poor white women depends on a large leap of faith because class considerations and intricate social traditions complicate the task of describing women's role and status in the antebellum South. Also much of the best evidence on family life comes from upper-class, mostly planter, sources.[10] This latter problem, however, is hardly insurmountable because enough yeoman letters and diaries (especially from the Civil War period) have survived to balance the well-mined plantation documents. And although class lines blurred on many important matters, these distinctions are important.[11]

After all yeoman women lived outside the social world of the plantation. Hundley—who was more objective, sympathetic, and perceptive than most observers—described farmwives as "modest and virtuous, chaste in speech and manners." Quite often "simple and unsophisticated," they were nevertheless devoted mothers and diligent housekeepers. Attired in calico or homespun, they had little time to ponder the issues of the day or to pursue an active social life. Their possessions were simple and practical: a table and some chairs, a bed, a mirror, plates, bowls, a teapot, and miscellaneous kitchen utensils. Their only reading matter was likely to be a Bible or a church magazine.[12] A life of hard work, a sometimes painful struggle for respectability, and a certain basic comfort set the boundaries of yeoman life.

Yet a property inventory with a brief sketch of an unassuming, pious, and respectable housewife paints far too simple a picture. The yeoman woman, who sometimes worked alongside her husband in a field, more often tended the livestock and garden, and in other ways contributed to her family's well-being, might achieve a limited independence in the household. At the same time, assumptions of female subordination in a man's world provided a rationale for simply pursuing one's own separate interests within the household. Security and satisfaction may have seemed far away from the realities of daily life, though most yeoman women, whether married or single, must have seen themselves as more harried than oppressed. Widow Jane Beale, for instance, had little money, but working hard for her family of nine children, she managed to send two sons to school. Yet only the aid of a generous brother and sister kept her precariously perched in the yeoman class.[13] For women in moderately comfortable circumstances, life meant continuous struggle against bad weather, low crop prices, importunate creditors, crafty merchants, and a host of other natural and human-made difficulties. Many pressing problems demanded immediate attention and left little time for thinking about either the justice or injustice of their position or for that matter alternatives to their present life.

When proslavery ideologues lyrically celebrated class unity in the Old South, their analyses contained a sizable dose of wishful thinking. During the slumps, large and small, that plagued the Southern economy before the Civil War, Southern stump speakers often resorted to a democratic rhetoric that declared the humble farmer and his wife as good as their wealthy neighbors. To be sure, the theme of class conflict was a muted one, often overshadowed by the larger and more salient issue of race, but it pulsed below the surface.[14] Men might lash out at politicians or even against the economic and political structure, but their wives were more likely to assail the hauteur of a privileged aristocracy. In 1857, Catherine Piper had sold some stove parts to wealthy Georgia planter David C. Barrow. After unsuccessfully dunning him once, she wrote a second, more pointed letter. Accusing Barrow of being insensitive to her financial plight, she even offered to accept a partial payment. "I hardly think that you realize the situation of the poor," she bitingly concluded, "as you have never had the misfortune to be so yourself."[15] Such statements cut to the heart of the problem. So long as yeomen and planters could both prosper, they might live together in peace. But in a political or economic crisis, the veneer of social unity might crack, and during the Civil War, it finally shattered.

Beneath the sometimes uneasy relations between planter and yeoman, a tension that often involved women as well as men, another world existed. In travel accounts and histories alike, the poor whites have either been ignored, treated with contempt, or made the butt of jokes. Where these women fit into the Southern class structure remains unclear, though even hostile commentators noted their generally sturdy sense of social justice, often including a prickly insistence that the rich meet their obligations to help the poor. Given the absence of reliable sources, determining how these women tried to make sense of their lives is often impossible. In one-room cabins that often contained no more than a bed, table, chairs, and some crockery, they lived out their lives in obscurity. With large families and little cash, many still used spinning wheels and wove their own cloth.[16] Did their resentment of the often condescending attitude of their more prosperous neighbors set them outside the mainstream values of the old South? Were they privately critical of the economic and political structure? Did race pride override doubts about slavery? Whatever the answers to these questions—and historians may never be able to answer them with much confidence— subtle and often unspoken class distinctions powerfully shaped Southern attitudes toward women and made the task of determining women's appropriate roles and status difficult, even in theory.

3

Although economic and social class has to be taken into account, Southern women encountered certain common expectations and problems. Girls growing up in the antebellum South faced the usual pressures to marry. Although some adolescents obviously questioned and even rebelled against their fate, most eventually became wives and mothers. At twenty-three, Carrie Hunter watched her friends fall in love yet feared the fickleness of men. "I feel like a ship cut away from its moorings drifting," she wrote in her diary. Yet she believed that "every young girl looks forward to marriage as the very probable course her life will take . . . and every girl is obliged to think about it a great deal." She had always assumed that she would find her chosen one but had come to have doubts. The single woman appeared "totally dependent on society . . . it is her duty to conform to it, and to promote in some degree its tastes."[17] In a culture that offered few other alternatives for women, the supposed comfort and security of home life seemed like the crowning ambition of female existence.

The South's rural isolation reinforced this way of thinking and made traditional domestic values and notions about woman's place easier to preserve and maintain. Living in the countryside or in small towns, most young girls could expect to meet only a few potential husbands and usually chose a relative or someone living in the immediate neighborhood. These young couples would then set up housekeeping near their parents, thereby reinforcing the strong family ties and intense localism that characterized Southern life even in towns and cities.[18]

For these new wives, the next step was dutifully to begin their reproductive lives. Biological destiny, at least as defined by most men and women, then meant a seemingly endless round of pregnancies. Although the demographic evidence is often thin, the manuscript census for any Southern county shows children spaced at intervals of two years or less—births only thirteen months apart were commonplace—and the Southern birthrate declined much less rapidly than the national birthrate during the antebellum decades. After ten years of marriage, Elizabeth Perry had been pregnant as many times (including four live births, two stillborn daughters, and four miscarriages). Hearing of a thirty-seven-year-old woman in St. Francisville, Louisiana, who had already borne sixteen children, Rachel O'Connor ruefully remarked that "her family may yet be much larger."[19]

Although the reactions of women to all these pregnancies ran the gamut from elation to terror, they apparently had little choice in the matter because the South lagged considerably behind the North in practicing any form of birth control. Most married women had children in rapid succession whether they wanted to or not. With a family of thirteen and no time for anything else, an exhausted Martha Battey could only note: "I have so many little children and no prospect of ever stopping." Even women determined to avoid pregnancy had little faith in their methods. Two girls were quite enough for Lizzie Clow (she especially dreaded "boy brats, noisy, rough things"), but she admitted: "I must not exult too much. I may be caught yet." Delayed weaning, abstinence, and coitus interruptus were evidently the only contraceptive techniques widely known and used in the South.[20]

Growing families—and all the work they entailed—placed an enormous physical and psychological burden on women. Most housewives actively managed their households, and even where slaves did much of the cooking and cleaning, white women sewed and devoted considerable time to child care. Farmers' wives tended gardens and livestock, occasionally helping their husbands in the fields. In East Texas, Frederick Law Olmsted met yeoman women whose "thin faces, sallow complexions, and expressions either sad or sour" offered silent testimony to their hard lives.[21]

Class differences affected the type and amount of housework done by Southern women, though few could have been dubbed "ladies of leisure." Jane Beale of Fredericksburg, Virginia, was a poor widow with nine children. She spent a typical day putting up pickles, cutting out cloth, dusting lamps, listening to children recite lessons, cleaning up the yard, whitewashing part of the house, cutting up peaches, mending clothes, ridding the beds of insects, and feeding and milking the cow. After getting her youngsters to bed, she sat down to chat with her brother Sam, with, of course, knitting on her lap. For more comfortably situated women, the tasks were different but only slightly less demanding. Along with her mother and half-sister in Marietta, Georgia, Mary Robarts worked hard to maintain a neat and respectable home. Rising early, she prepared breakfast and then hustled her nieces and nephews off to school. During a stroll through the yard, she looked after the ducks, turkeys, and chickens, reserving the afternoon for reading, writing, sewing, and another walk outside, though visits from neighbors and friends might disrupt this routine. In the evening she read aloud to the family. Planters' wives too had their daily chores, and most ran their households carefully. Yet they had much more leisure than the typical farm woman. Ella Thomas sewed, cared for her children, and worked in the garden but still had time to read popular novels and the four magazines to which, she subscribed.[22] Whether alone or with female relatives and neighbors women of all classes worked and generally worked hard. Despite the prevailing myth, the South never developed a class of idle women; each new season brought its own tasks to be added to the regular list of chores.

4

Over the years, work took a physical and psychological toll. On a day when the children were grouchy, the slaves unmanageable, and the men hungry and "savage," Susan Cornwall wished for a "huge pair of scissors to cut everything in my way." Much of this grumbling and exasperation was commonplace and hardly confined to the Southern states, but Southern housewives had even fewer alternatives to domesticity than their Northern counterparts. "What a tread mill existence it is to cook three meals per day the year round," exclaimed Abbie Brooks, "it seems to me I would rather die than to be bound in that way. I am sure there is no poetry in it, nor mental improvement, but some person has to cook."[23] She did not ask why it was always the woman who had to cook. Complaints about household drudgery seldom evolved into more general and hard-hitting critiques of the whole notion of separate spheres.

Indeed Southern women had little choice but quietly to fulfill their assigned roles. For those who no longer could stand their marriages, had grown fed up with child rearing, had become bored with the domestic routine, or simply longed for something better, there were few avenues of escape except to become an invalid. Running away meant losing property, risking social disgrace, and facing a still darker and more uncertain future. In the South, marriage signified a permanent commitment, a promise of security that seemed both tangible and attractive compared with the chimera of independence. Evangelical religion also stressed obligations over rights, and pious women learned to tolerate what they could not change.

For desperate wives longing to get out of a bad marriage, prospects were dim. Courts recognized legal separations and sometimes allowed women to keep their property, but separation was an infrequent remedy available mostly to wealthier women. Divorce too was difficult, especially in states that required the passage of a private bill in the state legislature to dissolve a marriage.[24] Though legislative divorce was a patriarchal bulwark that preserved both male honor and property, legal changes during the late antebellum period often favored the injured wife.

State legislatures gradually made divorce a judicial proceeding and expanded the grounds to include consanguinity, insanity or impotence at the time of marriage, and bigamy. More significant, every Southern state except South Carolina, which had no divorce law, eventually added adultery, cruelty, and desertion to the list. Lawmakers broadened the definition of cruelty and gave the courts wide discretion to determine what types of mistreatment constituted grounds for divorce. Some judges limited cruelty to physical abuse, but others considered verbal assaults, such as false accusations of adultery. Decrees awarding alimony during litigation also helped women.

The most important requirement for a female petitioner, however, was to establish her respectability beyond a doubt. As a plaintiff, she had to prove her good character, dedication to domestic life, and sub-missiveness toward men. In such cases, Southern judges became in-creasingly, though not uniformly, generous in awarding property and child custody to wives. Many tried to help the woman while preserving her subordinate status.[25]

In a way, these reforms appeared to challenge traditional social as-sumptions, but both judges and legislators saw themselves as protectors of women, especially of respectable and properly obedient wives who had been mistreated in some way. As paternalists, they tried to preserve clearly defined rights and obligations within marriage—rights and ob-ligations that could not be ignored even by the "stronger" sex. After all if marital abuses went unchecked, the institution of marriage itself might be in danger. Sentimental notions about women's moral superiority also made these men more responsive to aggrieved wives. By heeding cries for assistance and by granting relief from intolerable marriages, men in authority acted as defenders of supposedly weak and helpless women.

But these reforms also carried with them a cruel irony. Because of the powerful social stigma still attached to divorce—or even to separation—few women could or would take advantage of legal changes, and most either had to overcome their dissatisfaction or live with it. Plantation mistress Catherine Edmondston remembered the day when, as a young bride, she cried after her husband announced that "the first duty of woman was to attend to the cooking." After sixteen years of marriage, she herself had come to believe that "a well-ordered table—well cooked—and well prepared food is the keynote to health, happiness and usefulness!"[26] Years of housework tamed many a free spirit. The daily grind of sewing, preparing meals, and tending children forced the abandonment of other ambitions.

This psychological adjustment, however, came slowly and with great difficulty. The ideal wife never questioned her destiny, but flesh-and-blood women did. Married to a hotelkeeper in Marietta, Georgia, Louisa Fletcher admitted she dreamed of buying things beyond their meager means. Thankfulness for a loving husband, children, a home, food, clothes, and friends could not overcome her malaise. As a girl she had hoped for a good education and dreamed of becoming an "eminent scholar." She had also enjoyed music and regretted never learning to play the piano. Had she become a scholar or musician, she might have been able to "move in good society, and to live in good style, . . . to have a handsome house, handsome furniture, carriage and horses, rich wardrobe." But she would not give up present security to pursue a will-o'-the-wisp and finally had to "learn to be content" and never become a "complaining wife."[27] Giving up youthful aspirations meant accepting middle-age limits. Although men undoubtedly had to make similar compromises, a woman had fewer possibilities. For her, the frontier or the city did not beckon. Instead life revolved around husbands and children, and a search for a minimum of comfort and protection.

5

Reconciliation to a limited role in the home and in the larger society reflected women's often ambivalent attitude toward the world, an ambivalence that grew out of their religious beliefs. Charlotte McMurray had just learned that Louisa Hall was married and had recently given birth to a child. While rejoicing over an old friend's good fortune, McMurray paused to consider the "shortness and uncertainty of life, and the awful consequences of appearing in judgment before an infinitely holy God."

The warmth and safety of the home were deceptive snares for the unwary. Outside forces beat against this sanctuary. Ambition, vanity, and greed dissolved faith. For the rich, their possessions were as perishable as their lives; for the poor, release from suffering would come in the next world. Christian asceticism grew in the rocky soil of a hardscrabble life in the rural South. The devout took comfort in the promises of heaven and rejoiced that in the Apocalypse, all human-made distinctions would vanish.[28]

Such a vision of future bliss was especially powerful because Southern theologians and preachers, like their Northern brethren, maintained that female piety was natural. In their view—a view obviously shared by many Southern housewives—Christ-like women forfeited their own comfort for others. But if evangelical religion encouraged a certain mordant pessimism about human nature, fostered ideals of self-sacrifice, and reinforced notions of female submissiveness, faith seldom remained exclusively private or domestic.

After all, church membership was one of the few public activities freely open to women. Especially in the rural South, religion linked women to the world (even as it led them to shun worldliness and materialism) but at the same time left traditional sex roles intact. Ministers maintained that women found it easier than their menfolk to obey Christ because they had already learned to obey their fathers and husbands. "The fruits of regeneration," Virginia Cary emphasized, "spring from the docile nature of the weaker sex."[29] But the churches also offered security, comfort, and meaning to lives that might otherwise have seemed barely tolerable.

Even though evangelical religion preserved male authority (as represented by Christ, the Apostles, and the ministers), women eagerly embraced this faith. Membership statistics are notoriously unreliable, though Donald Mathews has conservatively estimated that twice as many women as men joined churches (the ratio may have been as high as four to one), and the disparity apparently was higher in the South than in the North. Mary Chesnut attended a crowded Sunday service where she saw only one man in the congregation. "It is plain why there is no marrying nor giving in marriage to heaven," she commented sardonically. "The church is the gate to heaven, and the church is apparently filled with women only going up there." Thomas R. Dew agreed. Women were devout because they had more sorrows than men, a greater sense of dependence, and a nervous system better suited to religious enthusiasm.[30] Such superior piety had its advantages—women could use it to convert recalcitrant men or to influence family decisions—but it also brought them into conflict with a more aggressive masculine world in which money-making, honor and what W. J. Cash once called the "helluva-fellow complex" competed against softer spiritual values.

In many ways evangelism then became a woman's crusade that not only provided wives and mothers with a greater sense of individual worth but implicitly questioned the legitimacy of the premium placed on aggressiveness in secular society. As the waves of revivalism swept across the country in the first half of the nineteenth century, women tested their power in the churches by promoting camp meetings and organizing ladies' societies to fan the flames of enthusiasm. Even sexual segregation broke down in the fires of revival, and during altar calls the response from the female side of the aisle was almost always the most impressive. Bolder women gave their testimonies at prayer meetings, led singing, and spoke in tongues despite opposition from ministers anxious to preserve their authority. Yet few dared run afoul of the Apostle Paul's injunction against women speaking in church.[31] The revivals opened up new opportunities for female religious expression, but the preachers tried, admittedly with mixed results, to keep such expressions within "proper" bounds.

Of course the long-term effects of this evangelical fervor are hard to gauge because then, as now, backsliding took a heavy toll among converts. The churches, however, gathered together believers who could sustain one another in time of need and these communities aspired to transform Southern society. Although the South fell behind the rest of the country in benevolent organization, Southern women collected money for buildings, taught Sunday-school classes, directed poor relief, and distributed tracts. For many churches, their fund-raising efforts were crucial for evangelism, expansion, and even survival. In making plans for a hospital-benefit concert, Carrie Shaffner commented that it was silly for women to withdraw from community life after they married.[32]

Such participation hardly affected well-entrenched ideas about female roles. After all, women had little voice in church government, and even the ladies' societies often depended on the direction and support of ministers and male elders. And as Suzanne Lebsock has shown in the case of Petersburg, Virginia, if women threatened to become too active in public benevolence, men might simply take over the organizations.[33]

Indeed church work seemed to offer women power on the one hand while reinforcing their powerlessness on the other. For example, even though in sheer numbers, women dominated the evangelical churches, men controlled discipline in the congregations, meting out harsher punishments at church trials to wayward women than to sinful men. Ministers sternly preached against the wickedness of fornication, but church officials, even if they were female, were much more likely to investigate and punish misconduct by women. In June 1857 a two-woman committee from a Baptist church in Carroll County, Georgia, visited Sarah Toomes, who was pregnant with no sign of a husband. On their recommendation, the congregation voted to exclude her from fellowship.[34] As women assumed new tasks and gained some influence within the congregations, they also ran into constant reminders of their subordinate status. But for most women that seemed a small price to pay for the benefits received, in both this world and the next.

6

In the Northern states, the road from church work to secular benevolence was short and direct. There women joined temperance, educational, antislavery, and moral-reform societies in which they implicitly challenged male prerogatives and practices. To be sure, Northern women followed many paths from benevolence to reform and most never became feminists. But in the South even fewer women organized and joined national and local reform associations, and even when they did, their efforts reinforced conventional class arrangements and domestic roles. Aristocratic ladies in Charleston, for example, worked with poor women and orphans, not only to ease suffering, but to convince the downtrodden that the local elite had their best interests at heart. Although these women were moved by the plight of the poor and sincerely wanted to assist them, they also hoped to turn such bedraggled souls into paragons of Victorian respectability.[35] By assuming that every woman should become a genteel housewife, cautious reformers kept charities politically and socially innocuous. An anonymous writer in *DeBow's Review* sounded the dominant theme when he praised Southern ladies for staying at home with their families and cultivating genteel manners rather than following the busybody example of their Northern sisters.[36]

Women's devotion to church work made them leery of Northern reform movements, which they readily associated with religious skepticism. The inroads of rationalism and science left little impression on the predominantly female congregations in the South. Indeed as the forces of change seemed to threaten their homes and society, women clung ever more tenaciously to the verities of their faith. Like bourgeois French women of the late nineteenth century, many yeoman and upper class women in the antebellum South showed a powerful revulsion against what might be described as modernity.[37]

Although some Southern men—especially among the intellectual elite—feared that women might succumb to the appeals of Northern feminism, they need not have worried. Even the most meticulous research has failed to show that Southern women's expanding roles in benevolent organizations produced anything resembling a feminist consciousness.[38] Few Southern women were either familiar with or sympathetic to what conservatives scornfully called "Bloomerism." During her honeymoon trip to Philadelphia, young Virginian Samuella Curd attended a women's-rights convention but dismissed the proceedings as "contemptible" because blacks and whites sat together during the sessions. In her strident attacks on female suffrage, Louisa McCord accused Northern militants of trying to destroy divinely created distinctions between the sexes. Women should exert their quiet influence at home rather than through speechmaking and voting; enfranchising women would surely "unsex" them. The true woman, McCord claimed, preferred caring for her family to tinkering with constitutions. In a clever twist on domestic ideology, she concluded that morally superior women should never sink to the level of degraded males stuck in the mire of partisan politics.[39] For such women, feminism seemed to inevitably lead to agnosticism, free love, and numerous other heresies.

The few Southern women with feminist sympathies—such as Mary Chesnut—confined their opinions to diaries and private conversations. In an upper-class home in Charleston, Emma Holmes enjoyed a spirited breakfast discussion about sexual equality because it "always makes me indignant to hear men arrogate to themselves such vast superiority over women, mentally as well as physically." At Grove Hill plantation in southwestern Virginia, Lucy Breckinridge listened avidly to a running debate about the relative virtue of the sexes. She decided that women were probably morally superior but that men faced greater temptations. Yet she drew back from taking the argument any farther. She regretted thumbing through a French feminist novel because "I do not like that kind of reading. It scares me of myself, and makes me rebel against my lot."[40] Such comments suggest ambivalence and may even have provided a slender foundation for future reform, but at the time feminism appeared irrelevant to the daily lives of Southern women and in many ways a dangerous doctrine that could well destroy the Southern home. For whatever gains women may have made in their private lives or in expanded opportunities to join charitable societies, they probably did as much as men to keep the South "safe" from the women's rights movement.

7

Yet even with these restrictive attitudes (and, of course, within the bounds of proslavery orthodoxy), the intellectual horizons of elite women expanded. In genteel homes, husbands and wives read to each other in the evenings; parents bought books and magazines for their children; on larger estates, women grew up with access to impressive private libraries (some even containing feminist literature). Based on her experience with the plantation society of coastal Georgia, Mary Jones warned her daughter against allowing housework to stultify her mind. "How degrading to the intellect is the way in which *young females particularly* spend their time!" she lamented.[41]

Plantation fiction has indelibly etched an image of a beautiful belle sitting on a veranda languidly thumbing through a romantic novel, and the myth has some slight basis. In many planter and yeoman families, young girls often read stories aloud while sewing or doing other household chores, and some found juvenile literature so alluring that they neglected their duller textbooks. Writers on women's character and domestic life deemed novel reading the besetting intellectual vice of females. One essayist warned that absorption in light fiction would cause girls to "lose their common sense" and neglect more practical works.[42] The ubiquitous popular romances threatened to pull women away from their household duties and stir longings for a life beyond their reach.

Educated parents therefore encouraged their daughters to read solid works of literature and history. William Hickling Prescott's volumes on Latin America and John Lothrop Motley's *Rise of the Dutch Republic* were particular favorites. Shakespeare (sometimes in expurgated editions), Dickens and other English novelists, the authors of classical antiquity, and religious works rounded out a typical reading list.[43]

But the reading habits of well-off and well-educated ladies present a far too elevated view of female intellectual life. Few women had either the time, the inclination, or the education to peruse such heavy fare, or romantic novels for that matter. Most read little beyond a few schoolbooks, the Bible, and some religious tracts—if they could read at all. In 1850 the estimated literacy rate for white adult females ranged from a high of 86 percent in Mississippi to a low of 64 percent in North Carolina. For Southern women the rate was four to sixteen percentage points lower than for Southern men. In contrast, the New England and Middle Atlantic states generally had female literacy rates above 90 percent, and only a few western states had rates as low as those in the South. Functional illiteracy was undoubtedly even higher than these figures indicate; many antebellum Southern women, like the wives of twentieth-century sharecroppers, read nothing.[44] Nowhere were Southern class differences more apparent than in the social distance between a planter's daughter devouring Tacitus and a poor white woman who could not decipher a sales receipt or sign her name.

Despite living in a society that for the most part discouraged their intellectual growth, some young girls painfully struggled to improve their minds, well realizing how much they had to learn. Contrary to popular belief, women were intellectually curious about many subjects, including science and mathematics. Judith Rives remembered how the girls in her family listened with fascination to their tutor's chemistry lectures and enjoyed making compounds in the laboratory. Beyond a love of knowledge, some women put forward strikingly modern reasons for obtaining an education. In Margaret Campbell's opinion, too many fathers and mothers saw their daughters as helpless and dependent, fit only to marry well so they could eventually support their aged parents. From her perspective, however, proper schooling made young women self-sufficient and placed them beyond "the necessitudes of fortune." During a fund-raising campaign for Wesleyan Female College in Macon, Georgia, one enthusiast even claimed that improved education would "bring equal pay for women doing the same work as men."[45] But few women perceived or tried to pursue such ideas, and even the best schooling failed to challenge older definitions of woman's place.

Even for the upper class, educational opportunity was by no means equally distributed because, for women especially, so much depended on the widely varying attitudes of parents. Ambitious fathers often took a keen interest in their daughters' education. In drawing up a reading list for his daughter Minerva, William Cain recommended history, geography, and good literature as more fit subjects for conversation "than dress or fiddle-faddle stories, that carry no information along with them."[46] But these men worried about more than the curriculum and often paid close attention to the smallest incidents of school life. Dr. Samuel D. Sanders, who sent his daughter Mary to a college in Columbia, South Carolina, advised her on selecting a proper roommate and offered precise instructions on how to study each subject. His standards were high; he wished her to excel in every department and stand first in her class. When she was ridiculed by other girls for being too diligent, he suggested that it was better to be considered dull and studious than vivacious and empty headed. Though pleased by her academic success, he was plainly disappointed when she dropped Latin.[47] Other fathers adopted a more distant and authoritarian tone. Mary Norcom must have tired of her father's endless epistolary lectures on hard work and other virtues, complete with warnings about the dangers of everything from night air to frivolous conversation. Constantly upbraiding his daughter for spending too much money, he cut off music and dancing lessons because of the expense. Even during vacations he sent along instructions on reading, exercise, and cleanliness.[48]

Why did Southern fathers take such pains with their daughters' education and even set aside money for it in their wills? Northern men might encourage intellectual independence in their daughters, who sometimes became feminists, but Southern planters and merchants had little interest in elevating the position of women. At most they hoped that spirited and undisciplined adolescents would grow into intelligent and respectable young ladies. And this required more than academic training. Girls had to learn the social graces and practical domestic skills. Charles Dabney wanted his sister Sarah to get a good education, not for its own sake, but because he thought learning useful for married women.[49]

Such a narrow definition of utility meant that a strong paternal interest in female education did not necessarily translate into political and financial support for better schools. The history of women's education in the nineteenth-century South is a story of brave beginnings and limited achievements. There was no sustained reform movement, and the improvements that did take place stemmed largely from the initiative of a few forceful teachers and administrators. Likewise, tight budgets slowed school expansion, though ideological barriers also stifled imaginations and slowed the pace of change.

Southerners who favored more and better schooling for women had to make their case without disturbing the social order or traditional sex roles. The Reverend George Pierce, a founder of Georgia Female College in Macon, discovered more "tinsel than gold in female education" and thought girls spent too much time with ornamental subjects, such as etiquette, music, and poetry. Instruction was often hasty and superficial, a mere prelude to entering fashionable society. Some women still believed they had to hide their intellect, though a Georgian hoped that "the days when the knowledge of making hoe-cake and hominy constituted the chief glory and highest ambition of half the rational creation are now past." And some wives and mothers bemoaned the lingering effects of outdated notions about the intellectual inequality of the sexes.[50]

Yet this rhetoric was far more progressive than the underlying assumptions. Southern educators agreed with Northern conservatives that schools for women should above all else turn out superior wives and mothers. In the developing republican ideology, maternal responsibility for training young citizens took priority over improving opportunities for women to achieve success outside the home. The well-educated woman fulfilled her destiny by helping men, not herself. What husband would not wish his wife capable of carrying on pleasant and intelligent conversations around the fire in the evening? But she should obviously not cultivate ideas of her own or challenge his thinking.[51] Educational reforms preserved traditional assumptions about woman's place and at the same time allayed domestic discontent by providing a temporary outlet for women's intellectual energies.

Of course even modest improvements could not help but alter in subtle ways the images women held of themselves and their sex. If women could benefit as much from knowledge as men, an anonymous North Carolinian suggested, they would also make "good teachers, poets, historians and even patriots, good managers of estates and families."[52] But just such a potential frightened nervous men who worried that a woman trained in the liberal arts would neglect her household chores, and such fears generated wildly contradictory arguments. In some mysterious and unspecified way, better schooling would improve women but not change them. The educated woman would still be the "heart" of the home whose "head" remained the husband, Richard Cook declared. Learning science, mathematics, or Latin would not free her from domestic responsibilities.[53]

Many tightfisted farmers would not even go this far and insisted that a woman need know only how to spin, weave, and read the New Testament. If young girls learned more about mixing chemicals than making bread, of what use was education? To spend hard-earned money on frivolous instruction in science, foreign languages, or music seemed the height of folly.[54]

Given such attitudes and the high costs of private schooling, the multiplication of female academies during the antebellum decades hardly affected the average Southern girl. Yeoman families could not afford the tuition, which usually ran to more than one hundred dollars a year, and most of these schools had fewer than one hundred students.[55] Only the elite enjoyed the luxury of sending their daughters to good boarding schools.

For these fortunate few, academies and "colleges" provided unprecedented opportunities for acquiring both knowledge and self-confidence. Although Southerners still doubted whether girls needed to study advanced mathematics, Latin, or Greek, reformers pressed for more history, philosophy, science, and mathematics in the curriculum.[56] During the 1850s, several schools added geometry and trigonometry. Astronomy, botany, and chemistry commonly appeared in the catalogues. So-called ornamental subjects—painting, drawing, needlework, and music—declined in importance, and surprisingly few institutions stressed the "domestic arts."[57] By 1850 a Southern girl of means could follow a curriculum in many ways comparable to that of her brothers.

But, as always, catalogue changes did not necessarily signify improvements. On the eve of the Civil War, women's education in the South was still severely limited, even for the most privileged young ladies. Teachers too often emphasized rote memorization over critical thinking and paid careful attention to the delicacy of their students. Women should learn to write, Eugenius Nisbet maintained, but not on controversial subjects; only "pure and holy" topics would do. They might study politics, so long as they did not become politicians. For both sexes, evangelical religion restricted the life of the mind; although botany was popular, the study of geology challenged biblical orthodoxy. And from the 1840s on, sectional tension stirred distrust of Yankee innovations. Southern nationalists called for educating daughters (and sons) in Southern schools to protect them from immorality and religious heresy.[58] All these forces diluted the effect of improved curricula.

Halfhearted reform efforts by administrators and tepid public support yielded predictable results. Most schools had neither the money nor the teachers to make needed changes. Northern and foreign travelers found

Southern women ignorant on most subjects; girls began their educations too late and stopped too early. Much of the ferment and excitement that had stirred the expansion and improvement of female education in New England was absent in the South. Rebecca Latimer Felton, the first Southern woman to become a United States senator, was graduated from Madison Female College in Georgia at the age of seventeen after only two years of classes. Many so-called colleges were nothing more than glorified academies. Sarah Morgan sorely regretted her superficial training, wondering why she had not had the same opportunities as her male acquaintances. She had taken advantage of every opportunity, but only ten months in school had left her little more than a "fool." All she could do about it was cry alone in bed.[59] If a young upper-class girl shed bitter tears, what about less fortunate women?

Efforts to provide schools for yeomen and poor whites ran up against frugality and class prejudice. Farmers and planters opposed the higher taxes on land and slaves needed to finance public education. Even with support from churches and benevolent societies, students from poor homes frequently felt out of place. Emily Burke paid the tuition for two "sandhill" girls to attend a Northern Georgia academy, but wealthy classmates with fine dresses and body servants ridiculed them until they finally left. Confining higher education to the more prosperous yeomen and the gentry merely added to the social isolation of female intellectuals. Sitting in rural Arkansas reading Herodotus, Mary Sims felt as if she were floating alone on a vast ocean of ignorance.[60] Educational reform simply widened the cultural gap between the elite and the mass of Southern women. New schools and courses drew a few young girls into a larger world while leaving many others behind to live much as their mothers and grandmothers had done.

8

Whether young girls acquired a good education, barely learned to read and write, or remained illiterate, they all lived in a society where the subordination of women was enforced by both custom and law. Under the common law, the husband held authority over his wife; her property became his, and after his death, his debts could become hers.[61] In equity law, on the other hand, women could make prenuptial agreements to guard their assets, but this device was not widely used and in any case contained many loopholes. On its face, a prenuptial settlement permitted

a woman to retain her property and shield it from her husband's creditors. But as Suzanne Lebsock has shown in a meticulous analysis of
equity jurisprudence in Petersburg, Virginia, prenuptial contracts preserved the family estate better than the woman's economic interests
because they did not always grant wives the unencumbered right to
dispose of their property. Legal ambiguities led to lengthy litigation,
especially over provisions concerning slaves and estate trustees. Whatever their drawbacks for women, men encouraged marriage contracts
to protect their female relatives from fortune hunters and wastrel husbands. George Douglass even advised his estranged wife, Hannah, that
if she remarried she should secure their children's rights to her estate.[62]
Such protection did not, however, prevent men from manipulating and
disposing of their wives' property through deception or intimidation.
Court decisions dealt only with extreme cases of conflict. In most upper-
class and nearly all yeoman families, men effectively controlled women's
property.

What makes much of the evidence so treacherous is the difficulty of
distinguishing between law and practice. Family papers suggest that
many Southern marriages were joint economic enterprises. Husbands
and wives often discussed the family business—whether plantation,
farm, store, or shop—and made decisions together. The evolution of
what social historians have called "companionate marriage" encouraged
cooperation, but as in other areas of family life, modern attitudes co-
existed with more traditional ones. Ann Thomas tried to dissuade her
husband from mortgaging their land and slaves to buy a plantation in
Louisiana, but he ignored her advice. When he died in the early 1840s,
she soon discovered that she had inherited a passel of debts.[63]

For many women, a husband's death brought his creditors down on
the estate like vultures. Anna Matilda King's husband, James, had invested heavily in slaves and sea island cotton. Caterpillars ate the crop,
and the debts mounted. After his death, creditors began seizing assets.
She begged one of the estate's trustees to safeguard the property inherited from her father because it was her only source of income for
nine children.[64] When it comes to money of course, relatives can be as
unmerciful as strangers in devouring a widow's inheritance. Some women
well understood the dangers and looked after their own interests. Ada
Bacot refused to stand security for her father on a loan because she
feared losing a small piece of property.[65] Given their anomalous position
in the Southern courts and the Southern economy, more educated and

sophisticated women relied on their own ingenuity and determination to safeguard their assets and rights.

For unless a woman administered her husband's estate, she might have little to say about its disposal. As real and personal property holdings grew in size and complexity during the late eighteenth century, fewer men, especially in the wealthier class, named their wives sole executors of their estates. Even in the nineteenth century as husbands began to leave property to their wives in fee simple rather than with conditions attached, widows still had little discretion over the disposition of family assets. Although many Southern wills divided estates equally between sons and daughters, large planters in North Carolina more often bequeathed slaves than land to their daughters.[66] Besides attempting to keep a family's farm or plantation intact during the next generation, some men also doubted that a woman could successfully manage on her own.

There was little that was uniquely Southern about this. After all property law was an ancient bulwark of the patriarchal family in the Western World, and even in the North expanded property rights for women may have had little effect on most families. By the same token, historians have exaggerated the conservatism of Southern property law. After the war of 1812, most states enlarged, however gradually, women's rights to inherit, manage, and sell property, and Mississippi was the first in the country to grant married women the right to hold property in their own name. Although reforms did not always give women full control over either real estate or slaves, public attitudes began to change. An anonymous writer in the *Southern Ladies' Book* argued that depriving married women of the right to dispose of their property was a "remnant of barbarism." In a republican society, women had to be independent and free—at least from the worry of being driven into poverty by an irresponsible husband. Even archconservative William Lowndes Yancey eloquently denounced the injustice of irresponsible men squandering their wives' estates.[67] Many such calls for change obviously contain large doses of paternalism, and men such as Yancey readily assumed their roles as protectors of helpless women. Beneath such sentimental appeals also lay the usual hardheaded desire to safeguard estates from importunate creditors.

Whether more enlightened laws really meant more enlightened public sentiment or not, legal reform failed to ease the economic burden of single women. The number of "spinsters" and widows increased during the nineteenth century, in part because more women chose not to marry or remarry. "Old maids" and widows alike trod a difficult path strewn with financial pitfalls. Merchants and peddlers saw them as easy marks and pressed their advantage; dependence on male relatives only added to the frustration and family tension.[68]

If single women and widows often felt depressed, they had good reason, and little wonder they often saw marriage as the only way to acquire security and a modicum of prosperity. To provide for oneself—let alone several children—generally meant a life of poverty. Female heads of households usually owned little or no real property, and even those who did held small amounts. For women who stayed in the same county between the 1850 and 1860 censuses and did not marry (or in the case of widows, remarry), there was little improvement. Some widows managed to build up their estates, but typically a woman was fortunate to be worth a few hundred dollars more in 1860 than she had been in 1850 (see tables 1 and 2). In counties with poorhouses, most of the residents were mothers with young children.[69] Besides suffering from legal and political disabilities, women found few opportunities for building a better

Table 1. Female Heads of Households: Real Property Holdings, 1850
Dollar Value of Real Property (Percentages in Each Category)

County	0	1– 100	101– 500	501– 1,000	1,001– 5,000	5,001– 10,000	> 10,000
Covington, Ala.	64.1	12.8	17.9	2.5	2.5	0	0
Dallas, Ala.	33.9	2.3	14.3	12.5	27.9	3.6	5.9
Coweta, Ga.	44.2	4.8	18.3	8.7	21.2	1.9	0
Natchitoches, La.	58.7	1.4	2.8	7.7	16.1	6.3	7.0
Attala, Miss.	64.2	7.5	17.0	3.8	6.6	0.9	0
Georgetown, S.C.	45.3	0	28.3	1.9	13.2	0	11.3
Sullivan, Tenn.	59.9	2.5	11.1	11.1	14.2	1.2	0
Weakley, Tenn.	41.2	5.2	39.7	7.7	5.1	0.5	0.5
Red River, Tex.	62.5	0	18.8	9.4	6.2	0	3.1
Halifax, Va.	56.0	4.1	15.7	9.0	12.8	0.8	1.5

Data gathered from the 1850 population schedules in the manuscript census for the following counties with the number of female heads of households in parentheses: Covington, Alabama (39), Dallas, Alabama (168), Coweta, Georgia (104), Natchitoches Parish, Louisiana (143), Georgetown District, South Carolina (53), Sullivan, Tennessee (162), Weakley, Tennessee (194), Red River, Texas (32), Halifax, Virginia (343). This census did not report the value of personal property. Counties selected represent various parts of the South, cash crops, and racial compositions. For the nature of these counties, see, James Oakes, *The Ruling Race: A History of American Slaveholders* (New York: Alfred A. Knopf, 1982), 245–47.

Table 2. Female Heads of Households: Real Property Holdings, 1860
Dollar Value of Real Property (Percentages in Each Category)

County	0	1–100	101–500	501–1,000	1,001–5,000	5,001–10,000	> 10,000
Covington, Ala.	49.3	4.3	20.3	14.5	8.7	1.4	1.4
Dallas, Ala.	36.5	0	6.9	8.4	25.1	12.3	10.8
Coweta, Ga.	43.9	2.5	9.6	12.7	26.1	3.2	1.9
Natchitoches, La.	44.2	1.9	8.4	9.7	22.1	4.5	9.1
Attala, Miss.	27.0	0.7	14.3	21.4	30.2	3.2	2.4
Georgetown, S.C.	61.2	1.9	15.5	7.8	11.7	0	1.9
Sullivan, Tenn.	58.4	1.9	7.9	8.9	18.7	4.2	0
Weakley, Tenn.	44.8	0.4	11.7	16.7	23.0	2.1	1.2
Red River, Tex.	29.3	0	20.0	14.7	21.3	5.3	9.3
Halifax, Va.	50.0	2.6	8.2	10.3	20.8	3.7	4.5

Data gathered from the 1860 populations schedules in the manuscript census. The number of female heads of households for each county is: Covington, Alabama (69), Dallas, Alabama (203), Coweta, Georgia (157), Natchitoches Parish, Louisiana (154), Attala, Mississippi (126), Georgetown District, South Carolina (103), Sullivan, Tennessee (214), Weakley, Tennessee (239), Red River, Texas (75), Halifax, Virginia (380). This census counted personal property in a separate category. Adding personal property to real property would place many of the female heads of households in the next-higher income category. Total property statistics are useful for analyzing the Civil War's economic effects on Southern women.

life. Of course some women married wealth or chose husbands who were likely to rise in the world. But for single women or widows who either would not or could not marry, economic mobility seemed to be for men only.

9

The straitened economic condition of most unmarried women both reflected and reinforced contemporary attitudes about their proper place. Indeed popular notions about female character and potential contained a good deal of self-fulfilling prophecy. Because many women owned little or no property, they had little chance of succeeding as farmers or planters; and so long as most businesses and professions remained closed to them, women usually could not save enough money to buy land.

Those looking for work outside the home soon discovered how few opportunities the Southern economy afforded women. The 1860 census listed housekeeper and seamstress as the most common occupations, though this information is misleading because wealthy widows who managed plantations were often classified as "housekeepers." Other women simply appear as "widows" or "at home." The census takers also ignored women who worked in their husband's stores or kept the books (sometimes a necessity to prevent their besotted spouses from drinking up the profits).[70] Because much of this information was gathered so carelessly and haphazardly, census data greatly underestimate women's contributions to the Southern economy, though better numbers would not exactly paint a rosy picture.

During the antebellum decades, increasing numbers of women worked outside the home, but mostly in traditional female jobs. Even in cities, seamstress and laundress remained the most common occupations. And though some women managed retail groceries, taverns, or other small businesses, they generally struggled along on modest incomes. If one's family was not reasonably well off, there were few other sources of capital. Elizabeth Carter sold small items out of her house in rural Arkansas and was glad when she earned five dollars a week. Any ambitious woman scanning a newspaper would find few openings except for sewing or caring for children.[71]

A housewife with a good-sized home might rent out rooms or even open a boardinghouse. Scattered entries in the manuscript census suggest that in this way some city and small-town women gained a steady income and even acquired considerable property. But all the work involved—including the constant strain of catering to cantankerous guests—made each dollar a hard-earned one.[72] Feisty boardinghouse keepers defied conventional wisdom about woman's natural passivity and dependence but soon learned how much initiative, imagination, and tenacity they needed for even modest success.

More commonly, women entered the antebellum economy as workers rather than as entrepreneurs. In the Northern states, industrialization created jobs but at the same time removed traditional crafts, such as spinning and weaving, from the household.[73] In the South, these changes took place much more slowly; a few factories complemented but did not supplant domestic manufacturing. In most parts of the South, the household remained the chief unit of production despite the appearance of a few factories. On the eve of the Civil War when many housewives and slave women still produced their own cloth, white women also made up more than 10 percent of the labor force (mostly in textile mills) in five of the future Confederate states.[74]

Fragmentary evidence offers only tantalizing glimpses into the lives of female factory workers in the Old South. Many were apparently teen-agers from the hill country; their earnings averaged five to seventeen dollars a month. Imitating the practices of Northern textile manufac-turers such as those in Lowell, Massachusetts, some employers provided dormitories for their hands, but a South Carolinian judged company housing in her area little better than slave cabins. Most factories, how-ever, were modeled on the Slater system and relied on the labor of widows and their children. Working conditions ranged from adequate to abominable. In Alabama, that peripatetic Northern commentator Fred-erick Law Olmsted saw scantily clad women and children shoveling iron ore and working as hard as any man. Some employers took a paternalistic interest in their workers' material and moral welfare while others fol-lowed a more coldly economic calculus. Child care for working mothers (if the children did not work in the factories themselves) was largely unknown except in Nashville and Charleston, which had special schools for these youngsters.[75] Yet these scattered facts leave many questions unanswered. What motivated these women to seek employment in the new mills? How did they view the transition from domestic to factory work? To what extent did these new enterprises disrupt family life and call traditional domestic ideology into question?

Whatever the effects of this movement of several thousand women from farm to factory, by 1860 the general employment picture was still bleak. Unskilled women with families to support toiled as seamstresses or domestic servants. Their reduced circumstances convinced some girls of the importance of staying in school. In a perceptive letter to her father, Lizzie Ozburn claimed that a properly educated woman could remain single and become economically self-sufficient. Although she surely ex-aggerated the prospects for such women, she also recognized their desire to avoid being dependent on men. "I love the English and northern people," she concluded, "because they believe in every one having an occupation or trade that will enable them to get a living for themselves any where."[76] Ironically, even a good education opened no such doors of opportunity in the South. As she considered her future, Lizzie Ozburn finally chose the one profession available to respectable Southern ladies: teaching.

In the nineteenth century, the schoolroom seemed a safe and proper place for women to practice their nurturing skills, and even in the South the number and proportion of female instructors steadily increased. Yet there was no concerted effort to employ more female teachers; few women held administrative posts, and many earned as little as two hundred dollars a year for a school term that in some places ran well into and even through the hot summer. Often mired in debt, they barely survived on such meager salaries.[77] Most schools and many academies had only one teacher, and if enrollment fell, she might find her income halved with little chance of ever recouping the loss. Governesses and private tutors fared no better. Women who offered music, dance, or art lessons in their homes could not make enough to support their families.[78] Little wonder that teachers wrote in their letters and diaries of being cast into a cold and heartless world.

Besides low salaries, the daily frustrations of dealing with rude, un-disciplined, and academically unprepared students gave young women little incentive to make teaching a career. Instead they often viewed it as a stopgap along the road to matrimony.[79] In salary and even prestige, teaching was only marginally better than more customary female oc-cupations. And given the paucity of real opportunities for either ad-vancement or financial independence, the growing number of women who entered the factories and the classrooms had many reasons to long for a more conventional life with a husband and children.

10

Because most jobs open to women in the antebellum South were either menial, tedious, or low paying, who could blame them for preferring the possible security of a family and home over uncertain advancement in an economy stacked against female enterprise? Except in a vicarious way through the experiences of fathers, brothers, and husbands, the arena of struggle and competition, where the dollar measured a person's worth, remained forbidden ground. Divorce and property-law reform touched the lives of relatively few women; likewise improvements in education largely benefited upper-class women. Church work and other forms of benevolence generally reinforced domestic ideals. In short, Southern households remained bastions of social conservatism.

As historians have continued the debate about whether Southern slaveholders were hard-driving capitalists or prebourgeois patriarchs, the distinct experiences of Southern women in both the planter and yeoman classes and their relationship to Southern cultural norms have largely been ignored. That most slaveholders hoped to turn a profit is difficult to deny, but if there was a haven for anticommerical values in the South, it was in the home. For in many ways women seemed more traditional and more prone to cling to older notions of propriety than their menfolk. Although the sources reveal little about the opinions of poor white women, substantial evidence concerning the views of plantation (and to a lesser extent, yeoman) women shows wives and mothers who, despite many problems and some complaints, fundamentally accepted or at least seldom disputed their assigned places and roles in the economic, social, and familial order. Women might sublimate a vague discontent in social activities or simply welcome the modest reforms of the antebellum decades, and those who thought about such matters might even marvel at how much women's lives could improve in such a conservative social environment or they might simply resign themselves to living with what they had little prospect of changing. When sectional tensions mounted and increasingly intruded into the domestic routine, most Southern women stood by the values of their culture because they had never examined or seriously questioned them. As both products and in some ways beneficiaries of a slave society, educated and articulate women in particular resented outside attacks on the South and defended their world against the forces of modernity, fanaticism, and abolitionism. Despite the grievances that some women nursed against the slave system and the latent class tension between yeoman and planter families—tensions that would erupt into sharp conflict during the Civil War—at the end of the antebellum period Southern society appeared remarkably placid. For the time being, the ambiguities of Southern domestic ideology papered over sexual and class divisions and at the same time magnified racial distinctions. Although the appearance of domestic peace and social consensus could be deceiving (and even if women's loyalty to a nascent Southern nation was not unshakable), it seemed solid enough.

CHAPTER 2

Defenders of the Faith

M ANY WHITE WOMEN HAD GOOD REASONS to internalize or at least to live with the economic and social values of the Old South, values that would be sorely tested but could survive even the fiery ordeal of civil war. And if women found comfort and security in rigidly defined sex roles, they, like those German women who supported nazism, felt an intense racial pride.[1] To paraphrase W. J. Cash, come what might they would always be white women.

Despite their own subordinate status in Southern society, many women directly participated in and benefited from a labor system far more degrading than patriarchy at its worst. Besides providing a domestic haven for slaveholding men, they reaped the rewards of exploitation and racial hegemony and at the same time became entangled in a complicated web of paternalism and cruelty, of sympathy and callousness, of pride and defensiveness.

As an important part of a racial and social hierarchy that also categorized people according to class and sex, female slaveholders identified with a reactionary social system that claimed to exalt and protect women. Some women of course recognized their anomalous position in an oppressive social order and condemned slavery as an immoral institution harmful to both races, but they are notable because they were so exceptional. By extracting a few juicy quotations from diaries and memoirs written several decades after the Civil War, historians have greatly exaggerated the amount of female antislavery sentiment in the antebellum South.[2] In fact few white women could transcend barriers of race and class to develop a sympathetic understanding of the slave's plight. Indeed the evidence of women either tacitly or actively supporting the institution is overwhelming.

Not only did they acquiesce in and benefit from slavery, but they also stood ready to defend it from outside attack. Even from their marginal position in the South's political culture, some women joined their menfolk in wrestling with sectional issues and, despite some reluctance during the early stages of the secession crisis, became ardent Southern nationalists.

1

Aside from isolated, occasional denunciations of slavery, most women seemed simply to have accepted the institution without questioning its legitimacy. Even Mary Chesnut, the most celebrated female critic of slavery, enjoyed the fruits of black labor all her life. She lived comfortably with her antislavery convictions and her slaves, relishing the luxury of clean, white sheets; fresh cream in her coffee; breakfast in bed; and plenty of leisure time to denounce slavery in her diary. Indeed her famous analogy between the condition of slaves and the status of women generally has mislead many historians into exaggerating white women's resentment of the institution.[3]

Other supposedly antislavery comments in diaries and letters often signify little more than momentary pique, and in most cases Southern women worried more about the burden placed on the mistress than about the suffering of the slave. From this perspective, white women who had to watch over, cajole, and punish the "servants" became the "real slaves."[4] At the end of a tiring day, slaveholders of both sexes often threw up their hands in dismay, but historians should not mistake exasperation for abolitionism.

As plantation mistresses and yeoman women went about their many daily tasks, they helped make slavery work. Far from being discontented and reluctant participants in the system, white women contributed much to its economic success. Many knew more about agriculture than their fathers, brothers, or husbands would have suspected or admitted. Some even immersed themselves in the details of cotton planting, crop diseases, and slave management.[5] Widows and single women, who made up about 10 percent of the slaveholding class, often ran farms and plantations on their own. Although the manuscript census frequently listed their occupation as "keeping house," these women took pride in their accomplishments. Dolly Sumner Lunt bragged about making forty-five bags of cotton on her own; after some experience with overseers, Rachel O'Connor decided she could do better by herself.[6] As some women struggled and others became astute and confident mistresses, they collaborated with men in buttressing the slave system.

2

A key question still lingers: did gender make a difference? Many young Southern girls learned to be women and slaveholders at the same time. Growing up with slavery meant quickly discovering what the institution demanded of women. Becoming acculturated into the system at an early age, girls usually looked to their mothers as models of the successful mistress. Most in fact recalled their mothers' treating slaves with kindness and patience. Although time inevitably clouded their memories and historians (along with some former slaves) have exaggerated the prevalence of "da good mistis," such paragons existed. These grand matriarchs of the plantation legend—along with those who fell considerably short of the ideal—helped create a complex and often tragic paternalism in which racial pride partly compensated for sexual subordination. When white women referred to slaves as their black family, they were not always trading in the coin of cheap hypocrisy. While at school in Staunton, Virginia, Kate Cox wrote about how much she missed her "devoted friends," describing in lyrical fashion the mutual duties and privileges of the two races. Because so many mistresses saw themselves as pious Christians caring for helpless dependents, they easily became complacent and condescending in their dealings with slaves. Although a certain gentleness softened the harsher features of bondage, it could not eliminate them. In South Carolina a former slave told how his mistress would pat the young blacks on the head and smile at them; but when the master cursed them, she walked away.[7] Humane treatment by the mistress and devoted service from the slave could build bonds of affection—bonds that did unite black and white families, bonds that helped the white women perhaps to salve uneasy consciences, and bonds that helped the slave survive.

Yet if female slaveholders *seemed* to wield their power less arbitrarily and brutally than white men—and the evidence on this question is often contradictory—their supposedly more humane treatment of black people contained its own subtle cruelties. Planning slaves' weddings, buying them Christmas presents, or weeping at their funerals could not eliminate the exploitative nature of the relationship. For slavery corrupted kindness, along with all the other tender emotions. There was a thin line between recognizing the slaves' humanity and treating them as amusing pets. One housewife slipped a slave child corn bread and sausage under the table—much as she would have done for a favorite dog. Privileges such as riding in a carriage at the foot of the mistress or sleeping under her bed proved equally demeaning. When white women interfered with the most intimate aspects of slave life, including the selection of spouses, they obviously showed little respect for blacks as people who could make their own decisions.[8] Paternalism may have lessened the physical cruelty of slavery, but it fostered dependence in both races and revealed the harsh psychological effects of bondage.

The thoughtless exploitation of black labor occurred daily in Southern homes, and even morally sensitive white women seldom noticed. In hot weather, slaves fanned their mistresses to keep them cool. White women remembered this as a pleasant feature of the old regime; slaves remembered being whipped for falling asleep.[9]

The slaveholders and their slaves lived side by side but in different worlds. The evidence suggests no particular sympathy by mistresses for female slaves; a Petersburg woman even whipped a pregnant slave.[10] Distinctions of class and race often blunted human sympathies. And despite notable examples of women who shielded slaves from punishment, many mistresses believed that blacks had to be dealt with firmly. Some agreed with male slaveowners and overseers that a flogging now and again kept slaves duly submissive.[11]

If white men struggled to control their tempers, so also did white women, and mistresses often exploded in sudden, unpredictable bursts of anger. When a South Carolina mistress laughed fiendishly as she whipped a slave, she demonstrated how female slaveholders could be and were every bit as cruel as men. Although no worse in this regard than men, some women also crossed the line from severity to sadism. Former slaves remembered mistresses who tied them to trees and hanged them by the wrists before vigorously applying the lash, often till the blood ran down to the ground.[12] And white women—who had good reason to be sensitive to any challenge to their authority—could not tolerate defiance. In some cases, their own dependent position must have made them especially testy when confronted by a disobedient or merely a negligent slave. Any show of resistance only redoubled the determination to make the blacks more respectful if not fearful. One Virginia mistress wedged a slave girl's head under a rocking chair, the better to flog the girl's writhing body; later a doctor had to push the distended face back into shape. Such brutality was seldom calculated or premeditated. In the heat of the moment, a mistress might strike out with whatever was handy. When her cook failed to heat a potato thoroughly, a Texas woman put the slave's eye out with a fork.[13]

In many ways, then, white women either tolerated or directly participated in the most horrifying aspects of slavery. Although some mistresses regretted, opposed, or even prevented slave sales—notably those that would have broken up families—women did not necessarily shun the dirty business of slave trading. They readily disposed of thieving bondsmen and expressed relief at the departure of troublesome slaves.[14] To overemphasize the kindhearted mistress is to ignore much contrary evidence; in a conflict between profit, convenience, and conscience, the head often overruled the heart.

After all, mistresses had an important economic stake in the institution. Whatever objections they might have to particular practices, they learned to live with them. Even miscegenation, that great chink in the slaveholders' armor that might have divided the sexes deeply, failed to shake the loyalty of most white women to the slave system.[15] As Ella Thomas noted in her diary, proper ladies either did not know about, would not acknowledge, or simply ignored the existence of miscegenation. They would certainly not mention it publicly. "Is it not enough," she asked, "to make us shudder for the standard of morality in our Southern homes?"

Even though women like Ella Thomas were bold enough to discuss the matter—at least in their diaries—their sympathies did not lie with the black victims: "I will stand to the opinion that the institution of slavery degrades the white man more than the Negro." In Mary Chesnut's much quoted comments on miscegenation, she too concentrated on the immorality of the masters, not the suffering of the slaves. Her famous lament that "we live surrounded by prostitutes" drove this point home. If Southern men, "like the patriarchs of old . . . live all in one house with their wives & their concubines," the true sufferers were not, she contended, the black women but their white mistresses: "Every lady tells you who is the father of all the Mulatto children in every body's household, but those in her own, she seems to think drop from the clouds."

In such a "monstrous system," white women remained innocent, untouched by the corruption all around them: "Again I say, my countrywomen are as pure as angels—tho surrounded by another race who are—the social evil!"[16] Historians have correctly interpreted these passages as an eloquent attack on miscegenation, but Chesnut's remarks also reflected deep racial and sexual phobias. Rather than denouncing slavery as a labor system or as an oppressive institution, she blamed the black women for luring white men into sin while white women preserved both their virtue and their naïveté.

In a sense, hiding from the problem was a white woman's most practical response and perhaps her only defense against the threat to home and family. For unless she was willing to brave a public scandal by deserting or divorcing her husband, she probably could not stop his illicit liaisons. A Mississippi mistress whose husband often molested black women advised a female slave either to submit or risk being killed. Admitting that her husband was a "dirty man," she sadly confessed to being powerless: "I can't do a thing with him." Beyond crying and praying, there was little relief from shame or the sting of neighborhood gossip. Some women attributed all the mulatto children on their farm or plantation to the overseer or other "white trash," thereby sidestepping the question of how to treat the misdeeds of a husband or prominent neighbor. Only rarely, did a brave woman challenge the conspiracy of silence. William Alexander Percy told how his Aunt Fannie had excluded from her guest list a wealthy man who lived openly with a black woman.[17] But such a bold attempt to uphold public morality and such a display of female assertiveness was unusual enough for Percy to recall it vividly more than half a century later. And even here his aunt was protesting against sexual immorality rather than criticizing the exploitive nature of the relationship.

A woman unable to stop or even question her husband's dalliances often punished the victim who was both convenient and vulnerable. An outraged mistress could therefore insist that the black woman involved be whipped or sold. Men seldom had to fear the fate of a philandering North Carolina master whose wife shot him dead.[18] In a situation where they held few advantages, aggrieved wives had little choice but to suppress their anger and suffer in silence.

Even those white women who might have been willing to turn their outrage against miscegenation into a more general assault on slavery itself faced the same problem that had always stymied abolitionism in the South. The idea of emancipation invariably created hesitation and second thoughts. Educated women in the Upper South had occasionally supported African colonization because, like Thomas Jefferson, they could not conceive of free blacks and whites living together peaceably. For women especially, emancipation conjured up frightening images of murder and even rape. "We are like the inhabitants at the foot of Mt. Vesuvius," Ella Thomas worried, "remaining perfectly contented among so many dangers." Although mistresses found comfort in the convenient fiction that their people were perfectly contented and would never consider rising in revolt, such assertions showed more hopefulness than confidence.[19]

These self-delusions (delusions, of course, shared by men) gave farm and plantation life—at least on the surface—a monotonously placid appearance. Slavery had always been a part of Southern life and seemingly always would be. Whatever their doubts or feelings of guilt, busy women suppressed them and became absorbed in their household duties. Others contributed directly to the most brutal aspects of slavery. Even mistresses who tried to ameliorate the institution's harsher elements proceeded cautiously and in any case lacked the economic and political power necessary to change the system. By somehow softening the relationship between master and slave, they also softened their own sensibilities. By extolling and sometimes living up to the ideal of the Christian mistress, they only strengthened slavery by concealing (at least from themselves) its oppressive character beneath a veneer of compassion.

3

"I have not a single doubt about the rightfulness of slavery," Louisa Davis declared during the secession crisis. Beyond accepting the institution as a necessary and proper system of labor regulation and race control, few female slaveholders had ever felt the need to defend a way of life that most took for granted. Aside from an unthinking racism which led them to consider most blacks to be either helpless children or stupid brutes, the philosophical and moral questions raised by the presence of slaves seemed arcane and largely irrelevant to the daily problems of field and household.[20]

But with the rise of abolition in the North, an intellectual and political defense of slavery suddenly became a practical necessity. The mounting agitation forced educated women at least to give some thought not only to justifying a labor system but also to defending themselves and their families against charges of immorality, oppression, and brutality. In her journal, Susan Cornwall drafted a detailed historical and cultural apologia. Asserting that blacks had never produced an important civilization, she portrayed the race as irresponsible, promiscuous, and barbaric.[21] Other women more casually accepted conventional proslavery arguments, perhaps interjecting them into conversations or making passing references in letters and diaries. Here too the intellectual rationale grew more out of personal experience than from philosophical reflection.

An exception was Louisa McCord, who wrote extensively and thoughtfully in defense of slavery. While attending school in the North, where her father, Langdon Cheves, served as president of the Second Bank of the United States, she had gotten into arguments with antislavery classmates over what she deemed their shallow and hypocritical opinions. She also had acquired considerable knowledge of complex political and economic issues. After returning to the South, marrying, and having three children—in others words, following the path of duty—she began writing long essays for Southern periodicals.[22]

Although accepting pseudoscientific racial arguments for black inferiority, McCord usually dealt with slavery as a question of political economy. Premising her arguments on the assumption of human inequality, she rejected abolitionism and feminism.[23] In her view, Negroes and women both needed protection from exploitation by the powerful; therefore, racial or sexual equality was "insanity." She especially excoriated British abolitionists (no better than "socialists and communists"), who would lower the white race to the primitive standards of the black race.[24]

By joining Josiah Nott and other ethnologists in contending that blacks were biologically suited for bondage, just as whites were suited for liberty, she made slavery the standard for comparing labor relations in America and Europe. "We love our negroes . . . as a father loves his children," she asserted in the classical language of paternalism. Those who shed crocodile tears over the supposed mistreatment of blacks in the South should compare the living conditions in the slave quarters to the misery of the English countryside or cities on both sides of the Atlantic. Echoing George Fitzhugh, she argued that slave society cared for its weaker members rather than casting them aside when they no longer served the interests of capital.[25] Not only had McCord embraced the values of her society, she had learned to defend them with a so-phistication and ferocity that might have seemed unfeminine but instead showed how women could both support and benefit from an oppressive social system.

In spite of this achievement, McCord's articles (like the work of other proslavery apologists) mixed pedantry with polemic. In two review es-says on Harriet Beecher Stowe's *Uncle Tom's Cabin*, she wrote no longer as a political economist but as an outraged Southerner. Along with contemporary and later critics, she questioned the plausibility of many scenes in the novel—as she put it, episodes filled with "vulgarity and absolute falsehood." Every piece of evidence that Stowe could muster against slavery, McCord dismissed as an aberration in an otherwise humane system. Instances of brutality not so easily disposed of, she attributed to the general weakness of human nature rather than to in-herent defects in Southern society. Her writing often degenerated into special pleading and logic chopping: breaking up families was not cruelty to a race that took marriage ties so lightly; if blacks were not inferior to whites, they could never have been forced into slavery.[26] But whatever the flaws in evidence and reasoning, McCord's essays demonstrated a truth she might have been loath to acknowledge: women could write on controversial subjects with an eloquence and verve equal to those of any man. But her essays also showed that educated Southern women who devoted themselves to intellectual pursuits would not likely ques-tion traditional sex roles or deviate from proslavery orthodoxy. In both attitudes and actions, both consciously and unconsciously, among the lettered and illiterate alike, most women remained bulwarks of the ancien régime.

4

By writing articles and even by commenting on slavery in their diaries and letters, women had entered politics. But they did so as defenders of the status quo in a world seemingly beset by frightening and uncon-trollable change. Thus despite her great interest in public questions, Louisa McCord drew the line at delivering public speeches. Believing that her sex was not strong enough to engage in political controversy, she also argued that women should avoid men's partisan squabbling. In her view, then, females stood both below and above politics. Their exclusion from public life rested not only on the peculiarities of feminine character but also on the convenient fiction of marital unity. "One of her [woman's] highest privileges," wrote an anonymous essayist, "is to be politically merged in the existence of her husband." In this way Southern men preserved peace in their homes and in the civic arena, a tranquillity seemingly welcomed by both sexes. If women ever did become active in politics, a Georgia clergyman warned, elections would become tumultuous as "patriotic amazons" tore each other's clothes to advance their candidates' cause.[27] That these "patriotic amazons" might aspire to office themselves was apparently beyond his wildest imagination.

But even in such a restrictive environment, women gradually became part of the political culture. In concentrating on the ballot box and courthouse, historians and political scientists have defined political participation too narrowly and therefore have ignored women's role in antebellum politics. After all politics takes place in the home as well as on the stump or at the polling place. During election campaigns, women could and did discuss candidates and issues with their families; bolder spirits even offered their menfolk advice on how to vote. Most of these conversations occurred informally and out of public view and even though the effects are hard to measure, voting cannot be isolated from home influences—including the opinions of women. Even the ultraconservative Thomas R. Dew suggested that men consult their wives before making political decisions for the family, thus implicitly conceding that women had ideas worth considering.[28]

Dew had a point. Some women closely followed politics and developed strong views on both men and measures. Several weeks after the presidential election of 1844, ardent Whig Elizabeth Bestor still smarted over the victory of "obscure Jim Polk." She had considered naming her new baby "defeat" but decided that in another four years she might have to rename him "triumph." Since women's political education occurred in the home, they usually echoed the convictions and prejudices of their fathers and husbands. But some women also disagreed with their menfolk, and a few even asserted their prerogative to follow an independent course. Rachel McNeill favored Know-Nothingism in spite of her husband's opposing views. "I am not an advocate of Woman's Rights," she wrote to a cousin, "but ... she should have at least the right to think and speak if not act."[29] This willingness to think without acting illustrated how tentatively yeoman and upper-class housewives broached public questions. In absorbing the political values and atmosphere of Southern society, women reaffirmed their commitment to domestic ideology and Southern cultural norms while expanding their own intellectual horizons.

As members of families obsessed with politics, the daughters and wives of public officials had unusual opportunities to cultivate their own views. Although in the nineteenth century few people could have named the wives of prominent politicians, these women often knew a great deal about politics. Looking for ways to advance their husbands' careers, they developed decided opinions on party strategy. Despite hoping that her husband, Howell, would obtain a seat in President-elect James Buchanan's cabinet, Mary Ann Cobb urged him not to take a position beneath his talents and astutely weighed the advantages of an appointment and its effect on his standing in Georgia. Her letters contain the usual claims about preferring domestic life, but they also reveal a woman of keen intelligence and intense ambition. Yet for every woman who reveled in public life or enjoyed cutting a figure in fashionable society, there was another who genuinely preferred a quieter existence. "The truth is I think domestic happiness and political life are diametrically opposed to each other," Laura Bryan perceptively observed. Families complicated political careers, and the expenses of public life devoured household budgets. In the fall of 1851, Varina Davis admitted to her parents that defeat for the Southern Rights cause (and for her husband, Jefferson) would ease the drain on the family's finances.[30]

Whatever their own reservations, politicians' wives often looked beyond home interests, taking a proprietary pride in their husbands' careers. They helped write speeches, answer letters, copy public documents, and, most important, plot strategy. In a series of letters written to her husband, Benjamin F. Perry, while he served in the South Carolina legislature, Elizabeth Perry showed solid political instincts along with the intensity and ambition her husband so noticeably lacked. Constantly prodding him to stay in public service, she dismissed his love for domestic life as "effeminate" and an excuse that would only comfort his political enemies. Yet she did more than play on her husband's ego and sense of manhood; she once criticized him for a hastily written newspaper letter that flattered his political inferiors, and she did not hesitate to question his judgment. When he strongly endorsed the Mexican War, she pointed out the dangers of alienating both the Whigs and the followers of John C. Calhoun. But only four days after writing this letter, she promised to stop making political suggestions and again become a "kind and sweet wife."[31] Perhaps she had offered one too many admonitions and had overstepped the bounds of feminine propriety.

After all even an Elizabeth Perry had to write and speak circumspectly. Like most Southern women whose interest and ambition revolved around their fathers and husbands, her political views remained of mostly private interest. Although beginning with the 1840 presidential election campaign, a few women attended speeches and rallies, they remained largely spectators on the political scene. When a woman dared write to a public official, either asking for political favors or soliciting views on the questions of the day, she generally adopted an effusively apologetic tone. In a letter to Andrew Johnson, Lizinka Campbell showed a clear grasp of politics but included the expected demurrer: "Of course being a woman, I can not pretend to understand these matters." Thus women became part of the antebellum political culture but did so cautiously. The fervent Whig lady who once accosted Jefferson Davis to offer a stern lecture on how Andrew Jackson and the Democrats had ruined the country by removing the federal deposits from the Second Bank of the United States was notable primarily because she was so exceptional.[32] To express such strong views in public went well beyond conventional definitions of feminine propriety. For women with emphatic opinions on public questions, the home remained their political arena.

5

For the most part, women's interest in politics remained sporadic, and even during the tumultuous 1850s, remarks on public issues appear only infrequently in their diaries and letters. Many busy housewives hardly seemed to notice the bitter and lengthy debates over slavery in the national territories. Though a few women became more politically conscious during the decade, most remained silent and apparently apathetic.[33]

If women rarely commented on such explosive issues as the Compromise of 1850, the Kansas-Nebraska Act, the Dred Scott decision and the Lecompton Constitution, they obviously did not think that such abstract and distant matters could affect their lives and families. In 1859, however, their relative indifference to politics suddenly seemed a foolish and dangerous luxury. John Brown's raid at Harpers Ferry—which appeared to strike directly at the Southern home—awakened many farmwives and plantation mistresses to the dangers of antislavery radicalism. More than previous insurrection panics, this incident made women from Virginia to Texas uneasy about the loyalty, not just of their neighbors' slaves, but of their own. "We feel that we can trust none of the dear black folks," young Susan Bradford confided to her diary. "I am afraid to say a word for fear it will prove to be just what should have been left unsaid." Vividly imagining wild-eyed Negroes pillaging, murdering, and raping their way through the countryside, Sarah Rodgers Espy prayed that "the women and children of the South be saved from their Northern murderers."[34]

This increasing anxiety about security also made party politics and elections seem more important. Although women apparently took little interest in the presidential campaign of 1860, beyond deploring the politicians' selfishness and divisions within Southern ranks, many finally concluded that Abraham Lincoln's election directly threatened their domestic tranquillity. The repeated secessionist charges that the victorious Republicans intended to foment servile insurrections and eventually enslave white Southerners struck an especially responsive cord in wives and mothers. Accepting the view of proslavery ideologues that white liberty and black slavery were inseparable, Grace Elmore prayed: "May we be worthy of our forefathers who resisted being trampled upon."[35] Yet excluded from direct participation in politics, women (and many men) still had trouble understanding much less embracing the more theoretical and legalistic aspects of Southern nationalism, especially the highly technical constitutional arguments for secession. For women living on farms and plantations, or even in towns and cities, only the more tangible dangers which so haunted their imaginations could rouse them from political lethargy.

Trying to generalize about secession sentiment, historians have ignored or minimized the complex response of individuals to the crisis. As part of a parochial culture, women weighed their immediate interests against more abstract ideals. They also remained dependent on men for political information and for cues on proper political opinions; those who listened to speeches or engaged in debates at home generally found secessionist arguments persuasive. "Better Carolina should be annihilated, better to be crushed by superior strength, than live under false colors," Grace Elmore declared. Some interpreted the election of Lincoln as a triumph of puritanism, greed, and demagoguery over sacred constitutional principles; others joined Jefferson Davis in summoning forth the history and spirit of the American Revolution to justify the creation of a Southern nation; the more rabid chaffed at delay and blasted Southern politicians for equivocating and hesitating when the times demanded prompt and firm action.[36]

In echoing the various shades of Southern-rights opinion in conversations, diaries, and letters, only a few women systematically analyzed the crisis, but their remarks show a growing political acumen and again suggest how women informally participated in Southern political culture. As the Gulf South states left the Union in early 1861, Susan Cornwall justified separate state action as a defensive response to Yankee coercion. "Do they [the Republicans] think then," she wrote angrily, "that we are as degenerate as our slaves, to be whipped into obedience at the command of our self-styled masters?" Ignoring the possible application of this rhetoric to the power relationships in Southern households, she called on her countrymen (and women?) to prevent a "sectional majority" from destroying liberty and urged the establishment of a Southern nation that would vindicate the past glories of true republicanism. In the future lay revolution and a rebirth of white liberty, for Cornwall did not shy away from arguing that the new Southern Confederacy had as its cornerstone a defense of African slavery and white supremacy.[37]

Even though such sophisticated expressions of opinion remained largely private, the secession crisis offered women an unprecedented opportunity for stating their views publicly. At such a critical juncture, state and Confederate leaders welcomed support from any quarter. After offering the requisite apologies for meddling in political affairs, several Florida women submitted a long letter on secession to a Jacksonville newspaper. They denounced the "submissive policy of Southern politicians" and traced the crisis back to the denial of Southern rights in California and Kansas. To avoid a future of black rule and racial amalgamation, they promised to emulate "our Revolutionary matrons," dusting off spinning wheels and looms for the sacred cause. The women of the South could then "reserve their crinolines to present to our Southern Politicians who have compromised away the rights of the South."[38] By implicitly questioning the manhood of some public officials, these women were not striking a blow against male hegemony in the home. Indeed such extreme statements glossed over the continuing hesitancy and dissension that plagued so many households.

The public appearance of unity belied private divisions, and the secession debates took place in homes as well as in mass meetings and conventions. Some women lived in families nearly torn apart by the crisis. The Civil War as a brothers' war has long been a historical staple, but the problem of conflicting loyalties affected women as well as men. Catherine Edmondston often debated secession with her Unionist parents and sisters, though she hated these confrontations and complained about politics intruding into private life. Yet she stuck to her convictions: "Now it [the Union] is no longer glorious—when it ceases to be voluntary, it degenerates into a hideous oppression. Regret it heartily, mourn over it as for a lost friend, but do not seek to enforce it; it is like galvanizing a dead body!" A visit from her sister Frances in February 1861 was ruined by their constant sparring over secession. Despite the personal pain it caused, she even disagreed with her father—a strikingly bold step for a dutiful daughter—and noted that it was the first time she had not yielded to his judgment. In a sense, she broke with both her family and her own previous beliefs in the sanctity of the Union. For her the American flag now became an "old striped rag," because it symbolized cowardice and vandalism, not to mention domestic discord.[39]

The effort to balance loyalty to family and country often made for hard choices and forced women into unfamiliar and awkward situations. As the Southern states declared their independence from the Union, some women declared their own independence from their menfolk's political opinions. Despite the fundamental conservatism of the slaveholders' revolt, the tumult shook up old ideas by presenting new opportunities for women to assert and test their power in the home and even occasionally in public life.

For young girls coming of age in the midst of sectional crisis, political acculturation began early. Twelve-year-old Susan Bradford received a book written by John C. Calhoun and soon learned the basics of Southern constitutionalism. Young ladies who previously had shown little interest in politics now delivered secession speeches to their classmates or, in the interest of fashion, sported secession cockades. But for many this was not simply child's play. South Carolinian Martha Washington remembered vigorously defending disunion during a family political debate. Her brother looked surprised but said: "I must treat your opinion with more deference hereafter."[40] Other men quickly discovered, whether to their amazement, chagrin, or pleasure, that women not only held strong convictions on public questions but would speak their minds.

Yet women's actions—as opposed to their words—more often than not reinforced their subordinate status in Southern society. After all secessionists promised to preserve, not transform, the Southern way of life. Making secession banners and cockades, rolling bandages, and stitching together cartridge bags all fit within traditional definitions of female benevolence. When young girls dashed about the towns and cities with subscription lists for flags and uniforms, they struck no blows for the emancipation of their sex. Instead their efforts became the subject of much postwar Confederate hagiography, a memorial to women who not only had served the South but who also knew their place.[41] Attending public meetings and sewing secession banners kept women on the fringes of politics, where they could do little more than applaud and sustain decisions made by men.

Did sex, then, make any difference in determining responses to secession? The question has no simple answer. Like Southern men, Southern women speculated about the meaning of disunion without arriving at any firm conclusions, their views ranging from wild optimism to mordant pessimism.[42] Yet from the beginning, and more so than men, women tried to understand how disunion would affect their families. Mothers especially doubted that secession could take place peacefully or that a civil war would be short and painless. In Charleston, Catherine Edmondston sat at breakfast enjoying the "luxurious and peaceful family scene," at the same time knowing "how in an instant it could all be changed—that horror and ruin might take the place of peace and comfort!" Women seldom considered war as an abstraction; they saw through the patriotic bombast to the horrors of countless personal tragedies. Their obsession with the local and the particular—a narrowness but at the same time an acuteness of vision—made their fears especially vivid and realistic. Grace Elmore did not dwell on general suffering but instead worried about the possible death of her brothers: "I purposely pictured my nearest and dearest brought home or worse still, I saw them among the slain and left on the battle field. The sounds that broke the stillness of the night were to me the groans of the wounded. . . . I saw my Mother in her old age shorn of her wealth, her two boys gone, her children scattered." Grace Elmore felt as if she "held the wolf to my breast and it devoured my heart, till I could endure no longer, and throwing my hands above my head I fell upon my knees and cried, 'Hear me oh God! Let this pass from me.' "[43] Although women were hardly immune to martial braggadocio and the accompanying illusions about a short, successful war, for many combat signified pain and sacrifice rather than glory.

The Confederate victory at Fort Sumter, Lincoln's call for troops, and the secession of the Upper South placed such misgivings temporarily in abeyance. Skeptics held their tongues and some women appeared grandiosely confident and fervently patriotic. "A nation fighting for its own homes and liberty cannot be overwhelmed," young Kate Stone trumpeted.[44] In the halcyon days of 1861, such clichés sounded like profound truth, but even as war fervor reached a zealous crescendo, wives and mothers could not help but ponder the future with dark foreboding. From her now precariously perched home near Alexandria, Virginia, Judith McGuire recoiled at the thought of what carnage a single battle would bring.[45]

The press of events, however, temporarily shut out such gloomy thoughts. Time grew short, and the troops had to be sent off to war properly. In doing so women wielded the familiar tools of their sex: the needle and thread. During the spring and summer of 1861, young ladies raised money, gathered material, and hurriedly sewed flags. Amid this frenzied effort, Susan Bradford mused, "This does not seem like war."[46]

She was right. Socializing blended with earnest preparations; domestic skills became public assets; excitement and enthusiasm could temporarily relieve misgivings. Much of this activity culminated in flag-presentation ceremonies; these rituals highlighted the contrast between the passive patriotism of women and the active patriotism of men for in spite of all their hard work, the ladies were often silent participants. Inhibitions against women speaking in public still prevailed. Not only were women supposed to keep quiet on such occasions, they were supposed to remain anonymous. After some Charleston ladies attended a ceremony for the Palmetto Guards, they were mortified to find their names printed in the newspaper.[47]

They need not have worried because their activities fell well within the most strictly defined bounds of female propriety. A Petersburg, Virginia, editor described the usual scene: "The ladies joined in with a zest that wreathed their fair faces with sweet smiles, and waved their snowy handkerchiefs with exultant pride and approval." Such syrupy romanticism inevitably oozed into the speeches men made on these occasions. By extolling both female patriotism and beauty, they expressed common expectations that war would only reinforce traditional social values. In New Orleans, Charles Conrad drove the point home: "Only in such gentle ways as this [sewing flags] are those of the softer sex permitted to express the deep-hearted sympathies which bind them to their country by bonds as strong as religious faith and enduring forever."[48] Loyalty, piety, and stoicism—all the old feminine virtues—therefore still defined woman's place in a Southern world on the brink of chaos.

With uniforms made and flags presented, the boys prepared to set off—whether by train, wagon, horseback, or on foot—to fight for their homes and families. The departure scenes had a set-piece quality; each person instinctively knew his or her assigned role. In cities, in towns, at country crossroads, the first recruits marched off to war while mothers, daughters, wives, sisters, and sweethearts crowded the station platforms and roadsides to watch. The mood of the day ran from lighthearted to solemn. A Virginia woman recalled how she and her friends associated battle "only with bands of music, gold lace, plumes, gorgeous trappings, prancing steeds and military display," with no premonition of the horrors to come. But the young girls of the Summit, Mississippi, Bible Society soberly presented Testaments to the Summit Rifles. A bit of sly flirtation, a few kisses, some last-minute admonitions, some nervous joking, and suddenly the men and boys were gone.[49] Romance, sadness, fear, prayer— all these seemed appropriate responses for women in the war's first months. Yet displaying female devotion to domestic felicity struck a sadly ironic note when the separation of families, which would soon become one of the war's many tragedies, had already begun.

In these last few moments together, women and men acted out their own small part in what would soon become an increasingly familiar and tragic drama. In Fredericksburg, Virginia, Betty Herndon Maury watched "some plain country people telling their sons and husbands good bye." She heard no complaints or regrets and saw few tears. One girl berated her sobbing mother for breaking down in front of the boys. "It will unman them," she warned. A stark realism dampened martial enthusiasm as macabre oddities cropped up even before the troops had left. On a trip from Virginia to Alabama, M. M. Jennings saw a soldier saying good-bye to his mother at a small depot. When the train started to pull out, he tried to jump aboard but his foot slipped. The woman saw her son crushed to death beneath the wheels.[50] Mars began exacting his bloody sacrifices long before anyone could have expected.

The women of the South were not simply victims or innocent by-standers to this national tragedy. Female slaveholders had struggled with and profited from a labor system that lay at the root of the conflict, and most white women had taken pride in the hegemony of their race. Despite their marginal role in the South's political culture, a few women had followed public affairs, and the sectional conflict aroused the interest of many others. They mouthed familiar words: *liberty, honor, Southern rights*; they excoriated the enemies of the white South: black Republicans, abolitionist fanatics, greedy capitalists; they even implicitly defended and tacitly supported a social system that exalted female subordination. In doing so, they took the lessons of their childhood—especially the idea of woman's special piety, understanding, and compassion—seriously and could therefore glimpse the human faces beneath the abstractions. Many could not embrace the blind optimism of the more fervent Southern nationalists. As they defended Southern orthodoxy, they also understood, however dimly, the consequences of secession. They saw their men going off to war; they saw them wounded; they saw them languishing in Yankee prisons; they saw them dying. Mourning dresses would become the fashion.

CHAPTER 3

The Civil War as
Family Crisis

O N THE MORNING OF MAY 11, 1862, near Jackson, Mississippi, Ann Hardeman watched her two sons leave to join the Confederate army. In her diary she assumed the role of the Spartan mother: "They are offered upon the Altar of Patriotism. . . . Our cause is a just and Holy one and God will protect the right."[1] Here was the patriotic woman, the belle ideal of the Lost Cause eulogist and romantic novelist, in the flesh.

Self-sacrifice and patient suffering had long been considered female attributes and, in the South, essential elements for maintaining both the honor of the woman and her family, especially during a crisis when the man of the house had to be away from home.[2] Most women understood these expectations well, and many fulfilled them. After the war, Southern orators lauded the Confederate woman, whose only regret was not having more sons to give for her country, and this legend of the anything-for-the-cause stalwart of the home front had some basis in fact. Everyone knew women who had cheerfully encouraged or sternly prodded their menfolk to enlist and kill as many Yankees as possible.

This ideal of endurance and fortitude exalted the passive female role. Active courage was for men; stoic suffering fell to women. Yet Confederates claimed to worship women even as they waged a war that from the beginning seriously disrupted domestic life. A war ostensibly fought for Southern rights—including the safety and independence of Southern families—destroyed the security of the antebellum world. By putting so many fathers, husbands, and brothers into the armies, the Confederates forced women to take on new and sometimes frightening tasks. Sexual confusion reigned as the course of the fighting seemed to make hash of traditional definitions of female propriety. Maintaining the familiar rhythms of family life became nearly impossible. From unconventional courtships to hasty marriages to family separations to child rearing problems to sexual tension to the constant anxiety about the safety of loved ones in the army, the war seemed to bring nothing but unsettling and occasionally terrifying change. And to women fell the burden of coping with this domestic turmoil while trying somehow to preserve the integrity, the honor, and in many cases by the end of the war the existence of their families.

1

If the war seemed to alter accepted definitions of appropriate female behavior, it left other expectations nearly untouched. Adolescent girls and even older single women trying to live up to antebellum social ideals faced an especially cruel dilemma: they were still expected to marry even though the war had taken away most of the potential husbands. "There is but few men at home," complained Mittie Williams to an unmarried cousin, "and what there is I reckon has declined the idea of ever marrying." With considerable joking about setting one's cap for some dotty old man or robbing the proverbial cradle, young ladies swarmed around any potential beaux left at home. The meaning of *potential,* however, changed to fit sometimes pathetic circumstances. Mary Chesnut listened to several friends debating the merits of wedding a soldier who had lost an arm or leg. One gloomily remarked that it would "be my fate to marry one who has lost his head."[3] Behind such grim humor lay ancient fears of spinsterhood. With each passing month, as more and more young men were killed and wounded, a quiet desperation (occasionally mounting to panic) spread among single women.

At the same time, the war considerably abbreviated the normal courtship period and lessened parental influence. Although chaperons had been de rigueur for the daughters of wealthy planters, they nearly disappeared after 1861 as young people acquired greater freedom of choice and more privacy. "This is an age," Elodie Todd advised her fiancé, "when secession, freedom and, rights are asserted. I am claiming mine and do not doubt that I will succeed in obtaining them." As a result, whirlwind romances produced brief engagements and hasty marriages as young women seemed to rush into matrimony with the first likely man. Adolescent girls supposedly had their heads turned by a military uniform and paid little attention to a potential spouse's background and character. In such exciting times, custom and expediency often clashed. In the spring of 1863, General George Pickett, conducting an especially fervent courtship of LaSalle Corbell, pressed the "lovely Sally" to disregard propriety, fly to his side, and marry him. She, however, deemed such a course unseemly and held him off until they could more properly wed in the fall.[4] But in an age given over to marriage mania, such hesitancy seemed quaintly old-fashioned, and the Picketts were more the exception than the rule.

Calls for prudence, judgment, and deliberation went largely unheeded. After talking with a young refugee from New Orleans, Ella Thomas could only shake her head in disapproval and disbelief. Married at fourteen and with four children, the woman had lost her husband in one of the Seven Days' Battles around Richmond, yet she joked about the handsome factory boys at Columbus, Georgia, and breezily announced her plans to remarry. Such recent widows competed with single women for a shrinking supply of men—the fewer the choices, the greater the urgency to find one. In 1861, Kate Corbin had bragged about avoiding entanglements with men and condescendingly noted how blind lovers were to each other's faults; two years later, she was planning her wedding at the insistence of her impatient fiancé. She did not like such last-minute arrangements but thought she had no choice: it was better to wed immediately than face a life of poverty alone.[5] Traditionalist tongues wagged over each new violation of the old rules of courtship and marriage. Order itself, an essential feature of proper family life, seemed to be threatened by the adoption of freer, modern practices, many of them imported from the North, censorious Southern nationalists might have added.

Few women could afford the luxury of being either deliberate, choosy, or entirely conventional because wartime hardships only intensified the pressure to marry. Economic reality, old social expectations, and innumerable contemporary examples weighed heavily even on the intelligent and the independent-minded. Living on the Grove Hill plantation in the Shenandoah Valley at the beginning of the war, sixteen-year-old Lucy Breckinridge had already thought long and carefully about the seriousness of matrimony: "A woman's life after she is married, unless there is an immense amount of love, is nothing but suffering and hard work. I never saw a wife and mother who could spend a day of unalloyed happiness and ease." Children fussed and cried; husbands got cross. Men could make their wives happy, she believed, but few did. Her aunt had died after seven years of marriage and five children, and she could not "help thinking that Uncle Wilmer is a bluebeard." God had cursed women more than men, she suspected, even though "Eve did not show more weakness than Adam."[6]

Despite these gloomy reflections and her obvious lack of commitment to traditional notions of family and female honor, however, Lucy Breckinridge doubted that she could or should avoid the fate of most women. By August 1862, she was preparing for a marriage that promised little happiness, refusing to believe the old lie that love would smooth out all problems. Apparently relieved when the engagement was broken off, by December she had resigned herself to becoming a "sweet old maid . . . one of those joyous spirits that ever 'make sunshine in a shady place!' "[7] However sincere the comments seemed at the time, she soon abandoned her resolution.

Young officers flocked to Grove Hill, fascinated by the vivacious but elusive Miss Breckinridge. During the last half of 1863, at least three of these men courted her, but she remained wary of making a bad match, even though her aloofness and detachment had begun to wear thin. "Women are so lovely, so angelic, what a pity they have to unite their fates with such coarse, brutal creatures as men, but some of them are *right* good," she wrote. In January 1864 she finally became engaged to a young lieutenant and enjoyed his company regardless of her nagging doubts about marriage. Men might promise the world before the wedding, but somehow reality always took the bloom off the romance. Should she sacrifice present happiness with her fiancé by getting married? Even with the date set for September, she felt uneasy. "It is woman's nature," she mused, "to love in a submissive trusting way, but it is better and safer to rely altogether upon themselves—poor creatures!"[8] After all these second thoughts, the wedding did finally come off, and Lucy Breckinridge's premonitions of disaster came true, albeit in an unexpected way. Shortly after her marriage, she died of typhoid fever.

Lucy Breckinridge's experience was hardly typical, but it does illustrate how the war complicated decisions on marriage, especially for young people who had qualms in the first place. Unexpected delays or hasty marriages with soldiers during brief furloughs made what was intended to be a permanent relationship seem impermanent. An air of impending tragedy hung over many wartime weddings, and most Southerners knew friends or relatives who had been killed in battle shortly after the ceremonies.[9] Yet human beings are adaptable and are able to shut out such unpleasant considerations. Women and men remained willing to take a chance even though they might not be able to establish a normal home life for several years—if ever. In so many ways the war made a mockery of dreaming and planning for the future as uncertainty and sudden sorrow made it more and more difficult for both sexes, but especially for women, to play their expected parts in the Confederate social order.

2

Because of its effect on families, enlisting in the army meant more than performing a patriotic duty, more than going off on a high adventure, more than reluctantly risking one's life. Trying to forestall objections from their wives, men regularly appealed to the idea of family honor. In this case, honor (or dishonor) was not exclusively masculine; women would share the opprobrium if their menfolk skulked about at home during a time of public danger.[10] "Better a widow than married to a craven" became a popular home-front motto.

The failure of either sex to behave appropriately during the crisis might well disgrace the family, and if men felt pressure to enlist, women felt equal pressure not only to agree to but to welcome and support the decision. All easier said than done, of course, and seemingly ardent patriotism often concealed inner reservations and painful ambivalence. Although Mary Blackford had heard mothers wish they had a hundred sons to send off to war, she was "not one of those heroines" and regarded it as "dire necessity only." Those who shared this reluctance in turn felt guilty for not being braver. Convenient excuses readily came to mind: a sturdy farmer could better serve his country by raising corn and caring for his family; a favorite son should stay home and not break his mother's heart.[11] As public duty and private interest became hopelessly entangled, second thoughts made women regret rash promises about making sac- rifices. Patriotism seemed easy, thought Sue McDowell, until the war touched home and loved ones, and then we "pine to keep them with us."[12] Parochialism may have complemented the reluctance to send men off to fight on distant battlefields, but thousands of women (and men) seemed trapped by their hypersensitivity to family reputation.

But once the decision had been made, however hesitantly, and a man had gone off to fight, the women left behind were supposed to remain cheerful and patriotic, their letters brimming with optimism and good cheer. Mail, the perennial herald of news, bearer of tidings, and servant of intimacy, became more important than ever when a long-awaited letter could strengthen, maintain, weaken, or shatter the bonds of affection. In both camp and home, letters became a mixed blessing. They could bring word of health and good fortune or reports of shortages, high prices, hunger, illness, and death. As the war dragged on, no news sometimes seemed preferable to any news. "I do not wish for letters," Kate Stone commented. "The sight of a letter turns me sick with apprehension."[13] With the lists of the wounded, missing, and dead lengthening, no wonder civilians opened each envelope with a mixture of delight and dread.

The problem was that even regular letters proved but a poor substitute for normal family life; indeed many letters show the futility of men and women trying to pretend that everything was all right. When such efforts failed, the worries that surfaced in these letters—or those that women more privately recorded in their diaries—not only reflected the stress created by danger to loved ones but also pointed to subtle changes in the character of Southern family life. Separation often reawakened dormant emotion in marriages, and mail conveyed affection in both directions. To be sure, much of it was couched in the conventional, stiff, and syrupy Victorian formulas of mutual worship. Yet despite their repetitiveness, the letters often had a spontaneous and touching quality. Samuel R. Latta admitted to his wife, Mary, that he was "not demonstrative nor . . . apt in words to express to you my love" but could better describe his feelings on paper than in person.[14]

In an age of coy respectability, layers of sentimentality concealed physical desire that had to be restrained or suppressed. Minerva Bone told her husband Robert how she missed kissing "those sweet lips and lovely face." Sublimated passion often broke through to the conscious mind in dreams, many implicitly sexual. Alpha Edge imagined her self being in her husband's arms again "hugin and kissin." And though rare, earthier comments occasionally appeared. A young woman identified only as Julia, after the usual admonitions to her fiancé (a Confederate soldier named James Higgins) to kill Yankees, recalled the pleasure they had taken on the bed and sofa, the delightful sensations when he "put it in the whole length." She then promised to love him with "all my hart and body dear Jim and will keep it closed fore you when you come home to break it open again it will be as tight as the first time you tried it."[15] If the war could bring forth such frank expressions of female passion, then what other unpredictable (and what most Southerners would have considered undesirable) consequences might result from the disruption of the old and tightly controlled rituals of courtship and marriage?

Of course most expressions of love were safely demure and romantic. Recalling the "days and hours" of happiness spent with her husband in words more sentimental than sensual, Kate Petty flattered him as one of "nature's noblemen," stressed her womanly weakness and even apologized for taking up his precious time reading her love notes. Life itself, she declared, revolved around his interests.[16] Again a brave attempt to pretend that somehow old family values could survive the war unscathed. Such reassurances of dependence belied the growing assertiveness and power that women now exerted at home, but conventional ideas about the relationship of wife and husband showed great resiliency. Lounging in front of a fire in the evening, reading aloud to each other, praying together—women longed for simple domestic pleasures. Sarah Yancey wanted her husband to return so she could again sit "watching your every movement and even trying to anticipate your wishes before they were expressed."[17] Such statements warmed men's hearts but became increasingly rare after the war's first year. Women busy with farms, plantations, and households had little time to worry about male prerogatives.

Indeed common expectations about feminine frailty and dependence now clashed with calls for stoic endurance and heroic sacrifice. A confusion of voices added to other wartime worries and frustrations, and women tried to play contradictory roles. Hoping to preserve their domestic influence, they also became impassioned patriots who tried to model their conduct on that of their Revolutionary War grandmothers. Worrying about how their men were faring in camp, many took an almost authoritarian tone in their letters. Mothers sternly lectured sons on duty, honor, and country and then fretted over everything from army food to spelling errors in letters.[18] Some women obviously wanted to govern their menfolk's lives long distance, but homey advice barely concealed the pain of sending young boys off to war. Not only was an idolized son leaving home "to become a man" (this chestnut about military life already had a long and dishonorable history), but he was growing up away from his mother's influence and out of her sight.

Above all, women feared the loss of moral authority, their most potent source of domestic influence. Wives and mothers pictured army camps as dens of iniquity in which evil lurked everywhere, ready to entice young boys to drink, swear, gamble, and (if one dared to imagine it) fornicate. Immorality, however, never originated with the beloved son, brother, or husband. Its source lay elsewhere: with the coarse, godless men who filled the Confederate ranks, just as their ancestors had filled armies throughout history, and with the camp followers who corrupted innocent young boys. Civilian and soldier alike often displayed a sad, and sometimes amusing, naiveté about human nature. Anna Clark, positive that "no foul oath ever polluted" her son William's lips, hoped he would emerge from the ordeal "pure and uncontaminated." Think of God and your mother, she advised, whenever temptation appears.[19] By assuming their traditional role as defenders of piety, women sought to preserve the family against the many unsettling changes brought on by the war while safeguarding the values of an evangelical culture.

If wives and mothers would eventually be forced into unfamiliar economic roles, many remained the great defenders what might be called domestic sentimentalism—the female as guardian of moral virtue. Women prayed for soldiers to put on the armor of Christian righteousness, and those who had long harangued men about the state of their souls now felt an even greater urgency. Julia Davidson feared her husband's reticence on religious topics meant that he was again drinking and swearing. Having exhausted other arguments, she pressed him to abandon the bottle with an appeal to the memory of his "sainted mother."[20]

The burdens of spiritual guardianship and the constant anxiety about the safety of loved ones steadily drained the physical and emotional strength of Confederate women. Many suffered from nervous headaches or debilitating depression; any unusual dream appeared as a frightening portent. If a wife had not heard from her husband recently, she concluded that he must be ill or wounded or dead. "I live only in the present," cried Florence King, fretting over her brother Henry. "The past is dreary and sad, the future black as midnight."[21]

Although Northern women obviously shared similar worries, Confederate losses, disappointments, rapidly approaching enemy armies, and mounting casualties threatened to overwhelm what appeared like increasingly futile attempts to hold families together during the war. Private jitters soon led to doubts about the cause itself. Premonitions of personal disaster easily turned into pessimism about the outcome of the fighting because individual anxiety naturally hurt Confederate morale.[22] The horrors of war, real and imagined, caused women to waver between despair and hope. One minute they envisioned their boys dying on a distant battlefield; the next moment, they looked forward to a joyous homecoming. But momentary optimism usually gave way to worry that domestic happiness had vanished forever, a pain both assuaged and intensified by religious conviction. Ella Thomas believed the grace of Jesus Christ sufficient for all earthly trials, including the loss of a husband. As she remembered her country's many widows, however, she fervently prayed that "this cup pass from me." On the other hand, Nancy Diamond feared that her unconverted son, "still outside the ark of safety," would be killed in battle without the news ever reaching home and of course without the boy ever reaching heaven.[23]

And if religious faith provided uncertain comfort, women also had to cope with their own isolation at home and doubt about their role and contributions to the cause. Some housewives obviously tried to lose themselves in their work, but mounting frustration often overcame their efforts. Celeste Clay hoped to "keep a stout heart" while dreading that her husband and brothers would all be killed. "I wish I could die for my country," she wrote gloomily, "and intend to if my darling falls." The daily tension made for wild daydreams. Susan Blackford thought it would have been better if she and her husband had both died "in those last delightful hours together" before his departure.[24] Fantasy and reality merged because who could any longer say what was improbable? The war undermined the customary distinctions between fact and fancy, between the normal and the bizarre.

In some ways trapped by their culture's particularly rigid definitions of feminine nature, many wives and mothers assumed that these intense bouts of anxiety were peculiar to their sex. Believing that most men, including her husband, lived in the present with little thought for the future, Rosa Delony did not think that men "were made to feel like women."[25] And although women too seemed mired in their daily problems, such statements show how antebellum assumptions about sexual differences persisted. Despite all the new strains on family life and their own intense emotions, women were still expected to endure whatever God or fate had in store for them. "I bow in submission," a North Carolina woman put it simply. If wives and mothers grumbled, they felt guilty because their suffering seemed to pale beside the dangers faced by the soldiers.[26] But uncomplaining passivity was difficult—even for women determined to maintain the old domestic routines. The "notable" Southern woman was no longer merely the embodiment of homey, pietistic virtues. She may have confessed occasionally to feminine weakness, but she also showed great strength and courage. In anger, and sorrow, and pain, she poured out her anguish in prayer while bearing her sorrows with dignity.

3

Although the experiences of real women formed the basis for the tales of heroic sacrifice that fill so much of the historical literature on the Confederate home front, more mundane incidents have generally escaped notice. Yet for most families the war changed daily life in many undramatic but important ways by intensifying existing conflicts and creating new ones. Ordinary problems, such as jealousy, pregnancy, childbirth, and child rearing, became more complicated. Separation compounded these difficulties by sapping the morale of soldier and civilian alike.

Despite the existence of miscegenation and a sexual double standard—however much historians may have exaggerated their prevalence in a culture increasingly shaped by evangelical religion—marriage was ostensibly a lifetime commitment and faithfulness the cement that made for permanence. But separation inevitably tested marital felicity. If, as the old saying goes, absence makes the heart grow fonder for somebody else, the Civil War seemed to confirm the truth of this folk wisdom. Regardless of whether the war loosened moral standards, as wars supposedly do, Confederates worried about the disruption of affection and intimacy. Insensitive husbands wrote letters home describing the beautiful women who visited the camps. Suspecting that his wife, Addie, was attracting admirers in Montgomery, Alabama, James Simpson wrote from Virginia that he intended to visit a "young married lady . . . who they say lets almost any body make love [i.e., flirt] and talk poetry to her."[27] Fortunately for James, Addie Simpson took such boasting in good humor. Other wives who were not so broad minded worried about their husbands' straying, and hardly appreciated enthusiastic reports about another woman's charms. And even though soldiers usually added the required paragraph about their spouse's unsurpassed beauty, wit, or intelligence and tried to patch things up with long apologies and pleas for understanding, the damage had been done.[28]

In a typical letter, Colonel Dorsey Pender bragged about the attractiveness of some more-than-friendly Virginia ladies. In a jocular but egotistical way, he noted how he had told them he was married, "for poor creatures I do not wish to destroy their rest." On receiving this bit of news, Fanny Pender exploded. After explaining how domestic chores and two screaming children had prevented her from writing as often as he expected, she then put in the knife: "I have never in the whole course of my married life done anything deliberately that I knew would pain you—your will has always been my law—and I have ever tried to obey to the very letter the commands of my Lord and Master." With an effective blend of submissiveness, wounded innocence, and subtle sarcasm, she twisted the blade, sharply asking why he kept referring to the women who had made such a fuss over him: "Was it to gratify your vanity by making me jealous, to make me appreciate your love still more?" Driving the point home, she wondered how anyone would dare "make such loose speeches" to her husband but suspected that he "must have gone pretty far for a woman to attempt such a liberty." What if their situations had been reversed and she had been the one flirting? It would be no "more immoral in me than in you," she wrote. "I did not think you would trifle with my feelings in that way . . . I had rather not hear these things. You cannot, of course, intend to give me pleasure by mentioning them." She agreed to forgive but would never forget: "Nothing you have ever said this whole of our married life—ever pained me so acutely or grieved me so deeply. I know you are sorry for it now, for you must feel it to be unjust, but it is enough to know that you could, in any mood, say so much to pain me." In defending her own character and none too gently chiding her husband, she displayed a prickly sense of propriety that was by no means confined to hotheaded males eager to respond to some imaginary insult. After all the Pender home seemed to be threatened by these brazen Virginia hussies and, even more important, by the typical male susceptibility to female flattery. Wartime separations created new uncertainties and doubts for many couples, thereby multiplying the opportunities for misunderstandings and irreparable damage.

Given their testy comments, and their typically Southern assertions of their own prerogatives and virtue, the Penders obviously disagreed over acceptable standards of behavior even though both seemed to operate within traditional Southern notions about male and female roles. Dorsey Pender apologized for his thoughtlessness but weakly countered that Fanny's remarks had been crueler than his. He bristled at being accused of "dishonorable acts" and excused his indiscretion, obliquely referring to his sexual needs at a post "lonely enough to satisfy a monk."[29] Fanny Pender apparently remained unconvinced by her husband's implicit defense of a sexual double standard. Whether this incident would have permanently damaged their marriage remains a moot point, for two years to the day after his wife penned her bitter letter, Dorsey Pender was mortally wounded at Gettysburg.

Although few couples seem to have shared the Penders' intense concern about infidelity, the war created other sexual tensions. If married women were supposed to produce children—and their high birthrate attests to how well Southern white women fulfilled this expectation—the war aroused new fears of conception by raising doubts and questions about the desirability of even having children when families remained separated. For soldiers' wives, the joy of a long-awaited furlough could not be unalloyed because it raised the possibility of an unwanted pregnancy. Shortly before her husband came home, one woman dreaded the "*horrible* nightmare which would always frighten away any little happiness that might occasionally cross my path." Few wives wrote or spoke so frankly; as in the antebellum period, many did not even mention pregnancy in their diaries. But prudery does not entirely explain their silence; perhaps the words *pregnant* and *alone* sounded too ominous. With her husband off fighting in Virginia, Harriet Perry prepared for the birth of their second child. Unable to sleep or take much interest in anything, she expected her beloved Theophilus to be killed because "war makes its widows by the thousands." She begged him to come home, but he could not arrange a furlough. Fortunately she had a neighbor to stay with her.[30] Other women bore their children without comfort or assistance.

The absence of the father—the marked incompleteness of the family circle—struck especially hard at women who long had accepted their own place in a social order that exalted male authority. And the birth of the child itself merely marked the end of one crisis and the beginning of another. Disheartened by the insensitive remarks of well-meaning relatives, mothers feared new babies would never see their fathers' faces. Whatever powerful notions of female dependency they might still harbor, in many homes women now assumed the entire burden of child care. Whenever her son misbehaved, Lou Wharton threatened to write his father, a tactic that had little noticeable effect on the boy's disposition. Although children naturally tested their mothers' control in a society that associated power with masculinity, the war years produced no lost generation of alienated youth. Women dealt with the daily challenges of discipline but seldom discussed them with their husbands. Instead they filled their letters with the homey tidbits that men savored: the appearance of baby teeth, the cute way a little girl's mouth looked saying *papa,* the distress of a son learning that his father had no little boys to hug in camp.[31] Yet many of these stories must have also made some men long for home more than ever while others realized that their distracted wives were only putting up a cheerful front.

The anguish of the Civil War, then, lies not alone in the destruction of the Southern economy or in the details of battles or even in the casualty lists, but in the stories of individual families and of the women who struggled to preserve them. In the summer of 1862, Theophilus Perry left his wife and two-year-old daughter in Marshall, Texas, to fight with the Army of Northern Virginia. As their little girl mischievously rummaged through the desk, Harriet Perry wrote to her husband about little incidents of home life, even circling the wet spot at the top of the first page where their daughter had planted many kisses for her daddy. One day the girl demanded her bonnet, announcing in a grownup voice that she was leaving to see her daddy. When a family friend asked where her daddy was, she answered that he had "gone to war and has to sleep on the cold ground." In the fall of 1863, she suddenly became feverish and died. Left alone with an infant daughter born the previous fall, Harriet Perry had only begun to deal with her grief when she learned that both of her brothers had been killed in battle. We must still look to God for comfort, she advised her husband, but their shared sorrow was short lived; in May 1864 Theophilus Perry was killed in the Battle of the Wilderness.[32] The Perrys' story is not a tale of unusual suffering, heroic endurance, or even bad luck. Instead it represents the experiences of thousands of families in an era when the tragic became the typical.

But anomaly is ever the handmaiden of misfortune, an effect heightened by cruel contrasts of condition. As always, suffering was relative: the Confederacy's yeomen and poor whites, many of whom also had responded to the siren song of Southern—not to mention racial and family—honor, shouldered burdens the wealthy often avoided. Staying at her father-in-law's house in Camden, South Carolina, Mary Chesnut marveled at how "our life here would be very pleasant if there were no Yankees." Because she had a fine library, a spacious bedroom, and time to knit, read, or write in her journal, her life was not a bad one and she felt secure in a world of economic and social privilege. Most families had no such margin of comfort. After only a few months in the army at the beginning of the war, Irish soldiers in Dorsey Pender's regiments were already receiving letters from home telling of starving wives and children. Lieutenant Colonel James Fremantle of the Coldstream Guards described farm households in Mississippi where the women scarcely had clothes on their backs. Cut off from communication with their husbands in the army and with little but fat pork to eat, they could only live out their days in uncertainty and despair.[33] Whether God smiled on poor as well as rich, whether the scales of justice would be balanced in time were problems for philosophers to unravel. Life went on even after dreams of prosperity and security had died, and the bonds of family seemed more fragile than ever.

4

Regardless of the natural tendency to focus their energies on immediate, household problems, the harried wives, mothers, and sisters of Confederate soldiers had to pay attention to events beyond their immediate neighborhood. In some ways the traditional area of feminine interest expanded as women became the ambitious wives of junior officers, worried relatives of captured and wounded soldiers, and mourners of the Confederate dead. But in each of these new roles, their actions still depended upon a relationship with a man and upon the performance of the well-established rituals of the woman left at home.

For despite the separation of husband and wife, the family's achievement and status would still be measured largely by what the man might accomplish as a soldier, politician, planter, merchant, artisan, or farmer. This was especially true for some wives of Confederate officers who saw campaigns and battles as opportunities for the advancement of their husbands' careers. But seeking a promotion for a spouse meant taking the extraordinary step of dealing with public officials. Except for clemency petitions, the papers of antebellum governors contain few documents written by women. From the beginning of the war, however, letters poured into Confederate and state authorities from women seeking commissions or special favors for their menfolk.[34]

The language of their petitions show how little the war changed the power relations between the sexes. Politically astute women appeared submissive and made the proper obeisance to masculine authority even as they shattered precedent. Alice Baldwin to Alexander H. Stephens:

"Emboldened by the knowledge that you are ever attentive to the request of a lady . . . ." Mrs. E. G. Rosser to Jefferson Davis: "Excuse the temerity of a weak woman in addressing an entire stranger . . . ." Mattie Hubbard to Zebulon Vance: "I know ladies are sometimes troublesome but I venture on your gallantry by asking for a few lines of information. . . ."[35] Instinctively understanding how to approach men in authority, they sounded the proper note of deference, then stated their request clearly and firmly.

Bolder women, whether they lived in Richmond or in a remote corner of Arkansas, also played army politics. Rosa Delony sent her husband advice on advancing his career, giving particular attention to the strengths and weaknesses of rival officers. Convinced that their men had not been aggressive enough in seeking promotions, other women sent importunate letters to commanding officers and politicians.[36] Yet these women remained the exception—a striking counterpoint to the thousands of others who simply waited at home for word of their men in the army. Such passivity intensified anxiety and eventually bred enormous frustration; following the course of the war and worrying about loved ones seemed poor substitutes for direct participation in the struggle for Southern independence.

As in all modern wars, many soldiers wrote letters on the eve of or the day after a battle. At home, women anticipated, looked for, but also dreaded receiving news. "Every time I hear a knock at the door," Susan Blackford told her husband, "I imagine it is a telegram telling me you have been hurt. . . . Life with me is made up of a tissue of hopes and fears." Even good tidings often were bittersweet. Emma Holmes learned that her cousin had survived the Battle of Gettysburg by seeing his name signed to a casualty report in a newspaper. "Thank God for his safety," she rejoiced, "but many of our friends and acquaintances in the long list have suffered." Waiting for word further frayed already raw nerves. Shortly after the Second Battle of Manassas, a North Carolina mother described the anguish: "Perhaps my precious child may be lying on the battlefield in death's cold grasp, perhaps in some hospital wounded and suffering. While I am far away suffering the torments of suspense and anxiety. But hope bears me up and I will still believe God has spared him until I learn otherwise."[37]

Chances were she would learn of her son's fate more quickly than in any previous war. The telegraph enabled newspapers to carry lengthy dispatches from the battlefields, but, ironically, improved communication increased anxiety. Despite the great volume of information, many reports were more alarming than revealing. Frances Robertson read that her brother's regiment had been in heavy fighting around Richmond, though the list of dead and wounded was incomplete. She could not stop worrying until she opened the wire confirming his safety.[38] Army telegrams, however, seldom contained such comforting intelligence. At best, civilians received widely conflicting accounts of battles and casualties. With haphazard mail service and the telegraph lines between the eastern and western parts of the Confederacy regularly cut by Yankee cavalry, the only news was often no news.

How did one interpret silence? After she had not heard from her brothers for several months, Kate Stone assumed they had been seriously hurt in the Seven Days battles. And when a newspaper reported that their brigade had been badly cut up and most of the field officers wounded, she was beside herself: "My heart leaps to my lips and I turn sick with apprehension whenever I hear a quick step, see a stranger approaching, or note a grave look on the face of any of the boys coming in from a ride." Distraught mothers asked Confederate officials for help in locating their relatives, but clerks simply forwarded the letters to department commanders who might not bother to reply.[39] Would another letter be appropriate? Should a wife or mother pack up everything to search for her loved one? Conventional definitions of the woman's role in the home provided no answers to these questions. To preserve a semblance of family life in the face of such nagging uncertainty stretched patience and endurance to their limits.

When a man was taken prisoner, the dilemmas multiplied because the relatives of Confederate prisoners received little information. It might take months to find out whether a soldier had been captured, and then many more months would pass before his release. Wealthy women tried to use connections with powerful politicians to have their relatives included in the next prisoner exchange; others tried to elicit official sympathy with stories of barbaric conditions in Yankee prisons. Mary Smith, for example, claimed that her husband was chained in his cell and subsisted on bread and water.[40] Confederate leaders could do little for the families. Prisoner exchanges required delicate negotiations, and the Northern government suspended them altogether in the summer of 1863 to impose more hardship on the manpower-short Confederacy. A dispute over Confederate refusal to return black prisoners further delayed matters until February 1865 when General Ulysses S. Grant renewed the exchanges.

In trying to gain a prisoner's freedom, women entered a political and logistical labyrinth. The task demanded assertiveness, persistence, luck, and, above all, influence. After Elizabeth Harding learned that her husband, William, was being held on Mackinac Island in Lake Huron, she worried that he would freeze without long underwear. Hoping to visit him, she dreaded applying for a pass to Provisional Governor Andrew Johnson, a man especially despised by Tennessee Confederates. Swallowing her distaste, however, she apparently convinced Johnson to parole her husband. She later assured William that his honor had not been compromised, suggesting that he return to prison if the terms of his release were not acceptable. Yet it surely must have galled her, if it did not shame her to have done business with the hated Johnson.[41] Again wives became entangled in the Southern obsession with honor at a time when they could ill afford to be so punctilious. Of course, upper-class women like Elizabeth Harding, who lived on a large plantation, might retain some of their pride and at the same time win their husbands' release. But when a woman had to beg for her husband's freedom before a "renegade" like "Andy Johnson," she had gone a long way toward compromising the family's reputation as well as temporarily redefining her own place both in and outside the household.

Whether or not the women left at home had assumed the task of preserving family honor—an idea that would certainly have shocked most Confederates—the typical family could do little but wait and pray. And even this small solace did nothing for their empty pocketbooks and their empty stomachs. Prisoners' wives successfully petitioned Confederate officials to receive their spouses' pay, but this pittance would scarcely feed and clothe their children. Disheartened wives and mothers crowded train depots waiting for the latest shipment of exchanged prisoners, anxiously searching for their relatives.[42]

When prisoners returned, the family circle would be complete once again, but what would happen to the household if the man were wounded or killed? Thousands of women faced the prospect of either living with disabled husbands or trying to eke out a living as widows in an economy that appeared to be falling apart. The combination of greater firepower, improved weaponry, and traditional tactics (such as frontal assaults on entrenched positions) made the American Civil War an especially bloody one. Each major battle produced long lists of wounded. Muskets, re-peating rifles, and rifled artillery tore through infantry lines and inflicted ghastly wounds. Lead bullets flattened as they entered the body, ripping tissue apart and shattering bones. Army surgeons hurriedly patched their patients together with little regard for preventing infections; am-putations became commonplace. Given the medical practices of the day, even a superficial injury might prove fatal.

For most families, information on wounded relatives was sketchy at best. Telegrams were tantalizingly cryptic or misleadingly optimistic. A report of a slight wound often preceded a death notice by only a few days. Many women had to rely on battlefield rumors, such as a vague account from someone who might have seen their man being hauled away in an ambulance. Tracing a wounded man through the maze of government hospitals and private homes used for convalescing patients was difficult, though women appealed to generals and politicians for help.[43]

Given the inefficiencies of the system, the only sure way to succor a sick or wounded man was to visit the hospital. Sad-faced women trudged from ward to ward, scanning the faces on the cots, their task sometimes complicated by army movements and frequent skirmishes. After losing two boys in the war, Hannah Coker became frantic when her third son, James, was wounded in September 1863 at the Battle of Chickamauga. She found him lying in a private home on Lookout Mountain, but when the Confederates retreated and the Federals advanced, he was not yet well enough to be moved. At last she tried to take her son home through the lines, but their train was attacked by bushwhackers and they were both thrown into a prison hospital at Louisville, Kentucky. Though they eventually were released, not until July 1864 did they get back home to South Carolina.[44]

Other women fared much worse. June May's husband was wounded in June 1862. "If my dear good husband is taken away from me then oh then what have I to live for?" she cried. "Oh if i was only with him" became her constant lament as she pictured him languishing in a Rich-mond hospital. He was in fact already on the mend—well enough to fight and die in the Second Battle of Manassas. But cruel ironies had already become so much a part of the war that both soldiers and civilians often appeared strangely benumbed. Stay at home or rush to a soldier's side? There were no pat answers, especially when reason and emotion dictated different decisions. Dorsey Pender met a North Carolina woman who had spent all her savings to visit her wounded husband in Virginia. She had walked the last two miles to camp through rain and mud, only to learn that he had been buried five days earlier. Pender handed her five dollars, realizing what little comfort the money provided. His comment on the incident was classically Victorian—predictable and sentimental—but true: "Many is the poor heart that will be broken by this war."[45]

To be sure, sudden death had never been a stranger to Southern society. A high infant mortality rate, epidemics, farm accidents, and murders had all scarred families. The Civil War, however, magnified the blows, rapidly piling grief on top of grief and adding bizarre twists to the normal passing of the generations. A Mississippi woman read in the *Richmond Enquirer* about an engagement in which a soldier in her son's company had been killed and only a few others were wounded or missing. By mid-1863 standards, these were light casualties and cause for rejoicing, but toward the end of the article she saw her son's name—the only man killed. The unreliability of news, official or otherwise, redoubled anxiety and put civilians on emotional roller coasters. A South Carolina mother who had just received word of her son's death was suddenly told that a mistake had been made, that someone had mixed up the names in a casualty report. As she welcomed this reprieve, a hearse drove up; it carried a coffin containing her son's body.[46]

Nor could these women simply go through the usual stages of grief. The war both extended and short-circuited the process because death itself became an uncertainty, especially when invading armies and internal disorder disrupted not only communications but the daily routines of many households. Hundreds of wives and mothers had no idea whether their men were dead or alive.[47] Were their relatives buried in a marked grave or simply thrown into a trench? Not knowing made it harder to accept the death, begin the formal period of mourning, and pick up the pieces of one's life. Some women simply could not rest until they had found the remains. The War Department regularly received letters requesting help in locating and returning bodies but could do little, especially when corpses were buried in areas occupied by enemy troops. After the Federals captured the Confederate archives at the end of the war, tracking down burial sites became even more difficult. Some women contacted people who had worked in the hospital where their relative had died. A Virginia nurse informed a widow that her husband had died about one o'clock in the afternoon (she was unsure of the date) of internal bleeding after an operation. She later reported that his false teeth had been stolen by someone on the burial detail; she could not arrange to have the body shipped home.[48]

If they found no helpful or knowledgeable person, women searched the hospitals and cemeteries themselves. A South Carolina mother traveled 450 miles to pick up her son's remains in Richmond. Riding the train home, she sat flicking flies off his body. She was fortunate that the corpse was intact. Other women found only bones to bring back in a satchel. Gathering them together for burial, however, closed a chapter of family history and the interment, whether immediate or delayed, made it easier to begin the process of living again.[49]

Compared to Northerners, Southern families stood a much better chance of having a relative wounded or killed; the Confederacy's smaller population, combined with Union military success, concentrated the anguish. Indeed the suffering intensified as the Confederacy shrank. In extreme cases, bereaved women died of shock, though eventually war inured people to horror. So quickly did one death follow another that most people had neither the time nor the emotional energy to become obsessed with a single tragedy.

Signs of grief appeared everywhere, strangely blurring the distinction between private and public sorrow. At a neighbor's plantation, Lucy Breckinridge counted fourteen women wearing black. "There were so many ladies there, all dressed in deep mourning, that we felt as if we were at a convent and formed a sisterhood," she wrote. Veiled faces at church services bespoke the somber mood of Southern society, but the war intruded even there. Inflation and shortages of black cloth prevented yeoman and poor white families from following the customary practices. Unable to buy mourning clothes, Jane Beale had to go about "with a stricken heart but no outward symbol of grief" for her departed son.[50]

The isolation of rural life and the intensity of family relationships made some women inconsolable. The old clichés about the healing qualities of time were not always true. On May 5, 1862, Willie Richardson was wounded at the Battle of Williamsburg; when his left arm was amputated, he quickly developed a fever and died. On the second anniversary of his death, Sue Richardson morbidly dwelt on her brother's pain: "I think I feel this day all the pangs of a wound and that my arm is being severed from my body." If she could only deal with the affliction by so closely identifying with her brother's suffering, she had hardly begun to go through the grieving process. Even shared suffering, the ancient healer of the bereaved, could be powerless against such overwhelming misery. Two years after her fiancé died at the First Battle of Manassas, Lula Oglethorpe described her torment in a letter to his mother. Although she tried to detach herself from the loss, claiming she had really only been the boy's close friend, three years later she was still pouring out her sorrow to the woman who would have been her mother-in-law.[51]

At the other extreme, women tried to assume their ancient role as impassive sufferers. When her brother died, a Mississippian felt that her "heart became flint." Women learned to steel themselves against calamity. A South Carolina mother reacted to her son's death by turning "white as a sheet, never uttering a word or shedding a tear." Observing this, Mary Chesnut asked: "Are our women losing the capacity to weep?" Perhaps so when the passage of coffins through small towns became a common occurrence.[52] The contrast between the emotionally unhinged and the unflinching stalwarts exemplified the difficulty of expecting supposedly weak, sensitive women suddenly and mysteriously to become strong during a crisis. The countervailing pressures of private sentiment and public expectation merely added to emotional turmoil.

In the midst of anguish and death—whether women grieved openly or hid their distress—the ideal of the Spartan mother persisted. Confederate orators and newspaper editors celebrated women who bravely laid their men on the altar of the sacred cause. A poor widow who already had lost three sons in battle told General Leonidas Polk that she was preparing her youngest, a sixteen-year-old, to enlist.[53] Such widely publicized stories undoubtedly elicited more sacrifices, but they simultaneously set up impossible standards while stimulating false hopes for the success of Southern arms, which ill-prepared women for the dawning realization that their loved ones had died in a losing cause.

For those unwilling to admit or even consider such a possibility, however, battlefield death remained a ritual sacrifice, best described according to the conventions of Victorian sentimentality. Watching a young captain die in a hospital, Kate Cumming knew what to write: "He has lost his life in defense of liberty . . . and when maidens come to deck the graves of our Southern patriots, they will not forget one who sacrificed all for them." "Martyr for the cause" and "died for his country" were phrases that came readily to lips and pen. And the words carried conviction, the conviction of an age in which patriotism was an uncomplicated emotion. "It is the death I would have chosen for him," claimed one widow. "I loved him for his manliness, and now that he has shown that manliness by dying as a hero dies, I mourn, but am not brokenhearted."[54] To the modern cynic, rising above personal loss with devotion to a higher cause seems implausible or possible only for revolutionary fanatics. In the nineteenth century, no one seemed surprised to meet people willing to give up so much.

The mounting casualty lists gave once easily made pledges of patriotic devotion new and more tragic meaning. Death touched so many homes. Yankee bullets not only killed Southern soldiers but struck at the heart of female loyalty to the Confederate cause. "Independence has few charms to me when the anguish of my heart is stretched to the utmost," wailed Fannie Robertson after her brother's death. "The victory at Richmond, Va. is a death knell to us." Even the promise of peace failed to comfort the brokenhearted. In Mary Chesnut's circle, several mothers agreed on a stinging epitaph for their sons: "Splendid young life sacrificed—in vain." Nor did such laments come only late in the war; in the summer of 1861, Harriott Middleton already paid more attention to the lists of dead and wounded than to reports of Confederate success. "The brilliancy," she commented, "seems very faint, amidst all this sorrow."[55]

Yet even widespread suffering could not overcome traditional social distinctions; pride of birth and class survived despite the wreckage of so many families. Aristocratic ladies fostered the illusion that somehow their losses weighed heavier than those of their poorer neighbors. To the wealthy in particular, the will of God now appeared more inscrutable than ever. Why would the Almighty take away so many of his once favored sons, the very flower of Southern youth, the future husbands, fathers, and rulers of the land? It seemed as if fate had conspired against all the brightest, noblest, and most honorable. When General James J. Pettigrew was killed during the retreat from Gettysburg, one of his relatives decried the capriciousness of death: "That so much labor and culture should be bestowed upon a man of so much genuine genius and capacity to come to this!!! and thousands upon thousands of useless mortals left to fill their ignoble place—questions arise which must be put down, for they cannot be answered without [illegible word] discontents unlawful for a Christian."[56]

Rather than indulge in such discontents or seek explanations where none could be found, most grieving Southerners clung more closely to their faith, however limited its consolations might be. For Lucy Breckinridge, always the guilt-ridden Calvinist, three lines of poetry gave meaning to the death of her seventeen-year-old brother John at the Battle of Seven Pines: "God takes our dearest even so; / The reason why we cannot know; / Helpless he leaves us crushed with woe." The faithful thumbed through their Bibles for comforting passages as well as prophetic explanations of contemporary events. No matter how hackneyed, old assurances about the dead being better off and expectations of the coming reunion in heaven gave the pious some relief from the sorrow that threatened to overwhelm believer and unbeliever alike.[57]

Such faith also wore thin, however. Too many men died, too many families mourned. Women struggled to maintain a semblance of stability by preserving as much of traditional family life as possible, but pain and death, separation, and suffering blunted their efforts. Wives, mothers, and sisters had to weigh once again their personal losses against their love for a struggling nation, and slowly the scales began to tilt away from sacrifice and toward self-preservation. Perhaps family honor had survived as women were forced to take on the task of safeguarding their families, but this must have been small comfort for those who realized that the war had destroyed so many of the sinews of home life.

CHAPTER 4

Southern Women and Confederate Military Power

M ARCELLA LEAGUE AND RUTH NICHOLSON lived in an impoverished county in northern Georgia; neither could write her name; neither apparently saw herself as a submissive female. When their husbands enlisted in the Confederate army, they refused to assume the role of the patriotic wife. Left with large families and no means of support, each dictated an affidavit claiming her spouse had gone off "without her consent and contrary to my will." Demanding that the president and secretary of war discharge their husbands, they threatened to sue the Confederate government for one hundred thousand dollars if their request was denied. Only able to scratch scratch an X onto the petition, they had nevertheless stated their case forcefully.[1] Somehow the war gave voice to the inarticulate.

Although few women so boldly claimed authority over their households, many begged and badgered Confederate officials for their menfolk's release. Mothers in particular sought the return of sons who had joined the army without their permission. Nearly all these petitioners expressed fervid loyalty to the Southern cause, yet many felt like Mary Scales, who argued that patriotism had to have limits: "I know my country needs all her children and I had thought I could submit to her requisitions. I have given her cause my prayers, my time, my means and my children but now the last lamb of the fold is to be taken, the mother and helpless woman triumph over the patriot."[2] Filling regiments with husbands, sons, and brothers devastated domestic life, but heeding the thousands of pleas for discharges and exemptions would have dangerously weakened the Confederate army. For a time the government might balance these considerations, by conscripting soldiers and adopting a liberal exemption policy. In the long run, however, such a jerry-rigged expedient was doomed to fail.

By the middle of 1862, fewer and fewer women willingly sent their men off to war. In a letter to Jefferson Davis, Virginia Thornton explained that her husband's "devotion to our country caused him to neglect his more sacred duty to his family." No longer did women write about heroic sacrifices on the battlefield. Instead they emphasized the far less dramatic but increasingly serious problems at home: high prices, shortages, and hunger. "What is to become of the women and children if you call out *all* the men?" a Mississippi woman pointedly asked Governor John J. Pettus.[3] Few civilians understood how desperately the Confederacy needed more soldiers to throw into the increasingly uneven struggle against Yankee armies. Unable to assess their country's needs, women were all too familiar with their own.

Their disenchantment grew as the war dragged on. Regretting that their sons had enlisted, soldiers' mothers advised other women to keep their boys at home. Desperation produced humiliating pleas for relief. When Margaret Thompson offered to throw herself at the feet of Georgia Governor Joe Brown, she undoubtedly was speaking figuratively, but many other women would have fallen to their knees instantly had they thought it would do any good. If mothers heard of some soldier returning with a discharge or furlough, they hoped their boy would soon follow.[4]

When traditional claims of family and community clashed with military necessity, wives and mothers seemed pathetically parochial in assuming that Jefferson Davis, the secretary of war, or some general had the time, energy, or interest to consider carefully each family's situation. Yet at the same time time their naïveté undoubtedly strengthened their case.

Though understanding little about army organization, Confederate laws, or War Department regulations, most women knew how to appeal to the hearts if not to the heads of powerful men. Wives who had lost their husbands quoted biblical admonitions on aiding the widows and fatherless. Their statements sounded stilted and melodramatic, even by nineteenth-century standards. Virginia Atkinson: "God bless you kind sir, your ear is open to the cry of mercy. Heaven will bless you, for you lendeth an ear to the widow's supplication." Mrs. J. M. McKee: "The yawning grave has closed over my dead husband and the widow at best is forced to tread a thorny path in this cold world." Such maudlin statements sometimes worked. Confederate leaders could never quite become coldhearted bureaucrats ignoring pathetic pleas and responding by the book, even though their subordinates had to take a more dispassionate approach. One of General Bragg's aides destroyed nine out of ten letters received from women. Jefferson Davis saw few of the desperate petitions that poured into his office.[5] Yet the War Department also bent the rules, granting discharges contrary to well-established regulations. Even after the Confederate government developed more hard-nosed procedures for dealing with the daily flood of requests, many officials refused to allow military necessity always to override humanitarian considerations.

As the conscription laws became increasingly complex, women themselves, slowly learning about loopholes and exceptions, worded their petitions accordingly. But in audaciously venturing into the public sphere—the traditional domain of Southern men—they soon discovered social and economic inequities that threatened to tear the Confederacy apart.

1

The chaotic system of volunteering and raising regiments, and after April 1862 the haphazard administration of the Conscription Acts, meant unfit men frequently served while the able-bodied stayed home. Although conscription brought in bodies, it did so at enormous political and social cost. Young boys and old men, the infirm and even the recently wounded filled depleted regiments. To many women at home, it seemed that the army took the wrong men at the wrong time, leaving destitute families to fend for themselves.

Even though most Confederate soldiers were between eighteen and thirty-five years old, underage boys also entered the ranks. Stirred by patriotic speeches and martial music, they ran away to enlist and Confederate officers eagerly mustered them into service.[6] Distraught mothers appealed to Jefferson Davis's instincts as a father to obtain the release of their sons from the service, a tactic that occasionally succeeded, but after the enactment of the first conscription law in April 1862, such paternalistic dispensations ended abruptly. Secretary of War George W. Randolph required a ten-year-old private's mother to prove that he had enlisted without her consent and to present a certificate of disability. If an underage boy volunteered with his parents' permission, the War Department seldom sent him home. A clerk usually explained that no "man" could be spared at the present time.[7]

This elastic definition of *fit for service* covered older men as well. The first conscription law declared men between the ages of eighteen and thirty-five eligible for service, but, much to the chagrin of many wives, this did not mean that those over thirty-five who had volunteered would be discharged. In February 1864, Congress made it worse by lowering the minimum age to seventeen and raising the upper limit to forty-five. In Reidsville, North Carolina, Mary Windsor worried about her forty-eight-year-old husband. He had served in a home-guard unit for three months, leaving her alone with a family of eighteen (including fifteen daughters and one son subject to constant seizures). With no one to look after the family farm, she vainly asked Governor Zebulon Vance for her husband's release.[8] No matter how militarily justified, each change in policy appeared arbitrary and unfair, especially to wives who had assumed that their husbands would never have to serve. The conscription of older men usually worked a greater hardship on women than the occasional recruitment of minors because these soldiers often left behind large families dependent on their support.

If age was a concern for the conscript's family, health was an even larger issue because the Bureau of Conscription literally snatched the halt, the blind, and the lame. The hazards of placing such men in the ranks should have been obvious. Maria Jones's brother had to crawl about camp like a child because he had no night vision; Nora Hayes's husband could not see well enough to distinguish a white man from a black one. By mid-1864, even deaf-mutes no longer escaped conscription.[9] Although disabled men made up a small proportion of the army, their presence not only symbolized Confederate desperation but also caused bitter resentment on the home front.

Even men who entered the army in good health did not stay that way long. More Confederate soldiers died of dysentery than from bullets. Pneumonia, tuberculosis, malaria, and mumps spread rapidly through the camps. The wives and mothers of consumption patients graphically described how their men spat up blood. In petitions to Confederate officials, women included gruesome details about their loved ones' ailments, bitterly observing that these men spent more time in bed than on duty.[10] Such pleas for relief, however, elicited more indifference than sympathy, more cynicism than assistance. Claims of disability were difficult to verify, and in any event, by the end of 1862, being able-bodied was no longer a requirement for military service.

The administration of provisions for medical exemptions failed to help and often created new problems. At best army doctors made hasty examinations, commonly passing men with bad limps, missing fingers, and other infirmities. Sarah Alsobrook complained about a gruff surgeon who had bragged he would "take every damn one of the men" and then declared her husband fit for duty despite his severe cough and heart palpitations. Nor did a certificate of disability guarantee exemption; local conscription boards might ignore their own physicians' advice, especially late in the war when the army needed every available man.[11]

Despite protests against such arbitrary procedures, little was done to reform them. Unscrupulous physicians and politicians solicited bribes for granting medical exemptions. After a series of run-ins with Confederate and state officials, a Georgia woman begged Governor Brown to rescue her husband—who had already been discharged twice—from overzealous recruiters who were after him again. The inefficiency and especially the irrationality of the system laid the groundwork for the black humor of twentieth-century warfare. Nancy Staley fumed at the injustice, not to mention the lunacy, of keeping her husband in the army in spite of his dropsy and kidney trouble, then refusing to pay his enlistment bounty because a surgeon had pronounced him unfit.[12] Joseph Heller's Yossarian would have understood.

Compared to the morass of medical exemptions, occupational discharges seemed a simpler matter. In exempting ironworkers in the first conscription law, for example, Congress had decided their work had strategic importance. But the wives of tanners, blacksmiths, shoemakers, and millers also believed their husbands performed important tasks, and under public pressure Congress added these crafts to the exemption list. Yet this only made the law more complex, and local boards often interpreted the statutes in their own exotic way. An occupation that exempted a man in one county did not necessarily apply in another.[13] Unlike farm women, who often could keep a place running in their husbands' absence, artisans' wives seldom had mastered their husbands' skills. These women depended on the earnings from the family business and naturally thought their men contributed more to the war effort by practicing a trade than by joining the army.

Conscription undoubtedly brought more men into the army, but from the civilian standpoint, it took away men sorely needed at home. In seeking discharges and exemptions, women sometimes exaggerated their men's infirmities or their youth or their importance in the local economy. The temptation to manipulate the system by stretching the truth was certainly great, and those who could write most eloquently were by no means the most deserving of relief. Yet even discounting embellishment and deception, the flood of letters and petitions that poured in to public officials contained striking evidence of how the draft had ravaged both family life and civilian morale.

2

The effects of conscription extended far beyond the alienation of individual soldiers and their anxious families. Even as they complained about the suffering of their fathers, husbands, sons, and brothers in the army, women more plaintively described their troubles at home. Ann Kidd was typical of those who now had to eke out a living on their own. A forty-five-year-old mother of nine living in Nelson County, Virginia, she was too weak to work in the fields. Her husband rented the land on which they lived, they owned no slaves, and she could not raise or harvest a crop by herself.[14] How she was supposed to manage under such conditions, no one could tell her. One thing sure, the Confederate government would eventually pay dearly for neglecting the Ann Kidds throughout the South.

The complex Southern kin networks eased some burdens, but large extended families exacerbated other problems. In caring for their relatives, people soon exhausted their own resources. A man might look after farms for brothers, parents, or cousins in the army, but by 1863 he too would likely be drafted. Consequently, one woman would suddenly become responsible for three or four families; mothers cared for daughters, daughters-in-law, and their many children.[15] And when they asked for the discharge of one of their menfolk, the secretary of war routinely instructed his clerks to "decline for the usual reasons."

Left alone with little advice from often taciturn husbands, wives faced an economic and emotional crisis. A long-accustomed dependence gave way to a new, unsought, and sometimes frightening independence. "I feel it is more than I can bear, as I have been accustomed to trust to him [her husband] entirely to manage and provide for the family having little or no knowledge of what ought to be done on the farm," a Mississippian admitted. Few Southern women had been taught how to support themselves, and as early as 1861 hunger threatened large families forced to live on a private's pay.[16] When public officials seemed unsympathetic, civilian resentment festered. To many women struggling to provide a bare subsistence for a once comfortable family, the sacrifices demanded of them no longer seemed reasonable. For yeoman families and poor whites alike, suffering bore little relationship to either their resources or their numbers.

The army's demand for men appeared insatiable. In pleas for discharges and furloughs, women frequently mentioned how many of their relatives were already in service: five sons from one family, three from another, two brothers and a son-in-law from a third—the burdens of war fell heavily on particular households and neighborhoods.[17] The deaths of husbands, the enrollment of each son who came of age, and financial hardship embittered the most ardent patriots. With two boys in service, Jennette Thompson angrily asked whether giving up a third son was necessary for Confederate salvation.[18] A dull weariness spread over the home front, and each new draft call drained morale, not to mention women's physical and emotional energy.

By 1862, wives and mothers increasingly cited their own poor health to justify bringing a husband or son home. The blind, the crippled, and the despondent flooded public officials with pathetic cries for help. The war now touched the most intimate recesses of family life. Their health shattered by work and worry, some women feared dying alone most of all. The desperately ill, often consumptive or cancer ridden, only wished to see their loved ones before the end came. A poor Georgia woman barely had strength to cook for her young children: "i am so feble i cant ceep from crying."[19] Although some of these women undoubtedly magnified and perhaps fabricated their ailments, their letters usually rang true. Most described their distress in simple and often semiliterate, but moving language.

Their words could not, however, change the fact that life was unfair. Calamities that never touched some families devastated others. Unhealthy wives had unhealthy husbands and sons in the army; a woman who lost one man to disease or in battle soon lost another. And the faltering Southern economy compounded their woes.[20] Yet women spent surprisingly little time cursing the cards fate had dealt them; they had not the strength.

In spite of women's best efforts, farms throughout the Confederacy fell into neglect. Crops rotted in the fields, the spring planting was delayed, and farm income, whether measured in dollars or food production, plummeted. Though living in the once prosperous Alabama black belt, Margaret Adams was running out of food for her eight children. In asking for the discharge of her husband, she seemed near the breaking point: "i have nary friend in the world no won do nothing for me ant no other chance in the world only for me and my little ones to go without cloths and something to eat."[21] Though she was obviously uneducated, her almost incoherent words well expressed a quiet desperation that was spreading through the countryside like an epidemic.

Poverty and eventually hunger entered more and more homes. With nothing to eat except dry corn bread, Narcis Nagle felt weak and sick and was unable to get out of the house. Like many other women, she saw her husband's discharge as her only salvation.[22] Such pleas sounded odd in a predominantly agricultural society where people were unlikely to starve, but formerly comfortable yeoman families now felt the pinch of shortages and high prices. As armies took more food and as refugees flocked to towns and cities, the remaining farmers could no longer feed the civilian population. Anyone traveling through the countryside could easily see the signs: gaunt faces of women and children staring vacantly from the doorways of run-down houses.

When they asked Confederate and state officials to discharge soldiers, women cited the need for financial support more than twice as often as any other reason (see table 3). Even in letters filled with complaints about health, anxiety, and the unfairness of conscription, economic woes usually headed the list. When the politicians and generals failed to respond to these problems, women became more protective of their families and less concerned about the future of the Confederacy.

The old debate over the effectiveness of conscription in supplying men for the Confederate army has been far too statistical and has ignored the domestic consequences of sometimes harsh and poorly administered policies. Even the most casual readers of the letters sent to Jefferson Davis, the War Department, and the state governors cannot help but notice the hopelessness of many Southern families. And the documents tell only part of the story, perhaps not even the worst part. Many women were no doubt too disheartened or too ignorant to apply for relief. Indeed as the plight of these families worsened, the crisis threatened to destroy civilian faith, not only in the Confederate cause, but in the Southern economic and social order as well.

Table 3. Reasons Offered by Women Seeking the Discharge of a Soldier from the Army

Reason	Frequency
Economic support	404
Soldier's health	193
Soldier is underage	137
Protect family	117
Civilian occupation of soldier	53
Enlistment without consent	36
Health of dependents	36
Soldier is too old	30
Soldier unfairly conscripted	15
Enemy forces approaching home	12
Soldier needs to complete his education	12
Family has become refugees	7
Soldier needed to settle an estate	5
Soldier is of foreign birth	3
Soldier has been wounded	2
Soldier enlisted when intoxicated	2

Source: War Department records and papers of the governors of the states of Virginia, North Carolina, South Carolina, Georgia, Alabama, and Mississippi. Because many official records were destroyed or lost, this count is heavily skewed toward Virginia, Georgia, and North Carolina. But with 536 documents, the sample is fairly representative. The total number of reasons given exceeds 536 because most women cited more than one reason.

3

Of course from the beginning of the war some women had sought ways to avoid making what they deemed unreasonable sacrifices. Even when discharges became harder to obtain, the clever turned the law to their own advantage. Each tightening up of loopholes in the Conscription Acts redoubled efforts to find new ones. Failure to obtain a man's release led the resourceful to petition for his transfer to a less dangerous post. If medical exemptions became harder to obtain, a new position with lighter duties might serve just as well.[23]

Transfers often had the additional advantage of moving a man closer to home, which the wives of convalescent husbands always claimed to have a healthier climate.[24] Yet these seemingly simple requests posed their own difficulties. Generals and War Department officials considered most transfers both unnecessary and inconvenient; such favors also smacked of special privilege and political influence, not to mention female interference in army administration. Women therefore had to approach public officials cautiously and circumspectly. "I ignore office seeking," claimed Carrie Bowie in pressing for her husband's return to North Carolina.[25] The disingenuousness showed through most such attempts to appear guileless and unselfish.

Staking out somewhat higher moral ground, mothers appealed for the protection of their sons. An Alabamian wanted her youngest boy transferred to his older brother's unit as a safeguard against the evils of camp life.[26] By invoking the traditional notion of shielding the innocent from a sinful world, these women failed to acknowledge that military necessity (or convenience) might outweigh their children's welfare. Although their rhetoric remained belligerently pro-Confederate to the end, mothers seldom accepted the argument that war had to destroy some families (and communities) to save others.

Women with less idealistic motives sought to find their men jobs safely removed from any fighting. Artisans' wives, for instance, petitioned for their husbands' detail to government arsenals and machine shops.[27] Like most modern wars, the Civil War generated conflict between the men in uniform and those safely employed in bombproof factories, government offices, and military staff positions. But charges of shirking and cowardice also reflected the class considerations so often at work. Aristocratic ladies warned their husbands against accepting a post or a salary beneath the family's dignity and accustomed standard of living. More appalling still was the prospect of a refined man's being exposed to the vulgar society of common soldiers.[28] To get a husband or son ensconced in a government job meant knowing the right people. At the same time, however, it fueled public suspicion of a "rich man's war and a poor man's fight."

What if a woman lacked the influence, persistence, or good luck to wrangle a soldier's exemption or transfer? Though they were a temporary expedient, furloughs were eagerly sought. Wives offered to nurse sick or wounded husbands at home, usually pledging to send them back to camp as soon as possible, or they requested seasonal help with a farm or plantation. Some obviously hoped that a temporary leave would become permanent.[29]

After all a furlough could do little to resolve the most pressing domestic problems, and women's letters and petitions often reveal how the war was slowly but surely destroying Southern families. A few days for their men to visit, to tend a crop, to look after the sick—that was all they asked. Ida Wilkom would have been overjoyed if her husband could have returned to New Iberia, Louisiana, for a month. Their infant son was dying, the other three children needed their father, and she had reached the limits of endurance: "I have tried every thing to submit to the will of God in tranquil resignation; but I find, a human being can suffer only according to his human strength."[30] Of course, if she needed her husband for only a month, she might get along without him altogether.

So Confederate officials reasoned as they shifted away from a policy that gave army commanders much discretion in granting short leaves to one that sharply curtailed furloughs. But even after generals capriciously canceled leaves and Congress enacted stringent restrictions on sending ill and wounded men home, some soldiers (and their female relations) still managed to beat the system. Too many "idlers" won official favor, Anna Booker grumbled, while their more deserving comrades stayed at their posts. On the other hand, when women listened to harrowing accounts of picket duty or bloodcurdling battle stories, they sometimes pressed furloughed husbands, sons, and brothers to extend their stay indefinitely.[31] Once a man left his company, odds were good that he would never return.

The inequities of discharges, transfers, and furloughs inevitably corrupted the conscription process, but the practice of wealthy men's hiring substitutes to fight in their place exposed even more dramatically the class bias of the system. The soldiers themselves resented and often ostracized the substitutes.[32] To many civilians, including their own relatives, men taking advantage of this escape hatch seemed little better than draft evaders or deserters. Given the strong social stigma attached to substitution, some women felt embarrassed and angry that their family's name had been disgraced, yet even here, subtle class distinctions appeared. Although some plantation mistresses encouraged their husbands to serve as a matter of honor, other genteel ladies seemed insensitive to the popular outcry against favoritism. In seeking a substitute for her brother, Elizabeth Wood claimed to be a true patriot: "I am and always have been a friend to my country, but while I think and care for my country, I ought not to suffer for the attention that is due to the gentler sex." Such women clearly expected special treatment for both themselves and their relatives, but few admitted it.[33]

If substitution favored the wealthy, especially large slaveholders, so did the infamous "twenty-nigger law." In October 1862, Congress expanded the list of exempted occupations to include owners and overseers of plantations with twenty or more slaves. Politicians hoped to maintain agricultural output and provide security for women left on the plantations but managed to do neither while pleasing no one.[34]

Martha Moncrief's thirty-three slaves worked only when the mood struck them, and she had been unable to find anyone to look after her place. If her son were not exempted, she would have to sell out. Similar appeals for discharges and exemptions poured in to the War Department from women who claimed they knew little about raising crops and managing slaves.[35] If the men were not released—as some of these letters clearly implied—the government could not expect plantations to raise enough food, either for the army or for the civilian population.

In petition after petition, however, women sounded the keynote: the need to protect helpless white families by preserving a "due subordination" among the slaves. In a typical plea for help, Sarah Stower claimed that no white male over six-years-old lived on any of five adjoining plantations in Adams County, Mississippi.[36] Mistresses also cited the alarming number of robberies and arsons committed by slaves. Assuming that Secretary of War James A. Seddon had already read many overblown accounts, Hattie Motley of Autauga County, Alabama, promised to spare him a "recital of monstrous woes, unheard of, except in the excited brain of some hypochondriac novel-writer." Though an invalid surrounded by large plantations where the slaves had no supervision, she tried to appear calm and unaffected, attributing her own fears to other, more easily frightened women. But a rape committed by a "Negro brute" on the daughter of a prominent attorney had spread panic among the female population—including Hattie Motley.[37]

By discharging fewer than a thousand planters and overseers (about the number needed to fill an army regiment), Confederate officials managed to stir resentment among the yeomen without satisfying nervous slaveholders. Mary Archer and her sisters lived alone with five hundred slaves distributed among five plantations in Claiborne and Holmes County, Mississippi; in her decided opinion, five overseers would have done far more for the country than five army privates.[38] And this was not simply the selfish plea of a pampered aristocrat. After all, plantations produced badly needed food, and the typical planter had hardly been lacking in patriotism. Often at the urging of their mothers, wives, and sisters, wealthy men had joined up at the first call for volunteers. Sue Walker's husband, for example, had enlisted without hesitation, but camp life had quickly destroyed his health. In approving his discharge, the War Department was not shielding a rich man from the suffering of his poorer neighbors.[39] Such a careful balancing of complex considerations, however, could not overcome the appearance of injustice. Small slaveholders and poor farmers gave claims of public necessity short shrift when their wealthy neighbors stayed at home.

But even the yeomen tried to take advantage of state and Confederate laws exempting overseers. More than half of women's requests for overseers were made on behalf of farmers owning fewer than twenty slaves. Confederate authorities agreed to abide by laws such as the one in Alabama that required the presence of one white man on any place with six or more slaves. In states without such laws, however, only planters with twenty or more slaves could obtain discharges, a legal anomaly that made politicians and public officials at all levels seem more high-handed. Fearing that her family would be murdered in their beds because the county militiamen merely went through the motions of maintaining a slave patrol, Addie Harris concluded that no one cared about the fate of small farmers.[40]

Many officials did appear indifferent to the needs of families who owned few, if any, slaves. But because of the public outcry, in May 1863, Congress limited the exemption of overseers to plantations owned by women and minor children. The new law primarily helped wealthy widows, but even they could hire only those men who had worked as overseers before April 16, 1862, and they would have to pay the Treasury five hundred dollars for the privilege.[41] Newspaper editorials and speeches about the plight of widows and orphans could arouse some sympathy in the most hardened politicians, though complex changes in the exemption laws did little for most women. Instead, Congress simply spread more confusion, undermined public confidence, and fostered sullen discontent.

Even those who supposedly stood to benefit from these laws crabbed about their uneven application. Lengthy wrangles with Confederate and state officials frayed nerves and increased frustration. Local conscription boards in Virginia, for instance, hesitated to release any man to supervise slaves. For its part, the War Department administered the law inconsistently, sometimes refusing to discharge overseers already in the army and at other times denying exemptions to overseers about to be conscripted. From Forest Station, Mississippi, Mary Christian claimed that unscrupulous army officers had demanded five hundred dollars to have her overseer exempted for one year, then hauled him away after only four months. Fed up with lies and rude treatment, she sent a fiery letter to Governor Charles Clark demanding that either her money be refunded or her husband, who was also in the army, be discharged.[42]

Mary Christian could not see beyond her immediate concern to the larger issue: the conscription laws and their administration raised some embarrassing questions. Why should a wealthy neighbor be allowed to pay five hundred dollars for a healthy young man to run his place, asked Annette Fauntleroy, when she, stiff with rheumatism, had four sons in the army, cared for two invalid daughters, and could not manage the few slaves she owned? If two young and vigorous men with overseers for their farms and no small children had been discharged to care for their mothers, Fannie Moss wondered, why had her chronically ill husband not been released as well? North Carolinian Martha Coletrane knew why and sarcastically suggested to Governor Vance that he should look after the welfare of the small farmers as well as Congress had safeguarded the interests of wealthy planters.[43]

This familiar litany of woe, however, fell on the insensitive ears of officials who had heard it all before. How many letters about forlorn widows, starving children, insolent slaves, and rotting crops had the War Department clerks read already? The daily flood of mail had numbed their senses if it had not entirely blunted their sympathies. Their replies became brief and impersonal; the secretary often scribbled "answer as usual" on the back of petitions—if anyone bothered to respond. Increasingly the harried officials scrawled across these documents the cruelest word in the bureaucrat's vocabulary: *file.*

4

The injustices of conscription and the seeming obliviousness of politicians, generals, and government officials to the suffering of Southern families did as much to destroy faith in the cause as defeat on the battlefield. Few women developed the cynicism of combat veterans, but they did become increasingly skeptical and bitter. Poor women *knew* the rich received most of the exemptions, though the scramble for special privileges pervaded all classes. Disappointed that her husband, who had been a shopkeeper before the war, had not been promoted, Julia Davidson advised him to seek a safer position as a printer. If that tactic failed, he might catch rheumatism just badly enough to secure a sur-geon's certificate of disability.[44]

Such ruses shocked and angered women who had patriotically sent their men off to fight. "This cruel War would end," a North Carolinian raged, "if all the loafers about, cowards and half Union men were made to enter the Ranks instead of lounging, sitting on Hotel benches or enjoying themselves . . . . I cant bear to look at them idling about, knowing that for them and theirs this cruel War was projected." As disaffection spread, feminine ire also fell on the officers—Harriet Strother called them "pompous well fed dandies"—who ate and lived well at the expense of the common soldier. Tales of bribery and rampant corruption in the Bureau of Conscription further outraged already disenchanted civilians.[45]

For many men and their families, the only logical escape from an inequitable system was desertion. Conservative estimates place the num-ber of Confederate deserters at 104,000, but it was probably higher. Soldiers denied furloughs, the sick and wounded whom surgeons had refused to discharge, men who had extended a forty-day leave into a sixty-day leave—all were likely to slip off temporarily or stay away for good. In pleading for the release of those caught, arrested, and impris-oned, women defended what their men had done by pointing to the desperate conditions at home.[46] Despite the stigma attached to desertion and some concern about family honor, women usually considered their absconding relatives more sinned against than sinning.

Indeed a painful ambivalence characterized the public response to desertion. After armed fugitives had stolen food and intimidated people in her neighborhood, Julia Jones rejoiced over the execution of several desperadoes.[47] Yet other women could not help but sympathize with those who fled from the conscription officers. Sneaking food to husbands hiding out in caves, the wives of deserters also led Confederate cavalry and home-guard troops on lengthy chases after phantom bands of out-laws. Other women hardly knew what to do: should they encourage their men to stay in the woods or persuade them to come home to protect their families?[48] Like many other wartime problems, desertion set class against class, neighbor against neighbor, and even wife against husband.

By intimidating, harassing, and occasionally assaulting civilians, con-scription officers ironically helped resolve these conflicts by turning more and more families against the government. Though no alarmist and normally cooperative with Confederate authorities, Florida Governor John Milton complained that raids against deserters in Taylor and Lafayette counties often drove the innocent from their homes. Throwing mothers and children suspected of abetting the renegades into jail only encouraged desertion. When soldiers came looking for a North Carolinian named Owen, his wife claimed he was dead. When they asked to see his grave, she roundly cursed the men. Colonel Alfred Pike then slapped her face, tied her thumbs together, and suspended her from a tree limb with a cord. Although she finally admitted that her husband was alive, once the men cut her down she reverted to her original story. They put her thumbs under the corner of a fence post, but again with no results. After investigating this and similar incidents, Thomas Settle reported that at least fifty women in the North Carolina piedmont had been similarly abused, including several who had been frightened into spontaneous abortions.[49] Such brutality extracted little useful information on the whereabouts of deserters and instead encouraged more men to leave the ranks.

Even if they did not know about such outrages against Southern civilians, many soldiers had already lost faith in their officers and the cause, and more often than not they deserted because of conditions at home. Shortages, inflation, and the impoverishment of the yeomanry made a mockery of patriotism. As one sympathetic Confederate colonel admitted, the explanation for most desertions in his regiment was no mystery: the men daily received letters from their families filled with plaintive descriptions of suffering.[50]

Whether intentionally or not, women encouraged desertion simply by recounting their daily problems. Many still tried to avoid complaining and, perhaps realizing that their men felt powerless to protect their families, adopted a deferential tone. A South Carolina wife still bowed to male prerogatives: "I think if your superior Authority knew my necessities and my situation and a house full of little children dependent entirely upon me." She realized her husband could not come home but obviously wanted him to. By upholding the wartime ideal of feminine bravery and by appearing ready to suffer more hardships, she may have convinced her husband that he must perform his masculine duty of protecting the family. Exaggerated accounts of civilian hardships were not necessary to induce soldiers to desert; the plain truth would serve just as well.[51]

However much women tried to conceal their despair and suffering, they could not put an optimistic gloss on hunger, and the soldiers saw through their efforts to keep up a cheerful front. Even if letters from home brimmed with hope, the men might receive more accurate news through neighbors in their regiment.[52] And though often loath to say so directly, many women wanted their men back regardless of means or consequences.

For despite brave efforts, spirits inevitably sagged, and the war's early optimists lost heart. Some wives sent word that everyone at home had given up and were fast becoming Unionists and insisted their husbands return at once. With by no means casual allusions to the poor food in the Confederate army, they also promised their men a good home-cooked meal. Speaking for thousands of others at the beginning of the war's last year, Kate Petty told her husband: "I cannot see one glimmering ray of hope that we will ever have any peace. Every body is whipped now."[53]

After the surrender, some men even blamed such faintheartedness for Confederate defeat. In the Richmond post office, according to a widely circulated story, a dead-letter bag was found containing hundreds of letters from soldiers' wives, all advising desertion. Although such reports greatly oversimplified the causes of the collapse, women *had* contributed to the decline of Confederate military power. After the war, Jefferson Davis dedicated his memoirs to "THE WOMEN OF THE CONFEDERACY . . . WHOSE ZEALOUS FAITH IN OUR CAUSE SHONE A GUIDING STAR UNDIMMED BY THE DARKEST CLOUDS OF WAR; WHOSE FORTITUDE SUSTAINED THEM UNDER ALL THE PRIVATIONS TO WHICH THEY WERE SUBJECTED." But in August 1863 he had stated publicly what everyone knew to be true: the Southern armies could better fight the enemy if all soldiers were present for duty. Many of the absent, he admitted, had left to save their families.[54]

From the beginning women had both sustained and undermined the war effort. Confederate propaganda notwithstanding, unity had proved as elusive in domestic circles as in political and military councils. Many women had sent their men off to fight in an outburst of patriotic zeal, but defeats and mounting casualties soon slaked their enthusiasm. So thousands scrambled to get their men discharged or detailed; others worked just as assiduously to arrange for substitutes, transfers, or furloughs. Even as they maneuvered their way through a maze of complex and contradictory state and Confederate laws, women too became victims of an iniquitous system. The wives of the Southern yeomen especially felt the injustice of a class favoritism and corruption that ran from the county conscription boards to the War Department. Probably by mid-1863, and surely by 1864, such women had little to lose by tacitly encouraging their men to desert. Yet even then the remnant of their fervent commitment to Southern nationalism survived. Indulging in a few last outbursts of fiery rhetoric directed at Southern laggards and Yankee invaders, many women did not realize or would not admit how much they had helped to undermine a cause they had once—and some still—so passionately embraced.

CHAPTER 5

The Political Economy of the
Southern Home Front

O F ALL HUMAN WEAKNESSES, materialism has received the most universal condemnation. Philosophers, ancient and modern, secular and religious, have denounced the single-minded pursuit of comfort as a corruption of the mind and soul. Southerners knew the pitfalls of greed but, like other people, periodically succumbed to the temptations of avarice. Bouts of selfishness alternated with orgies of repentance. The Civil War temporarily disrupted this cycle by ravaging the domestic economy and forcing people of all classes to redefine their relationship to the material world.

From the beginning of the war, a new asceticism pervaded many gentry and yeoman homes; the poor whites' standard of living hardly could have fallen much lower. Virginian Judith McGuire remarked on the change: "Economy rules the day. In this neighborhood, which has been not a little remarkable for indulging in the elegances of life, they are giving up desserts . . . . Personal indulgences are considered unpatriotic. How I do admire this self-denying spirit!" After 1862, even plantation mistresses had to watch their expenditures: "I am as careful of a lump of sugar as I used to be of a pound," Grace Elmore mused. But visions of cakes and candies still danced in her dreams.[1] Like the Children of Israel wandering in the wilderness but longing for the fleshpots of Egypt, many women now considered ordinary food and clothing more important than they could ever have imagined.

Shortages and inflation appeared immediately; familiar household goods either disappeared or became prohibitively expensive. Although shared suffering could unite Southerners in the spirit of common sacrifice, class divisions also appeared. The yeomen resented the apparent selfishness of their rich neighbors and cast a jaundiced eye toward Confederate economic policies as well. The burdens of war were spread too unevenly, and though government provided some relief for the destitute, poverty became the fate of all too many once comfortable or even prosperous families.

1

The government's voracious demands for food, clothing, and manufactured goods along with the Northern blockade and invasion squeezed the domestic economy. Housewives had to scrimp and improvise as so-called luxuries, and eventually many necessities, disappeared. "I never realized the varied needs of civilization," an Arkansas woman observed. "Every day something is out."[2] Most families felt besieged by uncontrollable economic forces as the new scarcity changed the habits of a lifetime.

Women who had never thought much about prices began recording the cost of everything in their diaries and letters. Jennie Lines, a struggling teacher in Atlanta, spent $18.50 for food that could be carried home in her hands. Toothbrushes for $2.50, large chickens for $3.00, bonnets at $60.00—each new price increase meant someone had to give up some item long taken for granted.[3] Even wealthy matrons watched for sales. Word of cheap sugar or bacon created mob scenes as an inflation psychology took hold. A barrel of flour or a cotton card that seemed expensive today would be dearer tomorrow.[4] When consumers timed purchases to beat price increases, they unwittingly drove prices higher.

Shortages complicated the simplest household tasks, disrupting daily life in maddening ways that few people could have anticipated. Mary Jane Lucas had only two dresses: a calico and a muslin. She asked her daughter in South Carolina to send some cloth because cotton material was not to be found in Charlottesville, Virginia. And then one could never tell about colors, given the poor quality of many homemade dyes used during the war.[5] She should have appreciated having two dresses—many farm women and poor whites had only one—but the supply of clothing was unevenly distributed. As late as 1864, merchants in Atlanta and in Huntsville, Alabama, had plenty of dry goods while stores else-where had empty shelves.[6]

Kate Stone might proclaim that fashion had become a "secondary consideration," but clothing still symbolized social respectability. After a cousin lent her a linen nightgown, Eliza Andrews reveled in an almost forgotten luxury: "I was so overpowered at having on a decent piece of underclothing after the coarse Macon Mills homespun I have been wear-ing for the last two years, that I could hardly go to sleep." She gazed at herself in the mirror and marveled at the changes brought on by the war. Outwardly devoted to the Confederate cause, she admitted weak-ening underneath: "I can stand patched-up dresses, and even take a pride in wearing Confederate homespun, where it is done open and above board, but I can't help feeling vulgar and common in coarse underclothes."[7] No leveling for her, even if class distinctions could be maintained only with underwear.

Other women were not so lucky. "My underclothing is of coarse un-bleached homespun, such as we gave the negroes formerly, only much coarser," seventeen-year-old Emma LeConte noted sadly. "My stockings I knit myself, and my shoes are of heavy calf-skin. My dresses are two calicoes (the last one bought cost sixteen dollars a yard), a homespun of black and white plaid, and an old delaine of prewar times that hangs on in dilapidated condition, a reminiscence of better days." Gone were the delicate petticoats and dresses once bought during shopping sprees in Charleston and other cities.[8]

Women who had never touched a needle suddenly made sewing into an obsession. "I am proud of making my own clothes," Martha Crussley announced, "If this were all this war costs us it would be a benefit to us." Countless tales of heroic seamstresses overdramatize but hardly exaggerate the challenges of clothing a family. Turning scraps or castoffs into usable garments required not only imagination but determination and endurance. "It seems funny to be wearing other people's half-worn clothes," Kate Stone commented wearily, "but it is all we can get."[9]

Yet skill and ingenuity could hardly compensate for the steadily rising price of cloth. In the fall of 1863, Josephine Habersham refused to pay $195 for a dress that had cost $9 two years earlier. Women shook their heads and wrote down the latest figures in their diaries and letters, usually with plenty of exclamation points. By the end of the war, clothing prices far exceeded the purchasing power of most families. After looking at a bolt of cloth selling for $45 a yard, Catherine Edmondston refused to spend the equivalent of three barrels of corn to make a simple chemise.[10] Only the wealthiest (and most frivolous) could any longer buy muslin, much less poplin or velvet.

The most ordinary material soon became prohibitively expensive. Take, for example, the simple calico dress—everyday attire for countless farm women. In early 1862, Margaret Preston thought calico dear at 75 cents a yard; by the end of the year, a neighbor was paying $2. The following year brought the price to $3 in Virginia, $4 in Alabama; by 1864, calico ran to $10 or more per yard.[11] The cost of a finished dress rose in proportion. A good buy at $20 or $30 in 1862, in Louisiana a calico went for $50 by the summer of 1863 and brought $150 the next spring.[12] When calicoes disappeared, the lowly homespun made a comeback.

Even as Southern industry expanded to meet the growing demand for uniforms, rifles, ammunition, and other supplies, the domestic economy became more primitive, reverting back to old methods of home manufacture. Southerners dusted off their spinning wheels and looms; wives and mothers learned the skills of their grandmothers. Making a virtue of necessity, the patriotic extolled spinning as a healthy activity for supposedly enervated plantation belles. But the early enthusiasm and pride of achievement quickly wore off. Mary Fleming and her sister carded and spun wool and cotton to prepare it for the wheel. The work began each morning and ended in the late afternoon or, if they had rested a bit, after supper. Like most women, they found spinning a tedious and exacting task that always went more slowly than expected.[13] Singing as they worked, their seeming cheerfulness could not overcome the drudgery and tiresomeness of the task.

Given the growing demand for homespun, whether out of necessity or as a symbol of devotion to the Confederacy, the poor now found their ancient skills much in demand. Adeline Graves could hear spinning wheels for half a mile around her house.[14] Weaving, knitting, and sewing all dovetailed neatly with traditional definitions of model womanhood. A popular song, "The Southern Girl with the Home-Spun Dress," acclaimed domestic virtue as much as it celebrated female patriotism: "My home-spun dress is plain; I know my hat's quite common too; / But then it shows what Southern girls for Southern rights will do."[15]

Despite their simplicity and popularity, homespun dresses were no bargain either for the women who wore them or for the Confederacy.

Because they washed so poorly, Kate Cumming would have preferred one plain calico to three homespuns.[16] To this humble wardrobe, the jauntier women might add a hat made of palmetto leaves—or corn shucks, straw, and various grasses—as the perfect accessory for Spartan attire.[17] Through scrounging and various makeshifts, housewives some-how kept their families clothed, but the task, and the worry, seemed never ending.

Ingenuity and perseverance might temporarily replenish a depleted wardrobe from head but not quite to toe. By 1863, cobblers got at least thirty dollars for leather shoes, and as refugees poured into the cities, prices soared to sixty dollars and more. Even the wealthy felt the pinch of ill-fitting, overpriced footwear: in September 1863, Mary Chesnut re-joiced at wearing her first reasonably comfortable pair of shoes in more than a year. Most families patched old shoes, made new ones out of scrap leather or experimented with other materials: alligator and squirrel skins, cloth, carpet, even wood. Others joined the many Confederate soldiers in going barefoot. Young Susan Bradford squeamishly objected that "the very touch of my naked foot to the bare ground made me shiver," but her slave mammy scolded her for being so fastidious when better folks suffered worse.[18]

Those fortunate families with clothes on their backs and shoes on their feet soon began to miss other common household articles. Forced to make their own soap and candles, women quickly discovered ingen-ious substitutes for many items.[19] But despite much experimentation, they could never find a replacement for coffee. Determined housewives tried roasting corn, wheat, rye, sweet potatoes, peanuts, and okra and dandelion, cotton, and persimmon seeds. All had the same drawback: they tasted nothing like the real thing. Women who had willingly given up many other small pleasures searched frantically for coffee at any price.[20]

Newspaper editors criticized selfish civilians for depriving soldiers in the field by refusing to make reasonable sacrifices, but surely reason-ableness lay in the eye of the beholder. Paper, candles, clothing, and coffee are in themselves small things, hardly noticed in normal times, yet people's lives are shaped by them in ways both obvious and subtle. One could write letters on bad paper for a time, read by the light of a sputtering candle, wear an old dress a little longer, or gulp down bitter Confederate coffee, but the cumulative effect exceeded the sum of these inconveniences. When the Confederate economy could not supply ordinary people with the ordinary things they both needed and wanted, morale plummeted. A longing for scarce "luxuries" did not immediately produce defeatism; empty stomachs soon would.

2

Soldiers' families could endure much so long as they had enough to eat, but by 1862 food shortages had struck many parts of the Confederacy and after 1863 hunger threatened many homes. When Sarah Morgan asked shopkeepers in Clinton, Louisiana, for flour, starch, sugar, and other household necessities, they laughed that anyone would still expect to buy such items.[21] Makeshifts and ingenuity could stretch supplies (and dollars) only so far; plates with meager portions bespoke hardships that even patriotic women would not abide indefinitely.

Housewives who could not raise all their food soon discovered that high prices made a nightmare of planning the simplest meal. Many recipes called for butter at $2.00 a pound or lard at $1.00 a pound or eggs at from $1.50 to $2.00 a dozen. If a dish had to be sweetened, sugar was $1.25 a pound, and a gallon of molasses for $10.00 seemed like a bargain. When wheat rose to $20.00 or more per bushel, flour disappeared unless one could pay at least $75.00 a barrel. Even corn, that great staple of the Southern diet, brought $5.00 or more a barrel by the middle of 1863. Anyone finding a bushel of potatoes for $5.00, had reason to celebrate. Except for bacon, which by early 1863 cost $1.00 or more a pound, meat vanished from many tables.[22] Anyone living near the front lines or in a city paid two or three times as much for these staples. The shock of hyperinflation hit Southern households hard, and even in rural areas food became prohibitively expensive.

Few people ate well. A good meal became an event worthy of detailed comment in diaries or letters. Turkey, ham, chicken, or mutton—ordinary fare before the war—seemed like gourmet dining. Some women with finicky appetites might grumble about eating corn bread and bacon all the time or claim to have delicate stomachs, but they could hardly afford to reject the most unpalatable fare.[23]

These skimpy meals had another depressing feature: monotony. Lucy Fletcher's family lived on rice and bread, with only occasional pieces of meat and no more than a pound of butter a week. Corn bread with sorghum, field peas, and milk made thousands of Southerners into involuntary vegetarians. Many families scraped by on two often identical meals a day.[24] How long women could watch their families growing thin, sallow, and lethargic without concluding that these sacrifices availed nothing was problematic.

Hunger cut across class lines, leveling social distinctions. Plantation mistresses could no longer take pride in being better off than their poor neighbors and kin. After giving up meat and poultry altogether, Susan Middleton's family lived on okra soup and tomatoes. Though they would have been loath to admit it, once prosperous families ate little better than yeomen or even poor whites. On Brokenburn plantation in Northern Louisiana, Kate Stone served family and guests alike a steady diet of corn bread, butter, and milk—all dished out in small quantities. Though relishing an occasional potato or chicken, she still scorned the fatback pork once reserved for the slaves. But by mid-1863, her family got by on flour and sugar with no meat except for an occasional slice of rancid bacon.[25]

She should not have expected much sympathy from her poorer neighbors, who often assumed that the wealthy still lived well despite the war. Indeed many plantation mistresses believed their hardship would be temporary. "I have never heard of genteel people starving," Harriott Middleton wrote confidently after her family's supply of corn had run out, "so I suppose something will turn up."[26] Perhaps God still smiled on a chosen few, but the pangs of empty stomachs suggested otherwise. Class pride could do little for hungry children. Instead of worrying about their loved ones in the army, most women devoted more and more of their physical, mental, and emotional energy to simply surviving from day to day.

The old hauteur proved costly for these new poor. Reluctant to throw themselves on public charity or their neighbors' generosity, they languished without seeking help. If the war did not destroy these families, it certainly lowered expectations and shattered dreams. Mary Smithie had married a country doctor, hoping to lead a respectable and comfortable life. By 1863 she could only see a gloomy future: "When this war is over we will be both naked and poor." At best they might put a little money into a small farm, but even this modest hope seemed wildly unrealistic.[27] Economic mobility had become a cruel delusion: the Confederate ideal was now simply to hang on to whatever was left.

In some ways the invisible and largely silent victims of the war, countless yeoman families slipped from a position of precarious comfort to one of desperate poverty. Harriet Perry lived without flour for six weeks,

feeding her children on fatty cakes and muffins. As various foods disappeared, women began counting the days, weeks, and months of fasting.
Pretending they were not hungry, mothers saved the remaining provisions for their ravenous children.[28]

But such acts of self-denial came at enormous psychological cost.
The traditional value placed on silent suffering seemed wildly unrealistic
when women had to shoulder such unprecedented burdens. Mothers
watched daughters and sons grow emaciated and listless; young children
fussed and cried. Tempers grew short at home, though discipline could
hardly have been maintained in such starving times. Anne Broidrick's
mother tried to spank her for some misdeed but stopped when she felt
the girl's thin arm. "I cannot [punish] my poor little half-starved children,"
she cried. "It is not naughtiness, it is hunger."[29]

Malnutrition seriously weakened the old, the young, and the ill, undoubtedly increasing the civilian mortality rate toward the end of the
war. Searching for food reduced families to packs of scavengers. After
living on corn bread, hominy, milk, and cow peas for most of the war,
one day Harriet Lang threw away a piece of stale corn bread. Thinking
better of wasting even a morsel, she brushed aside the ants and ate it.[30]

Stoicism, dedication to the Confederate cause, religious faith—all
seemed equally irrelevant and pointless. After all where was the vaunted
security of the Southern home? What good were the supposedly superior
values of Southern civilization? Widows in homespun walked to the
preaching on Sunday dragging along gaunt children whose vacant stares
revealed the depth of civilian hardship. Sally Taliaferro barely had enough
strength to record her anguish in a terse diary entry: "Very miserable
and wretched. Can get nothing to eat and no clothes for anybody. Can
hear nothing from my husband." Nor did most people believe their
suffering would end soon; the disconsolate feared the fighting might
never stop. "We have nothing but trouble and pesterment on account
of the war," Susan McLeod moaned, and she spoke for thousands.[31]
Families turned all their attention inward, searching for desperate ex-
pedients to get them through more weeks, months, or, if one dared think
it, years of want.

Yeoman families sold off slaves and land but still could not pay their
debts; dreams of economic independence disappeared. The growing
desperation bred social convulsions that even upset racial taboos. A
Louisiana widow had to sell her husband's clothes to Negroes. "It needs
no comment," Cora Watson exclaimed but then decided it did. "Nothing,

not starvation, nor nakedness could excuse it; no words can more plainly [express the] horrible deformity of the act. The bare fact is enough."[32] Easily said—until one's children whined for food. In condemning this poor woman, Cora Watson forgot the one mitigating circumstance confronted by thousands of Southern families: dire and unrelenting necessity.

On the margins of society, poor white women often lost what little they had, blaming conscription officers, the impressment gangs who seized their grain, or wealthy neighbors, but somehow they scratched out a living. In the hill country, women drove horses or oxen to make worn-out lands yield one more crop; some trudged through the fields barefoot. And their children worked just as hard. A sickly ten-year-old told her Sunday-school teacher that she could not read or write but proudly described her ability to iron, scrub, and cook.[33]

When planter families, yeomen, and poor whites all had to worry about where they could find food for their next meal, the crisis had come. High prices and scarcity first brought inconvenience, later hardship, and finally despair. Civilian morale not only rose and fell with news from the battlefields but wavered and finally plummeted when food shortages appeared. Women could not separate their own suffering from the travail of their nation. The shock waves that rippled through the planter class and the dire misery of the poor whites were severe enough blows, but the impoverishment of yeoman families—the backbone of the army and also of an economy no longer tied to cotton prices— would eventually prove fatal to the Confederacy.

3

A growing sense of helplessness only intensified the despair. Many families lived little better than the poorest Southerners had lived before the war. Of course the human spirit rebounds under the most unfavorable conditions, and, if anything, poverty intensifies the scramble for material comfort. When daily life offers few pleasures, the need for diversion, and even extravagance, becomes more urgent. The war placed a premium on women's ingenuity and especially their ability to discover an occasion for celebration and to find the wherewithal to bring it off.

For some war-weary families, Christmas filled the bill. Although the devout had long warned against turning a religious celebration into a heathen bacchanal, even among the pious, the day had gradually become an occasion of great festivity, especially for planters and the urban elite. During the war, the holiday brought a temporary exuberance to a distraught people. For women with relatives in the army and problems at home, Christmas offered a few moments of happiness in an otherwise dreary life. "If we cannot make a merry Christmas, we can have a happy one," Priscilla Bond suggested. Familiar decorations, favorite foods and drinks, and a brother playing Santa Claus recaptured the spirit of better days, and for a time blotted out the horrors of the present.[34]

In some upper-class homes, the yearly feasting proceeded as usual. Tables groaned with the specialties of the season: ham, turkey, oysters, plum pudding, and eggnog. Yet even for the wealthy the war forced small sacrifices. Julia Fisher fixed turkey, chicken, pork, oyster stew, cornbread dressing, chicken salad, and cornmeal pudding for Christmas dinner in 1863, though she could not help regretting the absence of fancy pies and cakes. "We try to console ourselves with the fact that we enjoy better health and appetites," she commented sadly. "We are always hungry—hungry the year round, but do not grow fat."[35]

Despite efforts to keep up appearances for the children's sake, women often succumbed to despair. Memories of happier holidays made present troubles seem unbearable. Even families who went to church, ate a regular Christmas dinner, and could afford presents found that the war had made the usual merrymaking ring hollow.[36] Minor disappointments loomed larger during the holidays; patriotism seemed so much harder when even the smallest pleasures had seemingly disappeared forever.

Each Christmas in the beleaguered Confederacy made both soldiers and civilians crave more than ever the amenities of life. Thoughts of delicacies, such as cheese and a "*real* sardine," made Ann Shannon Martin's visions of peace seem deliciously tangible. However much women still proclaimed their willingness to make the necessary sacrifices for the cause, their concerns had obviously narrowed and their words often lacked conviction. Julia Fisher stated the case bluntly but truthfully: "We want Northern comforts. It is tedious to spend half the time catching fleas and the other half in sleeping and eating hominy and rice. The thought of milk, potatoes and good bread makes us mourn for a return of good times."[37] But the good times showed no sign of returning, and the only way to obtain such "luxuries" was from a blockade runner or by trading with the enemy.

Publicly, Southerners dismissed the blockade as ineffective. "President Lincoln should have taken a peep at our dinner table," Lucy Irion crowed in mid-1862. "He would surely have raised the blockade in disgust. No signs of starvation there! The soup was quite as rich, the salmon quite as choice, and the meats, vegetables, pickles, sauces, wine, dessert, and fruits just as nicely served as any epicure could wish."[38] Yet many women realized what Confederate officials would not admit and some historians have failed to recognize: the blockade put immediate pressure on the Southern economy. As early as the summer of 1861, housewives complained of shortages and rising prices; by 1862 they regularly grumbled about the "closing" of Southern seaports.[39]

Even patriotic women covetously fingered foreign cloth or hunted for bargains in the most recent shipments. The more enterprising took matters into their own hands and smuggled everything from medicine to fancy dresses through the Federal lines. Well-dressed ladies concealed gray cloth (for uniforms), small arms, money, letters, and even cavalry boots in their hoop skirts.[40] Northern soldiers eventually caught on to these tricks and kept a sharp eye out for unusually shaped female Rebels who rattled or clanked.

In Confederate memoirs these exploits often sound more like spirited larks or elaborate games, but the line between patriotic subterfuge and trading with the enemy was a thin one. After the Confederate government refused to buy cotton, tried to impress it, or ordered it burned, resourceful plantation mistresses turned to the Yankees. Treasury agents reported women of all classes passing through the lines with bales of cotton to exchange for food, medicine, or luxury goods, often for resale to their hard-pressed fellow Confederates. And many of these female entrepreneurs had impeccable pedigrees. Sarah Polk, widow of the former president, for instance, after part of her crop had been destroyed by Confederate troops, asked permission to sell the remainder in Federal-occupied Memphis. Although other women made similar requests, Mississippian Martha Cragin beat them all for sheer gall. After admitting to doing business with the Yankees, she complained that Confederate pickets had burned several bales of cotton and had seized her driver, wagon, and oxen. In an amazingly restrained response, Governor Charles Clark seasoned his promise to get her property back with only a short homily against trading with the enemy.[41] Such a mild response could hardly stop this traffic, especially when women saw it as the only way to support their families.

Indeed, when Yankee peddlers appeared with wagons filled with coffee and the other goods so many Southerners coveted, the temptation could be overpowering. Although women who still had plenty to eat lectured their supposedly weaker sisters on the evils of doing business with the enemy, Jane Beale spoke for the desperate, who believed they had no choice: "Necessity has no law and I do not admire naked martyrdom, so we abuse the Yankees to our heart's content, but buy their goods still."[42]

This willingness to purchase food, clothes and other everyday items from any available source was only one sign of a larger economic and ultimately a political crisis. Far too often historians have pointed to the failures of Confederate fiscal policies without looking at their effects on the Southern home. Shortages and inflation of course not only caused widespread suffering and hunger but also created innumerable smaller but often important deprivations. Attempts to hold on to some vestiges of normal life—especially the everyday pleasures that could make larger sacrifices more tolerable—failed. As a result, faith in the Confederate cause declined, and calls for continued patriotic sacrifice were met with laughter, cynicism, anger, or disbelief. Women turned inward toward protecting their families, expecting little help from any quarter.

4

Such devastating economic problems demanded public solutions, but what historian Allan Nevins once called the organizational revolution that transformed the North never quite took hold in the South. Few citizens knew who was responsible for dealing with such widespread misery or how to marshal the necessary resources, even if they had been available. After all, the burden of government had always rested lightly on Southerners, who had paid low taxes and in turn received few public services. To many people, governors and state legislators seemed remote and their actions inconsequential, and public affairs seldom touched private concerns. The war changed all this. Decisions made in Richmond, especially on financial questions, now mattered to the average person.

Suddenly monetary and fiscal policy affected everyone, especially women trying to support their families. By the summer of 1861, complaints about depreciated Treasury notes had already become widespread. The absence of coins was a constant nuisance. Already hit hard by high prices, housewives also had to worry about changing their bills. Simple transactions grew complicated. A shopkeeper in Fredericksburg,

Virginia, gave Betty Herndon Maury two five-cent stamps and a row of pins back after she used a half-dollar note to pay for a spool of thread.[43]

The flood of paper money disrupted the domestic economy for the duration of the war. Commodity prices rose an average of 10 percent each month until a drastic currency reform in 1864 temporarily halted the hyperinflation. As early as 1862 some manufacturers and shopkeepers refused to take Confederate notes. In areas near the Federal lines, customers used Northern greenbacks, which often had ten times the purchasing power of the rapidly depreciating Confederate dollars.[44] The collapse of the currency forced a return to barter. Women exchanged pork, lard, tallow, salt, and iron for cloth. Near Atlanta, starving mothers combed the battlefields searching for minie balls to trade for food.[45]

No minor inconvenience, this monetary chaos spawned an economic and legal nightmare. A Georgia widow wondered whether her husband's creditors could legally decline payment in Confederate money. Unfortunately they could. By the end of the war, women seldom bothered to dicker with any merchant who still accepted Confederate notes because they assumed that anything bought with such worthless paper had to be a bargain.[46] After a frustrating day of shopping for scarce and overpriced goods, many simply threw up their hands in despair and cursed the Treasury Department. The hardships brought on by impressments and the Confederate tax-in-kind further fueled their outrage.

Although Jefferson Davis and Congress made remarkable strides in consolidating national power and harnessing the South's economic resources, bureaucratic snarls, political opposition, Southern parochialism, and public resistance undermined efforts to supply the armies, regulate industry, end speculation, and reduce inflation. Women with relatives in the service, limited resources, and large families came to see public officials as uncaring or hostile. Given the unpopularity of many government tax and spending policies, this reaction should have hardly been surprising. Yet a curious irony also appeared. Civilian disaffection spread despite unprecedented actions by government at all levels to assist soldiers' families.

In the war's first summer, poor women, mostly soldiers' wives with large families or struggling widows, began to petition Confederate and state officials for help. Large-scale public relief was unknown in the nineteenth century, and many women had little idea how government might aid them. Mahalay Hyatte, for example, simply asked Georgia's Governor Brown for a personal loan. And even when the poor requested army cornmeal to feed their starving families, they often appeared reluctant and embarrassed. "i have tried to do without calling for any help but i cannot hardly get bread for my children," wrote a desperate Virginian. Although women held on to old notions of self-reliance, by 1864 the disheartened vowed to head north if their suffering continued.[47]

But men rather than governments were supposed to support and protect their families, and old ideas of individual responsibility and masculine honor could not simply be tossed aside. President Davis and Congress therefore moved cautiously on the relief issue. In 1862, South Carolina Congressman William Porcher Miles proposed assisting the wives of missing Confederate soldiers who were waiting in Richmond for news of their husbands' fate. Although nothing came of this suggestion, in 1863, Congress authorized poverty-stricken counties to buy surplus food from the government. The exemption law of February 1864 required planters with overseers to sell surplus grain and meat to soldiers' families at considerably less than market prices. Wives and mothers eagerly took advantage of this measure but also wanted to buy food directly from the Commissary Department. Beginning in November 1863, the government distributed some tax-in-kind produce to poor families.[48] Any lingering opposition to public assistance fell victim to wartime necessity, though certainly politicians still saw themselves as the paternalistic protectors of helpless women and children. By their own lights, Confederate leaders had taken radical steps, but they never came close to meeting the enormous needs of destitute Southerners.

Private groups also tried to feed the indigent during the first two years of the war, and by 1863 nearly all the states had adopted some form of public welfare. Legislatures authorized counties to raise taxes for poor relief, though inflation quickly ate up these modest expenditures. By 1864 most state and county governments could not buy enough food and clothing to feed refugees and soldiers' families.[49] Individual states spent ten million dollars or more during the war on poor relief. It wasn't nearly enough. At best, the food and other items distributed to women and children provided a bare subsistence.

Besides general-welfare spending, several states bought up scarce commodities, such as salt, for resale at a low price. Beginning in 1862 a severe salt shortage appeared in parts of the Confederacy. Scraping dirt from smokehouse floors to salvage the salt yielded meager returns, and farm women eventually looked to the states for help. Georgia, for one, responded with an elaborate system for doling out salt to widows and soldiers' wives and their dependents. The commissary general sold half bushels to qualified buyers at a fixed price, generally $4.50—a bargain when the market price ran as high as $1.00 a pound. Despite these efforts, few families had enough salt; women complained about never receiving their allotment or their county's being shortchanged by the state.[50]

The distribution of relief was the chief bottleneck. Haphazardly drafted laws and decentralized administration guaranteed inefficiency and unfairness. In Alabama the wealthier counties received the most money because they could more easily meet requirements for raising local taxes. Furthermore, most states relied on local officials to distribute money and food to the needy, and whether police juries in Louisiana or sheriffs in Virginia, politicians could turn welfare into a patronage bonanza.[51] The welfare boards reduced or held up payments and applied harsh tests to determine eligibility. Wives living outside the county where their husbands had enlisted did not qualify for relief.[52] Officials wrangled over individual cases, often acting arbitrarily. Some women exaggerated their problems and received more than was justified while the more needy got little or nothing. Administrative problems made a welfare system that was by no means adequate on paper, worse in practice.

Even where relief operated efficiently, individual allotments remained pitifully low. North Carolinian Lydia Bolton received only three dollars a month from her county. "i ame a pore woman with a pasel of little children and i will have to starve or go naked," she informed Governor Vance. Trouble was, the Confederacy had too many Lydia Boltons and the burden of relief overwhelmed state and local governments. From 1863 on, more than a third of the families in Alabama depended on public assistance. Across the South, the amounts paid ranged from niggardly— six dollars a month in many North Carolina counties—to generous— twenty-five dollars a month in Athens, Georgia—and some counties provided nothing extra for dependents.[53] A woman with four children who received ten dollars a month, which was about average, could buy a pound of bacon, a bushel of potatoes, and a dozen eggs. Even combined with an army private's pay of eleven dollars a month, shoes and flour were beyond reach. What in total seemed like impressive expenditures by state and local governments was distributed among too many families and soon gobbled up by inflation. Welfare programs provided much needed succor but failed to prevent the collapse of the domestic economy.

5

In a society committed to localism, voluntarism, and noblesse oblige, destitute women more readily sought help from rich neighbors than from public relief. A South Carolina philanthropist purchased ten thousand bushels of corn for two dollars a bushel and offered it to soldiers' families for a dollar a bushel.[54] In New Orleans, Vicksburg, and several Alabama cities, prominent citizens set up "free markets," which made provisions available to needy women and children. These organizations reported impressive amounts of food distributed to large numbers of families, but like state welfare statistics, these figures are deceiving. Most of the benevolence occurred early in the war, the demand soon outstripped the most generous contributions, and, again, too many families received too little help. The Charleston Board for the Relief of the Families of Soldiers, for example, gave a mother and her children no more than twelve dollars a month in cash and provisions—hardly enough to live on.[55]

For the rural poor who proudly spurned the public dole, any organized assistance might seem degrading. Such impersonal help could not substitute for traditional, face-to-face handouts from wealthy neighbors. With a prickly sense of social justice, many poor whites still demanded that the planters meet their paternalistic obligations and grumbled more about the gentry's stinginess and indifference than about the inadequate payments from local relief societies or state welfare. "They [the rich] would sooner throw what they have to spare to their dogs than give it to a starving child," a Virginia woman informed Jefferson Davis. From the other side of this economic and social gulf, the wealthy accused the poor of ingratitude. Julia LeGrand berated the ragged women at the New Orleans Free Market for being too fastidious about the kind of tea they drank.[56] Rather than burying class distinctions beneath a spirit of general sacrifice, the Confederacy's economic woes widened the social and political distance between the haves and have-nots, stretching the conservative vision of an organic society to the breaking point.

No matter how much planters and merchants gave to the poor, they could not escape suspicion of using wartime shortages to line their own pockets. Blaming high prices on unscrupulous merchants who exploited the helpless, women wrote to public officials and denounced the knaves who hoarded provisions while families went hungry. Were it not for the selfish men who gouged the public, Kate Cumming claimed, everyone would have plenty to eat.[57]

The pious fully expected the Lord to punish the Confederate people for their mean-spirited selfishness, a sin compounded by the wealthy's excessive pride. In many ways, women remained the last defenders of domestic, anti-commercial values in a world seemingly given over to extracting profits from other people's suffering. "We are not humble enough," Julia Davidson advised her husband. "There is too much extortion too much speculation too much grasping after wealth, fame and power, *riches—riches*, everybody is striving to get rich. I tell you we must humble ourselves before this war will close. God will have the honor that is his due and if we will not honor him in prosperity and peace he will bring us to war and desolation and almost to famine in order to show us in what we have trusted that we have prided too much in our own strength forgetting the source of that strength."[58] Those who awaited divine retribution predicted that the wrath of the Almighty would fall most heavily on the rich. In the rush to enlist early in the war, wealthy men had promised to care for yeoman and poor white families but now refused to sell food to widows and their children. Much of this popular outrage focused on ardent secessionists who stayed home or on parasitic politicians who lived off the people's sweat and blood. "Wee that will worke has to give part of what we work and make to ceepe up the lazy wimen that don pretend to work," a barely literate South Carolina woman exploded. "I wish you [Jefferson Davis] would have all the big leguslater men and big men about towns ordered in to confederate serviz. they any no serviz to us at home."[59]

When the gentry testily defended themselves against such attacks, class ties proved to be far more powerful than gender. Sensitive about their own diminishing power in an unstable social and economic order, plantation mistresses grew impatient with poor women seeking charity. Ella Thomas coldly remarked that her father should sell his cornmeal for whatever the market would bring and not waste his generosity on "ungrateful wretches." When social distinctions were becoming harder and harder to maintain, any signs of social leveling seemed doubly dangerous. The loss of so much wealth could not destroy the vanity of born aristocrats. Despite being a refugee forced to buy cloth at the special prices offered to the poor, Eliza Smith resented standing in line for an hour with a "dozen or so greasy women and men."[60] Old habits died slowly, and the quondam elite still tried to act the part.

Social friction intensified because yeoman families suspected that the wealthy still used the legal and political process to their own advantage. The disparity of sacrifice galled the most. "The brunt is thrown upon the working classes while the rich live at home in ease and pleasure," Sarah Espy believed. In isolated communities, rumors about special favors granted to local planters set tongues wagging and turned cracks in the social order into deep divisions. After Mary Ann Cobb prevented her carriage horses from being impressed, her neighbors sullenly gossiped about how the well-to-do could keep their property while the poor lost everything.[61] But complaining about such injustices was pointless unless one was prepared to take action. Would the yeomen and poor whites simply tolerate class favoritism or did their accusations pose some unspecified danger to the privileged classes?

At the end of a ten-page tirade against speculators, Jews, and foreigners, a Georgia woman told Governor Brown about overhearing the wives of government contractors boast that if the war continued much longer they would be millionaires.[62] Although officials often filed such letters without responding, dismissing them as the work of cranks ignored a theme running just beneath the surface of these complaints: the implicit and occasionally explicit threat of violence.

Despite the South's long history of violence, there was no tradition of mass uprisings comparable to the food riots in Europe. In general, Southerners had favored more personal kinds of retribution such as dueling, lynching, or brawling to organized revolts directed at bringing about social change. The premium placed on individual and family honor left little room for either collective action or the direct expression of class hostilities. During the war, however, parts of the Confederacy became tinderboxes as refugees crowded into cities where the economy had already suffered from shortages and inflation. In the spring of 1863 the houses, markets, and municipal services in Richmond could not accommodate many more families. Although few beggars appeared on the streets, hunger gave rise to demands that the poor be fed. On April 1, Mary Jackson, the wife of a sign painter with one son in the army, met with a group of disgruntled women who decided to ask Governor John Letcher for permission to buy food at official government prices. If this tactic failed, they intended to take what they needed from the shops.[63]

Shortly after sunrise the next morning, Mary Jackson arrived down-town carrying a pistol and a knife. A well-dressed "lady" sat quietly talking to a "pale, emaciated girl" of eighteen who wore a calico dress that hung loosely on her thin body. When the lady asked if all the people milling about were planning a celebration, the girl archly replied, "We celebrate our right to live. We are starving. As soon as enough of us get together we are going to the bakery and each us will take a loaf of bread. That is little enough for the government to give us after it has taken all our men."[64] A crowd of women and men then marched toward the Capitol, picking up support from the nearby working-class neighborhoods along the way. When they approached the Governor's Mansion with shouts of "Bread or blood!" Letcher tried to stall them with promises of a meeting later in his office.[65] Paying little attention to him, the mob, now numbering around a thousand, stormed through the business district.

Looting warehouses for bacon or shoes but ransacking fancy shops as well, the rioters seized carts and drays to carry their booty. Despite its size, the crowd attacked fewer than twenty businesses, concentrating its fury against notorious speculators, along with German and Jewish merchants. Neither Mayor Joseph Mayo nor Governor Letcher—even when they resorted to threats of force—could disperse the mob.[66]

Then Jefferson Davis tried his hand. Urging the people to rally against the real enemy, the Yankee invaders, rather than turning on one another, he appealed to the rioters' patriotism.[67] Davis claimed to sympathize with the destitute but showed little understanding of their plight. Like other Confederate leaders, he refused to acknowledge class tensions, instead criticizing the rioters for stealing jewelry and fine clothing when they claimed to be hungry. Davis dealt with them like a Mississippi planter confronted by a group of poor white neighbors, throwing money into the crowd in a grand paternalistic gesture. Yet after the arrival of Virginia troops and Davis's grandiloquent appeal, the throng slowly melted away.

Who were these women who had so suddenly and dramatically taken to the streets? Most were married to factory workers, artisans, or farmers, and many had come in from the country on the morning of the riot. Employees of the Confederate uniform factory joined the mob along with at least two workers from the Richmond arsenal.[68] Many of these women claimed to be soldiers' wives barely able to scratch out a living in a city with impossibly high living costs. Although they blamed speculators for taking advantage of their misery, they also accused Confederate officials of worrying more about the welfare of planters than about widows, mothers, and starving children. Vowing to encourage their husbands to desert, they threatened a bloody denouement if conditions did not improve.[69]

But despite some noisy street arguments, no new outbreaks occurred. The War Department ordered the Richmond newspapers to suppress news of the affair, obviously fearing that women in other cities might follow this example. Authorities arrested forty-four women and twenty-nine men. At least twelve female rioters were convicted on various charges, but the final disposition of these cases is uncertain.[70]

The city's leading citizens learned little from the affair. Many denounced the mob as a band of prostitutes and thieves more interested in looting clothing and jewelry stores than in securing food. The genuinely poor had not participated in the riot, respectable people smugly assured themselves. As in most such episodes, politicians and newspaper editors preferred to find scapegoats—in this case Yankees and foreign-born agitators—than to probe for deeper causes.[71] Not only had women seemingly leaped out of the domestic sphere (though many working class women had not been there in the first place) and taken a powerful economic protest to the streets and given it strong political overtones, they also had exposed the fragility of public order in the beleaguered Confederacy.

The real danger was that food riots might spread disaffection and strengthen Unionists and other political dissenters. Shortly before the Richmond uprising, soldiers' wives had entered stores in Salisbury, North Carolina, demanding food at official government prices. Meeting resistance, they had brandished hatchets, intimidated merchants, and had carried away flour, molasses, and salt.[72] Similar raids occurred during 1863 in several North Carolina, Georgia, and Alabama towns.[73] Local officials either sympathized with the rioters or feared taking action; where troops were called in, they refused to fire on women and children. Communities closely knit by bonds of kinship and religion could neither suppress these outbreaks nor control the political and economic discontent that disturbed the usual placidity of rural and small town life. As for city folk, many of them still believed in a unified social order and refused to acknowledge that class divisions had been seriously widened by the war.

Even in rural areas, incidents of petty lawlessness often had strong overtones of class conflict. When poor white women "impressed" recently threshed wheat or waylaid government supply wagons along country roads, they challenged the most fundamental assumptions of a traditional society. Their actions aroused furious debate, dividing families, churches, and friends—in short, tearing at the very sinews of life for most Confederates.[74] Everywhere citizens reported a rash of burglaries. Ordinary thieves mingled with desperate mothers scrounging for food. The bonds of community cracked and sometimes broke. Once-friendly neighbors kept to themselves; families hoarded scarce commodities; suspicions grew along with hatred and paranoia.

Yet riots and robberies never seriously undermined the ability of national, state, and local officials to maintain order. Women rampaging through the business districts of Southern towns established no dangerous precedent; indeed after 1863 few such disturbances occurred. The internal threat to Confederate survival remained largely passive. Disgruntled women did not need to rebel; all they had to do was tell their men to come home. Disheartened families had little energy to protest, hardly conceived of revolution, and generally felt powerless against the large and often impersonal forces menacing them from all directions. As one cynical woman remarked, it mattered little who won the war—the Yankees fought for money and the Confederates fought for slaves.[75] Whatever the outcome, the poor would still be poor.

The people would not rise up in revolt against political and economic injustice, but in any case the crisis had come. Individual and family hardship on an unprecedented scale had ripped large holes in the social fabric. The war destroyed the precarious security of countless yeoman families and by no means spared the planters. By intensifying class tensions that had for the most part lain dormant during the antebellum period, the war also undermined the myth of a benevolent and paternalistic utopia. Old ideals crumbled before an all-consuming materialism that forced women into a desperate struggle for survival in the world. What shall we eat? What shall we wear? These would become the questions of the hour, and men—whether politicians, preachers, soldiers, fathers, husbands, or brothers—no longer had the answers. Patriotism and social conscience could hardly flourish among ragged, barefoot, and hungry women.

CHAPTER 6

The New Women of the Confederacy

"THE TIMES ARE MAKING STRONG WOMEN," reflected Kate Burruss early in 1864. "If they will be sure to stop at the right point, and not border on the masculine, it will be very well. I hope we are not to have our courage and sense put to such tests, but we have now much reason to fear that it will be so." Female courage and sense had of course been more than tested by this time, though Mary Chesnut doubted that the war would bring anything more than suffering to her sex: "I think *these* times make all women feel their humiliation in the affairs of the world. With *men* it is on to the field—'glory, honour, praise, &c, power.' Women can only stay at home—& every paper reminds us that women are to be *violated*—ravished & all manner of humiliation. How are the daughters of Eve punished."[1]

In several ways, both of these apparently contradictory statements ring true. Many lives would change dramatically during the war as women temporarily divided their attention between familiar domestic tasks and other, less conventional work on plantations, in hospitals, in businesses, in schoolrooms, in offices, and even in munitions factories. Yet contemporaries hardly expected such changes to have long-lasting consequences; women might step outside their sphere, but only out of necessity. Few people at the time saw the effects of the war on women as an issue worth much consideration one way or the other. Men and women alike seem to have assumed that wartime arrangements would be temporary, that women still performed largely *auxiliary* tasks in the economy, and that peace would return women to the domestic circle.[2] In both theory and practice, an essential conservatism prevailed, and Southerners had little trouble adjusting to seeing women in unfamiliar roles because they assumed that such arrangements would hardly change what modern historians call "gender ideology." Confederates did not see themselves as revolutionaries, despite attempts to identify with the Revolutionary fathers of 1776. Especially in domestic relations, they saw no need for a revolution that would create a "new" Confederate woman, and they would not have been very good revolutionaries anyway. Kate Burruss need not have worried; her sisters stopped at the "right point."

1

At the beginning, wartime necessity seemed to shake up the comfortable antebellum assumptions of a tranquil and well-ordered agrarian society. Of course planters' wives had always worked hard, organizing households and supervising slaves; more rarely, they had managed plantations on their own. As the men went off to fight, such exceptional circumstances became commonplace, throwing many women into the breach with little training or experience, pushing them to perform new tasks and make more decisions on their own.

In the first year of the war, plantation mistresses remained dependent on their absent men for advice on everything from butchering hogs to disciplining slaves. So long as they deferred to male judgment, the traditional sexual division of labor remained safely intact. Leaving a decision about buying boots to her husband, Sarah Hamilton Yancey wanted to make sure he would "not think I am assuming too much in managing all our business." Reemphasizing the point, she added, "I shall be very glad when I can turn over the management to you."[3] Were such women sincerely expressing doubts about their ability or merely soothing male egos? Probably a bit of each, because their new responsibilities thrust them into a situation filled with both peril and opportunity.

Most plantation mistresses went through periods of hesitation and uncertainty but could ill afford to be immobilized by doubt. Decisions on planting, cultivating, and marketing crops would not wait, and previous practice offered little guidance. Women played an important part in the transition from raising cotton and other staples to producing food—a complex process that left little time for worrying about what a husband, father, or son might think or for pondering questions of feminine propriety. Struck by the many changes in her life, Lizzie Simons listed the "unladylike" chores she had recently performed: unharnessing a horse from a buggy, rolling the buggy into the buggy house, reassembling a tub after the bottom had fallen out, leading a stray calf back home. Later on, this all seemed natural enough, but at the time, the adaptation to new roles and expectations was often incomplete. Catherine Edmondston sat one day in her storeroom watching the slaves at work while perusing a book on medieval history.[4] As her bondsmen labored and she read, half her mind rested in a more leisurely past and the other half dwelt in a tiresome present.

Housewives who had never examined a ledger suddenly had to keep the plantation books. Fearful that merchants and factors might try to take advantage of their inexperience by overcharging, they worked by candlelight to straighten out their accounts. In early 1863, Mary Jones spent the day counting cattle, hogs, and sheep. That night she could not get to sleep, overwhelmed by the sudden strain of managing her late husband's three plantations. Though obviously proud of what she had accomplished so far, she worried about preparing the tax returns.[5] The war made such calculations more difficult and at the same time more critical because the margin between profit and loss steadily narrowed.

Some plantation mistresses depended on overseers either to reconfirm or correct their decisions but often felt inadequate to the demands of their new responsibilities. Challenged by slaves who sensed the absence of experienced authority and by overseers who questioned their judgment, they simply floundered. In October 1861, Amelia Montgomery had run out of pork, molasses, slave shoes, and patience. The overseer had ruined the crop by letting the hogs run wild in the fields while he dallied with black women. Fearing her quarters would soon be "filled with mulattos," she whipped an old slave for suggesting the same possibility.[6] Yet this obvious displacement of anger hardly dispelled it. In great perplexity after only two months of managing the plantation, she wrote to her husband detailing her problems and asking advice, apparently feeling she had failed to fill his place.

But for every women whose nerve faltered or finances collapsed, another gained experience and confidence. The reliance on male advice and instructions, so characteristic of the war's first year, steadily diminished. Women soon became more familiar than their menfolk with a plantation's day-to-day operations. When her overseer did not begin slaughtering the hogs after a cold snap, Eliza Prince told him either to follow her instructions or leave. Willing to rely more and more on her own judgment, she decided to get along without him during the next planting season.[7] Such assertiveness undoubtedly surprised her overseer and perhaps herself.

In many ways, Amelia Montgomery and Eliza Prince represented the extremes not only of failure and success but also of despair and confidence. More typically, competence and self-assurance evolved slowly. Running her family's place in central Louisiana, Mary Pugh at first seemed uncertain and vacillating. When the slaves worked indifferently, she could only threaten them with unspecified consequences on their master's return, which she prayed would be soon. But after a month on the job, her outlook had changed remarkably. Although by this time a refugee in Rusk, Texas, she did not even complain when the overseer left. Instead, she went out each morning to direct the day's work with a new air of authority. "I never saw the negroes both better or happier and have no fear of any trouble with them," she proudly reported to her husband, Richard, and admitted getting on "much better playing overseer than I expected."[8] Mary Pugh did not see herself as a new Southern woman moving into a male bastion; necessity had forced her into taking charge, and she looked forward to ending the experiment.

Yet even the efficient and confident mistresses could hardly become too ambitious. After all they began directing plantation operations during the greatest crisis in the history of the Southern ruling class. All their other problems—whether with crops, livestock, or overseers—paled in comparison to dealing with the decay and eventual death of slavery.

Caught in this sea change, plantation mistresses tried to hold back the swirling tide by clinging to the familiar anchors of the ancien régime, most notably paternalism. Catherine Edmondston carefully weighed out the rations each day, apportioning them to the men, women, and children with the dignity and solemnity of a queen bestowing favors on humble subjects. Others visited the quarters each Sunday for Bible reading and religious instruction. Those who could still afford the extravagance of slave weddings presided over these affairs in the grand old manner.[9]

But this patina of tradition was just that: a thin veneer covering up unmistakable evidence of imminent collapse. Whatever pleasure they derived from displays of beneficence, mistresses eventually had to recognize that their world was about to come crashing down around them. Walking about her estate as she prepared to flee from Sherman's advancing troops, a South Carolinian recalled her "quiet home where I was always welcomed by . . . loyal vassals." Although women claimed to be sick with worry about how their slaves would fare without their kindly protection, they also wondered how they would get along without them.[10] Mistaking self-interest for sympathy merely added to the delusion of slaveholders who had long pictured themselves as the true friends of the black race.

The more women held onto the past, the more their actions revealed this other, harsher side of paternalism. The cliché "killing with kindness" well described the smothering affection of many women for their slaves, a cloying solicitude that still sought to govern the most intimate details of life in the quarters. For "da good mistis," like "da good massa," had more on her mind than Christian charity: behind her smile lay an obsession with control. Viewing blacks as pathetic and dependent children who little understood the tumult around them, mistresses bemoaned their loss of influence even as they welcomed any signs of its survival. When her old slave Rachel paid a visit only a few days before Robert E. Lee's surrender, Emma Holmes rejoiced to see her wearing the "respectable and becoming handkerchief turban" and frankly stated her preference for plain clothing in the "working class."[11] The very casualness of this remark revealed the unthinking way in which mistresses had imposed their will on "their people." Habits of command and expectations of obedience survived long after slavery itself had disappeared.

Always virtuosos of self-deception, slaveholders of both sexes highly valued any displays of faithfulness, hoping that somehow the institution—or at least its spirit—might survive. Former slaves later recounted how they had crowded around the mistress to listen to letters from the master or had tried to comfort her when trouble came or had even brought food to "their white family" after Yankee bummers raided the plantation. "I cannot see that the war has made them [the slaves] a bit different," wrote Susan Bradford in a fit of wishful thinking, "unless it has made them more particular to do their work well. I believe we can trust our servants for if they had any unkind feelings they would certainly show it now."[12] But would they? Could women believe their eyes and ears?

White mistresses' claims of expertise on the so-called Negro character rang ever more hollow. Mary Chesnut applied her acute powers of observation to slaves as she did to everyone else but wisely hedged her bets. "Not one word or look can we detect any change in the demeanor of these negro servants," she commented at the beginning of the war.

Yet she was too smart to be taken in: "They [the slaves] carry it too far. . . . And people talk before them as if they were chairs and tables. And they make no sign. Are they stolidly stupid or wiser than we are, silent and strong, biding their time?" She could not answer this question but soon noticed subtle changes in the demeanor of certain house servants. Her mother's butler, Dick, performed his duties as efficiently as ever but seemed more aloof and no longer paused for friendly chitchat. "He looks over my head—he scents freedom in the air," she suspected. As for the others, "they go about in their black masks, not a ripple or an emotion showing—and yet on all other subjects except the war they are the most excitable of all races. Now, Dick might make a very respectable Egyptian sphinx, so inscrutably silent is he."[13] How to interpret such silence became the question of the hour. Nervous mistresses watched their "servants" more closely but with little understanding and less confidence.

Their insecurity exposed the contradiction at the core of proslavery ideology. Despite common assumptions about the essential passivity and contentment of the slaves, nightmares of insurrection had often haunted the antebellum South, and the war exacerbated these fears. Proof of slavery's impending collapse appeared everywhere. Although whites had always complained about the inefficiency of black labor— even as they had exploited it—the war turned intermittent grumbling into a steady chorus of execration. In 1863 some Mississippi slaves went on a four-week vacation, refusing even to milk the cows. Expecting the worst, their mistress was "always thankful, when morning comes, that the house has not been fired during the night." The words *impudence* and *independence* cropped up time and again in descriptions of black behavior. Although Confederate memorialists later praised the "faithful darkies" who stood by their mistresses, contemporaries knew better. Slaves sullenly refused to do daily chores or performed their tasks with careless indifference. Yet most mistresses could not grasp or refused to see that black people might have their own goals and aspirations, that they might be using the wartime disruption, especially the discomfiture of their owners, to ease their own lot or even strike a blow for freedom. This failure of vision added to white women's exasperation. Lucy Muse Fletcher wished "the Yankees would take the whole race— they are so insufferably lazy & puffed up with their own importance."[14] Baffled, disappointed, and disillusioned, mistresses soon realized that each grudgingly completed task signified their own loss of power.

Just as women had begun to master the skills required for running a farm or plantation, their authority over their slaves steadily evaporated. If blacks could feel the shackles of bondage loosening, so too did whites. Giving orders that were not obeyed, losing one's temper, and then trying to maintain some semblance of discipline became a daily challenge. Susanna Clay felt sorry for the blacks because they did not know any better, but her slaves apparently knew a great deal, at least about avoiding work and behaving with a new sense of independence. "I try by 'moral suasion' to get them to do their duty and it sometimes succeeds," she commented ruefully. Two months later, her approach was yet more oblique: "I make no point except in the mildest language with ours." By the fall of 1863 she had lost command completely: "We cannot exert any authority. I beg ours to do what little is done." For exasperated housewives, it often became easier simply to do the chores themselves. Cajolery, threats of punishment, and tactful requests: whatever approach was taken, none seemed to make the slaves more obedient. Disgusted mistresses soon arrived at the point where they did not care whether their slaves did anything at all. "I shall say nothing," a Texas woman sighed, "and if they [the slaves] stop work entirely I will try to feel thankful if they let me alone."[15]

For the first time, white women discovered just how few blacks had really embraced the paternalistic ethos and how easily the supposedly secure bond between mistress and slave could be broken. The breach of trust was especially painful for mistresses who had long congratulated themselves on having elevated their slaves from a state of barbarism by caring for them like children. *Betrayed* was the only word that could describe their feelings. When supposedly spoiled dependents left without saying good-bye, often in the middle of the night, white women lashed out at the ingrates. The shock of favorite house servants deserting to the Yankees reverberated across the plantation South. Emotionally wounded mistresses feigned indifference, claiming that they were tired of bothering with the slaves anyway or even that abolition might best serve the interests of the ruling class.[16] But such rationalizations could hardly ease the pain of watching a world and its comfortable assumptions fall apart.

Forced to revise their view of their slaves and themselves, some women honestly welcomed emancipation as a release from the burdens of slave management.[17] Yet for most, the rejoicing was short lived. When the household servants left, women who had never before cleaned a room or cooked a meal quickly had to learn. Plantation belles, who had always prided themselves on having delicate hands, now skinned their knuckles and chapped their skin washing clothes. Even women who had worked hard before now tried their hand at unfamiliar tasks, such as milking cows.[18]

Whether they labored cheerfully or not, they marveled at the sudden change in their lives and, lying in bed at night exhausted, assessed the extent of the domestic revolution. Churning butter, making medicines, cleaning closets—all became part of a day's work. Sarah Morgan was astonished that she "could empty a dirty hearth, dust, move heavy weights, make myself generally useful and dirty, and all this thanks to the Yankees!"[19] Such experiences showed how managing a household on one's own or even working for wages outside the home did not necessarily foster a new sense of independence. Nor is this surprising given the persistent assumptions that despite all the changes wrought by the war women still needed the protection of a man. Too tired to enjoy her sudden "independence," the confident mistress simply lived from one uncertain day to the next. Black emancipation did not liberate the white mistress but instead further exposed her vulnerability to social and economic upheaval. The physical and psychological costs of this pseudoliberation seemed far too high.[20]

For even the pride women took in surviving on their own never quite overcame their sense that the times remained out of joint. Grimy and discouraged, harried housekeepers still looked for better days. "I did not have a cake for times were so hard," Carrie Berry wrote in her diary, "so I celebrated with ironing. I hope by next birthday we will have peace in our land so that I can have a nice dinner."[21] Some women would have defined a good meal as anything cooked by someone else. For despite the grit and humor that runs through these accounts, most plantation mistresses missed their slaves and would have readily welcomed them back.

But they would only have done so on their own terms because as slavery disintegrated, racism intensified. To many mistresses, including those few who felt ethical qualms about slaveholding, the blacks' wartime behavior reflected inherent racial characteristics: loyal slaves proved how little blacks valued freedom; runaways showed how most Negroes were ungrateful brutes. Although a few women understood the moral drama taking place, most had only pity or contempt for their fleeing chattels. "The characteristic of the negro is laziness," Grace Elmore noted, "few will work even for bread if not compelled to do so, and their greatest idea of freedom is not to work but plunder." Once free, she speculated, they would inevitably disappear in a ruthless competition with superior whites.[22] Other mistresses took a less callous attitude toward their former slaves but only managed to nurse a different set of illusions. Mary Jones, paternalist ne plus ultra, was sure that the "scourge" of freedom would fall with "peculiar weight" upon the unsuspecting Negroes. To her, the barbarism of Africa, the horrible consequences of emancipation in the Caribbean and the degradation of free blacks in New England made Southern slavery, whatever its imperfections and cruelties, seem a progressively humane institution.[23]

Indeed the threat of emancipation buttressed some white women's faith in slavery as an institution. Imaginations could no longer wander in the never-never land of lush plantations, kindly masters, and cheerful slaves, but the shock of black freedom showed once again how most white mistresses had been and remained committed to a proslavery world view. "Their [the blacks'] mission in America is accomplished," Harriet Moore argued, "The country is cleared for the white man and they will be colonized in some new country." Enjoying whatever solace these fantasies provided, many women turned to the catechism of white supremacy—their sole surviving bulwark against the revolutionary forces unleashed by the war. In words echoing those of Alexander H. Stephens in his cornerstone speech, Kate Mason Rowland intoned the litany of Southern orthodoxy: "We are indeed the most fortunate in the world, we peoples of the Confederate States, America. For we alone recognize & have founded society on the great principle of the inequality of races, & are thus far in advance of the age we live in. When this great truth & the system of servitude it entails shall be recognized by Europe, we will expand & be great & prosperous outwardly as one now fortunate & contented internally."[24]

Nearly drowned in a tide of sudden, radical, and wrenching social and economic change, many plantation mistresses searched for some sense of continuity as the foundations of their lives crumbled. The war had given upper-class women the chance to manage plantations, yet intractable problems on everything from crops to labor hardly made this opportunity a golden one. Less dependent on advice and directions from men, they ran their farms and plantations as well as could have been expected under trying circumstances, but their authority over their slaves steadily eroded. What power the war had given them, it soon took away. In the midst of seeming chaos, many women turned instinctively to the security provided by their culture's time-tested pieties, grasping at the remnants of family, class, and racial pride.

2

In the popular imagination, the war created few new images of Southern womanhood. Charity, tenderness, mercy remained peculiarly feminine virtues. Indeed the calls for women to engage in wartime benevolence stressed the moral superiority of females and made such work outside the home seem more acceptable and more respectable. When women nursed sick, wounded, and dying soldiers, they also nurtured conventional ideas about their own place and character.

The emphasis on voluntarism meant that women working in the hospitals would only do so temporarily and would not neglect their domestic duties. The first Confederate nurses simply opened up their homes to feed the convalescent and console the hopeless cases.[25] Before the government could establish a medical department, they raised money, set up hospitals near the camps, and opened wayside hospitals at railroad depots for sick and wounded men on their way home. The wealthy often paid for food and supplies out of their own pockets.[26] These efforts showed how dependent the Confederacy was on contributions from private citizens, but the aid associations lacked the resources and organization to handle the thousands of men who required more extensive and professional care.

For the duration of the war, the army hospitals also maintained a mixed character: they were staffed by paid physicians and nurses along with volunteers and occasional visitors, and sustained by public funds and private contributions. For women who worked in what generally amounted to makeshift facilities, the distinction between the volunteer and employee was never quite clear. Nursing was not yet an established profession—though the Civil War would begin the process—and volunteers complemented the work of doctors and ward matrons by gathering extra food, reading to the patients, writing letters, or simply listening and offering words of comfort. Arranging their visits on a more regular basis, women brought order to this normally haphazard benevolence. In turn, hospital aid associations gathered supplies and assigned helpers.[27]

Improved organization, however, did not mean that female visitors were always welcomed by either doctors, ward matrons, or the patients. These women had great potential for improving conditions but also could disrupt routines if not actually harm the men. Every ward had its quota of busybodies who claimed vast medical knowledge. Fannie Beers recalled two notorious cases: a seventeen-year-old girl who had killed a dysentery patient by giving him apple turnovers and a woman who loosened an amputee's bandages, causing him to bleed to death. Surgeons and matrons had to watch constantly for women smuggling in contraband food that the men craved but could not eat.[28] Although many of these volunteers obviously served the soldiers well, the insensitive and foolish gave the entire group a bad reputation.

Much of this activity remained both private and haphazard because the hospitals employed so few regular nurses—according to one estimate no more than thirty-two hundred in both the Union and Confederacy. Yet applications for positions poured into the War Department. Women who could not find jobs at home traveled to Virginia or wherever the armies were fighting; the impoverished wives and mothers of Confederate soldiers competed with refugees for the available openings.[29] In hiring nurses, hospitals followed no regular application or appointment procedures, and such administrative sloppiness further reflected the lowly status of Confederate nurses.

These women worked hard and long but did not earn enough money to be considered professionals. In the fall of 1862, Congress finally defined duties and set salaries. Each hospital was to have two chief matrons (forty dollars per month) to supervise the soldiers' diet; two assistant matrons (thirty-five dollars per month) to supervise the laundry; and two matrons in each ward (thirty dollars per month) to care for the bedding, feed the soldiers, and administer medicine. Additional nurses and cooks earned twenty-five dollars a month. Although convalescing patients and soldiers detailed to the hospitals also served as nurses, most matrons preferred women, as did Congress, which specified that females be used wherever possible.[30] But the hospitals could not find enough suitable applicants. Even though many chief matrons were wealthy widows or spinsters who donated their services, such paragons were hard to find, and complaints against matrons for inefficiency, callousness, and even carousing appear in the records.[31]

Whatever their qualifications and abilities, nurses could barely live on their salaries. One ward matron asked for permission to buy food at official government prices because her husband's army pay, combined with her own meager earnings, could not feed their four children. The class tensions that had developed in other areas of Confederate life also entered the hospitals. The contrast in dress, motive, and attitude be-tween well-to-do volunteers and poorer women who did the menial jobs occasionally erupted into nasty quarrels. Phoebe Pember contemp-tuously described the "many inefficient and uneducated women, hardly above the laboring classes" who worked in Confederate hospitals. Kate Cumming agreed that not enough "ladies" applied for these positions. She thought the laundresses far too fussy about their quarters and de-lighted in repeating gossip about these women's dancing with black men.[32] The mixture of benevolence, professionalism, and necessity made it difficult for women of such widely varying backgrounds to work to-gether harmoniously. Indeed, the familiar stories of altruistic angels of mercy reveal little about the complex lives of Confederate nurses, es-pecially the refugee women and soldiers' wives whose primary motive for working in the hospitals may well have been money.

Economic necessity inevitably clashed with expectations of disinter-ested benevolence. The high-minded volunteers exalting their own ex-ample of self-sacrifice could not understand how anyone could ignore the sacred call of patriotism. Kate Cumming advised young girls to "do what, in all ages, has been the special duty of woman—to relieve suf-fering." After serving in Mississippi and Tennessee hospitals for a year, she lashed out at the "rich, refined, intellectual, and will I say Christian" women who shirked their public responsibility.[33] Seizing the high moral ground, hospital matrons condemned selfishness without acknowledging their own mixed motives.

In the tradition of antebellum ladies bountiful and paternalistic plan-tation mistresses, some volunteers and nurses viewed hospital work as poor relief, a part of their customary obligation to uplift the downtrodden. Constance Cary Harrison described Richmond ladies "flitting about the streets," their slaves in tow carrying "silver trays with dishes of fine porcelain under napkins of thick white damask, containing soups, creams, jellies, thin biscuit, eggs *á la creme*, boiled chicken, etc., surmounted by clusters of freshly gathered flowers." When her mother offered one of these delicacies to a backwoods Carolinian, the man looked at her quizzically and stated a decided preference for greens and bacon. Despite the humor in this anecdote, some women treated ordinary soldiers with ill-concealed disdain. To yeomen and poor whites, one matron conde-scendingly sniffed, "gratitude is an exotic planted in a refined atmos-phere. . . . Common natures look only with astonishment at great sacrifices, and cunningly avail themselves of them, and give nothing in return, not even the satisfaction of allowing one to suppose that the care exerted has been beneficial,—*that* would entail compensation of some kind, and in their ignorance they fear the nature of the equivalent which might be demanded."[34] Yet these men had reason to avoid dependence on the wealthy, especially wealthy ladies. Southern notions of masculine honor made it difficult for proud soldiers to accept charity, even when they were lying flat on their backs in a hospital. Women who would serve only officers or soldiers from their own state reinforced the men's suspicions. Although most nurses and volunteers treated patients without regard to rank or class, social prejudice sometimes intruded.

And so did sexual tension. Flirtation in the hospitals seemed innocent enough, but for chief matrons, nurses, and patients alike, it sometimes became a serious problem. Sally Tomkins advised a volunteer to leave her "beauty at the door and bring in your goodness." When women innocently asked soldiers what they needed, many archly grinned and said, "A kiss." Some nurses thought most of the trouble came from rough and ragged poor whites, but even those who seemed to be gentlemen would make a pass at a likely-looking female. And sexual attraction ran in both directions. Kate Cumming overheard a pretty widow telling the doctors how much she enjoyed helping in the hospital because she had found a good candidate for a second husband. Her frank avowal shocked everyone, but she had simply stated what others were loath to admit.[35] If some soldiers saw women as little more than sexual objects, some women obviously accepted such an evaluation of their worth and behaved accordingly. Both class prejudices and sexual stereotypes limited the ability of Confederate nurses to perform their tasks, acquire self-confidence, and establish professional credentials.

The drudgery of daily work in the wards, however, soon took most of the romance out of hospital service. Besides cooking, changing linen, and dressing wounds, nurses scrubbed floors, wrote letters, and listened to the inevitable complaints. Mary Chesnut helped feed hominy, rice, and gravy to badly wounded men who had lost parts of their jaws, teeth, or tongues.[36] Although new patients arrived and problems changed, the days fell into a depressing pattern of madly dashing about with too little time for too many men—and everywhere death.

Women who had led sheltered lives suddenly confronted suffering and tragedy at every turn. Quietly reading from the Bible or singing hymns, they helped the mortally wounded accept their fate. Such experiences transformed squeamish girls. Closing dead men's eyes and cataloguing their personal effects made Phoebe Pember wonder whether she had "any feeling and sensibility left." At night she could hear the coughing and groaning of typhoid and pneumonia patients, although she had to save her strength for the more critically ill. Wearied by long hours, poor food, and cramped quarters, she and her comrades often became debilitated from contagious diseases; not everyone had the necessary physical or emotional stamina. After less than two months in a Virginia hospital, Ada Bacot could no longer stand the men: "Oh my to think of getting up early in the morning and going among them. I am so sick of the sight of them."[37] The daily horrors of the wards naturally sapped morale, but as the war dragged on, conditions only worsened.

The flood of sick and wounded men overwhelmed the resources of most hospitals; shortages and high prices turned nurses into scavengers. Like everyone else, these women had little good to say about the supply system in military hospitals. When food was available, matrons sometimes saved the choicest items for their families or favorite patients— assuming the omnivorous rats did not devour it first. By 1864, nurses at the Chimborazo hospital near Richmond gave the men dry pieces of corn bread and stretched their meager supply of flour to make tiny rolls so that each patient received something.[38]

Hospital societies took up some of the slack, but after 1862 their donations fell off rapidly, forcing even more reliance on individual charity. Several poor women sent corn bread and beans to a Newman, Georgia, hospital though they probably could ill afford such generosity. Nurses bought food for the soldiers with their own money or asked their friends to cook favorite dishes. But wrangling valuable provisions out of tight-fisted civilians required the negotiating skills of a Talleyrand. Fannie Beers scoured the Georgia countryside, visiting the homes of parsimonious and suspicious farm women. She praised their weed-filled gardens, admired their ugly children, and then casually mentioned the hospitals' need for food.[39] Her persistence and tact paid off, but such efforts were stopgaps at best.

As matrons, nurses, and volunteers wrestled with these problems, they assumed ever greater authority. Becoming more efficient, self-confident, and impatient with routine and bureaucracy, they inevitably clashed with the physicians in the hospitals. The most conscientious nurses often received little cooperation from doctors who had little use for women in the wards. At the Chimborazo hospital, the chief surgeon and his skeptical clerks carefully eyed Phoebe Pember, apparently fearing that her arrival marked the beginning of "petticoat government." She overheard a doctor remark to a colleague "in a tone of ill-concealed disgust, that *'one of them had come.'* " Some administrators would not allow women to visit the wards. Even those who kept their opinions to themselves offered gallant excuses about the hospitals' being no place for ladies. To Kate Cumming, the issue was justice: "The war is certainly ours as well as that of the men. We can not fight, so must take care of those who do." By asserting their right to do their job and receive due respect, nurses in effect acknowledged and accepted the limitations placed on their sex. With experience they became more assertive in dealing with surgeons, and eventually their competence and indispensability won them grudging acceptance.[40]

Yet women too sometimes felt out of place in the hospitals. Kate Cumming scorned the fastidious who were hypersensitive about their reputations. "A lady's respectability must be at a low ebb when it can be endangered by going into a hospital," she remarked caustically. In claiming never to have heard a vulgar or indelicate remark from any of the soldiers, she surely exaggerated. But she rightly blamed "false notions of propriety" for making women of ability and strong character hesitant to defy popular prejudice. Fathers and brothers seemed especially protective of adolescent girls.[41] Of course some women used these arguments as convenient excuses to avoid an unpleasant duty.

Many first-time visitors found hospital conditions so appalling that they never returned. Seeing badly wounded men or witnessing amputations, some fainted. Shortly after she began working in a Chattanooga hospital, Kate Cumming saw a stream of blood running off an operating table into a tub, which also held the patient's recently severed arm. On her way to the kitchen—just below the operating room—she frequently noticed blood oozing down the steps. And even if eyes adjusted, noses might not. The air in most wards was foul. "I dont like so much mess and so affluent odors," Lucy Bryan wrote in disgust. "It makes me sick to smell soldiers anyway."[42] Some young women with the best of intentions never got used to such conditions and decided they could serve better by sewing or raising money for the hospitals.

Although few mentioned it, many delicately bred young ladies dreaded affronts to their modesty. When applying for a job as a nurse, an Alabama woman discreetly inquired whether she would have to dress "stomach" wounds. In her first hospital job, Phoebe Pember learned how a "lively imagination" could easily conjure up embarrassing situations. Bringing chicken soup to her first patient, she feared he would express his thanks by rising out of bed in his skimpy hospital gown. After more experience she concluded that "little unpleasant exposure" normally took place and that no women should let "one material thought lessen her efficiency" but instead "*must* soar beyond the conventional modesty considered correct under different circumstances."[43]

Patriotism might overcome prudery, but complex ideas and emotions tugged would-be nurses in several directions at once, often making them deeply ambivalent about hospital work. Women were supposed to be brave and strong but at the same time remain loving and refined; endurance and perseverance were to characterize the actions of young girls who had been traditionally seen as weak and frivolous. Such contradictory and shifting expectations naturally confused women and made them uncertain about their proper roles and place. Were they stoically to endure the sights, sounds, and odors? Should they retreat to the safety of the domestic circle?

Although a few women went home unnerved from their first experience and had nightmares about the wounded and dying, most recovered from the initial shock, somehow learned to cope, and performed useful service.[44] More important, they pressured doctors and army officers into improving procedures. In a report to Vice-President Alexander H. Stephens that was reminiscent of Florence Nightingale's scathing critiques of British medical practices during the Crimean War, Mary Johnstone dismissed most surgeons as drunken political appointees unfit to run hospitals. She suggested a more careful classification of patients, the creation of receiving wards, and the installation of screens to shield convalescing soldiers from scenes of suffering and death. Other nurses told of wounded men who slept on straw in clothes that had not been changed since their arrival.[45]

In dealing with stubborn bureaucrats, arrogant surgeons, and cantankerous patients, women acquired informal political skills. Female administrators, such as Sally Tomkins and Juliet Opie Hopkins, wielded an authority that impressed and sometimes frightened their male colleagues. Like army officers and civilian leaders, they learned important lessons in organization. In their zeal for initiating reforms, women brought to the work previously untapped skills. The South's few female physicians either had to serve as matrons or as ordinary nurses. Ella Cooper, for example, had completed the curriculum at the Medical College of Cincinnati, but the faculty had not allowed her to graduate. "I am a woman and have been so trained to feel that a woman can not walk out of a certain routine, even to do good," she admitted. Though qualified as a surgeon, she was willing to serve as a nurse or even a cook. She thought the doctors were a "little astonished when they see me, to find that a woman can do something, [but] I presume it will not diminish their zeal or prove detrimental to the Confederacy."[46] This well-directed sarcasm might have amused other women, who, though not as thoroughly trained as Ella Cooper, ran the laundries, kitchens, and dispensaries with cool efficiency.

For once the official reports do not exaggerate: the accomplishments of Confederate nurses were impressive. Most matrons managed their wards as skillfully as the private hospital associations claimed, and their efforts markedly improved Confederate medicine where it counted most, in reducing the mortality rate. In hospitals run by men, the mortality rate was about 10 percent; in those run by women, less than 5 percent of the patients died.[47] Contemporaries attributed this difference to superior cleanliness, but better food preparation and organization also helped.

As it turned out, such achievements would mean little in the postwar South. Hospital work had for a time offered women a challenging new profession, which—despite low salaries—had bolstered their self-confidence and had given their lives new meaning and importance. But such benefits proved to be fleeting, and few men or women assumed that nursing had been anything more than a temporary job in crisis times for women who would ultimately resume their places as wives and mothers. Former nurses found few opportunities to apply their administrative skills outside the home and instead returned to domestic life. Although a few later became the subjects of syrupy obituaries, most died in obscurity.

3

Like most wars, the Civil War had many unexpected and unintended consequences that not only disrupted political and economic life but for a time changed the character of Southern homes and seemed to upset conventionally defined sex roles. Although women had managed farms and plantations, had supervised slaves, and had worked in benevolent associations during the antebellum years, the war also opened a few unusual opportunities in less traditional businesses and professions.

Of course anyone reading newspaper articles about enterprising women could misinterpret the effects of these changes. When contemporaries noted how more and more women were entering the labor force, they forgot those who had worked in factories and stores before 1861. Nor does a short list of female entrepreneurs add up to impressive gains for women as a group. That Ellen Elmore successfully managed her family's lumber mill does not mean that hundreds of women suddenly went into the lumber business. Peggy Cooper operated a ferry on the Pee Dee River in South Carolina, but exceptions were still exceptions. The female clerks who worked in stores seldom stayed there after the war. Although a few artisans' wives took over their husbands' trade, most struggled along to make ends meet and anxiously awaited their men's return.[48] Even when textile mills rapidly expanded and hired more female workers, this signaled neither the beginning of a Southern industrial revolution nor the emergence of a white female working class. The war might reshape domestic ideology in subtle ways, but it never seriously challenged old notions about women's work.

In fact class considerations gave women belonging to plantation and urban elite families even fewer options than their poorer neighbors. Factory work, running a small business, or even sewing at home hardly seemed respectable. Teaching therefore became the obvious choice for genteel belles and widows, and the war accelerated the feminization of elementary education in the South.

The departure of Northern-born teachers and Confederate conscription forced more schools—and especially the struggling academies— to hire women. The war nearly destroyed what had in any case only been a skeletal common school system and forced many academies and colleges to close, but after passage of the Conscription Acts, administrators could no longer be particular about gender in hiring teachers. A North Carolina minister even predicted that females would soon be instructing the "lower branches" in Southern colleges.[49] Despite these trends, however, few women had the training or inclination to become teachers. Of those who did, many taught only briefly, either marrying after the war or quitting when their finances improved.

As for the once wealthy women who joined the profession, they could not entirely lay to rest old doubts about propriety—what a Georgia woman called "the disgrace of giving lessons in music." For well-bred young ladies who saw only humiliation in having to work outside the home, even teaching appeared to be a slightly disreputable occupation. But such hidebound opinions may also have reflected a realistic assessment of the teacher's anomalous status and myriad problems. Having observed governesses at first hand, Sarah Morgan doubted that she could endure the "nameless, numberless insults and trials and the hopeless, thankless task." "I would rather die than be dependent; I would rather die than teach," she wrote, concisely defining the dilemma of many sensitive young women.[50]

If they could convince themselves, women still had to ignore community prejudice and persuade skeptical families. "My restless desire for independence is quite as strong as ever," wrote Madeline L'Engle. She had set up her own school and would no longer rely on her father's resources, even if it meant sacrificing her children's "social position." Hard times made class considerations less weighty but hardly made the decision to become a teacher simple or easy. In May 1864 Margaret Gillis was happily teaching on a plantation despite her husband's being "very much hurt at my perversity." He returned home on furlough in October and talked her into quitting, though for some unexplained reason, by January 1865 she had rejoined her pupils. "I had rather teach than do anything else in the world," she avowed; the domestic conflict continued, however, because her husband insisted that she would never take another school.[51] Despite wartime necessity and the old belief that women were uniquely qualified to nurture young children, the few available positions, along with the traditional roadblocks, prevented large numbers of women from entering the classroom.

A teacher's small salary often made the battle against such difficulties hardly worth the effort. Plantation mistresses paid tutors two hundred to eight hundred dollars a year plus room and board. Public school teachers seldom made more than three hundred dollars and often had to board with their students' families. Barely able to support their children in a time of ruinous inflation, some of these women appealed to state and Confederate officials either for relief or for their husbands' discharge from the army.[52]

Poorly paid teachers in turn found little satisfaction in their work. Idealistic young ladies who fondly remembered their own school days had their dedication tested by rambunctious students of modest intellectual ability and little motivation. "I love the care of children," Bettie Blackmore wrote enthusiastically at the beginning of the term, but a month later she was complaining about the rough boys who had enrolled after the harvest. By the middle of winter, discipline had become her primary concern. Even well-behaved classes made slow progress, and tempers grew short all around.[53] The search for respect, not to mention professional status, became more and more discouraging.

Hints of class prejudice appeared when aristocratic ladies taught in schools for yeoman and poor white children. As the formerly well-off left the relative isolation of the plantation or town house to mingle with the common folk, they could not leave their social biases behind. Emma Holmes was in many ways typical of these new teachers. A twenty-three-year old Charleston belle who had dreamed of becoming a "schoolmistress in a pleasant village among friends," in June 1862 struggled with two impish boys in a plantation school near Camden, South Carolina. Her class soon became larger, but she disliked working with children of "rather common parents" and missed city life. By October 1863 she had seemingly settled into a routine, confident of her ability to keep order and much more comfortable in the classroom. Yet moving to another plantation with eight children, she found her new scholars ignorant of the most common facts and in constant need of whacks from her ruler. Despairing of such "clod pates," she shortened the lessons to preserve her own sanity and often quarreled with her students' mother.[54] For many other teachers, initial excitement quickly waned. Soon they merely went through the motions, not from dedication, but mostly out of necessity.

The troubling question remained: what were the alternatives? Even the war had scarcely increased the options for most women. Southern businesses remained all-male operations, and a woman working in an office seemed a radical and unsettling innovation. As usual, only necessity opened up new positions for women. With so many men in the army, the Confederate government had little choice.

The Treasury and War departments hired female clerks, as did the Post Office Department, which also appointed a few postmistresses. Soldiers' wives, teenagers, widows, and refugees besieged these agencies with applications, many containing pitiable descriptions of domestic woes. Louisa Boulware, for example, could hardly feed her two orphan nieces in Richmond. She had already lost two brothers in the war, her parents had both died—her mother reportedly "frightened to death" by the Yankees—and her slaves had become too "changeable" to raise a crop. Secretary of War James Seddon found her petition worthy but had no vacancies.[55] Desperate women usually sought these jobs in vain; clerks gave their requests a pro forma response or simply filed them.

Nor was need necessarily the most important requirement for obtaining a position. Although Congress authorized the various departments to employ only "such females as are dependent upon their labor for support," it could not stop the use of personal and political influence. Inveterate diarist and War Department clerk J. B. Jones thought his department hired too many upper-class ladies while ignoring the plight of poor refugees. Octavia P. Taylor claimed that only friends of the secretary could get a job in the Treasury Department.[56] Many women understood how the system worked and gathered endorsements from powerful politicians and generals before seeking an interview.

Even geography favored the socially influential because most government jobs were in Richmond or Columbia, South Carolina. Yet obtaining a post where the cost of living devoured modest incomes could prove a decidedly mixed blessing. Women who signed Confederate notes in the Treasury Department earned six hundred dollars a year in 1862 compared to a male clerk's one thousand. After these amounts had been raised to nine hundred and fifteen hundred dollars respectively, in early 1864, the government increased the salary to three thousand dollars annually regardless of sex. Why the wage gap suddenly disappeared is a question with no easy answer. Congress never debated the issue, and there is no evidence that anyone was concerned about sex discrimination. Some members pushed for higher clerks' salaries by arguing that women could not live on nine hundred dollars a year, but they also may have been responding to constituent pressure. The Treasury payroll lists contain many names of women from prominent families with considerable political clout. Whatever the reason, the decision came too late. When the price of flour in Richmond went to three hundred dollars a barrel, many clerks undoubtedly wondered whether they could get by on what at first had seemed a generous pay increase.[57]

The situation was worse in the War Department, which had been much slower to take women in the first place. A few copyists worked part time in 1861, but during 1862 and most of 1863, no women were hired. As the draft siphoned off male clerks, the various bureaus added at least 129 women, more than two-thirds of whom were married. With salaries of fifteen hundred dollars a year—half those of the Treasury clerks—they could hardly support a family but were still better off than many other people. Copyists toiled at niggardly piecework rates—twenty cents per hundred words being standard—and illiterate washing and cleaning women received only six dollars a month.[58]

Besides working in the offices, women sewed uniforms, knapsacks, and other items—tiresome labor that earned the lowest wages. All across the South, the Quartermaster Department and the state governments ran what amounted to sweatshop operations, paying only thirty cents a shirt and a quarter for underwear. By 1864 the rates in Richmond had risen to two dollars and a dollar, respectively, but some senators charged that government contractors cheated the women out of part or most of their earnings. Despite pinchpenny wages and exhausting work, the Quartermaster Department had no trouble finding enough applicants for more than four thousand openings.[59]

During its final session, the Confederate Congress tried to remedy these inequities and relieve destitute workers. On January 5, 1865, ardent Southern nationalist William E. Simms of Kentucky introduced a far-reaching measure in the Senate. His bill would have increased the salaries of women in the Quartermaster's office and hospitals to the level of other government clerks' pay. The proposal also granted nurses and ward matrons free lodging and firewood and included substantial raises for ordnance workers, who could then buy rations and clothing at official government prices. Senator Robert W. Barnwell of South Carolina, a staunch fiscal conservative, sharply objected, claiming that no one knew how much work these women actually did. Other senators inveighed against providing charity or entered constitutional quibbles. A gutted bill, without the provisions for cheap food and clothing, finally passed both houses of Congress.[60] Despite pay raises ranging from 75 percent to 125 percent, Congress had hardly been generous. Doling out more depreciated Confederate dollars while refusing to help families buy necessities meant little with the Confederacy in its death throes.

This last futile gesture pointed up only the most obvious difficulty for women working in government offices. Besides the low salaries, they also had to face less tangible but equally troublesome problems. Although the "department girls" slowly won the respect of their superiors, they still met suspicion and hostility in other quarters. Gossip circulated about note signers who seemed excessively friendly with prominent politicians. Rumors of gross immorality, however, failed to address the real issue. In a blunt letter to the secretary of war, an anonymous correspondent went to the heart of the matter: the clerks were "lapsing into prostitution from their total inability to feed and clothe themselves with the[ir] pay" and innocent girls were being led into the "pathway of hell."[61] Despite the exaggeration in this statement, powerful economic pressures made respectability harder to maintain.

Although many women at first welcomed any government job as a godsend for their hungry families, their enthusiasm soon waned. Most jobs were neither rewarding nor exciting, and a few were downright dangerous. The Ordnance Department hired more than five hundred women to fill cartridges at a laboratory on Brown's Island in the James River. On March 13, 1862, Mary Ryan got a friction primer stuck in a piece of wood. She banged it on the table to knock out the primer. The blow set off an explosion that tore the room apart, hurling her into the air, catapulting some workers into the river, and scattering sixty others in all directions. Thirty-two women, many too disfigured for identification, were killed and at least thirty others were seriously injured. A similar accident in a Jackson, Mississippi, cartridge factory threw young girls into nearby trees, killing at least fifteen.[62] In both cases, most of the victims were indigent teenagers who would take any available job.

Yet even among the lowest-paid workers a new assertiveness—and occasional militancy—appeared. Piecework rates for filling cartridges and sewing cartridge bags had steadily increased, though never keeping pace with rising prices. In December 1863 at the Confederate States Laboratory in Richmond, women making $2.40 a day had successfully struck for a sixty-cent raise. During the war's last winter, ordnance workers also walked off their jobs. Ignoring official appeals to patriotism, they stood their ground until the War Department set up a store where they could buy food at one-fourth the market price. This settlement set no precedent, and similar protests failed. The Ordnance Department had a peculiar wage scale for salaried employees: in October 1864 married women received seven dollars a day but single females earned only five dollars a day. Three hundred unmarried women struck, but this time the government stood firm, firing them all and hiring new workers.[63] Arbitrarily determined salaries and the government's uncertain response to complaints not only illustrated economic and political inefficiency in the Confederacy but showed how male bureaucrats dealt with female workers. In Confederate rhetoric, patriotic women were indispensable to the cause; in practice, their treatment by both private and public employers suggests otherwise.

In defeat, these new Confederate women—who had served their country outside their accustomed sphere, faced psychological, social, and, most of all, economic crises. Plantation mistresses lost their slaves, the nurses no longer had patients, the currency so carefully signed by female clerks was now worthless. The war had opened doors for these women but had closed them just as quickly, and traditional notions about femininity survived more or less intact. Most Southerners saw the changes in sex roles between 1861 and 1865 as an aberration, an experiment launched out of necessity that would not be soon repeated. The Confederates had not promised a domestic revolution, and none occurred.

CHAPTER 7

Duty, Honor, and Frustration: The Dilemmas of Female Patriotism

I N THE SPRING OF 1861, Judith McGuire weighed the Confederacy's chances for survival with a curious blend of realism and romanticism. "We are very weak in resources, but strong in stout hearts, zeal for the cause, and enthusiastic devotion to our beloved South, and while men are making a free-will offering of their life's blood on the altar of their country, women must not be idle." Her spirit soared at the thought of doing volunteer work for the soldiers, but then she suddenly returned to earth, realizing how desperate the approaching struggle would become. "We shall be indeed dependent on our own exertions, and great must these exertions be."[1]

Southern women were familiar with several models of female behavior in wartime: the Spartan mother sending her sons off to fight the relentless foe; the daughter of Israel coming to her nation's aid at the moment of greatest peril; the Christian woman praying for the defeat of Satan's legions. But none of these historical archetypes exactly fit Confederate circumstances. Although a few women would take part in wartime political and military controversies or even defend their homes, no one called on them to become Amazons. However much rash young girls might clamor to march and fight, claimed an anonymous poet in the *Southern Literary Messenger*, their "feeble strength" prevented them from taking on a man's job.[2] Yet even as Southerners refused to invoke ancient examples of female warriors, they dared not push sentimental notions of feminine weakness too far. Women were supposed to preserve their soft and gentle nature but at the same time show devotion and courage.

Such ideological contradictions forced Jefferson Davis and other Southern leaders to hark back to a more recent and familiar time of testing: the American Revolution. To Confederates, the women of 1776 embodied both classical and modern virtues: stoicism, self-sacrifice, daring, determination. In hauling out old spinning wheels or reusing eighteenth-century dresses, their granddaughters of the 1860s might recapture this past glory. But flesh-and-blood human beings cannot model their lives on abstractions, no matter how revered. The Civil War presented its own challenges even though Southerners of both sexes continued to describe female roles in conventional language. Long after Judith McGuire's vision of selfless devotion carrying all before it had been shattered, Governor Joseph E. Brown was still rallying Georgians to the colors by praising the "noble women" who had "by their untiring energy clothed the naked and contributed millions of dollars to the support of our cause, and who like guardian angels, have ministered to the comfort and agony of the sick and wounded of every state."[3]

None of these endeavors threatened to "unsex" women or challenge male prerogatives. Despite the greatly expanded scope of this work, most Southerners thought of female benevolence in a constricted, Victorian way even though the war made old forms of charity inappropriate if not impossible. The Atlanta Hospital Association sold sugar to raise money for an "invalid ladies" home, but the Confederate government impressed its supplies. Who would make contributions when the soldiers commanded the lion's share of resources? The Sisters of Charity in Mobile ran out of funds for their female orphan asylum and unsuccessfully sought permission to buy goods from the Yankees in occupied New Orleans.[4]

By refocusing their efforts on war-related benevolence, women could act as true patriots within the limits of a conservative definition of female patriotism. But economic hardship, political conflict, and military disasters strained not only morale but also traditional notions about women's civic status. Frustrated by a whole series of public and private calamities, upper class (and even some yeoman) women who had always dominated antebellum charitable societies began to criticize politicians and generals, and in a few cases they even asked why they could not fight to defend their homes.

1

Like most wars, the Civil War relentlessly channeled energy in one direction. Working for the cause became more than a patriotic duty, it became an obsession. In the halcyon days of 1861, showering departing soldiers with food and clothing or greeting passing troop trains with armloads of provisions seemed easy enough. As late as March 1863, elderly women stuck loaves of bread on the bayonets of Texas troops marching through Richmond.[5]

In modern wars, governments encourage private contributions, such as bond and scrap drives, to give people a sense of participation in the cause, but the Confederacy required more than token generosity. The Southern people could not simply donate out of their surplus; many women gave away most of their bread or coffee. The meatless meal became a Confederate tradition, a symbol of patriotism, a way to save bacon and beef for the soldiers, but also a sign of the real sacrifices required for an underdeveloped nation to fight a war.[6]

Even the poorest women and their daughters could sew—what Emma Holmes called "a never-ceasing labor of love & patriotism." Knitting socks, making shirts, and stitching underwear helped housewives feel they were doing something important for their country, and in spite of sore, numb, and callused fingers, the dedicated counted their socks in the hundreds.[7] Sewing was clearly domestic and raised no touchy issue of propriety. When generals, politicians, and newspaper editors praised the devotion of Southern women, they in effect honored them for knowing their place in a conservative social order.

Besides safely channeling female energy and patriotism, sewing provided a new measure of female devotion to the cause. The term "famous knitter" appears often in letters and diaries, a stock encomium for these heroines of the home front. Such women served their country by giving up both their time and other interests and in some cases by sacrificing intellectual growth. When Lucy Breckinridge wrote in her journal, she felt guilty for wasting the time. Even notorious "bluestockings" abandoned their studies for basting and hemming. A friend of Emma Holmes who had always "lived wholly among books" and whose "ideas always seemed confused when she came in contact with the practical everyday world" gave up French and Italian to master the art of making a decent shirt.[8] Even though sewing opened new worlds for some women by making them feel more useful, it obviously closed off other possibilities.

At the same time, sewing broadened women's social horizons by bringing them together in groups. Although historians have exaggerated the isolation of antebellum Southern housewives who worked closely with family and neighbors on many common tasks, the war encouraged larger cooperative efforts outside the home. Less than two weeks after Fort Sumter, the women of Grace Baptist Church in Richmond met after Sunday services to form a sewing society, in effect serving as models of evangelical womanhood. For such volunteers the church became their primary spiritual and social outlet.[9] Though women often remained dependent on ministers and elders for money and advice, the sewing circles expanded feminine influence in the church while solidifying loyalty to both God and country.

In turning out everything from caps to sandbags, and sometimes supplying entire regiments, the aid societies made a significant contribution to the Confederate cause. Most circles met at least weekly, though many women sewed in churches, town halls, or private homes nearly every day. In the cities, energetic leaders established networks of committees, dividing the neighborhoods into wards headed by managers who were responsible for getting out the work on time, collecting dues, and raising money for cloth and other supplies. By drafting constitutions, electing officers, and handling daily problems, some women gained potentially valuable skills.[10] Upper-class matrons dominated these organizations, apportioning the tasks, scheduling meetings, and in many ways buttressing the local social hierarchy.

Although only a few detailed records of these groups have survived, by the end of 1861, South Carolina and Alabama each had around one hundred soldiers' relief societies. Some of these associations may have existed mainly on paper, but an active one could outfit several companies. Especially during the first months of patriotic fervor, secretaries reported an impressive output of clothing and blankets.[11] Behind the dull statistics in the minutes of the meetings were women cutting out cloth and piecing together garments with factorylike efficiency. If the war forced many individualistic farm boys into a new and exacting— some thought almost industrial—discipline, it also gave some women a taste of life in a more highly organized and modern society.

During 1861 and much of 1862, enthusiasm ran high as eager volunteers exhausted themselves for Southern independence. "I believe this war is to make a heroine even of me," Maria Louisa Fleet observed proudly, "I think of nothing all my waking moments but the soldiers, and what I can do to make you [her son Fred] or any of the needy around you more comfortable." Such zeal, however, was occasionally misdirected. The mania for knitting socks kept the soldiers' feet warm while leaving the rest of their bodies exposed to the elements. A South Carolina sewing society, which might have better invested its time and resources in looking after the ragged enlisted men, provided General P. G. T. Beauregard with a complete uniform.[12] Despite these occasional lapses of judgment, the sewing societies contributed much to the comfort and morale of the troops.

But women soon discovered that their enthusiasm outstripped their resources. Even the best-organized groups seldom had enough money to buy cloth. So like other parts of the Confederate war effort, outfitting the soldiers became both a public and private undertaking financed by individual contributions and by the War Department. The Confederate quartermaster sometimes bought the garments or paid the shipping costs to keep the aid associations afloat. As inflation depleted their treasuries, local groups asked state governments to buy the material.[13] Most states furnished cloth for the first two years of the war, but the burden of public relief soon made this impossible, leaving the volunteers to make do with their own resources.[14]

The financial crisis also forced women to act more aggressively in the public sphere. In what must have seemed to some Southerners a startling breach of propriety, well-dressed females stood on street corners and solicited contributions. One Charleston lady claimed to have collected sixty-four thousand dollars, but most women hardly raised enough to buy a few pairs of soldiers' shoes. Pennies collected from schoolgirls and small donations from hard-pressed families could barely improve camp conditions; inflation limited the good done by larger gifts. Even organized and well-publicized fund drives failed to meet the ever growing need.[15]

Fancy bazaars and raffles appealed to people who enjoyed the illusion of getting something for their contributions and also recaptured a bit of prewar elegance. Yet for the promoters, these projects involved more work than profit. Young women in Chapel Hill, North Carolina, sold fruitcake and fancy clothing, but even with a twenty-five-cent admission fee, they raised only a hundred dollars—about the average take for such affairs. In cities where wealthy women donated jewels, paintings, china, and furniture, bargain hunters swarmed around the tables. Although a New Orleans bazaar netted sixty thousand dollars for sewing supplies, such successes were rare, especially late in the war.[16]

The more lavish efforts raised more money for the soldiers, but at the same time they reinforced conservative definitions of woman's character and widened the social distance between rich and poor. A Union woman described the "lovely Creole girls present in exquisite toilets passing to and fro through the decorated rooms" at a New Orleans bazaar. Promotional techniques emphasized the popular image of women as shallow, giddy creatures. A Frenchmen visited a New Orleans fair where the "salesgirls are very pretty and had what it takes to clean you out." The most attractive ran the refreshment stands, smiling sweetly as they peddled sorry-looking chicken wings for outrageous prices. In a time of food shortages, such elaborate affairs also smacked of decadence. As Sherman's army approached Columbia, South Carolina, Emma LeConte marveled that women still had "cakes, jellies, creams, [and] candies" to sell. Speculators paid five dollars for charlotte russe and two thousand dollars for a large doll despite the incongruity of such spending in an economy on the verge of collapse. At other tables, yeoman and poor white women bought up palmetto bonnets, flour, and salt pork.[17] Although women of modest means made notable contributions to wartime benevolence, aristocratic women still dominated the larger public events.

To make money for charity and not coincidentally to enliven their social lives, upper-class women organized concerts and plays, though these amateur productions seldom raised more than a few hundred dollars.[18] The fashionable set preferred tableaux vivants, which became a craze in several cities. Young women from prominent families adorned themselves in costumes to represent the seceding states, various Confederate symbols, or fictional characters. Between the ornate stage scenes, bands played and children sang patriotic songs.[19] These affairs required careful planning and rehearsals, bringing women together and enriching local culture. Since a good turnout in a small city might earn anywhere from several hundred to several thousand dollars, the tableaux also proved to be the most lucrative fund-raising ventures.[20]

Despite their popularity among wealthy socialites, these performances often provoked controversy. In an evangelical culture that had begun to show signs of increasingly complex and serious class divisions, tableaux touched raw nerves. Speaking perhaps for families who resented such extravagant displays in a time of general austerity, ministers and their pious parishioners condemned tableaux as frivolous and sinful entertainment.[21] When women had to flout religious (and masculine) authority in staging tableaux, they defended themselves by appealing to wartime necessity.

But the critics had a point. Class prejudice and parochialism could limit the good done by the most generous and dedicated volunteers. Some women preferred sewing only for "gentlemen" from the "best families" while others wanted their contributions to go exclusively to regiments from their own community. Sidney Harding claimed to turn away hungry Confederate soldiers only out of necessity, but her description of one such incident suggests otherwise. "Two wounded came up—ugly, common, not much wounded," she coldly noted in her diary. Such condescension and hostility did not go unnoticed. Ragged troops marching through Richmond jeered at the fine ladies who stood cheering without offering them any food.[22] The plight of hungry and dirty soldiers no longer touched a responsive cord. Neither extreme need nor patriotism could overcome selfishness, clannishness, or upper-class indifference.

Declining civilian morale, a shortage of supplies, financial troubles, and rumors of corruption caused a sharp drop in support for soldiers' relief.[23] From the autumn of 1861 on, the number of women present at the meetings fell dramatically, and the minutes of the various aid associations and sewing circles often end abruptly in 1862. Some groups fined absent members or threatened to strike their names from the rolls but still could not improve attendance or replenish depleted treasuries.[24] In the end, only a few devoted souls—what the pious would have called a "righteous remnant"—remained active.

Soldiers' aid became another of the Confederacy's glorious failures. Although resources and determination eventually gave out, the women who ran the charitable societies deserved more than the often empty accolades they received during and after the war. Southerners typically tried to place this benevolence in familiar ideological categories, often repeating hoary sayings about female character. In recounting the success of a "ladies' fair" in New Orleans, a newspaper editor sounded themes that echoed through the rest of the century and beyond:

She [the typical woman running a booth] is beautifully timid and fearfully bold; showing the strength of the lion, and the meekness of the dove. Thrilling, provoking, indolent, passionate, variable, mysterious. Men die of love of these creatures, while the favored one exults. There is no sacrifice they would not endure, no whim they can not exhibit, no trifle they can not pursue, no danger they can not confront. Keenly sensitive to ridicule, jealous guardians of their sex, ever alive to the slightest breach of gallantry or tenderness, these creatures wield weapons of their own, scorning woman's rights, elections and politics. They would not enter the arena, they would not be jostled by the crowd. They know familiarity breeds contempt, and they stand aloof, fair and angelic, enlisting all the latent chivalry of that sex who boasts that they can be led through interminable labyrinths, but can not be driven an inch. Well do these fair creatures know that their weakness is their strength; their delicacy the seat of their power; their dependence their protection, and their smiles the axis upon which the busy world turns.

How such fragile "creatures" had accomplished so much or fit into a world view so riddled with contradictions, the editor never explained. Unsure of what to make of women taking a more active role in Southern life, such spokesmen invariably reverted to the themes of masculine honor and feminine deference. The soldiers expressed their gratitude in equally stilted language. "I wish you could have seen the smile of satisfaction which illumined the face of many a bronzed and scarred veteran in tattered uniform as he took his new warm flannel shirt," wrote Joseph Allston in words meant to strike a responsive chord at home. In a well-executed counterpoint to his pen portrait of manly toughness touched by feminine charity, he then praised the "thoughtfulness, care and affection of those dear ones at home for whom we are enduring hardship and danger."[25]

This familiar linking of active courage on the battlefield to passive courage at home sounded comforting to Southerners of both sexes. Women accepted such descriptions of their work because they saw themselves not so much as heirs of their Revolutionary grandmothers as exemplars of nineteenth-century womanhood. Mollie Colbert of Thomastown, Mississippi, repeated the usual rationale for women entering the world: "Knowing that we could not bear arms, and being unwilling to sit idle. . . ." Wartime benevolence meant an acceptance of limited roles. "The girls of this generation will be quite expert with our knitting needles," Melinda Ray predicted. "Altogether we will make model women."[26] Given such social and cultural assumptions, relief work provided a slender precedent for postwar reform—and an even weaker foundation for a women's-rights movement in the South.

2

Sewing circles and charity bazaars might provide some diversion for wives and mothers who had before devoted their full attention to home and hearth. The emphasis on obedience, loyalty, and by implication, subservience, struck a resonant chord in Confederate society.[27] Time and again, men and women noted that even though the members of the "fair sex" could not command armies or engage in politics, they could still advance the cause of Southern independence. After commenting at length on various public matters, a Mississippi housewife abruptly called "a truce to politics of which I am very fond, and, like most women, know very little about. Why should a woman of sense care to talk about anything but dress and her servants?"[28]

Others had exhausted these homey topics long before. Even during the antebellum period, educated women had participated—if only informally, indirectly, and subtly—in the political culture. The sectional conflict had stimulated awareness of public affairs, and the secession crisis had forced women of various classes to recognize the connections between public and private life. The war continued and intensified this acculturation even though women still exerted a marginal influence on government policy.

Plantation mistresses, daughters of the small-town and urban elite, and even farmwives often acquired decided opinions on politicians and generals. Even if these women were only a minority of the upper and yeoman classes and often lacked political sophistication, they generally agreed that defeating the Yankees would require much sacrifice. In some ways more realistic than their menfolk, they generally supported higher taxes and stronger economic controls, arguing that states'-rights dogmas must yield to draconian necessity. Showing greater flexibility and imagination than her husband, Varina Howell Davis maintained that "strict construction of our Constitution is incompatible with the successful prosecution of a war." Fearing that selfishness and greed would tear apart the social fabric, she despaired for republican liberty in a nation where the framework of government seemed inadequate for the crisis of civil war.[29]

Just as women called for a strong and effective war policy, so also did they favor bold and determined leaders; and more than most men, they stressed the need for unity. Unaccustomed to the give and take of politics, women wanted to believe in the new government and support its policies, and because they had grown up in a largely deferential, domestic environment, they naturally admired President Jefferson Davis as the embodiment of Southern ideals. Except for the wives of his critics, most politically conscious women stood by Davis during the first three years of the war, and some remained loyal to the bitter end. The pious exalted him as a model Christian, a man who bore his heavy responsibilities with dignity and humility. Sarah Wadley likened him to a second George Washington in his wisdom, coolness, and moderation.[30] In this way Davis became Bolingbroke's patriot-king, a rallying point for a young nation which badly needed one.

Perhaps because of their political immaturity, women also embraced the antiparty ideology of the early republic. Unable to see any virtue in bitter public debate, they accused Davis's detractors of helping the Yankees. Susan Bradford blasted the "weak-kneed cowards, who stand on street corners and criticize President Davis." Even many Charleston women refused to join the Rhett family, the *Charleston Mercury*, and other Carolina firebrands in abusing the president and his policies.[31] Quick to equate dissent with faintheartedness or even treason, those women who either publicly or privately expressed their views were much more likely than men to stand by the administration and its policies.

But as the war continued, women's growing political savvy was reflected by divisions within their own ranks. Expanded knowledge allowed some women to distinguish between responsible opposition and political posturing. In turn they blamed Davis for being timid, defensive, partisan, and stubborn.[32] Their views, of course, mirrored opinions offered by the newspapers and their male relatives, but they also displayed independent judgment. The government's obsession with Virginia and its neglect of the western Confederacy drew fire from perceptive female commentators. The Charleston woman who condemned the president for allowing Vicksburg and Port Hudson to fall while permitting Robert E. Lee's army to move into Pennsylvania showed considerable strategic insight.[33]

Like any group just becoming part of a complex political culture and debating public questions, astute Confederate women had a much fuller understanding of executive than of legislative power. The politically innocent often expect a single powerful leader to control the course of events and have little understanding of or patience with the deliberative process. Congress therefore became a natural lightning rod for female frustration and anger. Catherine Edmondston denounced the body as a "mill stone around the neck of our young Confederacy." The speeches and debates seemed endless and pointless, particularly with enemy armies advancing into the South. Small-minded politicians spent too much time squabbling over minor issues; men of character and vision, who could rise above low intrigue, seemed scarcer than ever. "Where are our big men?" a Richmond woman asked in exasperation.[34] Those who so sharply attacked congressional leaders perhaps displayed their naiveté, but even though they did not always understand the procedures, they were all too familiar with the results.

Men might carp about military strategy and political maneuvering, but women's criticism naturally focused in those areas that most closely touched the Southern home front: conscription, taxation, currency. Had Congress acted more firmly and expeditiously, "our independence would have been established long, long ago," Mary Davis declared.[35] Once powerful inhibitions against questioning public officials and their policies (and perhaps in some women a reluctance to question male judgment) had been weakened, the complaints came rushing out.

Even the normally reticent who had once feared being labeled with the derisive epithet *female politician* had run out of patience: "I write for my own amusement and not for men's eyes, I shall take the great privilege of saying what I choose," Mary Ezell noted in her diary. She then proceeded to pillory North Carolina Governor Zebulon Vance, as "incompetent for the work before him as a woman would be." But fewer women would have been so willing to disparage their sex; many concluded instead that they could not have ruined the country any more quickly or more thoroughly than the men in power. An anonymous North Carolinian denounced Secretary of War James A. Seddon as a "simpleton"; the ever feisty Elsie Bragg dismissed Louisiana governor Thomas O. Moore as an "imbecile." Although pungent, such remarks did not signify disaffection with the cause. To the contrary, women had little stomach for peace candidates or defeatist rhetoric and reserved their harshest attacks for politicians who hampered the war effort by underestimating the people's capacity to make the sacrifices needed for victory.[36]

This largely false and artificial distinction between shortsighted, cowardly politicians on the one hand and a virtuous citizenry on the other helped preserve faith in Confederate righteousness, especially the righteousness of the wives and mothers who had devoted their families and themselves to Southern independence. In fact much of this rhetoric was implicitly antimale as women blamed weak-kneed men for all the Confederacy's problems.[37] In a remarkable series of private letters, novelist Augusta Evans went a step further, partly cutting through this elaborate web of illusion, and adopted the gloomy rhetoric of the classical republican theorists. Corruption stalked the land; the South appeared headed toward anarchy or despotism. If free institutions rested on public virtue, she found little of it among her countrymen. "The great national ulcer—Demagogism—demands prompt cauterization," she insisted. The cause of impending disaster was universal suffrage, "an effete theory of utopian origin" that gave free rein to mankind's baser passions and allowed the common herd to rule over the wise and just through sheer numbers. With no faith in politicians, she succumbed to a discouraging and eventually an apocalyptic vision:

> The most radical of quondam Jacobinical democrats are at present gravitating rapidly toward centralization, consolidation and are quite ready to anathematize Jefferson as the prince of sophists, and almost prepared to yield allegiance to the dogmas and dicta of Hamilton. Strange, but immemorial paradox. Mankind plunges into cruel wars, into internecine conflicts in defense of principles which during the revolution they permit to slip through their fingers. Affrighted by the shadow of absolutism and abolitionism that brooded over Washington, the men of the South flew to arms, but three years of struggling have singularly modified their opinions, and I have been pained and astonished to find how many are now willing to glide unhesitatingly into a dictatorship, a military despotism even into a state of colonial dependence with gradual emancipation as a condition for foreign intervention and protection.

With the nation facing imminent destruction, she accused the wealthy of obsessively guarding their riches while placemen sold their country's birthright for patronage and power.[38] Although few women shared her sense of futility or her intellectual assumptions, many would have warmly applauded—even if they would not have entirely understood—her assault on ineffective leaders.

Anything was preferable to the endless temporizing of the politicians. Given their impatience with debate and delay, an impatience obviously shared by many men but also intensified by a limited exposure to politics and relative isolation in the home, women naturally placed more faith in the soldiers. Generals at least acted. By refusing to join the hue and cry against hapless commanders who lost a single battle, women displayed a clear preference for men who would risk failure over men who talked interminably but did nothing.[39] And when such bold cavaliers as Stonewall Jackson and Robert E. Lee won great victories, so much the better.

As a solid family man of the strictest piety who also happened to be an aggressive and hard-driving general, Jackson naturally won the accolades of Southern women. By 1862, admirers swarmed into his camp seeking uniform buttons and locks of hair, yet this upright and humorless man, whom contemporaries often compared with an Old Testament prophet, attracted more than simply sentimental adulation. Praising Jackson's boldness in the Shenandoah Valley Campaign, Judith McGuire was unruffled by tales of his mental imbalance because she believed that just such a "crazed" character was needed to beat back the invaders. Mary Chesnut agreed. Dismissing the romantic ideal of the "Christian soldier," she praised the "fanatic" Jackson who knew that "to achieve our liberty, to win our battles, men must die."[40] This seeming realism naturally concealed other delusions, especially the assumption that one decisive battle or commander would bring the war to a successful end.

In contrast to Jackson's rapid rise to fame, Lee's apotheosis proceeded more slowly, reaching its zenith long after Appomattox. As the only Confederate general whose presence guaranteed, if not victory, at least brave and ingenious persistence in the face of daunting odds, Lee naturally attracted many admirers who confidently exalted him as the last best hope for national salvation.[41] Lee embodied the ideals of masculine honor: honesty, humility, bravery, and boldness—characteristics that limned the myth of the Southern cavalier—and had not yet become the tragic hero of Lost Cause mythology.

Especially for women isolated from the fighting or at least from the madness, confusion, and random terror of the battlefield, the link between strength of character and victory remained simple and unbroken. In celebrating the virtues of P. G. T. Beauregard, Kate Mason Rowland expressed a naive but widely held belief in the certain triumph of the noble generals in gray: "With such honorable, high-minded commanders we cannot fail of success in this our righteous cause." But even Christian gentleman had to fight with abandon and become righteous avengers against the enemy, and many women believed that peace would come only after the Yankees had suffered all the horrors of war. South Carolina cousins Susan and Harriott Middleton wanted Northern blood to flow in retribution for destruction in the South.[42] The so-called softer sex suddenly seemed harder (contemporaries would have said more masculine); mercy no longer seemed a universal female trait.

Although many men would surely have shared these sentiments, most women who bothered to comment on military affairs deemed aggressiveness the one attribute necessary for success. Perhaps because of powerful inhibitions against the expression of female aggression, they vicariously reveled in confident generals and brave soldiers who struck boldly at the enemy. To the hesitant warrior, they offered no quarter. After the First Battle of Manassas, Betty Herndon Maury raged at General Beauregard for not attacking Washington though she quickly thought better of making such a daring remark and added: "I reckon he knows his own business best." Others pulled fewer punches, damning West Point-trained martinets who lacked martial ardor and timidly sat in camp letting opportunities to attack the Federals slip through their fingers. "Give us *Leaders!*" Catherine Edmondston exploded, "Leaders that can fire the Southern heart by *Action, hearty action!* & not depress it with a heavy dull defensive policy. Such a policy would suit the phlegmatic Dutchman, the calculating Scot, not the impulsive warm blooded Southron!"[43] In short, Southern men should act like Southern men. Yet the more dangerous underlying question went unspoken: why should these powerful exemplars of strenuous masculinity have to be shamed out of their lethargy by supposedly passive and retiring women?

Perhaps the women were not so passive and retiring anymore, and some had clearly grown bolder in speaking out on once forbidden topics. Indeed, after several staggering defeats in the Western Theater during 1862 and 1863—including the fall of New Orleans, heavy losses at Shiloh, and the disastrous Vicksburg Campaign—articulate women no longer blindly supported Confederate military leaders but instead began to lash out at any general who supinely retreated in the face of the enemy.[44] Although many unlucky commanders became temporary scapegoats, as the losses in the West continued, Braxton Bragg became a lightning rod for feminine ire. Elsie Bragg herself had often criticized western generals for being too cautious, egotistical, or rash, liabilities that her husband possessed in abundance. Women followed Bragg's retreat through Tennessee and the abandonment of Chattanooga with alarm, their spirits rising at news of the Confederate victory at Chickamauga but quickly plunging after the debacle at Missionary Ridge and the army's withdrawal into Georgia. Rumors of sharp quarrels between Bragg and his corps commanders added to the gloom, and some women blamed the general and his principal supporter Jefferson Davis for the abandonment of Tennessee.[45] With their attention riveted on the loss of territory, and with little appreciation for strategic or any other type of retreat, many women steadily lost faith in the army and the government.

Mounting criticism of generals and politicians indicated that women would now more readily challenge masculine judgment on any number of questions. Proposing that generals who failed should be hanged or shot, Elsie Bragg tartly remarked that "if our soldiers continue to behave so disgracefully, we *women* had better take the field and send them home to raise chickens." And a few took the short step from complaining to advising. Suggestions on strategy and tactics suddenly poured into Richmond and the state capitals. Move more troops here, strengthen defenses there—many petitions contained specific and firmly stated recommendations. Warning of Yankee spies in Jonesboro, a Georgia woman lectured Governor Brown on the need for more aggressive officers. She denied trying to set policy, but of course that was precisely what she was trying to do. Through all these letters and petitions runs a common theme: the politicians and generals should take whatever steps necessary to defeat the enemy.[46]

Those women attempting both to critique and change public policy had stepped, albeit gingerly and anonymously, outside the bounds of convention. Yet their calls for a more vigorous prosecution of the war reflected not only a fervent patriotism but also desperate conditions on the home front. Little wonder the word *attack* appeared so often in petitions, letters, and diaries. The need to regain lost territory gave women little stomach for holding actions and defensive warfare. Seventeen-year-old Lizzie Munford, for instance, thought the Confederate armies should take the offensive whenever the weather permitted.[47] However dubious such advice might have seemed to generals and politicians in Richmond, it signified a growing frustration among thoughtful Confederate women. By following and commenting on political or military questions, they could also now gauge their own powerlessness, for the apparent expansion of female participation in civic life had been modest at best and illusory at worst. Unable to take the field against the enemy or to shape government policies, a few women became more and more impatient waiting at home for their menfolk to either succeed or fail.

3

"Since females cannot bear arms" or something similar appeared in countless letters and diaries as women explained and justified their benevolent or patriotic activities. Even in a society with rigidly defined sex roles, such a stale formula could not satisfy everyone. For a few women, sewing, charity work, and domestic chores seemed poor substitutes for confronting the enemy directly. "If only I was not a woman," these words cropped up in much wartime writing and conversation. Such sentiments seldom expressed long-standing discontent but instead reflected a deep desire to serve the Confederacy where the need was greatest. For more venturesome women, everyday life during a time of national danger seemed decidedly humdrum. "But as I am unfortunately born a woman," Sarah Morgan complained, "I stay home and pray with heart and soul. That is all I can do; but I do it with a will." The departure of men for the battlefields only intensified this sense of dependence. Mary Latta worried about her husband in camp but jocosely offered to trade places with him. "I am only a woman," she wrote in a catch phrase of the day, "and must enjoy the comforts with which your hand has so freely provided—& who cannot share with you the privations & hardships you endure."[48] But such lighthearted repartee often concealed deep disappointment if not unspoken resentment.

The suppression of such desires led to wild daydreams. Though barred from entering the ranks of the Confederate army, women could indulge in martial fantasies. Young women who had come of age during the excitement of the secession crisis longed to serve their country in the field.[49] Zealots spoke of killing Yankees as the sacred duty of every true Southerner, regardless of sex, but only a few women seriously considered becoming soldiers. "I wish the women could fight, and I do think they might be allowed to do so in the mountains and in the fortified cities," Lucy Breckinridge wrote. "Their lives are not more precious than the men's, and they were made to suffer—so a leg shot off or a head either wouldn't hurt them much."[50] This curious statement epitomizes the dilemma of a Southern woman eager to aid her country. On the one hand, Breckinridge anticipated the female guerrilla fighter of twentieth-century warfare, but in the same breath she restricted women to the role of natural sufferer, whose pride sprang from the ability to endure pain. So what at first appeared to be a bold claim of sexual equality fizzled into another vapid admission of feminine weakness.

Because no one seriously called for women to join the army, most would-be warriors had more modest aspirations. In areas subject to enemy attack, their immediate worry became not the defense of their country but the defense of their families. Unable to rely on male protection—surely an unsettling thought in any traditional society—Nannie Abbott asked Virginia Governor John Letcher for a "brace of pistols." Another widow requested a Colt revolver, promising to put it to good use: "I have practiced shooting and I would not be afraid to defend myself."[51] The thought of delicate ladies wielding these weapons must have amused if not frightened public officials, but rural women were deadly serious.

Margaret Gillis did not even wait for the fighting to start. A week after Lincoln's election, she starting preparing: "Yesterday I buckled on a shot pouch, strung a powder flask around my shoulders, put a gun across my shoulders and went hunting." As a precaution against slave insurrections, plantation mistresses stockpiled arms and learned to use them. Typically, women gathered on a vacant lot to fire at makeshift Yankees. Such exercises seemed harmless and pleasant enough—unless Federal troops suddenly appeared in the area. In early 1865, when teenage girls near Tallahassee, Florida, met for pistol practice, they vowed to shoot themselves rather than be captured by the enemy.[52]

Desultory and individual measures of self-defense led directly to better-organized activities. Prominent women formed home-guard units to protect their neighborhoods, and their "rights, liberty, and honor," as a company in Athens, Georgia, put it. Daughters joined mothers in marching, drilling, and learning the vagaries of ancient pistols and muskets. In spite of their initially awkward and often humorous efforts to follow the procedures in William J. Hardee's *Rifle and Light Infantry Tactics*, these novices sometimes advanced to a fair level of skill. In Bascom, Georgia, nine women met each Wednesday and Saturday. "You know how nervous and timid Millie was," Bess Dell proudly reported. "Well now she can load a gun and fire and hit a spot at a good distance." Yet Bess Dell and her troop seemed to worry as much about their uniforms ("a tight-waist made of red calico and bound with blue") as about how straight they could shoot.[53] Ultimately, a bit of drilling on a warm afternoon seemed more social than martial, women playing at war.

No one, including the women taking target practice, expected these efforts to save the Confederacy or somehow turn women into warriors. Upper-class and yeoman women had not seen the war as an opportunity to overturn social assumptions with which either they had no quarrel or saw no hope of dislodging. Few had tried to challenge their society's definition of woman's place, and the collapse of the Confederacy largely cut off further experimentation. Only the leaders of charitable and benevolent societies still found a demand for their services in the postwar South, and even then widespread poverty deprived them of the wherewithal to carry on their work. Wartime bazaars, concerts, and tableaux gave way to smaller and in some ways pathetic efforts to raise money for disabled veterans, widows, and orphans. And despite the unprecedented participation of women in wartime political debates, Reconstruction provided few opportunities for them to enter civic life. Political comments disappeared from letters and diaries; public policy seemed ever more remote from and irrelevant to domestic concerns.

The war left women with some sense of accomplishment in a world beyond the home, but such memories faded quickly. In later years, most wives and mothers would more clearly recall, in many cases all too vividly, their families' travail, the shattering of hopes and dreams, and for thousands the terror of being left at the mercy of enemy armies.

CHAPTER 8

The Coming of Lucifer's Legions

THE INVASION OF THE CONFEDERATE STATES was more than lines on battle maps, more than the movement of men and matériel, more even than the occasion for bloody battles; it was a blow aimed at the heart of the Southern family. Military campaigns disrupted the economy and ravaged the home, but the psychological assault began earlier and lasted longer than the physical destruction. Rumors, false alarms, and imaginary phantoms frayed nerves before flesh-and-blood Yankees appeared.

For four years, thousands of women tried to comprehend the danger, prepare for the onslaught, protect their families, and finally to endure whatever the enemy had in store for them. They had little control over the events that would devastate their lives, but their responses transcended the legend of belligerent belles breathing fire against the bluecoats and created a much more complex and ambivalent legacy. Many women learned to tolerate, sometimes even respect, and in rare cases admire their occupiers. If geography did not exactly determine destiny, it exerted a powerful influence. In areas under siege or subject to frequent raids, the tension and turmoil lasted longer and required a different kind of courage and psychological adjustment.

Yet more than anything else the experiences of invasion and occupation shattered illusions of Confederate invincibility under the sheltering hand of Providence. Indeed the Southern soldiers, who were supposed to epitomize the highest ideals of Southern manhood, failed miserably to protect their homes. And when William T. Sherman's army cut its swath of destruction through Georgia and the Carolinas, mothers and children suddenly became military targets as the distinction between combatant and noncombatant blurred. No longer would sex provide immunity from the horrors of modern war, for the invaders not only tore up furniture and devoured food, they also tore at the sinews of faith and devoured hope. In Confederate rhetoric, brave men would protect defenseless women and children, but now the supposedly defenseless had to fend for themselves.

1

To Mary Greenhow Lee, the Yankee troops moving through Winchester, Virginia, were "the vilest race under the sun"; officers and men alike appeared to be the offscourings of the infernal regions. Confederate civilians readily succumbed to the paranoia fueled by their own propaganda.[1] "Yankee, Yankee, is the one detestable word always ringing in Southern ears," young Eliza Andrews raged. "If all the words of hatred in every language under heaven were summed up together into one huge epithet of detestation, they could not tell how I hate Yankees. They thwart all my plans, murder my friends, and make my life miserable." Mothers raised their children to despise the enemy, fretting lest their offspring fail to plumb the depths of Northern evil.[2] Emotion triumphed over reason, and, as always, truth became war's first victim.

Yet denouncing the ruthless foe also allowed women to sidestep the question of Southern war guilt: condemning the Yankees as the most hateful of God's creatures masked their own hatred. Women who hectored their men to kill as many of the enemy as possible hypocritically berated Northern women for doing the same thing.[3] This fierce enmity also helped women rationalize, modify, or abandon long-held ideas about Christian charity. Northern newspaper reports about sadistic Confederates contained some truth. Phoebe Pember visited a "pious set" in Richmond who collected macabre war relics. One "lady" kept a pile of Yankee bones near her pump so she could see them the first thing in the morning; another coveted a Yankee skull for storing trinkets.[4]

Such bizarre practices and hot words provided outlets for anger, but they also belied popular images of morally superior womanhood. "I take it out in 'cussing,'" Kate Sperry admitted in exasperation, "have become reckless—stonehearted and everything, hard and pitiless—never knew I was so vengeful." Many devout ladies forgot about vengeance belonging to God. Only by exacting a terrible price for Northern aggression could

Southerners justify the war's enormous costs. Calls for the mass slaughter of Yankee soldiers and shelling of Northern cities reflected this primitive standard of justice.[5] Such bloodthirsty sentiments poured from the mouths of genteel matrons; Union soldiers marveled at the vitriol of Southern ladies.

As good Christians, however, most of these women could not entirely sublimate more humane considerations. Outbursts of hatred often gave way to remorse. "I fear I am wicked all the time," Catherine Edmondston wrote, "for besides confusion & ruin, I wish to punish them [the Yankees] well for daring to come invade our land." Yet the temptation to hasten the day of divine judgment against the South's enemies was overwhelming. "I reckon it is sinful to have such feelings," commented a North Carolina woman who wished the Yankees consigned to hell, "but I cannot help it."[6] However wicked such sentiments might be, guilt could not suppress them; at best, shame created ambivalence toward shedding Yankee blood. To weigh the merits and possibilities of hatred and forgiveness became more than a theological question for many Confederate women. For those with homes directly in the path of Union armies, the issue was painfully practical.

But who knew what to expect or when to expect it? Rumors multiplied, the latest usually being no more reliable than its predecessors. Reports of approaching enemy troops sent women into a flurry of preparation. False alarms whipsawed emotions, and since no information could be relied on, the most fantastic stories became credible. Although the sophisticated soon learned to heavily discount the "latest intelligence," false hopes and fears kept civilians on edge.[7] Because of their isolation from public life, women became particularly susceptible to conflicting tales of great victories and crushing defeats; many hung their hopes on ropes of sand.

"I am like a prisoner awaiting his doom," exclaimed Emily Walker after Yankee pickets had been spotted near Alexandria, Louisiana. Women had nightmares about fleeing before the invaders without clothing or food. Sarah Morgan, crippled from a recent carriage accident, worried about burning to death in her house. Ceaseless unconfirmed rumors, not to mention retreating Confederate troops, unruly children, and insolent slaves, drove women to despair.[8]

All the while they struggled to decide whether to ride out the storm or flee. Families who stayed put battled against lethargy and a fatalism that threatened to immobilize them. "I know that I am sick with torturing my brain to try and find out what would be the right course to pursue," Stella Bringier wrote her husband as skirmishers approached their plantation near Donaldsonville, Louisiana. "If you were only here to tell me with four little children where can I go to, and how?" Anything now became endurable—except continued suspense.[9] Many just hoped the Yankees would come, do their worst, and leave so families could return to something faintly resembling a normal life.

Mothers keeping up a brave front for their families found unexpected reservoirs of courage. Impending danger spurred introspection. "I look at myself and can scarcely realize it is me," Priscilla Bond noted in amazement. "I am calm and have shed few tears." Of course the typical nineteenth-century woman was supposed to be neither composed nor dry eyed in such an emergency, but again the war modified popular images, temporarily displacing feminine weakness with feminine strength. A peculiar serenity appeared as the enemy drew closer. Sarah Wadley felt "*perfectly* free from fear" but at the same time experienced a "sort of exhilaration, a firm and healthy pulsation, the result of excitement but not agitation."[10] Some of these women merely deceived themselves, though many overcame faintheartedness with fortitude.

Self-possession allowed them to prepare their homes, their families, and themselves for the arrival of the Yankees. The first step was simply to hide things. Moving boxes into a cellar or attic would hardly fool determined pillagers, and imaginative women tried to avoid the more obvious ploys. Sarah Jane Sams removed all provisions to the bedrooms, stuffed clothing into mattresses, and crammed jewelry into nooks and crannies throughout her house. But uncertainty dogged these efforts, and women frequently changed their minds about where best to conceal some prized possession.[11]

Although a few women stashed valuables under skirts and bulky clothing, rather than risk rough handling by the Federals, most civilians preferred wells, cisterns, gardens, or the trusty woods. But a safe place was very much in the eye of the beholder and more than likely within sight of prying eyes—and not only Yankee ones. Women tried to fool their slaves and poor white neighbors by secretly burying their treasures late at night. Nothing better illustrates the breakdown of paternalism and the decline of community than this furtive digging.[12] Plantation mistresses, laboring and sweating, must have shaken their heads over the apparent inversion of the social pyramid.

Unless they still believed *their* Negroes could be trusted. Touching tales of mistress and slave carefully hiding family silverware from the rapacious Yankees became—and not without some slender basis of truth—staples of postwar memoirs and romances.[13] But such warm recollections told only part of the story. As the relationship between mistress and slave deteriorated, betrayal seemed more likely then loyalty. In Montomgery, Alabama, Sarah Follansbee and her trusted maid, Nancy, buried jewels and silver at midnight. Having second thoughts, she rightly decided to move the cache. Nancy led Federal soldiers right to the original hiding place; when they found nothing, the Yankees whipped her.[14]

With the enemy at their doorsteps and no one left to rely on, many women felt helpless, alone, and most of all defenseless. Some had only butcher knives to protect themselves. Grace Elmore nervously fingered the trigger of a five-shooter, wondering whether she would really have to kill a Yankee. At night, women slept in their clothes, ready to spring out of bed at any strange noise.[15] The waiting was nearly over: what had seemed at first impossible, then improbable, then likely, and at last unavoidable was about to occur. Just as past experience had not prepared women for the weeks (and often months) of nervous anticipation, so now they faced military occupation with little knowledge to guide them. Women who had grown up learning how to be dependent (or at least appear dependent) on men suddenly had to make many decisions for themselves, decisions that might well determine the future of their families. Again irony crowned tragedy. The Confederacy had promised to protect liberty in its classically republican definition, the safety of property and person, but few Southern women could now feel secure in either.

2

Whether or not most women were politically sophisticated enough to understand how the Yankee invasion endangered cherished liberties, they shared the Southern rural passion for the local and the particular. Rather than thundering against violations of abstract principles, they became furious about more concrete outrages. "It makes my blood boil," fumed Judith McGuire, "when I remember that our private rooms, our chambers, our very inner sanctums, are thrown open to a ruthless soldiery." Armoires would be torn open and filthy men would run their greasy hands over delicate petticoats. Though such chilling images might have given female patriots second thoughts, early in the war depredations only fueled their commitment to Southern nationalism. Amanda Worthington's reaction was typical: "But anything rather than submit to the Yankees! I'd rather live on grass & work my finger ends off—or indeed I'd rather die than give up to them."[16]

Little did she realize how aptly this statement forecast the immediate future of many Southern women. In a few hours, hungry soldiers could clean out Confederate larders, reducing formerly self-sufficient planters and yeomen to beggary. One family lived on animal feed mixed with hominy for several days after the Federals departed. Although many Northern soldiers hit plantations hardest because they blamed Southern nabobs for the war, most did not hesitate to ransack the homes of yeomen and poor whites. Common suffering temporarily overcame class differences as women worked with one another to gather and dole out what little food remained.[17] Such cooperation helped for a time but could not fill stomachs in neighborhoods stripped of provisions.

Many families lost more than food. Soldiers ripped bedding apart, trampled gardens, tore down fences and outbuildings, and left piles of rotting garbage in the yards. The extensive vandalism at Sarah Morgan's plantation home near Baton Rouge, Louisiana, was by no means uncommon. "Libraries emptied, china smashed, sideboards split open with axes, three cedar chests cut open, plundered and set up on end, all parlor ornaments carried off . . . piano dragged to the center of the parlor, had been abandoned as too heavy to carry off." The Yankees had also cut portraits out of their frames; muddy footprints remained where they had stood on the furniture. Upstairs, they had smashed the mirror on a mahogany armoire, emptied the contents, and knocked out the shelves. Worse than the wreckage was the invasion of privacy. The men broke into Sarah's desk, read one of her diaries, and made ribald remarks as they frolicked through the house bedecked in female finery.[18]

In a bizarre twist of fate, poor whites occasionally benefited from Yankee looting of their wealthier neighbors—becoming in effect the bottom tier in a primitive trickle-down network. As they scoured the countryside looking for scatted household items, once wealthy women sometimes found what the Federals had left behind in the hands of "common whites." An Irish woman was charging a fee for the curious to gawk at a portrait of Octavia Hammond's father that had been thrown away by the Yankees.[19] Social sympathy might have grown from the widely shared suffering, but the invaders also drove neighbors apart as families scrambled to save (or acquire) whatever they could.

Although no family's experience was typical and the soldiers themselves ranged from one who robbed Susanna Waddell in the "politest manner possible" to the most insensitive plunderers, women often had trouble making fine distinctions between gentlemen and scoundrels.[20] After all, even the best-behaved troops wanted to cow Southern civilians, and the unpredictability of the Yankees merely added to the terror. Some men enjoyed shocking pious women with blasphemous oaths, scrawling obscene graffiti on walls, or scaring children with bloodcurdling threats.[21] To women who had long heard frightening tales of Northern monsters, the bluecoats appeared capable of almost any atrocity. After all the line between verbal intimidation and physical abuse was not only thin but easy to cross.

When soldiers brandished whips and pistols against women who protested their depredations, they lent verisimilitude to the vivid and overblown newspaper stories of assaults on widows and young mothers. Although physical attacks on civilians were surprisingly rare, some Federals handled females roughly. After an Arkansas woman refused to hand over money to Yankee raiders, they shoved her right leg into the hot coals of a fireplace, burning her severely from the knee down. The leg had to be amputated, and she died two years later.[22] Such real brutality, along with lurid and often apocryphal tales, thoroughly frightened many women.

Of course, they worried about more than the destruction of property or possible violence. Beneath oblique references to "outrages against helpless females" lay fears of sexual assault. Like soldiers throughout history, the Federals thought about and talked about women constantly. Boys away from home for the first time sowed wild oats with camp followers, but they also wanted to meet more respectable girls. Fiery secessionists seemed particularly alluring but unapproachable; unsure of how to proceed, soldiers made crude remarks about looking for a wife among the daughters of a Southern household.[23] Sexual badinage, especially when it elicited a response from an attractive belle, was exciting.

But men sometimes moved from playful teasing to persistent harassment. In the spring of 1864 an Ohio private accosted a man near Harpers Ferry, West Virginia. "Have you any sisters?" he boldly inquired. "If you have I should like to fuck them. That was my business before I came into the service, and now I am fucking for Uncle Sam." This novel definition of patriotism failed to impress the officers of his subsequent court-martial, who sentenced him to thirty days hard labor.[24] Soldiers regularly intimidated mothers by threatening to rape their adolescent daughters, and even if they had no such intentions, rumors and scattered reports of sexual assaults struck fear in many households.

Even if talk did not usually lead to action, rapes did occur. Evidence on these attacks is sketchy because no one investigated the problem and women hesitated to report the crime.[25] Southern newspapers occasionally noted sexual assaults, but editors treated them garishly, wringing as much propaganda value out of the incidents as possible. Except as political symbols, the victims, usually described as suffering a "fate worse than death," hardly seemed to concern Confederate leaders.[26]

Although Southern accounts emphasized the helplessness of civilians facing Yankee pillagers, brutes, and rapists, women sometimes defended themselves not only verbally but physically. "Madam, do you know we sometimes divest Southern women of their clothes?" a Yankee officer leered at Evelyn Smith. Don't try it, she shot back, or he would never ride a horse again. An Arkansas woman fired twice at a soldier who had exposed himself. Frantic resistance, especially by several women at once, could be effective; screaming girls discomfited the Federals and usually shortened their stay.[27]

Accounts of courageous defiance—many embellished by the Federals themselves who grudgingly admired "secesh females"—have colored the interpretation of civilian-military relations in the occupied South and have caused historians to forget the thousands of women who endured invasion in sullen silence. Some simply stood on their dignity and refused to yield an inch. Sarah Trotter skillfully used this tactic when two soldiers came to her door demanding food: "I told both of them that I had nothing for sale and would not feed the enemies of my country . . . . I talked at least half an hour to one of them—he was polite & gentlemanly. I told him plainly tho kindly, how we all felt. He told me on leaving that he would tell his men no [*sic*] to come to my house—and I am sure he left thinking better of me than if I had fed him."[28] Yet Trotter's account makes this quietly determined approach sound too easy. Persistent pillagers, especially late in the war, were seldom deterred by a lecture—no matter how caustically or cleverly delivered.

The Federals eventually ran out of patience. A Louisiana woman enraged Union soldiers by saying she wished them "as far in Hell as a pigeon could fly." Such dramatic confrontations, however, sometimes became just plain ludicrous. A hapless bluecoat in Arkansas trying to haul away a dead hog met an angry housewife brandishing a club. Frustrated in his efforts, he "turned his ugly end towards her, pulled down his pants and emptied his bowels of [a] stinking load in her presence." Even this failed to move the woman, who coolly commented that she had lived around dogs all her life.[29]

For all the humor in such stories, defying the invaders was serious business and going beyond verbal sparring courted danger. Women waved shovels, pistols, or any other convenient weapon at soldiers who entered their houses. When a Yankee grabbed her brother's coat, Rachel Couch pushed him down the stairs, where her friend Sue Hunter gave him several good whacks with a broom.[30] Bold actions might succeed temporarily (and made for exciting anecdotes later) but showed as much foolhardiness as courage. Women themselves criticized such recklessness, fully realizing how vulnerable they were to the capricious mercies of the enemy.

Even the psychological satisfaction of defying the invaders quickly wore off. After all if women were not always "helpless" victims of the war, they were victims, and not only of whatever Yankees who plundered their property but of larger political and military decisions beyond their control. Their fate often hinged on geography. Families living along important roads or railroads, near strategic points, or in cities could expect a visit from the Yankees. Even refugees who had successfully evaded an enemy army often found themselves in the path of another.

3

Because so much of the South was invaded, it is possible to speak of the military experiences of Confederate women. Many families lived near battlefields or in cities under siege or in areas subject to frequent Federal raids or simply under military occupation. The precariousness of human life in modern war, the irrational character of combat, and the random terror inflicted by modern weapons suddenly became part of women's lives.

Those unlucky enough to live near battlegrounds or in towns and cities bombarded by the enemy faced obvious physical dangers but even more severe psychological stress. During the Battle of Fredericksburg in December 1862, Jane Beale spent thirteen hours on a damp basement floor as shells ripped through the upper stories of her house. Such an ordeal often left deep emotional scars, especially on children, who might cry out at night for weeks afterward.[31] Again women had to take on the traditional male role of family protector, providing reassurance to both their children and themselves. Panic sometimes triumphed over bravery, but these trials could also have a curiously benumbing effect.

Witnessing a battle, women often became transfixed. "It was a most peculiar and fearful sound," wrote Emma Holmes during a nighttime bombardment of Charleston, "the sharp scream or whiz through the air, and they [the shells] sounded exactly as if coming over the house. I was startled & much excited, but not frightened, but it produced a very solemn feeling. I lay with the windows partly open every moment expecting a shell might burst and kill me and the idea of dying alone, while others were so near was startling."[32] The careful attention to detail, the introspection, the sense of death's meaninglessness, and the grasping for psychological insight, all anticipate the better accounts of trench warfare during World War I. The passage also drives home the point that the American Civil War had more in common with the bloodbaths of the twentieth century than with the limited wars that preceded it. Emma Holmes had glimpsed the future of noncombatants in a world where violence would spill out of its traditional channels.

But from the depth of terror and despair, many women discovered how human beings adapt to the unbearable and soon described a battle or artillery duel as if recounting some everyday event. After Mary Waring and her friends nonchalantly watched the shelling of Spanish Fort in Mobile harbor from a third-story window, they moved downstairs for a pleasant lunch.[33]

The war might harden the most delicate sensibilities, but this equanimity, or perhaps resignation, was no good sign either for women or the Confederate cause. In extreme cases it signified what a later generation would call shell shock, a catatonic condition characterized by a listless acceptance of whatever might happen. Months of anticipating the enemy's arrival, hiding valuables, and protecting their homes had exhausted many women at the very time when they most needed their physical and psychological strength to cope with the perils of military occupation.

Although unyielding defiance became the model of female behavior most admired by Confederate propagandists, reactions to military rule varied. For every woman who sneered at the troops on the streets, others stayed indoors, afraid to go out, disheartened by their powerlessness.[34] Feeling trapped and at the mercy of the enemy, women conjured up classical fantasies of revenge. Watching "horrid soldiers" chop off the heads of her mother's chickens, Ella Washington "wished it were possible for me to see a guillotine take their heads off in just such rapid style."[35] The ideal patriot was not supposed to lose heart, but real people did, drifting along from day to day simply trying to survive.

Though women might long to strike some blow against the foe, their actions seldom matched their rhetoric. Kate Corbin talked of being "given over again unto Satan," but having learned better from a previous run-in with the Federals, she decided to "bridle" her tongue. Women slowly adjusted and found that life went on, even under enemy occupation.[36] However offensive the phrase *living with the Yankees* might sound, it accurately described the situation in many communities.

If the Federals stayed in an area for any length of time, officers frequently roomed with families. Women worried about having their children exposed to such vile creatures, and some huffily turned the men away, claiming they could not sleep in the same house with Yankees. But daily contact might eventually ease such fears. An Alabama minister's wife welcomed the generous payments from her new boarders and was even more pleased with their gentlemanly demeanor. Other women reckoned that taking in a bluecoat provided good insurance against pillaging.[37] After all political principles could not pay the bills, and necessity offered a convenient excuse.

Wealthy families had reason to cultivate the goodwill of their new masters. Not only would the officers prevent depredations, they might also arrange for the return of stolen property. If a woman could prove that she had treated Federal soldiers kindly, she stood a much better chance of receiving compensation for losses suffered from raiding parties. This all required delicate diplomacy and a good deal of posturing on both sides. Women played the role of helpless supplicants thrown on the mercy of gentlemen to the hilt, while soldiers relished acting as all-wise protectors and officers made a great show of listening sympathetically to female petitioners. In Huntsville, Alabama, General Robert S. Granger fawned over an attractive young woman who sought permission to send food through the lines. He handed her a piece of watermelon, gallantly offering her a handkerchief to protect her dress.[38] Women with money, beauty, or imagination learned how to survive and even prosper under the military yoke. Although the average family could expect little assistance, prominent citizens often received special protection.

Yet interaction between soldiers and civilians hardly became either routine or pleasant, and each side approached the other gingerly. Some women shied away from extended conversations and only slowly learned to see enemy soldiers as human beings. "Have condescended to chat a little with our sentinels," Harriette Cary noted. Although "rather hard cases," they listened patiently to her Confederate harangues. Eventually she accorded them grudging respect. "They seem faithful to their trust— which we endeavored to encourage by a little attention—so completely do we feel at their mercy." Standoffish at first, these relationships evolved toward mutual courtesy and even respect. When an Ohio soldier who had guarded her plantation was about to go, Mary Jones politely expressed her appreciation: "I cannot allow you to leave without thanking you for your kindness to myself and family; and if I had anything to offer I would gladly make you some return." His reply was equally conventional: "I could not receive anything, and only wish I was here to guard you always."[39]

Even at their best, relations between women and their "protectors" remained stiff and uncomfortable. Some women kept as much physical distance as possible between themselves and the soldiers guarding their homes. They also maintained a social distance. Even after a young lieutenant had kindly brought fruit for her sick children and carried the baby about in his arms, Cornelia McDonald would talk with him only in the hall, never inviting him into the parlor.[40] Barring a Yankee from the family's inner sanctum preserved at least a shred of a woman's finely honed sense of dignity and honor.

Civilians also had practical reasons for keeping the soldiers at arm's length. Too friendly a relationship could set local tongues to wagging about cavorting with the enemy. Sarah Morgan enjoyed a brief conversation with a Union officer yet refused to encourage such attention. "We are unaccustomed to treat gentlemen that way; but it won't do in the present state to act as we please. Mob governs."[41]

Although community prejudice certainly discouraged such contacts, women also felt inhibited by strict notions of propriety. In July 1863 a soldier searched Kate Foster's house for weapons. "He was very polite," she admitted, "but seemed too much disposed to converse with me, which advances I politely but decidedly refused to encourage." A month

later when another Yankee officer paid a call, she was even more reserved: "I did not ask him to take a seat but if he was on our side, I
should have a very good opinion of him, all but his flattery and I dislike
that even in a friend, coming from one of our enemies it is an insult."
By September, however, her determination began to waver. Having discovered that many of these visitors were gentlemen, she had to keep
reminding herself that they had after all ravaged her country: "If they
only wore our uniform how happy I should be to entertain them."[42]

This attitude mystified Union officers, who marveled at the young
ladies' coolness and discovered that social overtures or even simple
acts of courtesy elicited sharp rebuffs. As an Ohio soldier was politely
helping two Huntsville women into a carriage, one of them tried to slam
the door on his hand.[43] Such splenetic outbursts helped create the legend
of defiant Confederate women, but it also revealed anxiety and insecurity,
for bellicose females knew of other women who did *not* scorn the enemy's
advances.

By maintaining the polite fiction that no lady would have anything to
do with the "blue devils," upper-class women could hold on to the myth
of Southern social unity. Julia LeGrand treated the question of how to
deal with the invaders as a matter of etiquette, to be resolved with all
the panache of a prewar belle tactfully but firmly discouraging an undesirable suitor. "I would not be rude," she maintained, "for rudeness
in a woman is always vulgar, but you can freeze these young gentlemen
with such glances and quicken them with such politely pointed remarks,
that they will not wish to come again."[44] The war of course made such
an attitude seem quaintly out-of-date and even a bit eccentric. Carefully
drawn distinctions between plain courtesy, sly diplomacy, and improper
intimacy broke down.

Society became atomized as more and more people simply looked
after their own interests. Hypocrisy flourished. A Northern newspaper
reporter observed how women in Warrenton, Virginia, who during the
day refused to walk under the flag and plugged their ears when military
bands played national music, strolled through the streets at night with
Union officers. Even in Vicksburg, long a symbol of Southern resistance,
prominent belles danced with the Federals. "You remember how Miss
Lucy Rawlings wore the secession cockade," Alice Shannon gossiped.
"Now she tells the yankees that she always was for the union."[45] Although
staunch Confederates maintained that only poor whites would stoop

low enough to keep company with Yankees, daily scenes on the streets of Southern towns proved otherwise.

Out of these awkward flirtations developed serious courtships and intersectional marriages. Some girls bragged about their Yankee boyfriends or flashed engagement rings in front of envious or outraged friends.[46] Rare enough to elicit comments from shocked civilians, marriages between Southern women and Northern soldiers occurred often enough to raise doubts about unwavering female devotion to Southern independence. Arguments between those who spurned the enemy's advances and those who welcomed them showed again the fragility of the Confederate social consensus.

Unusual behavior at both extremes attracted much attention, but most women followed a course somewhere between defying and fraternizing with the enemy. Anna Robinson Andrews described the soldiers stationed near Shepherdstown, Virginia, as a pack of "Ruffians and drunkards" yet chatted with a polite officer and saw no reason to incite them needlessly. After all Southern men who advised stouter resistance hardly led by example. Cora Watson witnessed male courage firsthand when nine Union soldiers entered Holly Springs, Mississippi, in January 1864 and cowed a group of forty civilians. "These men—some of them once called brave—have stayed at home . . . until they have become so spiritless as to suffer a little band of less than one fourth their own number to come boldly in open day light, and rob them on the streets!"[47] Honorable men were supposed to protect their families, and their failure to do so left many women disheartened and confused. Uncertainty and doubt only compounded the misery of civilians living in besieged cities or in areas periodically occupied by the Yankees.

4

For most families, the pattern of invasion was similar—rumors, the sudden appearance of enemy armies, a brief period of pillaging, the equally sudden departure of the troops—with few variations from place to place, but geography and the fortunes of war could lengthen and intensify the ordeal. When at the end of an almost year long campaign Ulysses S. Grant's army drove Confederate forces back into the defenses around Vicksburg, Mississippi, enraged women screamed "Shame on you all!" as their bedraggled defenders came into the lines.[48] Familiar feelings of defenselessness spread rapidly as the Federals laid siege and shelled the city for forty-four days. The cannon roared around the clock, with only occasional pauses. Unrelenting tension produced despair and terror. When told that God would protect her, a four-year-old girl would not be comforted, fearing the Almighty had already been killed.[49] Her response was logical enough because the foundations of her world, including the religious faith of many adults, had been hopelessly shattered.

Most families could tell stories of near misses, providential escapes, or bizarre tragedies: a shell demolishing a bed right after an invalid woman had arisen; a child killed where she slept; a mother whose head was blown off, causing her twelve-year-old daughter to go into hysterical fits and die a few weeks later. Despite thinking herself fearless after a month of artillery barrages, one woman suddenly became unhinged when a shell tore through the upper part of her house and scattered fragments into the basement, where her family was hiding. "For the first time I quailed," she admitted, "I do not think people who are physically brave deserve much credit for it; it is a matter of nerves."[50]

But nerves usually did hold out, and women surprised themselves by somehow getting used to life under the guns. Some simply tried to keep up their normal routines and substituted frantic activity, including socializing, for fretful worrying. As one woman put it, "to sit and listen as if waiting for death in a horrible manner would drive me insane." She maintained her mental equilibrium by scribbling in a diary and reading Dickens novels in the dim light of a cellar.[51] As modern military strategists have learned, even the most fearsome shelling can make civilians more tenacious and self-sacrificing.

Families could withstand the bombardment because most were well entrenched, either in basements or in caves dug into the side of Vicksburg's many hills. Although women at first slept in their clothes on mattresses, as the siege dragged on, they laid carpeting, divided off rooms, and moved in bedroom and parlor furniture.[52] This appearance of homey comfort was deceiving, however. Young girls might entertain soldier boyfriends with candy, flowers, songs, a few hands of whist, and the promise of some innocent flirtation, but they could not get rid of the dampness that soaked through everything nor could they fend off hungry mosquitoes and the occasional rattlesnake that slithered through the tunnels. Women suffered from claustrophobia as well as fear of being buried alive. Penetrating shells collapsed entrances, scattering dirt and debris everywhere, sometimes injuring the occupants, and occasionally killing them.[53]

At first, civilians welcomed hungry soldiers into their caves for a meal, but by early summer the city's ravenous defenders were stealing from women and children. Families tired of corn bread, then gagged on greasy bacon and musty pea meal, but finally wolfed down small birds, mule meat, and even rats.[54] Although hunger probably had more to do with ending the siege than the bombardment, the women and children of Vicksburg had learned firsthand how warfare had changed. Grant had brought the war home to Southern civilians in a new and terrifying way. Shelling a city filled with women and children and then starving it into surrender portended the horrors of total war.

For all their intensity and concentrated terror, sieges did have a clear beginning and a decisive conclusion. The people of Vicksburg could at least try to pick up the pieces of their lives after the surrender. In areas subject to intermittent invasion, occupation, and skirmishing, uncertainty, worry, and fear became part of everyday life for months and even years. Fighting in the Shenandoah Valley of Virginia illustrates this process well. Both sides trampled over the lush farms and indiscriminately raided corncribs, chicken coops, and pigpens. As early as October 1861 the Federals appeared in force; by March 1862, General Nathaniel P. Banks's army occupied Winchester, the largest town in the valley.

"Suppose we'll have to consider Winchester Yankeedom—though I'd rather be in Devildom any day," Kate Sperry noted glumly, feeling "ready to cuss the whole herd and piously wish them in Hades." Time confirmed her judgment of the Federals: the "meanest set of poor white trash I ever beheld." Yankee cavalry galloped through the valley, stealing food, tearing down fences, and burning buildings. To the southeast in Front Royal, Lucy Buck fumed as the "wretches" coolly surveyed her property. "To think that they should dare come here and pollute with their footsteps the dear old familiar home-spots sacred to the memory of so many dear associations!"[55]

Stonewall Jackson's brilliant campaign relieved her pain and temporarily liberated the area, but these hard-fighting veterans soon marched off to join Lee's forces near Richmond. Civilians awaited their fate, troubled as much by uncertainty as by fright. Even military occupation seemed preferable to month after month of momentary hopes quickly dashed. The once fiery Kate Sperry hoped that if the Yankees did come back to Winchester they would stay for good and restore mail service.

She did not have to wait long. The day after Christmas, soldiers broke windows in Cornelia McDonald's house, threatened to demolish the furniture if they were not given breakfast, and stole most of her firewood (though they later *sold* it back to her). By January 1863, Northern cavalry was again sacking homes in Front Royal.[56] This pattern continued for the rest of the war, with Union and Confederate forces alternately occupying and retreating from the valley.

By early 1864 many families had left. Those who stayed behind could do little but protest the destruction. After her house was burned, Henrietta Lee informed General David Hunter that she was a "helpless woman whom you have cruelly wronged" but nevertheless poured out her anger in a letter that is a minor masterpiece of vituperation:

> Hyena like, you [Hunter] have torn my heart to pieces! for all hallowed memories cluster around that homestead, and, demon-like, you have done it without even the pretext of revenge, for I never saw or heard of you. Your office is not to lead, like a brave man and soldier, your men to fight in the ranks of war, but your work has been to separate yourself from all danger, and with your incendiary band steal unawares upon helpless women and children, to insult and destroy. . . . I ask who that does not wish infamy and disgrace attached to him forever would serve under you? Your name will stand on history's pages as the Hunter of weak women and innocent children; the Hunter to destroy defenseless villages and refined and beautiful homes—to torture afresh the agonized hearts of widows . . . the Hunter with the relentless heart of a wild beast, the face of a fiend and form of a man. Oh, Earth, behold the monster![57]

Of course the howls of outraged women could hardly arrest the momentum of a war that had come to embody cruelty and an utter lack of concern for any individual's welfare. In holding enemy generals to old-fashioned standards of honor and even in declaring their own helplessness, women failed to understand how the nature of warfare had changed. Families no longer simply suffered from the deaths of loved ones in the army or from economic hardship; increasingly, women and children became casualties in their own right.

All that remained was hatred, fierce and unrelenting but impotent. When an Ohio colonel told Lucy Breckinridge and her sisters that they would have to marry Yankees because "that's the way to build up the Union again," she wanted to shout that they would marry black men first but held her tongue. Arguing with a triumphant enemy seemed pointless. Wishing the Yankees dead would not make it so, but women wished anyway.[58] The embittered victims of invasion and occupation at least managed to find a focal point for their wrath: a Yankee demonology. Union generals became objects of execration because they had waged war against women and children. Reigning over this pantheon of villains was a man of unequaled malevolence, the true prince of darkness: William Tecumseh Sherman.

5

However much women might hate Grant, Hunter, or Benjamin ("Beast") Butler—the nemesis of fiery New Orleans belles—somehow Sherman was different. Long before the famous Georgia and Carolina campaigns began, Southern civilians had already endured invasion, depredations, and occupation. Yet their suffering had been incidental to the achievement of some military objective. What made Sherman different was his carefully calculated determination to carry the war to the Southern home front with no other military purpose in mind.

And again women had to raise an uncomfortable question: where were their protectors? In begging her husband to come home from the army, Julia Davidson blasted male cowardice: "The men of Atlanta have brought an everlasting stain on their name. Instead of remaining to defend their homes, they have run off and left Atlanta to be defended by an army of women and children." With the flour and bacon gone, she prayed: "God help us for there is no help in man." Her husband could not get a furlough, the family moved several times, and they ended up living in a single room.[59] For Julia Davidson and many other Georgia women, the advancing Federals did more than drive people from their homes; they undermined faith in widely held social and cultural assumptions. So much for the vaunted superiority of Southern civilization—and Southern men—when women and children stood alone against the Goths and Visigoths. Retreat may not have emasculated the men, but it made them appear supine and powerless.

This feeling of impotence only made the Yankees seem more formidable and Confederate propaganda more believable. After all these barbarians did war against innocent families. Hyperbolic rhetoric suddenly seemed all too accurate when Sherman openly stated his objectives. "Until we can repopulate Georgia, it is useless for us to occupy it; but the utter destruction of its roads, houses, and people, will cripple their military resources," he confidently predicted. Assuming this departure from conventional strategy would be received skeptically in Washington, he dramatically announced: "I can make this march, and make Georgia howl!" Reporting that the army was well supplied but had no corn, he ominously added that they could "find plenty of forage in the interior of the state." Although at the beginning of the famous March to the Sea, Sherman ordered the foragers to gather food along the way—leaving each family with enough for subsistence—and not enter private homes, use abusive language, or take wagons, horses, and mules from poor farmers, these instructions were often honored in the breach.[60]

Sherman's men sowed more confusion and fear than any other Northern army. The reverberation of cannon, the cracking and popping of small arms, and the rumble of wagons off in the distance announced their coming. Terror sometimes immobilized women who never recovered from the first wave of panic. As the Federals advanced through the Georgia countryside, women prepared for the worst, realizing, perhaps for the first time, how defenseless they were against a relentless enemy. Foraging parties and bummers arrived first, often demanding to be fed. Though usually eating in the kitchen, some tried to humiliate or simply enrage the "Reb women" by insisting on elaborate meals served on fancy china in the dining room.[61]

Unrestrained pillaging became all too common, despite halfhearted measures by the generals to keep it under control. Even soldiers who refused to abuse women and children hardly hesitated to strip a place of food. Cows, hogs, and chickens became rare sights, except in Yankee hands; corn, potatoes, turnips, butter, and milk disappeared from dinner tables as raiding parties went about their work with an almost savage thoroughness.[62] What the soldiers could not or would not bother to carry away, they burned—especially cotton, fences, and outbuildings.

Besides provisions, the men hauled off personal items. They may have begun their work in the kitchens and pantries, but they soon ranged into bedrooms, rooting through drawers, tearing carpet from the floor, and smashing children's toys. A Northern newspaper reporter observed some foragers scattering one family's belongings all over a yard. He saw bedding ripped apart, dead chickens and pigs lying about, and a captain lugging away all his arms could hold while four frightened women huddled inside the house.[63] By carting off items of no military value—including treasured heirlooms—the Yankees showed a certain method in this seemingly mad carnival of destruction. Not only did they strip families of food and other necessities, they seized or destroyed irreplaceable pictures, documents, and other mementos. They struck at the heart of the home, tearing at the sinews of memory that bound families together and to past generations. In ransacking houses, they in effect ravaged habit and tradition, destroyed the commonplace, and left lasting scars, on the land and the people.

Women had expected barns and outbuildings to be looted, but the vandalism of their homes showed how war had become ever more undiscriminating and brutal, even invading the recesses of private life. Those who could watch silently as the enemy grabbed livestock and food reviled the rough-handed men who pawed through their personal possessions. Despite the psychologically crushing effects of Yankee raids, the Confederate woman's legendary defiance still occasionally burst forth—in both Rebel songs and harsh invective. When Sherman's men entered Milledgeville, Ann Green walked through her house loudly singing, "We live and die with Davis." With more optimism than realism and more wit than conviction, women's sharp tongues could neither conceal nor compensate for their anguish and despair. These harangues meant little to the Yankees, except perhaps some momentary amusement or consternation, but for women they provided some emotional catharsis as well as a sense of standing up to the conquerors. "The first damn Yankee that sits at this table, I will kill," one woman screamed. Some nearby soldiers might have taken her up on this threat had her friends not convinced them she was mentally deranged.[64] Few women attempted to go beyond muttering brave words or making empty threats. Knowing that only scattered cavalry brigades and militia units filled with boys and old men stood between them and Sherman, most held their tongues and bowed to the necessity of the hour. For nearly everyone, the time for foolhardy confrontations had long passed.

In a curious way, Sherman's army both fulfilled and baffled female expectations. To many women, the soldiers appeared like devils sent from Hell to prey on the weak and helpless. "Do the annals of civilized—and I may add savage—warfare afford any record of brutality equaled in extent and duration to that which we have suffered, and which has been inflicted on us by the Yankees?" Mary Jones cried. "Such was their blasphemous language, their horrible countenance and appearance," wrote her terrified daughter, "that we realized what must be the association of the lost in the world of eternal woe. Their throats were open sepulchers, their mouths filled with cursing and bitterness and lies."[65]

On the other hand, the vilest creatures would have had trouble living up to the advanced billing given this army, and women were sometimes pleasantly surprised when the officers—given Southern views on caste and class, many had a snobbish respect for *officers*—turned out to be gentlemen. Even foragers occasionally apologized for the brutality of less scrupulous colleagues. Some generals tried to prevent the looting of private homes by posting guards, and plantation mistresses asked for protection as a matter of course.[66]

Because not everyone received such kindly treatment, Sherman's men unintentionally exacerbated Confederate internal conflicts, especially the class divisions, which had already been widened by wartime economic dislocation. Generals and officers might act as the gallant protectors of plantation mistresses or engage in gay repartee with beautiful belles, but the Northerners found the more typical Southern female to be a pathetic, bedraggled creature. Dirty, toothless, vulgar, and constantly dipping snuff, she appeared in many ways sexless. Even though such haggard-looking women only exemplified the sad condition of many yeoman and poor white families, like Northern travelers before the war, Sherman's soldiers mistakenly described a two-tiered class structure of extreme wealth and dire poverty. They failed to realize what the war had done to families who had once lived in modest comfort until they heard shy-looking housewives suddenly curse the "damned war" to anyone who would listen to their complaints. Some disaffected women told Northern newspapermen their husbands had been forced into the Confederate army and they had always opposed disunion.[67] Political, economic, and cultural unity had long since disappeared; women who had once ardently supported Southern nationalism appeared lukewarm if not disaffected.

Whether the people of Georgia had also lost the ability to endure hardship remained an open question. Certainly the physical and psychological devastation had more effectively shattered morale than Sherman himself could have hoped for or predicted. Reverting to the familiar images of her evangelical faith, Mary Jones felt like a modern Job beset by a host of troubles:

All our pleasant things are laid low. Lover and friend is put far from us, and our acquaintance into darkness. We are prisoners in our own home; we dare not open windows or doors. Sometimes our dear little children are allowed under a strict watch and guard to run a little in the sunshine, but it is always under constant apprehension. The poor little creatures at a moment's warning— just let them hear 'Yankee coming!'—rush in and remain almost breathless, huddled together in one of the upper rooms like a bevy of frightened partridges. To obtain a mouthful of food we have been obliged to cook in what was formerly our drawing room; and I have to rise every morning by candlelight, before the dawn of day, that we may have it before the enemy arrives to take it from us. And then sometimes we and the dear little ones have not a chance to eat again before dark.[68]

However overdrawn and melodramatic, Mary Jones captured the growing despair of many other families.

A careful listener might still hear Rebel songs or outbursts of Rebel rhetoric, but the spirit of most female Rebels had been broken. Plantation mistresses had learned how war could intrude on the most bucolic isolation. Farm women who had never left their county suddenly came face to face with young boys from Iowa and Indiana and Wisconsin in circumstances not designed to make their outlook more cosmopolitan. By the time Sherman's men reached Savannah, they had left behind them not only a track of devastation but homes and families filled with despair, sorrow, and most of all bewilderment, mixed with dread for the future. Who could any long dream of some miraculous deliverance? The collapse of hopes and dreams—for individuals, families, and the Southern nation—seemed all but complete. Wives and mother might try to pick up the pieces of their lives, but for many there were few pieces left.

All these emotions merged into a new, sardonic humor. Some Georgia women asked Sherman's men why they did not take out their anger and frustration on the state of South Carolina, the home of Calhoun, nullification, and states' rights extremism. Indeed many South Carolina women had heard that the Federals would throw off all restraints once they had crossed the Savannah River. In fact even most Palmetto State belles no longer donned the secession cockade or breathed fire against the Yankees; the most ardent female patriots saw little but gloom in their nation's future. Looking back on even the recent past with a tragic nostalgia and becoming increasingly obsessed with their private agonies, they listlessly awaited their fate. In Columbia on Christmas Day 1864, Grace Elmore foresaw only relentless destruction: "The time has come in which every trifle in our home life has a mournful value as belonging to a time of rest and comfort that will soon be among the things that were. The days of our home are numbered, and I feel very much like one who is watching the last hours of one near and dear to thee. . . . Our old life of ease and comfort is spent, and our advent into trouble and care, uncertainty and poverty almost here. Indeed our minds go beyond the present and we already experience what that life will be; and even the happy laugh of childhood is painful in its glee, so unconscious of the bitter fate that overhangs its sky."[69] Rumors and false reports might revive hope for a day or so, but even the optimists now gave in to despondency.

The energy and determination that remained went toward protecting home and family, although preparing for the onslaught seemed pointless given the recent experiences of many Georgians. Any acts of defiance became mostly perfunctory—and a bit silly. Bravely singing "The Bonnie Blue Flag" as the Confederacy entered its death throes seemed less courageous than pathetic. Claiming that she verbally "fired volley after volley of rebel shot" at two Yankees who came to the house, Emma Holmes explained why women still bothered to put up a brave front: "Oh, how I enjoyed being able to relieve my bottled wrath and show the spirit which animates the Southern women. I did not forget my character as a lady but I taunted them with warring on women & children."[70] The admission that harsh words served personal rather than public needs meant that the last pretense of resistance had disappeared. With the Confederacy on the verge of collapse, fewer women bothered to play their assigned role in the great drama or even go through the motions. Only the shell of the legendary Confederate woman remained.

In February 1865, after feinting toward Charleston and Augusta, Georgia, Sherman's army of sixty thousand headed north into the heart of South Carolina. With nothing between them and the invaders except Confederate cavalry and nearly worthless home-guard units, women scrambled to secure their property and keep food out of enemy hands. Families who had scrimped for months suddenly became gluttons, hungrily stuffing themselves with hams and turkeys before the Yankees arrived. Adopting a more imaginative ploy, one woman dumped her meat into the yard, covered it with flour, and then, with a proper look of naiveté, told the soldiers that stragglers had sprinkled it with something called strychnine.[71] Clever tricks, however, failed to deter the troops from plundering houses, often with a savage relish; thoroughness and relentlessness became the hallmarks of Sherman's army in South Carolina as the soldiers vented their fury on the state that many considered to be largely responsible for starting the war.

"We lost everything." These words appear time and again in the post mortem accounts of the raids on Carolina farms and plantations. Provisions, clothing, furniture, jewelry—all seemed fair game for Sherman's men. At Anna Thomas's house, soldiers scattered the loot on the parlor floor but left much of it behind; several days later, another group rummaged through the fancy dresses looking for presents to send home. Nor were young children exempt from these depredations. Near Columbia a soldier grabbed a doll and piece of soap away from a six-year-old girl.[72] Such indiscriminate pillaging rapidly demoralized families, especially when the Yankees did not keep most of their booty and instead left behind them a trail of castoff household goods between Savannah and Columbia.

However unrestrained, the pillaging had a clear purpose. If Sherman's men seemed to spare no one, they still preferred to plunder wealthy planters. On Adele Allston's rice plantation, two soldiers hauled all the linen and furniture from the main house. Smashing the banisters, tearing out locks, and taking doors off their hinges, in a few hours they had reduced a symbol of Southern pride to a pathetic shell filled with the refuse of departed glory.[73] Such scenes of desolation—along with the smoldering barns and trampled fields—became constant reminders of how far the mighty had fallen. Although by the abysmal standards of conquering armies in other wars, Sherman's troops acted with restraint, such lessons in comparative history were lost on the Southern female population.

As the last soldiers departed, women began assessing the damage but first had to search for any food that had been overlooked or carelessly dumped on the ground. Given the thoroughness of the looting, most families found little. Anyone who still had a cow—or any livestock for that matter—seemed fortunate. Anna Thomas's mother found potatoes hidden under flagstones and roasted them in the fireplace. A bit of meat, grist, hominy, sassafras tea, some jugs of sorghum, a barrel filled with corn still on the cob rounded out the depleted larder.[74] Despite her heavy losses, she should have been grateful; her family could at least stay warm at a time when many others were homeless.

As the two wings of the Federal army meandered toward Columbia leaving behind smoking ruins and a countryside stripped of provisions, a deadly calm punctuated by occasional panicky outbursts spread over the South Carolina capital. By the first week of February, when the Yankee columns approached the Congaree River, the emotional energy needed to sustain any kind of resistance had dissipated. Noting the calm demeanor of many citizens, Grace Elmore ominously compared the atmosphere in Columbia to the sang-froid of French aristocrats imprisoned in the Bastille, "that philosophical rather than reckless spirit that accepted and used everything cheerful and bright in their prison life; a spirit which enabled them to laugh and chat with gayety though they knew in the next few hours they would be headless."[75] Too many women seemed dangerously detached from reality. To avoid coming to grips with a dark future, they still lived in a dream world where trouble was always far away or happened to someone else. On the evening of February 15 when the first shells fell on the city, Grace Elmore steeled herself for the ordeal: "How accustomed we have become to war. Tonight with the almost certainty that tomorrow the Yankee shall rule, we sat for the last time and chatted around the tea table."[76] As families aimlessly went about their daily tasks, Sherman's men entered the city.

Under orders to destroy public buildings, railroad property, factories, and machine shops, on February 17, General O. O. Howard's corps also ransacked private residences, determined, as they put it, to "humble the pride" of the South Carolinians, especially the women. Peering fearfully from behind drawn curtains, the social leaders of Columbia saw fires rapidly consuming the city—and in a sense their own lives. "By the red glare," Emma LeConte wrote the following day, "we could watch the wretches walking—generally staggering—back and forth from the camp to the town—shouting—hurrahing—cursing South Carolina—swearing—blaspheming—singing ribald songs and using such obscene language that we were forced to go indoors." Soldiers broke into houses, soaked beds with turpentine, and set them ablaze. Harriott Ravenel recalled how her house had been saved only because the Federals had started small fires in the closets but had gone off to plunder elsewhere, giving the family time to extinguish the flames. A few soldiers still tried to douse the fires; others maliciously cut water pipes and fire hoses.[77]

As the sack of Columbia proceeded, women and children crowded onto the grounds of the lunatic asylum, a cruelly fitting place of refuge from Sherman's madmen; there they rested on mattresses and wrapped themselves in blankets or pieces of carpet to keep out the cold. The looting of private homes continued. "They stole for the mere pleasure of stealing," Grace Elmore believed, "for they made no use, nor could of much they stole and destroyed." While the Yankees plundered her house, she uttered a familiar but pathetic lament: "If I were but a man how firm would be my arm to strike." As the fire added to the frustration of women seemingly deserted by their menfolk, it also briefly reawakened a new fury against the invaders. "My whole nature is changed," Grace Elmore wrote as the last of Sherman's men passed through the city. "I feel so hard, so pitiless. Gladly would I witness the death of each of those wretches. . . . God grant they may suffer in their homes, their firesides, their wives and their children as they have made us suffer."[78]

Whatever temporary relief the troops' departure might provide, in some ways, the worst was yet to come. The silence of desolation, coupled with fear of the future, completed the demoralization of women left to sort through the smoldering ruins. Food was the most immediate concern. "Starvation seems to stare us in the face," Emma LeConte recorded. "Our two families have between them a few bushels of corn and a little musty flour. We have no meat, but the negroes give us a little bacon every day." The once prosperous felt humiliated if they depended on handouts from their former slaves, but the poor became desperate. Famished mothers threatened to break into the large houses and take any food they could find.[79] Again the invasion had put new strains on the Southern class structure and caused the resentment of many yeomen to boil over. Talk of a bread riot sounded ominous but seemed pointless when so little food remained for anyone.

Even when the pious turned to their Bibles they found too many painful reminders of their own suffering. Mary Chesnut recalled the Book of Exodus: "They are everywhere, these Yankees—like red ants—like the locusts and frogs which were the plagues of Egypt."[80] Fatalism and defeatism had at last overwhelmed even the South Carolina firebrands.

The movement of Sherman's army into North Carolina was largely anticlimactic, a final blow directed against an already dispirited people. When the bummers reached Fayetteville, one woman politely asked for a guard. "You'll git no protection," snapped one soldier. "That's played out long ago," another grinned. And so it had. The troops seized food, clothing, dishes, silverware, and jewelry with as much relish as they had plundered towns in Georgia and South Carolina. Sherman's rough-looking men shocked Tarheel women, who had seen little of the enemy. "The house was so crowded all day," Janie Smith wrote in disgust, "that we could scarcely move and of all the horrible smelling things in the world— the Yankees beat. . . . I don't believe they have been washed since they were born."[81] Despite rumors that Joe Johnston had laid a trap for Sherman or that Lee was heading for North Carolina, even false hopes had largely disappeared.

Only a truncated and skeletal Southern nationalism survived the war, all Lost Cause rhetoric to the contrary notwithstanding. Four years of worry and sacrifice had hardened emotions and shattered illusions, but hatred was a poor substitute for patriotism. Two days after Lee surrendered to Grant, Janie Smith indulged in a common fantasy of revenge: "If I ever see a Yankee woman I intend to whip her and take the very clothes off her back. . . . Where our Armies invade the North I want them to carry the torch in one hand & the sword in the other. I want dissolution carried to the heart of their country. The widows and orphans left naked and starving just as ours were left."[82] Dreams of retribution had long haunted Confederate minds, especially for those who could not directly strike a blow against the enemy. Powerlessness and ennui overwhelmed women as they suddenly plunged into the tragic mainstream of human history. In destroying civilian morale, Sherman's men brought the war home to Confederates regardless of sex; few Southern women could any longer feel immune to the vicissitudes of the world outside their homes.

Whatever shrillness in tone lingered in many private and public remarks made by white women who had lived through the march, it merely signified despair, agony, and hopelessness. The worst had finally happened, and they had to submit, whether with good or ill grace, to the enemy yoke. For every Janie Smith, other women joined those in Fayetteville who quietly and gratefully received food from the Yankees.[83] Hatred could not feed hungry children, as Sherman well knew. Nor would the wounds inflicted on Southern families, or the blows stuck against class pride, be quickly forgotten. The spiritual malaise of the Confederacy's final days would not soon disappear.

CHAPTER 9

Refugees and Revelers

T HE TERM *American refugees* has a curious ring; the adjective and the noun seem oddly joined. Americans long have assumed that becoming a refugee, like so many other historical tragedies, happens only to strange people in foreign lands, yet during the Civil War, thousands of Southern families fled from invading armies. This large floating population intensified political unrest and class conflict, disrupted agriculture, and uprooted rural society. Women headed most refugee families, making the hard decisions about where to go, how to get there, what to take along, where to live, and how to survive. Large problems and petty annoyances dogged efforts to provide for their families. Their experiences and the inevitable clashes with new neighbors sorely tested the capacity of Southerners not only to make sacrifices for the Confederacy but also to give up outmoded social practices.

If the juxtaposition of *American* and *refugee* startles the eye, the title of this chapter must seem a perverse mistake; no one associates refugees with revelry. But the migration of displaced families into towns and cities created a complex social life, and to emphasize only the suffering of these people misses several ironies. Although families from all economic classes were impoverished by the war, polite (and not so polite) society survived, whether in small communities, near army camps, or in the more glittering environs of Richmond, Charleston, or Mobile. And some wealthy people continued to live well, seemingly oblivious to the general suffering and sometimes indifferent to the course of the war. Amid hunger, sorrow, and despair, a sadly pathetic decadence appeared. In the lives of refugees and socialites, extremes met with a shattering effect on Confederate unity and morale.

1

The crisis began in the summer of 1861 as Federal armies moved into Southern territory. Many women refused to budge until the Yankees were literally on their doorsteps. For the more prosperous farmwives and plantation mistresses, becoming a refugee meant abandoning prized possessions and allowing family heirlooms to fall into the hands of Yankee cavalry, poor white neighbors, or slaves.[1] But even a decision to flee from the enemy meant little if there was no place to go. "Shew me a safe point and I'll go tomorrow," Jane Pringle declared, "but no such happy valley exists in the Confederacy." Practical objections arose immediately; after all, women did not act for themselves alone. Cornelia McDonald made the obvious but critical point: "It is not an easy matter to move about with seven children in the best of times but now it seems next to impossible."[2] For all the discussion in Southern homes, the questions of if or when to depart had no pat answers. For women brought up to feel dependent on men, making such a decision could be frightening in and of itself.

"I am but a poor weak fearful woman," Jorantha Semmes wrote in asking her husband's advice. Men enjoyed offering sage counsel—often couched in words that emphasized female helplessness—but could not quite determine whether proper Southern ladies should risk flight or endure Yankee occupation. Some thought women should never abandon their homes while others offered detailed suggestions on what to pack, how to travel, and where to go. George W. Scott even sent his wife a diagram showing how to pitch a tent.[3] But if contradictory and sometimes sketchy recommendations were frustrating, many husbands, fathers, and brothers offered no help at all, their reticence giving women little choice but to take matters into their own hands.

Unable any longer to depend on male advice, more women had to assume the traditionally masculine responsibility of planning for their families' future. Only a month after the war began, many Northern Virginia housewives left their homes. By 1862, this early trickle of refugees had swelled to a flood all across the Confederacy; from Kentucky, Tennessee, New Orleans, the Virginia Peninsula, and the Shenandoah Valley, mothers and children flew before the invading armies. The capture of the Mississippi River line and Chattanooga in 1863 forced more and more people into less and less territory. In 1864 and 1865, Sherman's march through Georgia and the Carolinas cut through the heart of a shrinking Confederacy, sending some women packing for the second or third time. By early 1864, Francis Turner had already moved ten times, including one dash through the woods with babe in arms. Uncertain when to go, women feared being caught in a general stampede and losing all their possessions.[4] Whatever the doubts and dangers, at least a quarter-million Southerners left their homes during the war.

These refugees came from all social and economic classes, though each new wave contained a goodly number of the wealthy. Farmwives could seldom afford to abandon their homes unless they could move in with friends or relatives living in a safe place within the Confederate lines. Poor women had even fewer options.[5] Most refugees eventually ended up in towns or cities. Richmond, Raleigh, Columbia, Atlanta, Mobile—all attracted hundreds of families. Even towns in Texas grew rapidly. None of these places had enough housing, food, or public services to accommodate the rapidly increasing population.[6] And if anything, the psychological disorientation was more serious. Women who had spent all their lives on farms often knew little about where to move, and the world outside their immediate neighborhood appeared strange and frightening.

Once a family had chosen a new home, many other decisions loomed before them. Packing was not only hard work but also emotionally draining; going through the accumulation of a lifetime to determine which items to take drove home the refugees' desperate plight. Wealthy women unable to give up their treasures loaded wagons with heavy trunks and household furnishings, which later had to be sold or simply dumped along the road. A fortunate few shipped carpets, furniture, and clothes ahead to their new homes. More typically, housewives could pack little and even had to do that in a hurry. One South Carolinian stuffed chickens that had just been roasted into jars filled with preserves; some families left with no food. As they rode along in trains or wagons or on horseback, the refugees took stock of what they carried with them and, more painfully, what they had left behind.[7] Unable to forget the past, they were ill equipped for the future. At best, a wagon filled with bedding and provisions or some clothes hastily thrown onto a railroad car constituted the whole of a family's worldly possessions; many women fled without a change of clothes and with little food.[8] Slowed by the scarcity and expense of transportation, they made their way by any available means: train, wagon, horse, or on foot.

Whatever the conveyance, a primitive democracy of the road developed. Wheels fell off, horses pulled up lame, rain drenched everything, making families traveling in wagons dependent on help from any quarter. Few could now be excessively fastidious about their associates. When Yankee artillery threatened Fredericksburg, Virginia, in late 1862, Georgia Congressman Thomas R. R. Cobb saw "gentle ladies dressed in furs trudging through the mud, poor little children huddled in go-carts and ox-wagons."[9] To watch the procession of once proud plantation mistresses along country roads undoubtedly gave some satisfaction to yeoman women who had felt the sting of social snobbery. In the mire or in the dust, former social distinctions meant little, and the quondam elite could no longer be picky about what they ate or where they slept. Humble farmhouses became the unlikely resting places for the South's first families.

Of course such experiences could not instantly turn haughty aristocrats into social levelers. En route to Columbia from Greenville, South Carolina, riding unceremoniously in a farm wagon, Lizzie Smith complained about having to share a bed with two other women in a filthy hotel room. Comic encounters occurred when poor women offered well-dressed ladies a pinch of snuff. Yet the yeomen easily detected contempt and condescension in the manner of upper-class refugees, and many closed their doors to travelers. Sidney Harding thought the "piney woods" people in Louisiana standoffish and inhospitable, but they had little reason to welcome those who had so often ignored or ridiculed them.[10] Habits of deference waned with every advance of the Yankee armies and at every sign that the Southern ruling class no longer stood invincible against the world.

Even on the railroads the social hierarchy broke down as women and children of all classes rubbed elbows. A bemused Mary Chesnut watched stout ladies being pushed through the windows of cars leaving Columbia just before Sherman's arrival. Refugees clambered onto troop trains or crowded into hospital cars where the sights, sounds, and smells of the sick, wounded, and dying nauseated the heartiest travelers. Under the best of conditions, journeys were long, uncomfortable, and interrupted frequently by breakdowns and derailments.[11] Trying to move children and household goods in the middle of a civil war became so complicated and exasperating that many women must have regretted the decision to leave their homes.

Dirty hotel rooms, cold meals, and jostling with one's social inferiors made stops along the way as unpleasant as the trips themselves. Staying with a poor white family in Northern Louisiana, Sidney Harding covered a grimy mattress with shawls and skirts, but between the filth and some voracious bedbugs, she still could not sleep and sat on the floor crying. Sarah Morgan found conditions in Bonfouca, Louisiana, equally appalling. A narrow bed for three women, a creaky table, an old mirror, a bottomless lounge chair, and an armoire filled with corn were bad enough, but in the middle of the room stood a large pile of dirt, around which the mosquitoes swarmed when they tired of feasting on the guests.[12] Rather than reflecting on how the other half lived, plantation refugees too often remained snobbish and condescending. In some ways, social prejudice intensified even as economic distinctions were being leveled beyond recognition; ironically, the very women who had once shown such disdain for their yeomen and poor white neighbors now found themselves uncomfortably close to these same people. Despite the generosity shown to refugees in many homes, they more often recalled only the horrors of the journey.

Unlike most refugees who had neither the time, energy, nor inclination to record their experiences, Kate Stone carefully described how five women, two boys, and several slaves traveled from a plantation northwest of Vicksburg to Tyler, Texas. The first leg of the journey in April 1863 was a hot, six-hour, bayou trip in an "immense dugout" to Delhi, Louisiana. There, refugee baggage was "just thrown in promiscuous heaps—pianos, tables, chairs, rosewood sofas, wardrobes, parlor sets, with pots, kettles, stoves, beds and bedding, bowls and pitchers, and everything of the kind just thrown pell-mell here and there." Soldiers, women, children, and slaves milled around trying to find a train to take them away; families slept on railroad cars because the town had few hotel rooms. Kate Stone fell ill and had to stay in a rooming house with dirty bed linen and no place to bathe. Living on corn bread, milk, and fat bacon, her family finally set out for Monroe despite rumors that speculators there regularly fleeced refugees.

Forced to take a mule train from Monroe to Minden, the Stones found poor accommodations and worse food in the farmhouses along the way; tired of having doors slammed in their face, they camped out for the rest of the trip. Near Bellevue they could at last buy milk, butter, chicken and fruit— sumptuous fare by refugee standards. Once they crossed the state line, however, ticks, fleas, bedbugs, and snakes became more plentiful than either food or hospitality. Watching a dozen dirty men in Lamar County, Texas, eating a coarse meal on a greasy tablecloth off dishes washed in a nearby duck pond, Kate Stone suddenly lost her hearty appetite, a rarity for most famished travelers. Later her family stopped at a farmhouse where cats and dogs scampered near a filthy dining table. "We tried to eat without seeing or tasting to sleep without touching the bed. . . . We certainly had found the dark corner of the Confederacy," she scribbled in her diary.[13] By late fall they were living in Tyler but had little money or energy left. Starting fresh might have a few attractions but also meant many new problems.

Whatever sense of accomplishment refugees must have felt when they had arrived in their new homes, their troubles had just begun. In the towns and cities where most families settled, renting, much less buying, a house became prohibitively expensive. After several frustrating days spent looking for a place in Richmond, Judith McGuire decided that wealthy people cared little about suffering refugees. Rooms listed in newspaper advertisements as warm and spacious were often cold and cramped. But most families could not be fussy about anything except cost. In August 1862, Emma Holmes thought sixty dollars a month for part of a house in Camden, South Carolina, was "extortion"; a year later in Marietta, Georgia, one hundred dollars a month for several rooms seemed like a bargain; by September 1864, single furnished rooms in Richmond went for more than one hundred dollars a month. If landlords did not think a family could pay more, they evicted the family and raised the rent for the next tenants.[14]

Regardless of the price, contemporaries had little good to say about refugee housing. The word *Spartan* aptly described most places. White-washed walls, cracks in the floors, no curtains, few windows—common features of the ramshackle buildings where many families lived. In Richmond, Cornelia McDonald glumly sat on a box, eating off a chest in the center of her single room; for cooking she had only a small skillet and a teakettle. On summer days the heat prostrated mothers and children in small and poorly ventilated rooms; at night they tossed fitfully on pallets (beds had become an outrageous luxury). Living in dark hallways or damp basements with vermin and disease still somehow seemed preferable to having no place to stay.[15]

Most refugees would have relished a peaceful night in a modest frame or brick house, but desperation and ingenuity produced some makeshift accommodations. Families slept on church pews, in stables, carriage houses, tents, and caves. In Atlanta, mothers and children moved furniture and carpeting into abandoned boxcars, placing marble steps along the sides as reminders of vanished gentility. From South Carolina baggage cars came the strains of light music from pianos and guitars played by delicate fingers. But such jury-rigged quarters, in spite or perhaps because of their many defects, provided security. Unlike dwellings where landlords raised rents or evicted families to make room for their friends, few people coveted a drafty boxcar. Luxury or even comfort became optional. "If I could only get to some quiet nook, some lodge in a vast wilderness, . . . I think I should be happy," mused Judith McGuire after being shuffled among hotels, houses, and single rooms in Richmond for more than two years.[16] In a world of incessant anxiety and sudden tragedies, where families living in abandoned cabins seemed lucky, this longing for permanence became a cruel delusion.

Uncertainty and suffering touched all classes. In overcrowded cities, even once comfortable refugees ate sparingly and suddenly had to worry about where their next meal was coming from. In Charleston, a former plantation mistress survived on hominy, bacon, and corn bread; in Clinton, Louisiana, Sarah Morgan hungrily ate beef with a spoon and corn bread with her fingers and drank water from a dirty cup; another Louisiana family lived off fish caught by the girls and a tomato plant found in an abandoned garden.[17] As strangers, these women seldom had a network of neighbors or kin to sustain them. Their former economic and social status often meant little in their new homes.

And if upper-class refugees led a hardscrabble life, yeoman families barely survived. Poor women and children meandered along country roads with little idea of where to obtain shelter or food. During Sherman's march, a Northern newspaper reporter found several families huddled under a bluff, where they had lived on berries for three days. A fourteen-year-old girl had died, and the others had become so weak from hunger that the body lay unburied. Fate piled disaster atop anguish, often heaping more troubles on the already destitute. Women whose homes had been burned by the Yankees then lost their remaining possessions in boardinghouse fires.[18] Although deprivation had become the common lot of many families, refugees faced the problem without the psychological anchor of familiar and friendly surroundings.

Under such circumstances, accommodation became the key to survival. Women learned to live in their new homes by talking and working together, by sharing problems with other refugee families. Psychological adjustment took several forms. Perennial optimists saw many others worse off than themselves and thanked God for small blessings; others got by on patriotic fervor and hatred of the Yankees. Social diversion or an active imagination could also ease nervousness and worry. Judith McGuire enjoyed a quiet ride through the Richmond suburbs, where for a short time she could forget about the war and her family's misery. Yet reality always returned. "I am aroused, as from a sweet dream," she sadly admitted, "to find myself a homeless wanderer, surrounded by horrors of which my wildest fancy had never conceived a possibility, in this Christian land and enlightened day."[19] Though faith still sustained the weary and downtrodden, some refugee women naturally had trouble believing that God would somehow protect them from harm.

Increasingly, the Lord seemed to only care for those who looked after themselves—and even that was no certainty. Many refugees had no choice but to rely on handouts. Poor women carrying babies walked to Goldsboro, North Carolina, to beg for food and a place to stay. But for hard-pressed families, *charity begins at home* was more than a cliché; it was a formula for survival. From necessity rather than hardheartedness, housewives hesitated to feed refugees when their own children went hungry.[20] Despite the South's tradition of close-knit families, some women turned away their own relatives. As invading armies captured more and more Confederate territory, prices soared, food grew scarce, and the social fabric unraveled.

In many communities, clannishness and suspicion intensified hostility toward the refugees. The people of Montgomery, Alabama, Marsha Shorter claimed, "have hardened their hearts, they don't heed the cries of the starving women and children . . . Al[abama]. soldier wifes draws money every month while the Florida soldiers families are entirely without." County governments denied relief to "outsiders," a policy that often excluded the neediest families.[21] The Confederacy paid a high price for this parochialism. Reflecting their constituents' prejudices, local and even state politicians proposed "caring for our own first." More than states'-rights ideology or any innate conservatism, provincialism often encouraged cruel indifference.

Long-standing sectional tensions within the states made some refugees even less welcome. Beginning at least as early as the eighteenth century, relations between the low country and up country of South Carolina had been strained and occasionally violent, and the migration of planter families to the interior early in the war exacerbated the tension. Farmers refused to sell provisions to low-country aristocrats, whom they blamed for starting the war. Susan Middleton accused the " 'best' people in Columbia" of extorting money from the homeless. "I do not believe, if we had gone to the heart of Connecticut, we should not have fallen among such a set of *screws*," another woman complained.[22]

And despite conservative faith in the class unity of an organic society, economic grievances produced bitter social conflict. According to Mary Chesnut, the boardinghouse keepers of Richmond made their roomers "assume the patient humility of a poor relation"; from the other side of this cultural divide, the residents of Tyler, Texas, contemptuously dismissed refugees as renegades. Even religion, rather than fostering charity and tolerance, provided new opportunities for waging a social cold war. What Kate Stone called a "battery of hostile eyes" greeted refugees walking into a church; a Lynchburg, Virginia, pastor pointedly told visitors to sit in the gallery—the traditional place for slaves.[23] This powerful symbolism showed that regardless of previous wealth or station, displaced women and children fought an often losing battle for social acceptance.

But refugees could be equally cool and provincial. Making no bones about preferring their old homes and friends, their tactless comments often raised the hackles of sensitive natives. Yet refugee women naturally dwelt in the past and fondly recalled the familiar sights, sounds, and smells of their old haunts. As they went back over the large and small events of their lives, the modest homes left behind now seemed like palaces, and in the warm glow of hindsight, crotchety neighbors became dear friends. Such fond recollections helped to shut out the present and provided a psychological defense against unpleasant reality. For refugees painfully adjusting to their new surroundings, spare moments allowed them to think over what might have been. Waves of homesickness welled up and temporarily overwhelmed any determination to build a better future. "Everyone speaks of the high spirits and cheerfulness of the refugees," Sidney Harding wrote perceptively. "They little know of how many sad hours we have."[24]

And for those who refused to make the necessary concessions to change, suffering only persisted and intensified. Elizabeth Middleton Smith sensitively analyzed a typical case among the South Carolina plantation gentry: "Mary takes her reverses badly. All this time she has lived in luxury, ran the blockade for fine dresses, tea, coffee, sugar, & despised those who had not the means to do the same . . . . Now everything is gone, carpets gone, groceries & food gone, & Mary is cast down to the point we have all been for a long time and thinks herself the most wretched of women."[25] Clinging to the past, to vanished wealth and status, added to the pathos and created hard feelings all round.

Too many upper-class matrons displayed a remarkable ingratitude toward their new neighbors. Although a kind woman in Lincolnton, North Carolina, had rescued Mary Chesnut from an expensive hotel, the inveterate diarist harshly described her benefactor: "This mine hostess is young & handsome, very well educated, talks well, seems so lady like & kind . . . . N.C. aristocracy as far as it will go—but does not brush her teeth—the first evidence of civilization—& lives amidst *dirt* in a way that would shame the poorest overseer's wife. May we teach them that Godliness is *only* better than cleanliness. A Lady evidently she is in manners & taste! & *surroundings* worthy a barbarian."[26] This coldly superior tone naturally gave offense at the very time refugees most needed the sympathy and support of strangers.

Even generous and hospitable relatives and landlords soon tired of such arrogance and could not entirely bridge the social gap. Folk wisdom has it that no house is large enough for two families, and the history of Confederate refugees proves the point. New and awkward living arrangements magnified the usual tensions. Tempers grew short; in-law problems exploded into nasty quarrels; annoying personal habits became unbearable. Refugees living in the most pleasant homes with the most amiable people still coveted a place of their own. Women with a strong sense of self-sufficiency and accustomed to running their own households chafed at staying under someone else's roof; becoming beholden to another person galled people who now had little left but their intense pride. "I was never destined to live in any way but the most independent," Annie Sehon lamented, "I must have a home of my own, for such is my disposition that I cannot feel entirely at home and at liberty to do as I please in any but my own home."[27] Ironically, the kindness of their hosts probably intensified their discontent.

For even in the best of circumstances, loneliness seemed the refugees' common lot. Memories of family and friends cast a cloud over their present lives. Women who appeared pale and gaunt suffered as much from emotional problems as from nutritional deprivation, and homesickness hit young women especially hard. Elizabeth Collier fantasized about being a child again so she could have someone to cheer her up; after all boredom could be almost as deadly as depression, particularly for adolescents. Charleston refugee Emma Holmes found up-country Camden relentlessly dull. The natives usually kept to themselves; afternoons and evenings dragged slowly without the diversion of pleasant company; local belles rode and walked together, oblivious to her ennui. Her diary became a record of slights and insults suffered at the hands of people whose "low breeding and disagreeableness" constantly grated on overwrought nerves. A reading club that might have brought refugees and local women together never got off the ground, and Emma Holmes gave in to self-pity: "I sometimes become almost misanthropic. Here everything is so utterly stagnant & monotonous that I have absolutely nothing to interest me. I read & sew & knit, till my brain and arm are weary and I have no one who sympathizes with my tastes or pursuits, who can enter into my feelings, or enjoy what I do—no one to discuss the books I read." Despite finding a kindred spirit among the Charleston exiles, her mood improved only slowly.[28]

Pretending indifference at not being invited to dances and parties, refugees ridiculed native social life. Kate Stone scoffed at the dirty, shoeless Texas women who donned old-fashioned hoopskirts that Louisianians had given up three years before and claimed that "there must be something in the air of Texas fatal to beauty" because she had "not seen a good-looking or educated person since we entered the state."[29] But she could not hide her hurt or despair.

Many refugees did more than pour out their vitriol in diaries and letters. Responding to clannishness with clannishness, they usually clustered in their own social circles. The fashionable set turned rented houses into salons for entertaining Confederate officers and cut quite a figure in front of local rivals. Refugee women wearing silk and satin desperately tried to recapture the social triumphs of a more prosperous past and at the same time show up the native belles who had snubbed them.[30]

The sounds of music wafting from refugee homes and the window silhouettes of dancing couples struck contemporaries as curious. Such gaiety and frivolity appeared unseemly, if not vulgar. But from Mobile to Richmond, the displaced elite fought for a place in high society. In a Warm Springs, Georgia, hotel, where many wives of Confederate generals and politicians stayed, stylish refugees appeared each evening in opera dresses to play cards and dance the night away.[31] Social affairs could not cure homesickness, but they could temporarily relieve the symptoms. Women who had given up nearly everything they owned, had traveled in uncomfortable wagons over bumpy country roads, had often lived in run-down houses on meager rations, retained a spark of spontaneity, an instinct for finding pleasure at unlikely times in unlikely places.

2

Despite the war, the search for amusement—any kind of amusement—proceeded apace, widening class divisions and in the end further lowering morale (and morals). Surely the asceticism demanded by the Confederate experiment had some limits. If refugees grew tired of self-sacrifice, other civilians too refused to give up simple pleasures. After a day of pleasant conversation, young Susan Bradford admitted she had "laughed as heartily as if there was no war" but claimed to do so "only to lose sight of it for a while."[32]

If such respites were all too brief, they might also encourage an unhealthy flight from reality. Adults and young people alike wavered between condemning and encouraging frivolity. Because of these ambivalent attitudes, recreation often failed to lift sagging spirits and instead fostered guilt. "I did not dance last week but I have danced this year and when I think of my country and my own exile life, I feel sometimes if my heart were sadder it would break," Lizzie Hardin confessed near the end of the war. Balancing pleasure with pain, and indulgence with sacrifice became more and more difficult. Young women who condemned merrymaking sounded prematurely somber and harshly critical of their more carefree contemporaries; others seemed thoughtlessly gay. After several months of refugee life, even Kate Stone gave up her aversion to society: "I did not think two months ago I would ever dance or care to talk nonsense again. But one grows callous to suffering and death. We can live only in the present, only from day to day. We cannot bear to think of the past and so dread the future." For despite her belief that pleasure seeking was usually empty and futile, she could not help but enjoy her family's successful social debut in Tyler, Texas.[33]

Whether war inhibited social life or provided a convenient excuse for self-indulgence, it also added a new dimension to the relations between the sexes. With families separated, entertaining the soldiers became a solemn and patriotic duty. By extending this hospitality, mothers fulfilled their traditional nurturing role while their daughters mastered the homey skill of playing sentimental tunes on the piano. Yet the war inevitably loosened the bonds of convention. Staid propriety competed with less noble impulses. According to some officers, the presence of pretty young women near the camps undermined discipline. Concluding that the "boys and girls were getting rather too dissipated," Colonel Louis Bringier forbade more than one picnic or ball in any week. Such restrictions angered young ladies and their would-be beaux. When soldiers stopped visiting homes near Woodville, Mississippi, Kate Burruss grumbled that "the girls have as dry a time as usual escorting each other about the country, but looking decidedly drooping. We will all be old maids."[34]

Beneath such playful remarks lay more serious concerns. After all not every man in uniform was equally worthy of female attention. Genteel mothers encouraged their daughters to set their caps for the presumably better-educated and more-respectable captains and majors instead of the so-called common soldiers. Besides polite conversation, an ideal evening consisted of women playing the piano while officers sang in their fine strong voices. Respectability, culture, and well-defined sex roles evoked the central themes of midcentury Victorianism.[35] Although some women ignored social class or rank in welcoming the troops, the vaunted democracy of the Confederate army manifested itself more in poor discipline than in egalitarianism during off-duty hours. Officers sought women of their own class, and vice versa.

Both sexes embraced the romantic expectations of their age. Women tried to act like refined ladies while the men played the role of gallant cavaliers. On July 4, 1861, some ten thousand visitors, most of them female, flocked to the army camps around New Orleans. On this and similar occasions, women watched the men drill, parade, and fire their guns. Finely dressed ladies strolled among the tents, distributing food, clothes, and religious tracts. Wealthy belles brought Madeira, French brandy, champagne, fruit, ice creams, cakes, and flowers in their picnic baskets. To express their appreciation, the soldiers serenaded their visitors and performed their fanciest parade maneuvers.[36]

These public ceremonies, along with their private counterparts opened up new and unconventional opportunities for flirtation. Casual dalliance put a premium on insincerity, but the war suspended the normal rules of courtship and made encounters between the sexes, if no more honest, at least less stilted. New and freer practices naturally shocked the older

generation, which had grown up in an era of chaperons and other restrictions. Some parents considered soldiers dirty, ill bred, and lecherous
but had trouble keeping their girls socially quarantined. Bowing to the
inevitable, Josephine Habersham allowed her daughter Anna to entertain
soldiers because she thought that "a young girl should become accustomed to the society and attentions of gentleman when young so that
her head will not be turned by the first man who notices her!"[37] Such
thin rationalizations only promoted latitudinarian standards of respectability.

Men assumed their uniforms gave them the right to speak to any
woman without a proper introduction, a liberty sometimes resented but
generally welcomed. In what seemed at first a scandalous breach of
propriety but soon attracted little notice, ladies visited army camps
without a male escort. Such a change, which appeared dramatic at the
time, rested on a polite fiction. "We never think of requiring an introduction to a soldier, as we have perfect confidence in them," Kate Cumming naïvely maintained. "To be in our army is a passport. The men
are all gentlemen—at least I have found them so thus far."[38] But she
made this comment at the beginning of her work in the hospitals. The
Confederate army contained its share of crude, unscrupulous, and smooth-
talking bounders, and not all soldiers seeking female companionship
preferred respectable young ladies.

After all, women's obsession with men in uniform could have dangerous consequences, and the mutual attraction was not purely platonic.
The often priggish Emma Holmes feared that two Charleston girls were
"going to ruin" because they had rouged their cheeks and jumped out
of windows to meet soldiers.[39] These worries were not simply products
of an overactive imagination because apart from sedate parties, camp
visits, and sentimental music, another social world flourished, a world
of cruder and earthier entertainment. Soldiers on the march reported
women in every community eager and willing to accommodate their
sexual needs. Some poor women obviously sold themselves to feed their
families; others took advantage of their husbands' absence to enjoy
themselves. Reports of widespread debauchery and a rising number of
illegitimate births seemed to confirm the worst suspicions.[40] Contemporaries blamed the war for lowering the moral standards of both sexes
by making momentary pleasures seem more important. Yet the evidence
on the supposed wickedness of yeoman and poor white women origi-

nated mostly in camp gossip and the comments of hostile observers, including Northern soldiers.

Then too the line between promiscuity and prostitution was often a thin one. Prostitutes followed the armies and strolled the streets of Southern cities; some ostensibly worked as laundresses or disguised themselves as soldiers. Generals issued orders banning "lewd women" from the camps, but many regiments still reported three or four new cases of venereal disease a month. With thousands of soldiers stationed nearby, Richmond naturally became a center of vice. Although the city had always had bawdy houses, well-dressed courtesans now drove pedestrians off the sidewalks. One brazen madam opened a brothel across the street from the YMCA Soldiers' Hospital; her women appeared at the windows trying to lure convalescing men inside. Attempts by the mayor to close such establishments produced a flurry of arrests and much publicity, but fines and jail terms halted business only temporarily. The worldly-wise editor of the *Richmond Enquirer* noted wryly that whores had traveled with armies throughout history and that men should hardly condemn women for entering a profession that catered to masculine weakness. Yet the streetwalkers were not simply entrepreneurs taking advantage of an expanded market for their services. As Congressman Warren Akin sympathetically remarked, many poor women had no other choice: "Husbands and fathers are in the army, food difficult to obtain, temptation great, and opportunity abundant, and the simple hearted go to ruin."[41]

Much of this forbidden world remains hidden from view. Respectable people passed it by without comment. In many ways, the cultural distance between genteel matrons and the Richmond prostitutes illustrates both the centripetal and centrifugal forces tugging at Southern society. Economic hardships and shared suffering pulled people together but at the same time pushed them apart by making social distinctions both more important and more difficult to maintain. As the economic basis of class differences declined, social prestige, however tenuous, acquired greater value. When economic discontent and doubts about the government's war policies turned into class resentment, even yeomen and poor whites became more and more touchy about their status. Judith McGuire, a remarkably acute observer, recorded a revealing incident involving "two ungrammatical country women" riding on a stage in the Shenandoah Valley. When the coach was stopped by Confederate pickets who asked to see passes, these women sharply replied that white folks needed no passes. "I ain't none of your dear madam," one exploded, "I'se just a free white woman, and so is Kitty Grim, and we ain't no niggers to git passes . . . . Now I'se done talking." She spent the rest of the trip cursing the Yankees and the slaves, telling all who would listen that the war was being fought to save rich folks' "niggers."[42] Distrust, anger, and a prickly sense of pride prevailed among people buffeted about by social and political forces they only dimly understood.

The elegant life of the Confederate elite took place in a world almost beyond their comprehension. Yet they suspected that the rich lived, as always, off the sweat of the poor. For despite general suffering and deprivation, fancy parties, balls, and receptions continued. As simpler folk relished the few pleasures left them or worried about entertaining the soldiers, a more lavish social life flourished among the privileged in Richmond. For a while it seemed that the traditional core of Southern society—a sturdy yeomanry who had lived neither spartanly nor sumptuously—would disappear, leaving the destitute and the decadent to fight over what was left of the Confederacy.

3

These social fissures appeared early in Confederate history. Whatever its military and political rationale, the movement of the national capital from Montgomery, Alabama, to Richmond, Virginia, had important social consequences.[43] Many old-line Richmond families watched the arrival of Confederate politicians, generals, and their wives with a mixture of bemusement and contempt. To members of this closed society, Jefferson Davis and his wife, Varina, seemed like unrefined westerners at best and ambitious parvenus at worst. Although Varina Davis had been a successful Washington hostess, the haughty Virginians, and especially the hypercritical South Carolinians, remained cool and aloof.[44] Even Mary Chesnut, a staunch supporter of the Davis administration and an admirer of Varina's patience and good humor, thought her occasionally coarse, jealous, and petulant.[45] From the beginning, Varina Davis seemed overwhelmed by a flood of visitors; and despite her enjoyment of society, the pressures of being constantly on call made her chary of even the mildest criticism.[46]

At levees, receptions, and at the simple teas—which the high-toned disparaged for being too informal and democratic—Varina Davis labored mightily to please her husband's associates. Constance Cary, a reigning belle of Confederate society, probably best understood the first lady's character. She described her as warmhearted and impetuous, witty and thin skinned—a complex combination of strengths and weaknesses. Although Varina was no beauty, was prone to putting on weight, and was occasionally aloof (some snidely referred to her as "the empress" or "Queen Varina"), she presided over official Richmond with an intelligence and amiability that won her and the president many friends.[47]

Yet despite her best efforts, Varina Davis could never placate her critics or her husband's political enemies and their powerful female allies. Lydia Johnston's sarcastic remarks on the "royal family" added venom to the quarrel between Joseph E. Johnston and Jefferson Davis. After the first year of the war, however, she usually traveled with her husband and no longer poisoned the social atmosphere in Richmond.[48] That task fell to Charlotte Wigfall, wife of the Texas fire-eater and vocal administration critic Louis T. Wigfall. From the first she and her daughters had disdained Varina Davis as a "coarse western belle," and by 1862 they openly snubbed the first family. Petty quarrels, fueled by gossip on both sides, reverberated through the capital and beyond. Aristocratic families in the Southeast avidly discussed the Davises' latest faux pas; when Varina Davis left Richmond in the spring of 1862 during McClellan's Peninsular Campaign, rumors about her cowardice, Yankee sympathies, or worse circulated in fashionable drawing rooms.[49] Ever more sensitive to the political attacks on her husband, Varina Davis could not calm the stormy social waters. Entertainment at the Confederate White House was either too sumptuous or too meager, the first family either too ingratiating or abrupt, the conversation either too frivolous or too grave.

These controversies soon spilled over into a more general discussion of propriety in Confederate social life. The pursuit of pleasure seemed to mock the heroic sacrifices of soldier and civilian alike. "If Spartan austerity is to win our independence, we are a lost nation. I do not like the signs and fear the writing on the wall might in time come to us," Phoebe Pember warned. Sensitive women could hardly enjoy a dance or reception without thinking about their husbands, brothers, and sweethearts in danger. Of course the pious had always frowned on frivolous entertainment, but the war added new force to their arguments and even made some young people unusually sober minded. At twenty-two, Kate Stone already sounded cautiously middle-aged: "I feel out of place with a party of gay young people. Their mirth jars my heart. Life seems too sad a thing to spend in talking nonsense. I feel fifty years old." The lengthening casualty lists cast a shadow over feeble attempts at merrymaking. "Instead of parties we have been almost every week to a funeral," Kate Corbin reported gloomily.[50] Such depressing thoughts led a few disheartened Confederates to suggest a moratorium on social life for the duration of the war.

But Southern society had always been divided between a church-based popular culture and a more secular and extravagant upper-class culture. The war only intensified the conflict between evangelical self-restraint and hedonistic indulgence. For members of the Southern elite torn between these competing ideals, the best solution seemed to have it both ways. Wealthy Richmond women sewed and knitted for the soldiers, though Joe Johnston thought they overplayed the part of Roman matrons. Even austerity could be ostentatious, and public patriotism might obscure less-elevated motives. Constance Cary and other young women held "starvation parties" at which no refreshments were served. The music, dancing, and tableaux vivants provided entertainment for the soldiers (generally officers) and made women who usually dined in style feel they had given up something for the cause. Those with no taste for even this small sacrifice ate beforehand.[51]

Some elegant women refused to go through the motions of self-denial. Parties, dances, balls, receptions, and endless teas filled their social calendars, burying unpleasant thoughts in constant gaiety. Mary Chesnut later described these "days of unmixed pleasure, snatched from the wrath to come," and few participants looked beyond their immediate gratification. In June 1863, only two months after the Richmond bread riot, Phoebe Pember attended a party with the Cary sisters and a bevy of local belles where she ate strawberries and ice cream and promenaded with some handsome "cavaliers."[52] This callous pursuit of enjoyment naturally produced a reaction. The thoughtful and pious began asking hard questions about public virtue.

Debates among the restrained, the indulgent, and the slyly hypocritical took place in many Southern homes, and patriotic critics did not always get the best of the argument. With Richmond under increasing enemy pressure, James Chesnut tried to rein in his exuberant wife, Mary. Vainly trying to assert his power as "master of his own house," he forbade her to attend any more tea parties—an order she regularly ignored or circumvented. He raged, she appeared penitent, but the pattern kept repeating itself. When he suggested they stay home out of consideration for others' misery, she exploded: "And go mad? Catch me at it! A yawning grave—piles of red earth thrown on one side. That is the only future I ever see. . . . No, no. I will not stop and think."[53] Of course she often did stop and think, but her husband had a point. However common in wartime, the relentless search for amusement appeared out of place in the beleaguered Confederacy, an ominous counterpoint to the sacrifices being made on battlefields and in Southern homes.

Contemporaries bemoaned the effect of social extravagance on the female character. An outraged Emma Holmes criticized the "ultra fashionables, who seem to have forgotten alike the dead & the living and who with grass scarce green on the graves of their brothers, cousins & other near relatives, have shared in all the gaiety of the past winter." Worse yet, too many heedless young girls were acquiring "fast" reputations. Soldiers ignored young ladies who refused to waltz or polka, dances considered risqué by refined matrons. Adopting a classically republican argument, Harriott Middleton warned that "liberty always falls rapidly into license." And gossip from the low country supported her assertion. Confederate officers claimed they only had to "open their arms and the Charleston ladies rush into them"; their less-inhibited comrades preferred to hold the girls on the sofa rather than on the dance floor. In what Susan Middleton considered a profane mockery of the Sabbath, young people met each Sunday evening to "sing psalms until the clock strikes twelve, when the band begins to play and the company dances till daylight."[54] Such affairs struck a discordant note in a dying nation. Men and women alike seemed hell-bent on a final fling.

If dances seemed inappropriate, sumptuous dinner parties appeared even more out of place when so many families went hungry. Yet fashionable Southerners still crowded around tables filled with the finest food and drink. Mary Chesnut's diary often reads like the menu from a fine restaurant: pâté de foie gras and *dindon aux truffes* when recovering from an illness; oysters, ham, turkey, partridges, and good wine on Christmas Day 1863; terrapin stew, gumbo, juleps, claret cups, apple toddy, whiskey punches a month later; a "luncheon to ladies" with Varina Davis, consisting of ducks, olives, *suprême de volaille*, chickens in jelly, oysters, lettuce salad, chocolate jelly cake, claret soup, and champagne.[55] A few planter families fared just as well, even though most of their neighbors felt the pinch of shortages and inflation. A refugee in Shreveport, Louisiana, who had been eating too much rich food ruefully commented that "good living is a queer thing to complain of in these days of starvation."[56] The poor could not have fathomed such a remark but *knew* that the war's sacrifices were not being equitably shared. Feasting in the midst of famine only fueled the fires of class hostility and further alienated the already disillusioned yeomanry.

Seemingly oblivious to the consequences, the wealthy continued to spend their money and indulge their whims. In a rare blast, a Mobile editor blamed Confederate women for abetting the "extortioners" by purchasing what they wanted regardless of cost. Urging housewives to follow the example of their Revolutionary mothers, he feared that "many are joined to their idol pleasure and forget every noble impulse in bowing at the shrines of vanity." Yet inflation encouraged people to spend their rapidly depreciating Confederate notes; in the cities, fancy carriages epitomized these orgies of extravagance. And with necessities priced out of reach, even families of modest means occasionally bought some frivolous luxury.[57] The virtues of frugality seemed irrelevant when people saw little point in saving for such a bleak future.

A fin de siècle decadence gripped the Southern ruling class during the last year of the war. In Orange County, Virginia, only a few weeks before the Wilderness Campaign, a medieval tournament was staged, complete with thirteen knights, a queen of "love and beauty," and four maids of honor. After the jousts had been completed, the gentlemen and their ladies danced through the night. This oddly timed throwback to the misty legends of the cavaliers showed the lengths to which Southerners would go to find diversion. Eugenia Holst bitingly accused the Charleston elite of "dancing on the ruins of their country."[58] To be sure, the Yankee invasion curtailed such affairs in most parts of the Confederacy, but as long as Richmond held out, the social madness could proceed in a final rush toward oblivion.

During the war's last winter, life in the Confederate capital seemed more glittering than ever. In 1864 alone Mrs. Robert Stannard, the reigning queen of Richmond hostesses, spent more than thirty thousand dollars on food and entertainment. The long casualty lists, desertions from the army, and the tightening enemy grip on Petersburg—Richmond's life line to the rest of the Confederacy—could not halt the parties, balls, and private theatrical productions. Less than three months before the Confederate evacuation, Sallie Bird wrote a sadly appropriate commentary on Richmond's last binge: "There has been and is considerable depression here and yet people have dances and weddings and bands serenade (delightfully too) and ladies dress and walk the streets as if there was no war. Only the soldiers, the full hospitals and the wails of the bereaved tell us constantly of this dreadful war."[59] But the breakup eventually came, the nation died, and the cries of the partygoers faded.

Refugees and revelers defined the extremes of Southern society. The conflict between self-sacrifice and self-indulgence was never resolved. Pious women had called on the Southern people to restrain their passions and appetites, but many had embraced a live-for-today ethic. These cultural battles, though by no means reflecting any clear-cut class divisions, had nevertheless shattered social unity.

The Yankee invasion, the displacement of thousands of families, and the social tensions caused by the war itself had also changed women's world, even if only in small and temporary ways. Early in the war, General Joseph E. Johnston had noted the increasing seriousness of many young girls: "The most frivolous are hushed and awestricken in the presence of griefs that stalk like ghosts in our midst. Poor little butterflies, the gloss is brushed from their wings and they droop wearily on the stalks of broken flowers, flowers and butterflies struck down in the storm!" Although a few wealthy women threw themselves into the frantic gaiety of the Confederacy's final days, even for the ruling class the war eventually delivered an inescapable blow aimed at the heart of their social assumptions and self-confidence. In a sense, then, both the flight of the refugees and the parties of the Richmond elite marked the collapse of civilian morale—a loss of faith that affected everyone from the poor white mother with eight young children to the society belle. Mary Chesnut supplied the appropriate epitaph: "We must sup on death and carnage or go empty."[60]

CHAPTER 10

From Exaltation to Despair

S PARTAN MOTHERS, HOME FRONT STALWARTS, unshakable optimists, fiery rebels, fervent patriots—all popular images of the Southern woman at war. Confederate propagandists (with help from Northern soldiers and newspaper reporters) created these ideal types, and such paragons did exist, but for most women, devotion to the cause was no simple matter. Especially after the war's first year, commitment wavered, faltered, or disappeared, and the pattern was complex. Some women remained consistently hopeful or gloomy—seemingly oblivious to the course of events—while others rejoiced or despaired at every report of victory or defeat.

Civilian morale did not rise, level off, and decline like lines on a chart; place, time, and individual circumstances naturally complicated the process. Whether living in plantation houses or small cabins, women had to assess, in ways both simple and sophisticated, their relationship to the Confederate crusade and to the Southern social order. Religious beliefs, political assumptions, economic class, social relations, and personality all shaped their views of the war, and the interplay of public and private events made both intellectual and emotional responses highly volatile and unpredictable. From the balmy months of 1861 on, diversity rather than uniformity characterized home-front opinion.[1] Yet these individual variations could not conceal the general decline of civilian morale. However tortuous the process, the erosion of faith became a fact of life, especially for women, who grew ever more aware of their own powerlessness in the world of affairs. In the end, battlefield losses and the shattering impact of modern war—with all the horrors of economic strangulation and military occupation—created both a theological and cultural crisis.

1

Confederate assumptions of early and easy victory had a seemingly firm religious foundation. In the halcyon days of 1861 the confident assertion that "God is on our side" echoed across the South. Betty Herndon Maury believed the Confederate nation to be under "special protection." To many women, the Lord was no passive observer of the conflict but instead actively guided the Rebel armies. After a minor victory at the Battle of Big Bethel in June 1861, Julia Tyler rejoiced: "How can it be otherwise than that? The hand of Providence should assist this holy Southern cause." The North's superior numbers meant nothing when weighed against the strong right arm of the Almighty.[2] Although their evangelical Christianity might have made women wary of so closely tying human purposes to divine ones, enthusiasm overwhelmed judgment.

The rallying of clergy and their congregations to the Confederate cause produced a rhetorically potent civil religion. Patriots wrapped themselves in a mantle constructed from equal parts of militant Southernism and evangelical fervor. Skeptics pointed out the irony of carrying on a bloody war in the name of Christ, and Mary Chesnut wondered how men dared to "mix up the Bible so with their own *bad* passions."[3] Yet the optimism generated by the First Battle of Manassas and other early victories temporarily held such reservations in abeyance, and a bedrock of religious faith buttressed the struggle for Southern independence.

In this evolving Confederate theology, the South became the new Israel, God's chosen people, who would soon be delivered from Yankee oppression, and this divine favor fell on individuals as well as the community. The Lord bestowed on people the physical and spiritual strength necessary to endure any hardships.[4] Such an unwavering belief in divine protection anchored daily life, sustained hope, and, above all, helped women make some sense out of the war. And for a time the course of events seemed to vindicate their confidence.

But from the first a painful ambivalence greeted news from the battlefield, even news of great victories. Those who still thought that defeating the Yankees would be both a quick and easy task could no longer maintain that it would be a bloodless one. Celebrating the rout of the Federals at Manassas could not shut out more unpleasant reflections. When Confederate generals failed to follow up on their success by capturing Washington, civilians grew impatient, frustrated, and testy. From her Northern Virginia vantage point, Emily Voss more realistically appraised Confederate strength. Despite the panicky retreat of the Northern soldiers, she knew about the formidable fortifications around Washington. Comparing Manassas to the bloody battles chronicled in the Old Testament, Jane Beale predicted that the Yankees, like the ancient Babylonians and Assyrians, would soon renew the attack with even larger numbers.[5] Obviously the blood already shed had a sobering effect. Although the casualties were light by the meat-grinder standards of 1863 and 1864, sellers of mourning cloth did a brisk business, and across the South women attended funerals for local boys brought back from the front.[6] In the summer of 1861, these services attracted attention and comment; soon they would pass largely unnoticed.

As armies prepared to go into winter quarters during the fall, war news was either scarce or entirely unreliable. Reports of skirmishes appeared along with the inevitable rumors. Given the public thirst for information, improbable tales of great victories easily found an audience. Although women soon grew cynical about newspaper accounts, stories that the European powers had intervened or that a Southern army had taken Washington circulated throughout the war—often during lulls in the fighting. " 'Prisoners of Hope'! yes we are indeed prisoners but to a most delightful tho delusive jailer," moaned Catherine Edmondston, "We have become quid nuncs & watch the papers to see what more we can find to rivet our chains with."[7] As she well recognized, rumors fed both hopes and fears. This explains why civilian morale did not move in a single and certainly not in a simple direction, especially during the autumn and winter months.

In the South's agarian culture, winter allowed time for reflection on both private and public matters. The domestic routine continued, but with less time spent working out of doors in gardens or fields, women too might pause to consider the probable course of the war. Yet as housewives weighed both their personal anxieties and their country's future, they often chafed at their inability to contribute more directly to the cause. "Oh, this inactive life when there is such stir and excitement in the busy world outside," Kate Stone lamented, "it is enough to run one wild. Oh! to be in the heat and turmoil of it all, to live, to live, not stagnate here."[8]

With more spare time and limited war news, imaginations often ran wild, shifting rapidly and suddenly between hope and despair and in many cases simply reinforcing the opinions of both natural pessimists and born optimists. For doubters, the plight of widows and orphans added private sorrow to public woe, and even those who believed the South would never be subjugated wondered whether the struggle was worth the cost. "The mind grows weary of constant war. At times I feel too gloomy to write," Mary Ezell confessed. Nor did such statements simply reflect momentary despair. In a few cases, defeatism had already set in. A South Carolina mother rejoiced at her son's confidence but could not share it: "I see only ruin to the country and a farewell to white liberty."[9] At the other extreme, the interim between campaigning seasons could renew hope. Might not 1862 bring a series of brilliant victories and Southern independence? After all, people easily confuse desires and expectations. The Yankees were quickly sinking toward anarchy or despotism—or so the newspapers reported—and a rapidly maturing Confederacy stood ready to meeting any challenge.[10] Such beliefs showed women's psychological resilience and revealed a persistent faith in the future. Although the beginning of the new year was typically a time of serious if not somber reflections on the past, in the private writings of Southern women the harbingers of gloom by no means drowned out the prophets of victory.

Any unified notion of morale ignores the fact that different publics, not to mention individuals, held widely divergent and often contradictory views on the course of the war.[11] Sometimes bitter debates between ardent Southern nationalists, lukewarm Confederates, Unionists, and the apathetic added to the confusion of voices. After all, at this stage any imaginative person could find reason either for cheerfulness or despondency. And since women occupied such a marginal position in public life, these divisions of opinion hardly seemed that important. In a sense, women could more easily form independent judgments because they could not vote, did not have to pay much attention to political speeches or what passed for public opinion. At the end of the war's first year, few Confederates of either sex realized the potential harm that could be done by disaffection on the home front.

2

Then suddenly in February 1862 the real test of civilian morale began. The loss of Forts Henry and Donelson forced the Confederates to abandon Kentucky and much of Tennessee. For women from Vicksburg to north-western Georgia, this disaster produced an unexpected and almost de-bilitating sense of insecurity.[12] For the first time, they had to face the possibility that the South was losing the war—and thousands of young men—and that their own communities might soon be invaded and oc-cupied. The carnage at the Battle of Shiloh further suggested that the war would continue at enormous cost, with mounting casualties and with uncertain results; lost territory would not be regained quickly, if ever. As death struck more and more families and domestic tragedies multiplied, hopes for a short and victorious war faded rapidly.[13]

"What can't be helped must be endured patiently," a Virginian wrote resignedly. Silent suffering had long been considered a feminine virtue, but the war severely tested this assumption. Patience soon wore thin, and women longed for a renewal of physical and spiritual energy in the South. Too many men skulked about at home rather than serving their country; planters and overseers refused to enlist or joined militia and home-guard units; able-bodied young men lounged about, oblivious to their patriotic duty.[14] Women sometimes wanted their own menfolk dis-charged, but in general they called for all the able-bodied to come to the aid of their country. Again the behavior of Southern men often mocked the ideals of masculine honor, forcing wives and mothers to become guardians of their family's reputations and in many ways the most ardent defenders of the Southern cause.

For the time being, women could compensate for their own frustration and powerlessness by exalting the quasi-religious character of the Con-federate crusade. Jefferson Davis and other leaders frequently pro-claimed public days of fasting, humiliation, and prayer, and these occasions offered women an opportunity to display their patriotism. "I can but believe that the prayer of faith has this day ascended as from one heart and one voice, although ten thousand knees have bowed in humble supplications at the throne of our Divine Redeemer, Jehovah of Hosts," Mary Jones enthused. All across the South, devout women re-sponded to the call, filling churches and private homes with worship-ers—as usual, mostly female.[15] Repeating the familiar petitions for mercy as part of a larger evangelical community brought comfort to families and strengthened social ties among women.

Stay-at-home men seldom attended these prayer meetings, and their tepid response to the call of religious duty and to the defeats of the spring compounded the morale problems at home. The apparent lethargy of the menfolk only intensified women's indignation and despondency, even as they tried to ward off or deny their own loss of faith. Positive thinking no longer worked, and some confused the public crisis with their personal anguish. To Sarah Wadley, wracked by doubt, peace seemed a distant and fading memory: "I mourn for my country, mourn for my loved ones, yet I feel sometimes as if I have known inward conflict, a conflict of passion and duty, of good and evil far more difficult to bear than even this heavy burden." She tried to remain hopeful about the future, but others gave up the pretext. "We are to be conquered," Elizabeth Pinckney stated flatly, "and all our fine young men sacrificed." Again that word *sacrifice*, mouthed so easily before and now seldom appearing without the adjective *pointless*. Despite the thousands of men already dead or wounded, the Confederacy appeared lost beyond redemption. Nor did these pessimistic thoughts plumb the depths of despair. Melinda Ray saw no end to the suffering: "I believe it [the war] will last forever & if the men are all killed I don't want to live."[16] Often left alone at home, isolated from the course of events, women could only react to war news; their powerlessness in turn only made them more downcast.

Despite new outlets for expressing Christian commitment, the war also exposed the limits of faith. Women found it harder and harder to add "Thy will be done" to their prayers amid personal tragedy and national crisis. Although people often turned their hearts to God in times of adversity, discouragement and suffering sometimes fostered skepticism, cynicism, and even agnosticism. "This is a fast day by Jeff Davis's appointment," Susan Cook noted, "None of us have regarded it though. The prayers and fastings of one or two will avail nothing."[17] Sophisticates might scoff at the steadfastly devout, and religious fervor did decline, but for the time being a solid core of faith survived.

Because women responded out of their own experience, hopelessness scarcely could sweep all before it so early in the war. Each person had to interpret events for herself or himself. The defeats in the West clearly eliminated much of the early overconfidence, but they did not necessarily destroy trust in the ultimate triumph of the Confederacy. Overcompensating for the inroads of despair in their own lives, some women bitterly condemned neighborhood malcontents. "It drives *me mad*," fumed Elizabeth Collier, "when I see & hear desponding persons, who are brave enough when the enemy is kept at a distance but let their homes be menaced let them have to give up one single comfort & they are speedily transformed into a set of miserable croakers, traitors they will prove in the end." Nor was optimism a simple function of geography. One might expect women far from an invading army to persevere, but many whose homes stood directly in the enemy's path were surprisingly sanguine.[18] With the fate of the Confederacy still hanging in the balance, the optimists and pessimists—and everyone in between—would debate the future. But as the arguments flew back and forth, the war continued. Catherine Edmondston had truly called women "prisoners of hope." And so they remained. Each new report from the battle front, whether true or false, and the constant rumors, kept them on psychological tenterhooks.

General George B. McClellan's drive toward Richmond during the summer of 1862 seemed to vindicate the doomsayers. From the Battle of Seven Pines to Lee's last counterattack at Malvern Hill, reports of heavy casualties did as much as the spring defeats to dampen morale. Women vividly imagined the dead and wounded lying unattended under a scorching Virginia sun. The coffins and returning wounded brought home to the most isolated household the terrible cost of civil war. Noting how many aristocratic South Carolinians already had been killed, Mary Chesnut thought the "best and bravest of one generation" have been "swept away." Temporary and always short-lived victories could not compensate for the death of so many promising young men because the enemy would inevitably return. Perhaps Virginia was doomed after all.[19] And the slaughter never stopped, regardless of battles lost or battles won. Even when Lee launched his invasion of the North in the fall of 1862 and astute women well understood the strategic and diplomatic stakes involved, most assessed the price of failure in human terms.

The South could never replace the flower of youth already lost, but the North seemingly had a bottomless pool of manpower. "They come like the frogs, the flies, and locusts, and the rest of the vermin which infested the land of Egypt," groaned Judith McGuire. Advantages in numbers and resources, so readily discounted in 1861, now seemed insurmountable when viewed through the usual year-end gloom. With so many empty chairs around the fireside, the Christmas holidays became particularly depressing. Cornelia McDonald felt like the prophet Jeremiah weeping over the slain of Israel. Unable to remember the names of the battles, she kept searching for meaning in all the sacrifices but found none.[20] At the end of 1862, Southern independence seemed farther away than ever; increasingly obsessed with their own suffering, families teetered on the verge of despair if not disaffection.

Even the coming of a new year could not rekindle hope. In looking over the past several months, Emma Holmes considered her diary little more than a "record of death." The same old questions arose. When will the war end? Would this be the year? The answers, however, had changed. Few women believed that the butchery would stop in 1863. Instead the devout remembered the prophecies about false cries of peace that would precede the coming of Christ's kingdom or even speculated that a Confederate collapse might cause the trumpets of the Apocalypse to sound. Human contrivances, including Southern society itself, counted for nothing. "I have no longer any faith in civilization, learning, religion—anything good," Julia LeGrand concluded mournfully.[21] The dull inactivity of winter fed this hopelessness, exaggerated fears, and in many ways immobilized women throughout the South.

Optimists were still around, but they either spoke in more muted tones or used more extreme and illogical arguments to shore up their confidence. Distraught widows and mothers now seldom mentioned the achievement of Southern independence; instead they merely prayed for the destruction of the enemy. Violence had become an end itself. Wild talk of fighting to the last man (or woman) and turning the South into a desert before surrendering to the Yankees seemed more irrational than brave.[22] Many women had difficulty playing the role of the fiery Southern belle, and some withdrew into their own world. Unable to stand all the bad news, Myrtie Candler "ran into the yard to find consolation among my fruit trees, my horses and my negroes. Here was safety. This could never change."[23] But if the first two years of the war had proved anything, it was that all things changed and that the appearance of stability was delusive at best. Even if peace did finally come, for many white women their old way of life seemed gone forever, and even their religious faith seemed threatened.

The spiritual lives of Southern women became more unstable as they wavered erratically between reassurance and desperation. Traditional prayers for the safety and salvation of relatives and friends grew more urgent. Many women took a mechanistic and self-centered view toward prayer, bargaining with the Lord to preserve a loved one's life. Believing that faith had brought their men home safely, they failed to consider that the husbands, sons, and brothers of many equally God-fearing women had died.[24] Because women believed that the Almighty determined who would survive a battle—however fuzzy they might be on the theology of the question—they put their God and their beliefs to an unreasonable test. Therefore the death of a friend or relative could send women into abnormally severe bouts of depression, elicit intense guilt, and more readily destroy faith.

A similar process eventually undermined confidence in the Southern cause, though at first the Lord appeared as the omnipotent guardian of the Southern nation. Surely God would heed the prayers of his people and protect them from the vile Yankees just as he had protected the ancient Hebrews from the idol-worshiping Canaanites. This view of history—which pervaded family devotions as well as church services and other public ceremonies—made lost battles and other temporary setbacks meaningless in the larger scheme of things. Women could endure much so long as they could believe in a final victory. They found comfort in the familiar passages of Scripture and devotional maxims about God working in his "own good time." After all, miracles usually occurred during the darkest hours. In spite of the disasters of early 1862, Cornelia Noble refused to despair: "The Lord's arm is not shortened that it cannot save. Oh may he now turn and save us."[25] By 1863, however, such unambiguous faith had nearly disappeared and the devout could not help but ask whether all the bloodshed had served any useful purpose.

Even the dramatic Confederate victory at Chancellorsville could not lift the gloom. Scanning the newspapers filled with more lists of the dead and wounded made rejoicing difficult. "I can see nothing but desolated homes, and broken hopes," Harriott Middleton wrote. "We seem to make so little impression on the North, the men we kill are foreigners, and there are hundreds of thousands more to fill their places."[26] Those women who could celebrate Robert E. Lee's tactical brilliance had trouble conceiving that the result had been worth the cost. Good news from the battlefields hardly seemed much better than bad news. Regardless of the outcome, the casualty lists piled up—so much blood spilled for nothing. After the fall of Vicksburg in July 1863, Sarah Wadley wondered whether God had forsaken the South. "All is dark. I cannot look ahead.

I shudder to think of the future" became her litany of despair. She paradoxically affirmed that the Confederacy would survive and the people's liberty be preserved, though such statements no longer carried much conviction.[27]

The Battle of Gettysburg should have completed this process of demoralization, but curiously it did not. In many parts of the Confederacy, wildly inaccurate accounts led women to believe for a month or more that Lee had soundly whipped the Federals and was marching on Philadelphia or Baltimore or Washington.[28] And even when the worst was known, wishful thinkers deftly turned disaster into a test of Southern faith and argued that such a crushing defeat would at last arouse the people to make the sacrifices necessary for victory.[29] But by this point in the war, geography began exerting a larger and larger influence on civilian morale. Ironically, the Yankee invasion created pockets of optimism in those areas cut off from any reliable war news. For with notable exceptions, such vain hopes flourished in direct proportion to one's distance from the fighting.

On the fringes of the rapidly disintegrating Confederacy, women bravely kept up their courage by disregarding or reinterpreting recent history. Grasping at straws took several forms. Recalling the history of the American Revolution, Harriet Moore maintained that the loss of cities and territory to the enemy would not be fatal to the Southern cause so long as the armies remained in the field. The Northern draft riots also revived rumors that the Yankees would soon be fighting among themselves. Yet surely these statements masked inner doubts for women who, though loath to admit it publicly, knew that the Confederates were whipped.[30] And so the delicate balancing act continued among women who could face reality, those who sought to adjust reality to their own hopes, and those who ignored reality.

As disaster followed disaster, the nervous strain grew, but the long roll of war dead became the one inescapable fact of life. Gettysburg's terrible toll touched, at least indirectly, countless Southern families. Catherine Edmondston knew eleven young men killed in the battle; two months later she spent a day visiting eight households, all in deep mourning. The most ardent patriots began to add up the cost of war, usually by counting the number of their loved ones already lost or presently in danger.[31]

By late July the cumulative effects of the Vicksburg fiasco, the slaughter at Gettysburg, and several smaller defeats had cast down the sophisticated and naive alike. "I as a woman may not know how great the reason for so deep a gloom," a Georgian confessed to Alexander Stephens, but she realized that the Confederacy was threatened from several directions. Old bromides about darkness always coming before the dawn and silver linings in the stormiest clouds readily came to mind, however little comfort they might still provide. For many women, the psychological disintegration became all too apparent. "When I think of probabilities and possibilities," Judith McGuire admitted, "I am almost crazy."[32]

And even though the Confederacy had somehow survived its worst year on the battlefield, at home civilians reeling from the twin blows of shortages and hyperinflation could find little on which to hang hopes for the future. By fall, despondency ran deeper than ever, cutting into the core of patriotism. Mary Boyden bitterly welcomed winter because at least the cold weather would temporarily halt the bloodshed. Women now seemed willing to sacrifice anything—including Southern independence—for peace. Dissension and selfishness tore at the social fabric, and for once the end of the campaigning season could not revive expectations of victory or peace. Grief simply ran too deep. Funerals, words of sympathy—all the traditional means of coping with death—failed to assuage the pain. Straining to describe the overwhelming sorrow in a small Arkansas town, Virginia Gray simply declared: "Poor women! Poor everybody!"[33]

Looking back over 1863, Cora Watson spoke for thousands in calling it "this saddest, dreariest year." The wind, snow, rain, and bitter cold that swept over much of the South on December 31 seemed altogether a fitting conclusion. January 1, 1864, brought forth the usual prayers for peace, but fewer women than ever expected them to be answered. Many joined Kate Garland in "lamentations for *our heroic* dead" even as they felt their devotion to the cause slipping away.[34] The ideal of the Spartan wife and mother seemed cruelly out of place when the war continued without apparent purpose or end.

Despair produced bitterness and cynicism. The dead seemed like so much cannon fodder needlessly offered up on the altar of a lost cause. "Is anything worth it? ... this awful penalty we pay for war?" Mary Chesnut asked. And the new year would only add to the number of casualties. Already, the war had consumed the "flower of youth," the "bravest and best" as many contemporaries described the killed and wounded. Watching a parade of young Alabamians on their way to Virginia, Carrie Hunter thought about how many of these smiling boys would never come home. Everyday sights, ordinary pleasures brought no relief and in some ways only increased the despondency. Seeing the roses of spring burst into bloom, Catherine Edmondston sadly remarked that many women could not forget their grief long enough to enjoy the beauty.[35]

A crisis in theological confidence rooted in the earliest months of the war threatened to overwhelm the hardiest female patriots. The belief that God would surely preserve the Southern nation faded rapidly; for women especially, the emphasis shifted away from corporate salvation back toward personal salvation. They prayed for inward peace as much as for Confederate victories because civil religion seemed a poor substitute for individual piety. Evangelical truisms soothed the bereaved, and a rereading of Scripture offered at least some answers to difficult questions. Even Mary Chesnut, who often commented on events with sardonic detachment, found the Bible, especially the Book of Job, a source of comfort during the Confederacy's time of testing.[36]

National and private woes—confusingly mixed in many women's minds—naturally added to the otherworldly emphasis of evangelical religion. Those with one eye toward heaven could more easily live with wartime suffering because they had hoped to be reunited with the Confederate dead in the near future. The devout assumed that the souls of men killed in battle would be saved, though the doctrines of original sin and eternal damnation raised doubts about the final resting place of many soldiers. For evangelicals the vision of redemption had often overcome fears of death, and some women more than ever looked forward to release from their temporal suffering.[37] This turning inward symbolized a basic inability to cope with severe economic problems, the heavy battlefield losses, and the constant psychological strain, but few women could entirely detach themselves from the larger issues surrounding their country's fate.

The contradictions between personal and national salvation became unmanageable. To still believe in a covenant between God and the Southern people required more faith than many women could muster. By 1862 and certainly by the end of 1863, divine protection of the Confederacy seemed a most doubtful proposition. So instead the devout held that God still ruled over the universe and that the fate of the Confederacy, however, uncertain remained in his hands. But such trite affirmations raised troubling questions about God's omnipotence and the holiness of the Southern cause. Why, for example, would an all-powerful God allow his chosen people to suffer at the hands of mammon-worshiping infidels? To avoid such theological conundrums, women often fell back on familiar evangelical formulas. "But the Lord is king," proclaimed Cornelia McDonald, "and He can bring us peace in His own good time, and in His own way. We must learn to trust Him, and believe that He will do all things well." Yet a disturbing ambiguity also surfaced. Two weeks after the Battle of Gettysburg, Sarah Espy tried still to affirm that God would scatter the South's enemies, but for the time being he had "given us over into the hand of our cruel foe." Rather than being nestled in the loving arms of the great Jehovah, the Confederates stood before the judgment seat suspended between heaven and hell.[38]

Given the devastating effects of this psychological and spiritual crisis, Unionists suddenly received a more sympathetic hearing. Ardent patriots now shared the public stage with the disillusioned and the disaffected as the unity of the Southern home front crumbled. Three years of war had slaked the enthusiasm of even the female fire-eaters. Lost battles, lost territory, and, most important, lost lives had changed minds. Faith had given way to questions, then to doubt, then to pessimism, then to gloom, and finally to hopelessness. Even though most Southern women would never have admitted it, it was only a short step from hopelessness to alienation and an even shorter one from alienation to desiring peace regardless of the consequences.

3

Surely the price of war had become too great. In the spring of 1864, General Ulysses S. Grant led the Army of the Potomac in a determined and ultimately successful drive on Richmond. For the men on both sides, the fighting in the Wilderness brought a new terror and confusion. For women watching the newspapers and waiting for the latest word from the front equally uncertain about the outcome, the meaning seemed clear: death and destruction on an unprecedented scale.[39]

The toll of dead and wounded from the Wilderness, Spotsylvania, and Cold Harbor merely completed the demoralization of Confederate civilians. In Tallahassee, Florida, Susan Bradford saw women scanning the bulletin boards for the names of their relatives. " 'Killed, Wounded, and Missing,' " she cried, "I seem to see them in letters of fire when I wake in the night." Cornelia Phillips Spencer spent a Sunday evening visiting a recently widowed friend: "There she sat with her four fatherless children weeping, weeping." Words failed to comfort; those not in mourning wondered why they had been spared. The bloodletting had seemingly gone on forever. What made these new horrors worse—and anticipated the charnel house of World War I—was the absolutely meaningless sacrifice of human life—"precious blood poured like water" according to Emma Holmes[40]

By the summer of 1864, the range of female opinion had narrowed, hovering somewhere between weary hopefulness and unrelenting gloom. Those who could not grasp the portent of Grant's offensive or Sherman's march still looked for encouraging signs.[41] Some could at least adopt a life-goes-on attitude. Mechanically performing daily tasks might shut out thoughts of the war for a morning, an afternoon, or an entire day.[42] But for most women any appearance of disinterest barely concealed intense anxiety, and in many homes, despair had become constant. "The roll of death is fearful—the cruel monster is insatiable," Emma Holmes cried.[43] By the end of the year, depression blanketed the home front.

On December 31, 1864, dark clouds and a chilly rain capped off a terrible year in Columbia, South Carolina. Even young girls had lost their usual resilience. "Hope has fled," Emma LeConte sadly conceded, "and in its place remains only a spirit of dogged, sullen resistance." But any talk of defiance rang hollow. Words of hope or faith either disappeared from diaries and letters or appeared perfunctory. The disheartened had trouble describing their emotions or the atmosphere in their homes and communities. Kate Cumming wearily commented on the destruction and death in stilted language: "Our land is drenched with the blood of martyrs! Her fair hills and valleys, lit by blazing homesteads and echoing to the booming of artillery and the roar of musketry. The very air is rent with the groans of the wounded and dying, and the wail of the widow and orphan."[44] But stale words and phrases could no longer encompass the horrors of the Civil War; an elegant, formal style seemed madly inappropriate for such a cataclysm. Imagination itself had failed.

The novelty of suffering and sacrifice had long since disappeared, leaving behind a dull and steady pain often heightened by new tragedies. The optimists of 1861 had become the fatalists of 1865. Some barely clung to sanity. Families, homes, and Southern society appeared doomed, assailed from without and decaying from within. "War is devastating and separating hearts which were once united," Abbie Brooks feared, "while immorality sweeps over the land, and religion burns dimly in the misty atmosphere." Nor would the nation's ruin be short lived: "This country will be unable to recover for generations to come."[45]

To the devout, all these trials appeared to be a fulfillment of biblical prophecies, though their exact meaning remained hidden. At least as early as 1862 and intensifying in each succeeding year, a corroding sense of despair and doubt—intensified by so many difficult and sometimes unanswerable questions—spread through homes and even churches. That God ordained each event, for good or ill, became harder and harder to believe. Sarah Wadley failed to grasp the Almighty's "inscrutable designs" despite her abiding confidence in the righteousness of the Southern cause. All the deaths seemed incongruous with any divine plan or else signified some larger disturbance in the universe. "God shows he can *make troubles* & disregards our puny efforts to make it for ourselves," Mary Chesnut wrote with her usual flair for irony.[46] After 1863, even the pious echoed these sentiments though they usually tried to conceal private doubts behind public professions of faith.

For many evangelicals, the Old Testament idea of national sin helped explain Southern troubles even if it did not make them more endurable. "Pridefulness . . . ingratitude, violence, profaneness, blasphemy and oppression reign in our Midst," Cornelia Noble wailed, sounding the proper note of lamentation. The Confederates deserved to suffer for their transgressions; the people had abandoned the ways of God to pursue selfish interests and pleasures.[47] Only a modern Jeremiah could reawaken dead consciences and restore the nation to the Lord's favor.

And if the Confederates did not repent of their sins, God would surely allow their enemies to overrun the land. But how long this punishment would last was anyone's guess. Such convictions readily become a theology of despair because the people did not turn away from evil, and so even late in the war they had not yet reached the depths of agony. Christians therefore had reason to fear that the fighting would go on from generation to generation. Yet, ironically, these affirmations also provided some slender hope for the eventual vindication of Southern honor and rights. Once God had scourged the South, he would then turn his wrath against the North. A few days before Lee's army surrendered, Margaret Ramsey speculated that if Southerners put their faith in the Lord rather than in men, the Confederacy might revive and prosper.[48]

This chain of reasoning had several weak links, however. If the sins of individuals caused the nation to suffer, earnest women had to assume some responsibility for the fate of the Confederacy. Feeling both confused and guilty, they blamed themselves not only for their own spiritual shortcomings but for the apostasy of their country. Given this framework of explanation, disasters on the battlefield logically stemmed from innumerable acts of personal disobedience. Although the laments that filled the wartime diaries of Southern women often reflected the normal soul searching of the evangelical conscience, many connected—however awkwardly and incompletely—their transgressions to the woes of the Confederacy.[49] And in the back of many minds remained the nagging worry that neither the Southern people nor the Southern nation deserved redemption, that God was destroying Southerners and their society because of their unrepentant character.

Had the Lord then abandoned his chosen people? Lucy Breckinridge came perilously close to questioning the Almighty's judgment: "It is so hard to believe that war is a punishment to a nation administered by a merciful and just God. If it was a fiery ordeal through which we would come out purified and humbled, I could see the mercy of it; but it [seems to] me that people are more reckless and sinful than ever. It ruins our young men and has an immoral effect upon everyone. But, of course, it is just and wise, as God orders it so." Maybe, but many other women would not have added the final, qualifying sentence that barely kept her statement within the bounds of orthodoxy. Echoing Christ's words from the cross, Lizzie Hardin cried out: "My God! My God! why hast *Thou* forsaken us?" The bedrock of faith suddenly appeared fragile. To trust in God, to utter the Christian's historic prayer "Thy will be done" became ever more difficult and for some women impossible.[50]

And even as both resistance and faith waned the war followed its relentless course, a nightmare of death and destruction without end. From her refugee quarters in Chester, South Carolina, Mary Chesnut watched Confederate troops marching off to join Joe Johnston or perhaps Lee: "the last gathering of the flower of Southern youth." That they would die in battles that decided nothing and that more mothers would weep seemed foregone conclusions. Searching for scapegoats or mouthing empty recriminations about what might have been no longer mattered. Such women as Grace Elmore and her mother sat in the ruins of Columbia, silently watching the shadows of the flames from their fireplace dancing on the walls. Each bravely tried to cheer the other, but with little success.[51] The end had come. The Confederacy was slowly and surely dying, defended by two depleted and exhausted armies. Women prayed that the fighting would stop before all their menfolk died. Those who had faithfully written in their diaries from the beginning of the war abruptly fell silent, too disheartened to describe the nation's final days.

Even the women of Richmond, so used to rumors, alarms, and invasion, had to somehow at last face up to the collapse of their hopes and dreams. Food shortages and inflation had plagued the capital since the beginning of 1863, but by March 1865 women staggered in the streets from hunger; families lived on greens because they could not afford a piece of fatback pork. On the day the Federals entered the city, a woman sat munching a hard biscuit to avoid being captured on an empty stomach.[52] The articulate and educated might still try to recapture the climax of this unfolding tragedy in their diaries or letters, but most devoted their remaining energies to surviving the chaos of military conquest and whatever might follow.

As the Federals poured through the abandoned defenses, anarchy reigned. The looting of government storehouses began at once; women and children ran through the streets, hauling away bread and other supplies; both sexes seized barrels of whiskey or scooped up the precious fluid from the streets and gutters. Women of all classes carted off provisions. The explosion of powder magazines, fires at the arsenal and the Tredegar Iron Works, and continual shelling added to the terror. In a last, pointless burst of defiance, Kate Mason Rowland wrote that it was better for families to be burned out of their homes than to abandon property that could be used by the invaders.[53]

Although a few women huffily avoided contact with the occupation troops, most Richmonders were too emotionally drained or hungry to notice or care. Many were simply glad if soldiers protected their property and even made friends with the young sentries. But above all else, women welcomed the sudden abundance of reasonably priced food. Fiery Rebels who refused to draw Yankee rations were in the minority. One young girl clapped her hands when the Federals arrived because there would at last be plenty to eat, but she devoured so much rich food that she soon died. More typically, women neither embraced nor spurned their conquerors; instead they merely bowed to necessity. "I'll take anything I can get from the Yankees," one mother rationalized, "They haven't had any delicacy of feeling in taking everything we've got."[54] In the end, flour and bacon took priority over any last-gasp defiance.

But such actions reflected less equanimity than despair. The physical and emotional exhaustion also signified a spiritual malaise, for surely the wicked had triumphed. Ethie Eagleton remembered that "the prayer of the righteous availeth much" but still wondered whether there were enough good people left to make the Confederacy worth saving. William Faulkner recaptured the sense of futility in a brief description of a Methodist service: "I reckon there is a time when even preachers quit believing that God is going to change His plan and give victory where there is nothing left to hang victory on. He just said how victory without God is mockery and delusion, but that defeat with God is not defeat. Then he quit talking." But whether God was with the South in defeat remained an open question. Speaking for thousands of others, Grace Elmore simply asked: "How long, oh Lord, how long?"[55] Of course even in such depths of despair women could not abandon their ancient beliefs. If the war had destroyed many of their theological premises, they still clung to their faith, no matter how attenuated it had become. In the midst of national tragedy, the tradition of the Christian home nurtured by Christian women remained as powerful as any ideal that survived the war.

Four years of war, alternating moods of hope and despair, and the Confederacy's great crisis of public confidence had ended suddenly and undramatically. Most women had not followed a straight or even a jagged path from optimism to pessimism or from self-sacrifice to selfishness. Women naturally refracted their opinions on the war through a prism of personal experience; military events never wholly dictated home-front attitudes. Unionist sentiment—sometimes geographically concentrated but to some degree present in nearly all parts of the Confederacy—created at first small and harmless but later wide and dangerous divisions among Southern women. Complex economic, social, and psychological forces tugged at both reason and emotion, pulling women in often unexpected directions.

So, too, the evangelical cycles of sin, repentance, and reassurance fit well the seasonal rhythms of an agrarian culture; and throughout the war, women's morale had followed a similar pattern. The tide of victory and defeat, survival and death, had torn at the Southern psyche, making civilians subject to the erratic mood swings of a manic-depressive. Hope, defiance, and faith had competed against despair, resignation, and doubt. For women in particular, extremes of confidence and gloom came readily because they so often found themselves isolated from public affairs— the world of politicians and generals. But whether they welcomed, accepted, seemed indifferent to, or could never adjust to the outcome of the war, their struggles and troubles had not ended and for all too many had only begun. Just as white women had sustained and later lost their faith in the Confederate crusade, so now they would have to rebuild their lives, the lives of their families, and ultimately a new society in a strange and forbidding world.

CHAPTER 11

Defeat

FOR WOMEN WHO HAD PRAYED AND WORKED for the Confederate cause, the end of the war marked the beginning of a new emotional crisis. Peace brought its own troubles, and defeat—so unthinkable, so overwhelming, so crushing—cast a pall over daily life. Whether old beliefs and assumptions could survive in the conquered South remained an open question. To comprehend and somehow live with the collective and individual tragedies while making a new life in a world turned upside down became an often impossible task. Devout women still tried somehow to fathom God's purpose while others sought catharsis in words and acts of defiance against the Yankees.

But the intense feeling and strong commitment of the war years had either vanished or appeared as quaint survivals of a recent, but now suddenly distant past. The war left in its wake a complex legacy. For most women, public activities became less important as individual struggles intensified. In its simplest definition, *reconstruction* meant rebuilding, and women still performed important economic and social tasks, but the civic life of the Confederate period largely disappeared. Private concerns, especially the still desperate plight of many families, now took priority, and even educated, upper-class women took only a desultory interest in the politics of the Reconstruction era. A few dedicated women worked hard and long to enshrine the Lost Cause, but poverty, social insecurity, and other domestic problems became the dominant themes during this age of shrinking opportunity. And the essential conservatism of Southern women—for sure, a conservatism often based more on habit and inertia than conviction—survived and indeed flourished.

1

As the news of Lee's surrender and the collapse of the Confederacy spread rapidly in the spring of 1865, some women still tried to ignore or deny that the end had come. Yet living on wild rumors or false hopes only delayed the inevitable.[1] Because many women had strongly identified with the Confederate cause, defeat struck at the foundations of their existence. "We are paying the forfeit of our delusions and mistakes," Cornelia Phillips Spencer commented perceptively. Much that was familiar had vanished, and many of the once wealthy and powerful felt like aliens in their own land. Adolescent girls who had known only conflict and war seemed even more adrift and alone. In January 1865, Emma LeConte mourned a generation grown up too soon:

> It [the war] commenced when I was thirteen, and I am now seventeen and no prospect yet of its ending. No pleasure, no enjoyment— nothing but rigid economy and hard work—nothing but the stern realities of life. These which should come later are made familiar to us at an age when only gladness should surround us. We have only the saddest anticipations and the dread of hardships and cares, when bright dreams of the future ought to shine on us. I have seen little of the light-heartedness and exuberant joy that people talk about as the natural heritage of youth. It is a hard school to be bred up in and I often wonder if I will ever have my share of fun and happiness.

Gloom spread across the South like a dense fog. The sense of loss made a few women frantic, causing them to sob quietly or restlessly pace through halls or around yards.[2]

The bright sunshine of spring and summer heightened the contrast between past and present, between the unappreciated pleasures of what now seemed a golden age and the endless suffering of the here and now. "Oh, I wish we were all dead!" cried Susan Bradford from her father's plantation in Leon County, Florida. "It is as if the very earth had crumbled beneath our feet." For refugees returning home, death and destruction stalked their old haunts. A numbing and relentless pain followed in the wake of the Confederate surrender. "My heart became dull and heavy,"

Judith McGuire noted in her diary, "and every nerve and muscle of my frame seems heavy too. I cannot now shake it off."[3] Drifting along from day to day without anchor in a stormy sea of change, women often seemed aimless and disoriented, even in the familiar surroundings of hearth and home.

Uncertainty and fear, no doubt intensified by the lingering effects of wartime propaganda, spread through the countryside. Whatever their individual prospects, many women would have agreed with Annie DeMoss: "We cling to the past—we endure the present—we have no future." Too many questions—about the economy, about the freedmen, about the Yankees, about postwar society—remained unanswered and probably unanswerable.[4] Like the South's down-and-out politicians, articulate women saw few prospects for improvement and so readily succumbed to an almost apocalyptic despair.

Especially for upper-class and yeoman women who had given up so much for the cause, defeat became both a public and personal tragedy. In this psychologically innocent, pre-Freudian age, Southerners might have trouble labeling or even describing various mental disorders, but they instinctively knew what had caused them.[5] Depression had afflicted women throughout the war and in some ways worsened afterwards, making normally busy housewives lethargic. Catherine Edmondston lapsed into a "drowsy dream," often falling asleep in a chair or sitting "benumbed" for hours. The stultifying effect of the surrender eroded the core of personality. Octavia Otey had doubts about her own identity, feeling somehow detached from her body, as if she were watching someone else suffer.[6] Women (and men) used most of the classic avoidance mechanisms and even though only the most privileged could afford to indulge their emotions for long, the ennui persisted and often intensified the emotional and spiritual turmoil.

"Hard thoughts against my God arise; questions of his justice, of his mercy arise, and refuse to be silenced; because unsatisfied by reason; and so night and day in every moment of quiet I am trying to work out the meaning of this horrible fact, to find truth at the bottom of this impenetrable darkness," Grace Elmore wrote amid the ruins of Columbia, South Carolina. Even to the less introspective, the Lord's will seemed an unfathomable mystery.[7] For at least the last two years of the war, pious women had wrestled with hard theological questions, and though peace subtly changed the content and meaning, answers came no more easily.

The issue of national reunion—not to mention the presence of Northern garrisons in the Southern states—forced the devout to frantically search their Bibles for the appropriate historical analogies. Like the ancient Hebrews, who had been forced to make bricks without straw in Egypt, the Southern people seemed slow to acknowledge and repent of their sins. During the war, pious women had called for national purification; in defeat the need appeared even greater. But whether the disheartened Confederates would find grace or would, in Grace Elmore's words, "seek the flesh pots of Egypt, turn our backs on freedom, and let the river of blood be spanned by the hand of the foe" remained in doubt. A year after the surrender, Susan Cornwall saw corruption everywhere, people wallowing in "drunkenness, profanity, and other vices" with "honesty as rare as true godliness." Self-interest prevailed over self-sacrifice as Southerners aped the Yankees in a mad rush for the almighty dollar. Fanny Atkisson agreed that "human nature is ten fold deeper in iniquity— than before—deeds are openly committed now, that a few years ago, persons would have been horror stricken at the bare mention."[8] Although decadence had sometimes characterized upper-class society during the glory days of the Confederacy, a more general moral collapse appeared to be just one more result of military defeat. Evangelical culture had always produced these stock jeremiads, but the surrender of Southern armies afforded new opportunities for bewailing the sins of the present generation.

Yet in believing that somehow God could turn national disaster to a good purpose by teaching Southerners important lessons and by calling for patient submission to the divine will, women could avoid questioning the Lord's judgment and mercy. Such familiar affirmations, however, proved even less comforting in peace than they had been in war.[9] Simply learning how to live in such radically changed circumstances became far more important than pointless speculation about the past or continued defiance of fate.

For most women, this adjustment did not mean either resignation or apostasy; the experience of Lizzie Hardin typified the complexity and incompleteness of the process. After spending most of the war as a refugee in Virginia, Tennessee, Alabama, and Georgia, this twenty-six-year-old Kentuckian returned home to Harrodsburg. Like many other embittered Confederates, she began to "almost . . . doubt the faith in which I have been trained. Sometimes I fear I am becoming an infidel." Casting aside these thoughts as "wicked," she tried to believe that God had planned some greater destiny for the South but kept wondering why the Lord did not strike down the proud Yankees. "Sometimes I can't tell what I think or believe," she moaned, "With individuals it may be said the next world will compensate them for their sorrows, or punish them for their sins; but for the nations there is no hereafter. Their accounts must be balanced in this world." Prayers, fasting, and bloodshed had availed nothing. For Lizzie Hardin, understanding the course of recent history and resolving religious doubts remained elusive. "I wish I had the unquestioning faith of a child," she admitted. "I feel like one who is groping in darkness and yet responsible for every step he takes."[10] While preachers juggled their theology enough to exalt the now vanquished cause and at the same time provide their congregations with some sense of eternal security, pious women followed their example, sometimes losing their faith, occasionally becoming hopelessly depressed and spiritually disoriented, but finally coming through the ordeal.

Clinging to the bedrock of evangelical religion provided at least some comfort in a world of storm and stress. During the war, with so many families separated, women had taken on more and more responsibility for sustaining Southern spiritual life, both at home and in the camps.[11] Their influence had extended into the churches, even though most congregations steadily shrank during the war. The churches had of course remained important social centers, especially for women who wanted to swap news about relatives in the army or meet soldiers home on leave. Yet as attendance at worship fell off, and Sunday services had become more exclusively female than ever, dissatisfaction grew. Frustrated by the limitations placed on female activities by ministers and elders, Jorantha Semmes had tartly remarked that praying was "all the women and children can do."[12]

After the war, the revival of church life offered solace and stability for the brokenhearted and disillusioned. But even then women in mourning often stayed home, and congregations became embroiled in the political and social conflicts of the day. In towns and cities occupied by Northern troops, Sunday worship itself brought painful reminders of national humiliation when soldiers crowded into the pews. Although there are no reliable statistics on postwar church membership or attendance, in many areas the number of the faithful seems to have dwindled temporarily to the righteous remnant mentioned in Old Testament prophecy.[13] For families too downhearted or poverty stricken to join a church but who retained at least some part of their evangelical faith, the practice of piety, especially during first year or two after the war, became increasingly private. Even in the traditional practices of the Christian faith, public opportunities for female participation appeared to diminish.

Prayers for humility, resignation, and strength served individual needs regardless of their seeming irrelevance to civic life. Women still saw themselves as bulwarks of faith in a world of sudden and frightening change.[14] By turning their devotions inward, they could hold on to a traditional theology without having to square their assumptions with the harsh realities of everyday life in the postwar South. In a sense then, an other-worldly religion could also be a psychologically practical one. Visions of heaven might help women forget their suffering on earth and in their very intensity safeguarded the faith of fathers (and mothers) from the dangerous inroads of modernity that advanced steadily under the aegis of Yankee cultural imperialism.

But in the long run such efforts were doomed to failure because however successful wives and mothers might be in turning their homes into bastions of evangelical commitment, they could no longer isolate their families from the course of history. Dreams of the afterlife could not shut out the effects of defeat as economic, social, and political upheaval sent shock waves through the Southern countryside. A few women might still react sharply against Yankee attempts to reform Southern ways, but private concerns often overwhelmed attempts to act like the staunch Confederate women of popular mythology. The unreconstructed seldom expressed their reactionary views outside their homes, and the widely reported encounters with Yankee soldiers on the streets of Southern towns and cities meant little more than a contrived release of psychological steam by a small number of women. The spirit of defiance was largely gone; action seldom matched rhetoric, and even the rhetoric cooled off.

2

Those women who still tried to breathe fire against the enemy simply lived up to the expectations of Union soldiers and Northern travelers. At the same time, greatly embroidered tales about "secesh females" reassured anxious Southerners of both sexes that somehow faith in the righteousness of the Southern cause had survived.[15] And by waging a social cold war against the Yankees, women might also avoid admitting that their wartime sacrifices had gone for naught. Infuriated by the anti-Southern cartoons in *Harper's Weekly* and *Frank Leslie's Illustrated Newspaper*, Eliza Andrews took off her slipper and "beat the senseless paper with it." But she did not confine her wrath to Northern sources. "I am more of a rebel than ever," she wrote indignantly, "and it makes me furious to see how many Union men are cropping up everywhere."[16]

She did not say *Union women*, for like other die-hards, she blamed Southern men for giving up too soon. As Confederate soldiers wearily trudged home after the surrender, they met women who begged them to continue the fight. These stalwarts berated anyone who appeared too ready to accept the situation, too willing to surrender their manhood to the conquerors, too anxious to pursue the main chance.[17] Such women made up a small minority, but to dismiss their comments as the meaningless ravings of empty-headed teenagers or naïve matrons would overlook the deep psychological scars left on both sexes by the war.

Indeed some Confederate veterans worried about how women would respond to defeat. Whether their concerns stemmed from sexual anxieties or a feeling of lost honor, some men even wondered whether Southern belles might suddenly turn indifferent to their now not so dashing heroes in gray. If anything the bravado shown by those women who refused either to adjust to or in extreme cases even admit Confederate defeat must have reassured nervous men. Criticism of male cowardice never turned into a more general assault on female subordination. The war portended no domestic revolution; and despite great strain, traditional definitions of appropriate sex roles still held sway in the Reconstruction South.[18]

After all, the rebel viragoes so popular in Northern newspaper propaganda hardly proved or even suggested that defeat had emasculated Southern men. Instead these women admitted to feeling deeply humiliated themselves and often mouthed commonplace notions about holding onto honor even in the midst of disaster. Choking on the words *submission* and *subjugation*, impatient firebrands still dreamed of someday renewing the battle against the Yankees.[19] Although never as obsessed with honor as their menfolk, women nevertheless still valued it. If anything, they took a more protective attitude toward both their men and their family's reputation after the war. Yet these efforts to somehow keep alive old hopes and dreams rested on a disturbing irony. Ultimate vindication depended on fate, divine favor, and Southern men; this left women with the humble task of praying or simply hoping for the best.

Safeguarding the reputations of both families and the Southern people in general also meant indulging in a great deal of wishful thinking. To proclaim bravely that the South would rise again, that perhaps the Confederacy would someday be reborn, that the blood of the slain would be avenged gave upper-class and yeoman women some relief from the nagging fear that war had been nothing but a quixotic crusade.[20] In acting as guardians of the sacred past, Southern women joined in restoring the old domestic order. After all, the ideal Southern woman could not properly preserve memories of the Confederacy or offer hope for the future glory of the South without either embodying herself or at least extolling the classical virtues of wife and mother.

Although this cultural struggle to preserve Southern identity reinforced passive female roles, both Northern and Southern men knew how women could fan the flames of sectional bitterness. Even if some called for reconciliation and forgiveness or said nothing, a small but vocal group specialized in Yankee baiting. Mary Steger spoke for the irreconcilables: "Every day, every hour, that I live increases my hatred and detestation, and loathing of that race. They [Yankees] disgrace our common humanity. As a people I consider them vastly inferior to the better classes of our slaves." Even the highly articulate struggled to find words harsh enough to express their enmity. Augusta Evans blasted New England as "that synagogue of Satan." After returning from a trip to New York, she colorfully decried the decadence of Northern society: "The men are effeminate, selfish, most unscrupulously grasping, and utterly devoid of national pride, or disinterested patriotism;—the women are masculine, Amazonian,—strong-minded, imbued with heinous heresies, both social and religious; the children—heaven help them!—are not children, but miniature women of fashion and progress,—and pitiable manikins already chanting paeans to the Golden calf."[21] Few women engaged in such polemics, and even those who did confined them to diaries and private letters. However much they longed to defend Southern interests, women seldom participated in the rancorous and occasionally violent public debates of the Reconstruction period; whatever influences they may have exerted with their menfolk, they did so privately.

To fearful Union men and Republicans who worried that Southern homes remained "nurseries of treason," any female assertiveness, however limited, seemed dangerous enough. Whether by instruction or example, some women certainly tried to inculcate their children with a deep loathing for the Yankees. "Fear God, love the South, and live to avenge her," was Hannah Rawlings's new catechism. Such lessons obviously overrode religious teachings about forgiveness and mercy. After telling of a Savannah mother who never allowed her children to utter the word *Yankee* without some "opprobrious epithet," such as *hateful* or *thieving* attached, Eliza Andrews admitted that "even this is too mild for me. I feel sometimes as if I would just like to come out with a good round 'Damn!' "[22] Her religious convictions obviously helped curb her tongue, and like most women she kept such thoughts to herself. As with so many others who still felt intense loyalty to the Confederacy, she had to figure out how old beliefs would shape future actions.

To fervent Southern nationalists now living in a reunited country, the dilemma of national identity became more painful than ever. Bowing to necessity and acknowledging the sanctity of the Union meant repudiating one's birthright and betraying those who had sacrificed their lives for Southern independence. So young women kept their Confederate flags flying, brazenly waving them before Federal occupation troops, while older women joined their daughters in singing Rebel songs and displaying pictures of Rebel heroes.[23] In doing so, they remained ardent champions of ideological purity, the uncompromising defenders of the Confederate past.

For such true believers, avoiding contact with the Yankees became a most sensitive point of pride. In towns and cities in particular—at least after hungry civilians had finished devouring Yankee rations—a new sullenness and sometimes outright hostility appeared. During the early months of military occupation, few "respectable" women appeared on the streets and those who did veiled their faces.[24] This social ostracism continued for several years. Although women claimed to welcome "respectable" Northerners into their communities and homes, their definition of respectability was a narrow one, limited to those who embraced Southern political and racial mores.[25]

When fiery belles and their mothers did battle against the Yankees in the only available arena, the social circle, they exemplified and confirmed old notions about acceptable female behavior. But words and even acts of defiance could barely relieve frustration, nor did they have much effect on either Northern Republicans or Southern leaders. If men felt politically impotent during the early years of Reconstruction, women had even less influence on public affairs. Although some had paid close attention to the unfolding sectional conflict and had freely commented on and even tried to shape Confederate policies, Appomattox brought this nascent activism to an abrupt end.

3

During the early years of Reconstruction, female interest in politics quickly waned. Having just arrived from England in 1866 to live on a Georgia plantation, Frances Leigh noted how most women seemed to dwell on the past and cared "less about what is going in Washington than in London." Few any longer bothered to comment on public questions in their letters and diaries, and political discussions apparently became much less common in Southern homes. If women usually ignored state or local elections, they paid even less attention to national contests.[26] Partisan politics seemed increasingly irrelevant to daily life when the South's future in the Union remained so bleak and uncertain.

And this hopelessness inevitably led to apathy. Even the radical Republicans, the bête noire of Southern politics, received little notice in family documents and discussions. To women, these men served as distant symbols of malevolence endangering the South in a frightening but ill-defined way. Endless debates in Congress over Reconstruction policy surely boded ill, even though the threat seemed neither immediate nor tangible to most families.

For housewives concerned about the local and the particular, abstract political questions acquired meaning only in a specific social context. Therefore Northern occupation troops—whom Jeanie Young called the "blue coated dogs of despotism"—became natural lightning rods for political frustration and anger.[27] The presence of these soldiers rubbed several sensitive nerves. When the men promenaded with well-dressed black women, upper-class white women in particular keenly felt the racial insult. Ever sensitive to claims of caste and class, they denounced the Yankees as dangerous levelers. Besides flaunting their black "wenches" in front of respectable ladies, the troops held what outraged white natives tagged "miscegenation balls," supposedly drunken and noisy "orgies" lasting well into the night.[28]

Of course white women might find the soldiers attractive, and this possibility created some anxious moments for Southern white men. Not only did they feel the humiliation of being conquered and occupied, they often felt powerless to protect *their* women from the social advances of the brazen Yankees. The image of the fiery belle spurning the attentions of an impudent bluecoat became, if anything, even more important after the war, but the reality of the situation was far more complex. Young girls and widows—and not all of them poor whites by any means— sometimes viewed the soldiers as potential husbands rather than as dangerous enemies. Prominent hostesses regularly entertained officers of "good birth," showing that social snobbery could override political prejudice. The sight of the men sauntering about the streets with local women on their arms outraged many Southerners, and though some women confidently claimed that none of their friends would stoop so low, the harshness and frequency of the comments suggested other- wise.[29] But for all the fury these incidents elicited, they were generally more spectacular than representative. Not enough intersectional mar- riages took place to heal the wounds of civil war or to upset the cus- tomary relations between the sexes in the South. Caution and confusion prevailed with conservative social instincts generally winning out.

Certainly many Southern women knew their assigned part in this social drama and played it to perfection. When the Federals flew the Stars and Stripes over streets and sidewalks, they pointedly avoided walking under this hated sign of subjugation. Haughty belles hiked up their skirts and turned aside whenever they approached a sentry, but in one Texas town the local commander refused to abide such displays. With the regimental band playing "The Star Spangled Banner" and "Yankee Doodle," he or- dered a recalcitrant old woman and her daughter to march back and forth under an American flag hanging in front of his headquarters.[30] Such small incidents usually amused the soldiers as much as they infuriated the women, but they also portended the larger and more intractable problems of Reconstruction. "As we rode through the city [Charleston]," General Cyrus Comstock observed in December 1865, "I saw several who called themselves ladies make faces at the Yankee officers with us. It is useless to say they are only women—they express openly what their husbands or brothers feel but do not show."[31] Yet women had stated their opinions much more openly and forcefully during the war. With the onset of Reconstruction, most educated and articulate women simply ignored politics, and soon grew, if not exactly acquiescent, at least accustomed to having the Yankees around.

For even as Southern politicians spoke of preserving honor and lam- basted Northern Republicans, most women suffered in silence. Sensitive about the brittle emotions of their menfolk returning from the war, many trod lightly to avoid infringing on masculine prerogatives. But such restraint could not help but make women uneasy. Though conceding that men faced the most severe trial, Grace Elmore admitted that her sex also suffered: "Women can bear it, 'tis their province to endure, and they at least are prepared for the feeling of personal humiliation, which every man must experience; but the chief bitterness to them is to witness the chafing of those high strung men, most dear to them, under the conqueror's rule."[32]

Yet these same women could not entirely defer to male political judgments and became embroiled in public controversy in spite of themselves. Because of the confusing and often contradictory requirements in the various military departments, some women had to join Southern men in taking an oath of future loyalty to the Union.[33] In areas under Federal occupation, both sexes had to swear allegiance to the United States to receive mail, collect rent, run a business, qualify for Army relief rations, or even get married. For young women eager to wed but unwilling to forsake their convictions, secretly taking the oath in their homes at night partly salved their consciences. Some girls joked about becoming old maids for their country, though others refused to sacrifice themselves. Fortunately for those torn between principle and practicality, the requirement was easily evaded.[34] Despite the humor apparent in many comments on these episodes, the symbolic dilemma was serious enough. Aping male rhetoric, many women drew a fine distinction between acceding to the inevitable and repudiating their birthright.

Only starvation or some other dire need could justify taking the cursed oath, but the line between necessity and rationalization was by no means clear. Did yielding to force violate one's conscience? Scrawling a signature across a piece of paper under duress meant nothing. "Who considers it binding?" Catherine Edmondston explained. "It binds one no more than a promise made at the pistol's point to a highwayman!" But she hardly believed her own excuses, and beneath her apparent equanimity, resentment seethed: "Yes, Yankee nation . . . you cannot fathom the depth of hate, contempt & rage with which you have filled the breast of every true Southron. You have lowered our standard of morality. You have sullied the purity of our integrity. You have made us say with the lip what we did not intend to fulfill with our *acts*, made us promise what we will not pay, & for all this we hate you."[35] Her fury remained largely impotent. Defiant rhetoric still provided some brief escape from a world of defeat and subjugation, and even if most women preferred simply ignoring public questions, a few joined Southern political leaders in perpetuating a fantasy world of white and black, of heroes and villains, of saviors and tyrants.

Realistic assessments of the South's political situation remained as rare as hard currency in the ravaged land. Southerners of both sexes had too often ignored varying shades of Northern opinion, and they had paid a heavy price for their failure to distinguish among friends, enemies, and neutrals. The spring of 1865, with its many jolts and surprises brought on by Confederate defeat and Lincoln's assassination, was hardly a propitious time for acquiring greater political sophistication, especially for women who could find no safe or acceptable way to express their views or vent their anger. Men too felt these historical shock waves, but for women the blows went deeper, striking at the heart of domestic life. Who could any longer believe in the myth of Southern men as the invincible protectors of their homes? Yet rather than questioning the honor of Southern men in general, which would have been both subversive and dangerous, female critics concentrated their anger on a supposedly small group of political opportunists who seemed to be making fatal concessions to Northern demands. Less than a week after Lee's surrender, Carrie Hunter complained that "submissionists" had already begun "raising their dragon heads in our very midst." Domestic gloom reinforced such political pessimism, though few women had recovered enough from the Confederate collapse to sort out their experiences or make decisions about the future. Kate Stone sounded the dominant chord of despair and powerlessness: "Now, most seem to think it useless to struggle longer, now that we are subjugated. I say, 'Never, never, though we perish in the track of their endeavor!' Words, idle words. What can poor weak women do?" Not much, as they watched their "nation" heading toward anarchy, tyranny, or even monarchy.[36]

Yeoman women who had sacrificed so much during the war must have felt especially vulnerable but at the same time had to devote most of their energies to helping their families eke out a living. So too did many once wealthy matrons, who found it so hard to give up their old habits of command over both their slaves and Southern social life. *No reunion, no reconstruction* became a popular cry for women who still pined for the good old days. "What can ever bridge over that fearful abyss of blood, suffering, affliction, desolation, and unsummed anguish stretching through these past four years?" Emma Holmes asked, "The blood of the slain heroes cried aloud against such an end—as if end it could be. Peace on such terms, is war for the rising generation." Only bayonets could subdue proud Southerners; they would avoid any feigned love for the Union. "I have always been down on Reconstruction," Ella Cooper declared, "and never should one Southern man accept it with my consent. I opposed it to the last. They can force it on us, but I say 'never accept it.' "[37] High-minded women swore to at least preserve their dignity when they had little else left.

The emphasis on personal honor, which had so pervaded antebellum Southern politics, not only persisted but flourished. Despite their lack of influence in the public arena, elite women still equated their "country's" reputation with their family's and with their own. "Let us resolve to do our duty," Ella Thomas advised, "The South has a glorious record. Let us not dim her glory by senseless humiliation. Let us retain our dignity."[38] Although men too lived in a make-believe world of unbending resistance, women elevated foot dragging from a tactical maneuver to a solemn duty. Such bravado undoubtedly masked uncertainty, anxiety, shame, and a little guilt, but it also held male politicians to an impossible standard of purity.

Women who still closely followed political developments and who spurned any compromise or patched-together Reconstruction even considered the conservative policy of President Andrew Johnson unacceptable.[39] Unlike Southern politicians, who hoped to play off Johnson against the Republicans and somehow take advantage of divisions in Northern opinion, they remained skeptical and pessimistic. Even when the president could still hold his own against congressional opponents, Emma Holmes feared that Northern radicals—in her mind no better than the French Jacobins—would triumph. Nor did the National Union movement, Johnson's ill-fated attempt to form a conservative party supporting his administration, arouse much enthusiasm. Cornelia Phillips Spencer dismissed the scheme as "claptrap"; Ella Thomas thought any displays of sectional reconciliation a "disgrace" so long as Jefferson Davis languished in prison.[40] More often, women simply ignored this complex factional maneuvering and instead emphasized the need to maintain principle against the threat of trimmers and compromisers.

Officeholders and newspaper editors who worked with President Johnson for a speedy restoration of the Union became in Spencer's telling words "feeble" and "servile," but the crisis of confidence ran much deeper. "Cowards" who had stayed home during their country's hour of need too often defeated Confederate veterans in postwar elections. Southern men no longer acted like men; instead they appeared as pusillanimous favor seekers and time servers.[41] Once again, however, attacks on male politicians did not evolve into more general assaults against a male-dominated political order. Disillusioned women did not translate their fury into activism and instead stoutly refused to join the Northern advocates of female suffrage. Especially for the impoverished members of the Southern elite, political interest remained narrowly focused on sectional questions, and the harsh rhetoric belied women's essential passivity.

When Congress passed the Reconstruction Acts in 1867 and constitutional conventions began meeting in the former Confederate states, a few educated women responded in the old language of sectional extremism. But their rhetorical excess mounted in direct proportion to their inability to stem the tide of revolution. Novelist Augusta Evans charged that the South had fallen into the hands of the "insensate Jacobins who now rule us ruthlessly at Washington." Warming to her theme while mixing historical analogies, she mourned the sorry state of a once-proud people: "More pitiable than Poland and Hungary and quite as helpless as were the Asia Minor provinces when governed by the Persian Satraps, *we* of the pseudo 'territories' sit like Israel in the Captivity; biding the day of retribution . . . that must surely dawn in blood upon the nation that oppresses us." But faith in any kind of divine retribution had nearly vanished. Instead women (and men) grasped at political straws: that the Supreme Court would overturn the Reconstruction Acts or that a political reaction in the North would drive the radicals from power.[42] But none of these dreams came true, and conservatives could only watch in horror and disbelief as a new ruling class took the reins of power.

Elections (with former slaves voting and even running for public office) and the drafting of new state constitutions turned the familiar Southern world upside down. Race war seemed to threaten the countryside as "mean whites," carpetbaggers, and blacks gained control of Southern politics. Denouncing the "mongrel crew" meeting in Montgomery, Sally Perry complained that Alabama had become a "slave state"—obviously missing the irony of her word choice.[43] Although such statements seemed to crackle with the old fire, the coals of rebellion had been banked. Denunciations of congressional policies in the late 1860s marked the last sustained outburst of female defiance—a final blast against the despised Yankees and their Southern allies. Most white women fell silent.

The bitter and often violent struggles to redeem the Southern states from the Republicans received little attention—even from women who had often commented on public matters in their diaries and letters throughout the 1860s. Zuleika Cleveland wrote a long poem detailing the evils of radical rule and calling for the overthrow of the carpetbaggers, and an occasional remark on political violence or elections cropped up in family papers. Nancy Willard, for instance, blamed lazy and apathetic white men for not driving the Republicans out of Bossier Parish, Louisiana.[44] But hers was an isolated voice crying out in a wilderness of political indifference. As state after state fell back into Democratic hands, women turned their attention inward—toward their families, themselves, and their souls. The wartime struggles, the agonizing adjustment to defeat, and the bitter experience of Reconstruction could seldom overshadow the trials of domestic life. The turbulence of postwar politics had not opened up new opportunities for women but instead had reinforced their role as the guardians of the home and of Southern traditions, no matter how irrelevant those might be to life in the postwar South.

This futility, though seldom explicitly acknowledged, appeared most clearly in the cult of the Lost Cause. As unofficial preservers of Confederate memory, elite women fulfilled postwar expectations about their proper role. Although some of these women eventually joined the temperance movement and a few even became suffragists toward the end of the century, their activities seldom stirred controversy or threatened traditional power relations between the sexes.[45] The widows and daughters of Confederate soldiers often dedicated their lives to enshrining their loved ones' sacrifice. Turning their eyes toward the glorious past rather than toward a troublesome present or uncertain future, they added new layers of mythology onto a culture already heavily encrusted with myth.

The ladies of the Lost Cause managed to forget the unseemly parts—especially conflicts within the Confederacy—and eventually rewrote the history of the war. By lionizing the dead from a revolution that had failed they bravely tried to rescue Southern heroism from oblivion. As early as 1866, Southerners celebrated Confederate Memorial Day, which eventually became an official holiday in ten states. Placing flowers on the graves, praying for the fallen champions, and extolling the nobility of the Southern soldier all became part of a standard ceremony that struck just the right notes of sentimentality, spirituality, and patriotism.[46]

Such sporadic, local efforts served for a time—especially during Reconstruction, when women lacked the wherewithal to do more—but they could not meet the need for larger and more permanent commemoration. Women eventually organized Confederate memorial associations, which gathered soldiers' remains for proper burial and placed simple markers on each grave. Although Augusta Evans noted the cruel irony of honoring men whose blood had been shed in vain, she campaigned for the erection of a thirty-foot monument in Mobile, Alabama. Raising money for such ambitious projects in the poverty-stricken South was no small task. In the first two decades after the war, most memorial associations did little more than look after the cemeteries, and only in the late 1870s and 1880s did the first substantial monuments appear in town squares. Even the Lee Monument Association in Richmond was forced to send out agents across the South soliciting contributions.[47] Perseverance eventually paid off, and the limited resources available made women's achievements in these organizations that much more impressive. Yet in a society that still relegated women to largely ceremonial public roles, these periodic celebrations of the sacred past reinforced the most reactionary characteristics of Southern culture.

The unveiling of Confederate monuments showed the persistence of established sex and class relations in microcosm. The fashionable ladies of the community—usually dressed in white, symbolizing the purity of their patriotism along with their racial status and presumed moral standing—gathered for the ceremonies. Even though women had raised the money for the construction, men typically presided at the unveilings and delivered the speeches. Their addresses celebrated an organic unity that had not always characterized either the antebellum or wartime South, but these men also acclaimed the sterling qualities of Confederate women. According to Thomas Nelson Page, the mothers, wives, and daughters of the fighting men had endured the harder part of war by patiently waiting for news of their loved ones.[48] Such speeches nicely combined a reaffirmation of Southern virtue with a sentimental view of the Southern home while ignoring the class divisions, declining morale, and the social tensions that had wracked the Confederacy.

Elaborating on themes from Confederate speeches and editorials, postwar orators lauded Southern women as the modern counterparts of the Roman matron and the Spartan mother—both models of womanhood that could hardly threaten male prerogatives. To be sure, even as they praised the Confederate woman's patience, fortitude, and selflessness—the usual fireside virtues—some speakers admitted that female patriots had toiled in hospitals, camps, and government offices.[49] But these unprecedented activities had not sparked a domestic revolution. Conservative ideology readily accommodated the extraordinary Confederate woman by making her a model of self-sacrifice rather than of self-assertion.

The course of war and reconstruction therefore confirmed what most Southerners considered to be fundamental and natural sex differences. "When men have flagged and faltered, dallied with dishonor and fallen," declared ex-Confederate General Matthew Calbraith Butler in 1888, "the women of the South have rebuilt the altars of patriotism and relumed the fires of devotion to country in the hearts of halting manhood." Confederate women then outshone Confederate men in two respects, wartime dedication and postwar tenacity, and managed to shore up their menfolk in private as well as public life. The devoted labor of the sturdy farmwife or determined plantation mistress also became an important theme in Southern literature from Ellen Glasgow to William Faulkner. In Faulkner's first Yoknapatawpha novel, the old maid Virginia Du Pre acerbically compared the Civil War experiences of men and women for the generation of 1914:

> Men can't stand anything. . . . Can't stand helling around with no worry and no responsibility and no limit to all the meanness they can think about wanting to do. Do you think a man could sit day after day and month after month in a house miles from nowhere and spend the time between casualty lists tearing up bedclothes and window curtains and table linen to make lint, and watching sugar and flour and meat dwindling away, and using pine knots for light because there aren't any candles and no candlesticks to put 'em in if there were, and hiding in nigger cabins while drunken Yankee generals set fire to the house your great-great-grandfather and you and all your folks were born in?[50]

When the men returned home from the war sullen and depressed, women had to goad them into continuing to scratch out a living for the sake of survival and family honor. By joining the memorial associations and later the United Daughters of the Confederacy, women in effect reassured uneasy men that their strength would buttress rather than undermine the social order and that their energies would flow in perfectly safe channels.

Though often allied with New South promoters, the women who decorated soldiers' graves and raised money for Confederate monuments looked toward the past more than the future. A Mississippi preacher rightly described them as the "perfect embodiment of the righteous principles of the Southern people." They explicitly acknowledged their dependence on male guidance and rejected the dangerous doctrines of Northern feminism. "We meet not as new women clamoring for rights," declared the Ladies Memorial Association of Montgomery, Alabama, in 1898, "[but] we assemble under the protectorate of the United Confederate Veterans."[51] Such statements acknowledged what men and women both knew: the war had left the familiar web of relations between the sexes largely intact.

"Years ago we in the South made our women into ladies," declared Quentin Compson's father in Faulkner's *Absalom, Absalom!* "Then the War came and made the ladies into ghosts. So what else can we do, being gentlemen, but listen to them being ghosts?"[52] But fine ladies, even ladies who had become ghosts, could not survive off memories of the past or hatred of the ever-present Yankee. However much the wounds of defeat and family tragedies festered within their minds and souls, life went on, and the needs of the body could not be ignored. And whether yeoman and poor white women shared in the political sorrows and agonies or not, many of the once proud and mighty had been humbled and impoverished. Even in their reduced circumstances, so readily apparent to anyone visiting the Reconstruction South, women had to eat. And eating, not to mention feeding the men and children and making clothes and generally rebuilding lives in an economy mired in depression, became the all-consuming problems that challenged female ingenuity, tested families, and kept women out of public life.

CHAPTER 12

Reconstructing the Domestic Economy

B ORN IN 1845 on a plantation in Washington County, Mississippi, Amanda Worthington had grown up in relative ease and comfort. As an adolescent, she might have looked forward to making a good marriage and living out her life as a plantation mistress. But the war came, and like thousands of other Southerners during the fall of 1865, she mourned a world destroyed: "None of us can realize that we are no longer wealthy—yet thanks to the yankees the cause of all unhappiness, such is the case. As long as I thought we would conquer in our just cause, I cared nothing for the loss of property for I felt as if we would still be rich if we had *Our Rights* & *Our Country* left us—but now they are lost too, & *we have* suffered *in vain. In vain*! there is where the bitterness lies!" Poverty prolonged the emotional and spiritual crisis of defeat because the devastation of the Southern economy left few house-holds untouched. For husbands and wives, for widows and their children, for single women, for the genteel and yeomen alike, destitution defined existence. Nannie Rayburn described the reign of want: "Poverty is a tyrant, and he has a Roman sway over the Confederacy now and like a Nero, he uses his cruel power."[1]

More than the Yankees, more than politics, more than the traditions of kinship, domesticity, and evangelical religion, poverty shaped daily life and became the war's most enduring legacy. An economy of scarcity forestalled social change and reduced many women to eking out a bare subsistence. To most Southerners of both sexes, the proper feminine sphere of activity remained the household, and the heroic activities of

Southern women—which soon became staples of Lost Cause legend—generally had domestic settings. Peace left thousands of widows simply trying to survive; Reconstruction also meant the reunion of husbands and wives long separated by war. Although women seemed less inclined after the war to write in their letters or diaries about the intimate details of family life or about how the war had changed their marriages and their relations with their children, they did comment at some length about economic, social, and racial problems that so often plagued them. Indeed the struggle for survival, a struggle that must have often seemed endless in the postwar South, provided the social context for both women and men to redefine—or, more accurately, re-establish—"proper" female roles.

Trying to rebuild farms and plantations without slaves sorely challenged yeoman and upper-class women alike. To hang on to the past, to compromise with necessity, or to plunge ahead into some new endeavor—white women tested all these strategies. In social life, and especially in race relations, the foundations of the old order crumbled, leaving women confused, depressed, and even frightened. Whatever opportunities the new free-labor economy offered them, many would have agreed that the disadvantages far outweighed the benefits.

1

Although women had expected peace to relieve their financial burdens, wartime shortages continued even as inflation eased. Haggard housewives and lethargic children still gathered around tables for sparse meals. The standard of living declined for all classes except for the very poor or the very fortunate. In Mobile, Alabama, Northern reporter Whitelaw Reid found striking evidence of the economic collapse: worn sofas, furniture missing pieces of veneer, ragged curtains, and floors without carpets. As late as 1867, letters poured into the office of the New York Southern Relief Association from Georgia, North Carolina, and Virginia telling of orphans without clothing or food.[2] And among the many requests for aid came forlorn pleas from members of prominent Southern families, one-time leaders of society, now barely surviving.

Emancipation, wartime destruction, and a sharp drop in land values wiped out wealth, leaving planters' wives and widows in precarious circumstances and forcing some to abandon their homes. In the cruelest irony of all, a few planter families lived in cabins once occupied by their slaves, who now sought, as free people, to escape the scenes of their bondage and establish new lives of their own, ironically showing a spirit of initiative and independence that belied white racial assumptions.[3] Indeed this display of black independence and self-assertion seemed to mock white attempts to restore old ways of life. Although the Southern elite recovered at least part of their wealth and social standing, the war had shattered their self-confidence and their esprit as a ruling class.

In 1869 a Northern army veteran touring Civil War battlefields for a Boston newspaper met a former plantation mistress scavenging for scraps of bread on the streets of Montgomery, Alabama. "Here my husband was honored where I am now a beggar," she said pointing to the Capitol. Melodramatic perhaps, but in the wreckage of their civilization some women still acted like genteel ladies, refusing to eat coarse food or do menial chores. Proud widows lived quietly, letting no one know of their desperate situation. "There is nothing disgraceful in our poverty," Maria Fleet advised her son. "We come of an honest stock on both sides of the house and can't help being poor—you have nothing to be ashamed of, some of the best in our land are now reduced."[4] Arrayed in the tattered finery of better days, dignified ladies upheld the old standards of respectability with barely the means to keep up appearances.

In doing so, they often struggled along without much help. As determined women began picking up the pieces of their families' shattered lives, domesticity acquired new meaning. To restore the day-to-day intimacy of marriage after long periods of separation must have been difficult, though few women commented on the emotional (and certainly not on the sexual) aspects of this problem. What is clear is that economic woes subtly reshaped many marriages. Wives whose husbands had returned from the war physically or emotionally crippled had to manage the household finances. The appearance of increasing assertiveness and success by women alarmed some men, but they need not have worried. Despite the domestic contretemps, women challenged male prerogatives obliquely if at all. Family letters contain the usual complaints about a husband's laziness or poor business sense, though female folk wisdom had always emphasized male helplessness. Rather than usurping the authority of the "stronger sex," wives slowly acquired influence in important though undramatic ways in the home.[5] In these evolving relationships, Southern couples found adjustment if not contentment without permanently upsetting the balance of power between the sexes. New household routines and attitudes changed individual marriages but scarcely affected conventional definitions of what marriage should be.

The vagaries of the postwar economy and men's frantic efforts to support their families in the grand manner produced far more disillusionment than rebellion. Ella Gertrude Thomas and her husband had seldom discussed finances, and she had always deferred to his judgment. Unfortunately, he had invested much of the money inherited from her father in slaves and Confederate bonds and had borrowed money from her relatives several times. War had steadily reduced the family from what Ella Thomas called a "state of affluence" to a condition of "comparative poverty." But she still did not realize how her husband's mismanagement, extravagance, and questionable business ventures threatened their security. In November 1868, Jefferson Thomas finally admitted that he would have to declare bankruptcy and that they might lose their house in the country and their store in Augusta. In December he persuaded her to sign a mortgage for their town property.[6] Such stopgaps, however, failed to avert the final collapse.

By May 1869, Ella Thomas knew the worst and described the past two years of their life as a "death struggle." Creditors had seized all the goods from the store, and the building was to be sold at auction. Though suspecting for some time that her husband's business affairs had become hopelessly snarled and admitting that they had lived beyond their means, she had felt powerless to avert disaster. Blaming her husband for the losses, she nevertheless conceded that her own pride and stubbornness had also contributed to their troubles. As a faithful wife, she could not separate her self-esteem from his. "My life, my glory, my honor has been so intimately blended with that of my husband and now to see him broken in fortune, health and spirits," she wrote. To hide her shame, she put on a fancy dress and took the family carriage into town, but preserving appearances became a losing battle. She exchanged some old dresses for a new bonnet and had to sell a diamond ring—a gift from her father—to pay the servants' wages. Jefferson Thomas suggested renting their store and selling goods on commission, but she talked him out of this dubious undertaking. Citing ruinous rates of interest and the money needed to pay clerks, she gradually reined in his impractical impulses, and at the same time grew more critical of his business sense. After a heated argument about the prospects for making money from plantations in Burke and Columbia counties, she poured out the frustration in her diary: "Most men dislike to admit that their wives own any thing. It is all masculine 'my' and 'my own' which they use and in polite circles it would be considered in bad taste for a woman to say 'my plantation,' 'my horse,' 'my cows' altho they are really as much her own as the dress she wears."[7]

Yet Ella Thomas remained loyal to her husband, and even when they quarreled over her efforts to economize, she enjoyed receiving his extravagant gifts. Though fearing the loss of property inherited from her father, she kept such thoughts to herself and tried to meet society's expectations for the dutiful wife:

> Men go into the world and endeavor to retrieve their loss and come home depressed, dejected and irritable, glad of a safety valve for the annoyance of the day. They come to wives who have been fretted with careless servants and crying children, fretted by little worries while the ever present thought of debt is pressing like an iron weight upon them. They come expecting to find a soothing welcome, gentle words and loving glances . . . I try to do my duty. I have a bright fire, do my best to have tea ready . . . to have the children taken to bed directly after tea knowing how essential perfect quiet is to tortured nerves. I have the will to do this but my cook had tea late and this was annoying to Mr. T and seating himself in an attitude of abject dejection his head aching if a child touches his chair & so nervous that the least thing annoys him.

As the Thomases lost more and more property, including the family plantations in Burke County and the plantation inherited from Ella's father—both of them became testy. He did not seem to appreciate that she now did the housework without servants and even berated her for not understanding the ways of the world. For the rest of the decade they scrambled to remain solvent but could barely pay the smallest bills after her relatives called in her husband's bad debts. Ella Thomas ended up teaching school and taking in boarders, though even these heroic measures only slowed the pace of the family's decline.[8]

If Ella Thomas had descended from a comfortable upper-class life to a more precarious existence, many yeoman women faced greater difficulties with less margin for error. Learning what crops to plant and acquiring other agricultural skills did not destroy the assumption that farming was men's work. Even wives who took on new responsibilities neither welcomed them nor saw them as an opportunities for self-assertion. Although antebellum travelers had occasionally seen white women plowing in the fields, the sight became common during Reconstruction. But these women toiled in the sun because they had little choice in the matter, and their chances of escaping the grinding poverty of the postwar South were slim. Dreams of economic success or even obtaining a modicum of comfort had long since vanished from many yeoman homes. Such blighted prospects also made ordinary household chores suddenly more onerous and monotonous. With four children who always seemed to act up when she was most tired, Emily Bealer grimly undertook endless rounds of cooking, cleaning, and sewing. Worrying constantly about money, without wood or coal in the middle of winter, and unable to dress her children well enough to send them to church, she sat down at the end of another long day with just enough energy left to record her weariness: "As usual, with a feeling of discontent at being a drudge with hands hurting and real longing for other pursuits, I finished my kitchen duties and then changed my dress and cut out a pair of pants for Pierre."[9] However much their stories might have varied in detail, many other women would have recognized this spirit of sad resignation that hung over so many Southern households.

When the politicians and newspaper editors praised the stamina and determination of Southern women, they forgot about those who broke under the strain. Postwar poverty only added to the problems of women who would not have had an easy life anyway. Margaret Gillis made her first mistake by marrying a Methodist minister, an odd choice for one reared as a strict Baptist. His tight-fisted parishioners in Lowndesboro, Alabama, did not want to pay him a decent salary and expected her to teach local children for a ridiculously low fee. "I am a preacher's wife," she wrote with a mixture of realism, sorrow, and disillusionment. "I must work all the time for other people for nothing. Still I must live, I must dress decently and the clothes of my family must always be in order." Pregnant with her second child, at age twenty-nine life seemed insufferable. Forced to go about in the rain or cold, she resented having to perform acts of charity for others when her family had nothing to eat but fat bacon and corn bread. And even then busybodies gossiped about the preacher and his wife wallowing in luxury. By September 1868 she had fallen into a severe depression: "This may be the last entry I shall ever make in my journal, and were I to express all my feelings they would be as dark as midnight."[10] A few days later, Margaret Gillis died of complications in childbirth.

But such quiet desperation had long characterized the lives of poor whites, and during Reconstruction, their lot hardly improved. Freedmen's Bureau agent John W. De Forest described the ragged-looking, ignorant women who came to his office in Greenville, South Carolina, begging for food. Many of them smoked pipes, wore no shoes, and did not know their own ages. When the widows of Confederate soldiers lived in drafty shacks with no money for clothes and little for food, justice and mercy seemed far away. Because few of these women wrote letters or kept diaries and in any case were generally illiterate, all too often our glimpses of this hidden world must come secondhand. In September 1865, Kate Stone stopped at a ramshackle two-room cabin in Hopkins County, Texas. Eight people lived in these cramped quarters; the women had no ribbon, lace, or anything else to spruce up themselves or their home, not even a comb to run through their badly matted hair. Kate Stone could see beneath the dirt and squalor and appreciate the genuineness of their hospitality.[11] Yet even with her sympathetic attitude, she had trouble bridging the social and cultural gap.

To Northerners traveling through the Southern hill country and piney woods, slack-jawed, vacant-eyed women and children seemed barely alive. Even after allowing for exaggeration and class prejudice in such accounts, the poor white family appeared hopelessly mired in the past, caught up in a daily battle for survival with few plans and slender prospects for the future. What careless observers deemed laziness represented despair more than any inherent character defect; the women had little reason to believe that working hard and acting respectably would relieve their poverty and cultural isolation. Then too their families kept growing along with their other problems.[12] Always chary of criticism, poor white women resented being preached at, shunned advice from meddlesome neighbors, and so became ever more clannish and standoffish.

Relations between the various classes had been strained during the war, and peace failed to restore social harmony. In hauling away some expensive furniture from an abandoned plantation, an Alabama woman scoffed at the pretensions of folks who considered themselves better than other folks "just because they owned niggers." In a depressed agricultural economy, the privileges and patronizing attitude of the large planters still stirred resentment. Yet emancipation also added to the economic and social insecurity of poor white families, and they lashed out at the safest and most convenient target: the freedmen. "We poor folks was about ekil to the niggers, about being hard put to it to live," a North Carolina woman complained, "Now they's free they don't do nothin' but steal, and how we'll live I don't know." Any progress made by blacks only intensified this hostility because poor whites chafed at the smallest changes in social customs. Another North Carolinian vowed never to let a black sit in her kitchen because "white folks is white folks, and niggers is brought up to know their place."[13]

There was more at work here than racism, and postwar poverty upset old hierarchical values. While the blacks were free, many white women, including formerly wealthy plantation mistresses and the proud wives of yeoman farmers, felt they were in economic bondage, dependent on handouts from neighbors or benevolent societies. During Reconstruction, New Orleans ladies, demurely hiding their faces behind thick veils, crowded into the mayor's parlor each morning to apply for assistance. They told of property lost in the war, of hunger, of illness, of husbands in prison; a Louisiana widow simply informed the New York Southern Relief Association that she needed everything.[14]

The requests for help overwhelmed local and national aid societies, in no small part because the families who normally would have contributed to these efforts could now barely support themselves. In Georgia and Alabama, hundreds of mothers came down out of the hills seeking food; many had walked ten or twenty miles with young children. Given the size of the problem, the usual bake sales, raffles, and fancy dress balls raised only enough money to provide temporary relief for a few families. From Adams Run, South Carolina, Claudia Legare effusively thanked the director of the New York Southern Relief Association for a gift of twenty-five dollars, though her seven children must have quickly eaten up such a pittance.[15] Most poor women had either to manage on their own or rely on the uncertain generosity of wealthy neighbors.

The ancient traditions of noblesse oblige survived in small towns and the Southern countryside. Wives and widows of Confederate generals raised money for veterans' families through circular letters filled with heart-rending tales of suffering. The emphasis was clearly on helping the deserving poor. Writing for the *North Carolina Presbyterian*, Cornelia Phillips Spencer proudly told of distributing ten dollars among half a dozen families who had kept themselves clean, worked hard, and respected biblical teachings. In suggesting that other Christian women follow her example, she further revealed the condescension of much postwar benevolence: "Extremes meet—and I have often seen among my poorest neighbors—(always referring to the virtuous honest poor) specimens of the same delicacy, generosity, and genuine good breeding that are so charming among the gently born and bred. To go much among our poor neighbors, to be in habits of friendly intercourse with them and of familiarity with their simple annals, is to learn to think better of human nature."[16] Despite and perhaps because of the economic leveling caused by the war, social distinctions gained added importance. Conservative views of class relationships survived the destruction of the old economic order.

For their part, poor women resented the haughty demeanor of their would-be benefactors, but they too shared Southern notions of dignity and honor. The barely literate Louisa Hughes asked Alabama Governor William H. Smith for a loan so she could make a crop. Her husband had recently died, and their four young children had little to eat. At the end of her sad letter she promised to repay the money once they got back on their feet. But pride got in the way of seeking help, and many women waited until matters had grown desperate if not impossible. Despite her obvious need for government rations to feed her three small children, invalid Eugenia Carew pathetically clung to her self-respect: "I begin to feel as if I should economize my strength or I will make myself more of a dependent. How I hate the word, but I do feel myself to be one."[17]

Yet pride proved to be poor sustenance in a land where widespread poverty shattered old dreams and stifled new ones. Single women or widows trying to support their children faced an uphill struggle for mere survival without even considering the prospects for economic mobility. And unlike their Northern counterparts, Southern widows received no government pensions. Public officials did little, not even bothering to study the problem or even count the number of widows and orphans. And though there are no reliable statistics, widespread destitution obviously overwhelmed the inadequate private relief efforts.

By 1870, many female heads of household owned little or no property and in some counties the plantation elite nearly disappeared (compare tables 4 and 5). Emancipation, falling land values, and increasing property taxes made what few acres women owned nearly worthless. For many farmers and plantation mistresses, comfort and security seemed like distant memories. Not only had the war destroyed the wealth of the once prosperous, it had also devastated the formerly large and respect-

Table 4. Female Heads of Households: Total Property Holdings, 1860
Dollar Value of Total Property (Percentages in Each Category)

County	0	1–100	101–500	501–1,000	1,001–5,000	5,001–10,000	> 10,000
Covington, Ala.	5.8	23.2	20.3	14.5	26.1	4.3	5.8
Dallas, Ala.	20.7	1.5	6.4	3.9	17.7	12.3	37.4
Coweta, Ga.	5.1	15.3	17.8	11.5	28.0	10.2	12.1
Natchitoches, La.	22.7	5.2	11.0	12.3	15.6	9.1	24.0
Attala, Miss.	10.3	3.2	12.7	10.3	38.1	5.5	19.8
Georgetown, S.C.	42.7	3.9	15.5	8.7	16.5	6.8	5.8
Sullivan, Tenn.	20.1	25.7	13.6	8.9	22.4	6.1	3.3
Weakley, Tenn.	7.5	11.7	25.9	11.7	28.1	7.9	7.1
Red River, Tex.	10.7	8.0	12.0	14.7	24.0	12.0	18.7
Halifax, Va.	28.9	15.0	7.9	5.8	14.2	10.3	17.9

Source: See table 2.

Table 5. Female Heads of Households: Total Property Holdings, 1870
Dollar Value of Total Property (Percentages in Each Category)

County	0	1–100	101–500	501–1,000	1,001–5,000	5,001–10,000	> 10,000
Covington, Ala.	69.2	3.0	16.1	9.2	10.0	0.0	0.0
Dallas, Ala.	36.3	2.0	10.9	12.9	26.6	6.0	5.2
Coweta, Ga.	39.6	3.2	14.3	15.5	24.6	2.0	0.7
Natchitoches, La.	62.8	9.7	10.6	9.2	10.6	2.4	3.4
Attala, Miss.	35.3	7.2	14.1	20.9	20.1	2.0	0.4
Georgetown, S.C.	66.0	1.0	12.4	9.3	10.3	1.0	0.0
Sullivan, Tenn.	15.6	9.3	27.3	14.5	27.0	4.8	1.4
Weakley, Tenn.	19.6	9.5	32.1	23.2	11.3	3.6	0.5
Red River, Tex.	25.5	10.2	27.5	14.3	13.3	2.0	7.1
Halifax, Va.	53.3	4.0	15.3	8.4	14.4	1.7	2.9

Data gathered from the 1870 population schedules in the manuscript census. The number of female heads of household for each county: Covington (140), Dallas (248), Coweta (252), Natchitoches (207), Attala (249), Georgetown (97), Sullivan (289), Weakley (268), Red River (98), Halifax (347). I have added the real- and personal-property figures from this census to arrive at the total-property figure. For the limitations of the 1870 census data, see the detailed discussion in Jonathan M. Wiener, *Social Origins of the New South: Alabama, 1860–1885* (Baton Rouge: Louisiana State University Press, 1978), 229–39.

able yeoman class while swelling the ranks of the poor whites. Even those who owned land found that running a farm or plantation with free labor in a depressed economy meant nothing but a life of hard work, constant worry, and mounting frustration.

2

During the war, female slaveholders had contended with the vicissitudes of taxation, impressment, recalcitrant slaves, and, most of all, the threat of emancipation. Peace removed some uncertainties but created new ones in an economy where stability remained as elusive as prosperity. In Charleston, plantation mistress Caroline Gilman stood, like Mrs. McIntyre in Flannery O'Connor's short story "The Displaced Person," surveying the wreckage of her past, feeling the urge to break with that past, yet making plans to repair the long-neglected family cemetery.[18]

And if the fictional Mrs. McIntyre had long ago decided that she could not rely on anyone—white or black—to help her, many real-life women in the postwar South soon reached the same conclusion. According to legend, courageous plantation mistresses rolled up their sleeves to begin anew, and here legend does not stray far from the truth. Recouping a family's losses or refurbishing the old homestead absorbed most of their energy; a few widows became so successful they could afford to spurn marriage proposals. For most women, however, making a modest living was now their highest ambition. Sarah Hine and her husband could barely afford to rent a plantation in Thomas County, Georgia. While he tended the fields, she tried to make the dilapidated house into a home. Milking the cows and raising chickens, she sold milk and eggs in Thomasville and eventually hired a servant to do the cooking, ironing, and washing. Keeping a piano and some silver plate as mementos of genteel respectability, she cheerfully wrote to a friend that they were growing more comfortable all the time.[19] A modicum of security, perhaps (and not much by antebellum standards), but she had fared much better than many of her neighbors.

For plantation mistress and farmwife alike, a host of troubles—some merely bothersome, others potentially disastrous—dogged their quest for economic self-sufficiency. The unsettled labor situation compounded the usual difficulties caused by flood, drought, and crop failure.[20] Even seasoned planters scrambled to make money, and women often regretted their inexperience. During the war they had learned to plant, harvest, and market crops and some had even kept their own accounts, but the tasks hardly became easier after 1865 and the problem of confidence persisted. "Woman as I am, & ignorant of planting affairs," an Alabamian confessed, "I think, indeed feel sure, my being there [the plantation] in person will make things work more smoothly & successfully." Many other women too doubted their own ability but still tried to take charge. The shortage of capital, declining land values, and wildly fluctuating crop prices magnified small mistakes into fatal errors. Large estates ate up more and more money for less and less profit.[21] Often unable to hire enough hands, women saw the weeds take over productive fields and the grounds of beautiful estates fall into neglect. Whether they could even hang onto their land appeared at best problematical.

After several exasperating months on a plantation in Quincy, Florida, Clara Elizabeth Barrow felt angry and betrayed: "It really has seemed to me that every body combined to rob me pitilessly of the heritage to which I was justly entitled. I met these efforts with but a weak woman's weapons, and have done what I could to stem the tide of oppression." Unreliable overseers and rising labor costs forced even careful plantation mistresses to plunge deeply into debt. Ann Faulkner declined her brother's invitation to move in with his family because she wanted to support herself, but the desire for independence exacted a high price. After paying her taxes and laborers, she had little money left and like many other women struggled with overdue bills and the threat of bankruptcy.[22] Such women naturally felt trapped—unable to abandon their land, their homes, their ties to plantation life—but at the same time facing an unrelievedly dark future.

For those torn between holding on to and giving up the old way of life, yearly losses forced a decision without making it any easier. One might cut back operations or simply sell out, but long-time plantation mistresses seldom gave up even at the risk of their physical and emotional health. The daily stress of managing a large estate under the least-favorable conditions produced overwhelming perplexity, self-doubt, and occasionally severe depression. Mary Chesnut's cousin sobbed constantly about her poverty and the helpless condition of her three young children; worry and debt finally drove a friend of Maria Fleet into an insane asylum.[23]

Because so many men had died or returned home from the war disabled, women still had to run farms and plantations, though at a decidedly unpropitious time.[24] Those who succeeded were usually older widows or younger women who later married and turned the responsibilities for managing the property over to their husbands. For a woman to run a large plantation still struck people as a novel experiment with dubious prospects, and the most determined mistresses found it hard to obtain respect, much less credit, from male planters, bankers, and storekeepers.

Hostility to enterprising women also distorted market operations and slowed economic growth.

A series of letters written by Suzanne Keitt to merchant and cotton factor William A. Carrigan during 1878 and 1879 illustrates the anomalous position of female planters in a depressed economy. Sinking under an avalanche of debts and in danger of losing her late father's plantations in Marlboro County, South Carolina, she considered various means, including a legally questionable transfer of property, to avoid the demands of importunate creditors. Vowing to go into court rather than surrender any of her land, she decided that "it would be weakness to yield further." Obviously as proud and stubborn as any male member of the South Carolina aristocracy, she felt confident about working her family's former slaves and offhandedly dismissed rumors of an impending black exodus. Yet the plantation accounts frequently fell into arrears, forcing her to ask Carrigan for advances against the next crop and even for a loan of six cotton bales. Acutely aware of being a woman in a traditionally masculine preserve, she diplomatically reassured him that she intended to behave properly: "Don't think me unreasonable and grasping. I am only determined to merit a 'well done' by showing the honorable energetic business talent of my honored father." Yet in asking for an extension on a loan, a lower interest rate, and more control over the sale of her cotton, she insisted on equitable treatment: "You must also grant me with it [the loan extension] certain privileges whereby I will be enabled to do business with the advantages of a man. If I am to do the work of a man, I must have his tools. In other words, I must have the necessary funds to make advantages."[25] Although such assertive language seldom appeared in the letters of female planters, her remarks cut to the heart of their dilemma. Facing the common problems of debt, too much land, and uncertain credit, she also worked under the added burden of prejudice against her sex. Solving one difficulty too often came at the expense of creating a new one. And even after plantation mistresses could put their finances in order, they still had to deal with a labor revolution.

3

As slavery had disintegrated during the war, white women glimpsed the future of Southern race relations. Disliking what they saw and trying to ignore the consequences of Confederate defeat, many fully expected emancipation to be gradual. Surely slavery would be replaced with some other form of forced labor; whites and blacks living and working together in a free society seemed beyond imagination. But regardless of desperate attempts to believe that somehow old ways would survive, emancipation came. Former slaveholders could hardly consider themselves masters and mistresses any longer and instead had to grapple with the reality of what had once been unthinkable.[26]

In this painful period of adjustment, gender made a difference. Many white women had worked more intimately with slaves, especially house servants, than had their fathers, husbands, or brothers. By seeing themselves as the grand matriarchs of paternalistic tradition, they had seldom viewed slavery simply as a labor system. Although farm women might have been more hard nosed in dealing with slaves, they just as often aped the opinions and practices of their wealthier neighbors. If this more personal approach to the institution could mean either an easier or harder life for the slaves, it inevitably made it more difficult for many white women to give up their old ways of management.

After all, no one could foresee the consequences of this economic and social upheaval, and uncertainty if not fear characterized the response of many white women. Most mistresses simply gathered the slaves around the farm or plantation house for the fateful announcement. Some dropped the news like a thunderbolt from heaven; others made elaborate speeches filled with admonitions about hard work, the responsibilities of freedom, and the dangers of listening to smooth-talking Yankees. The emotional tension ran high and after months of postponing this confrontation with the inevitable, distraught mistresses broke down. Despite their best efforts to appear stoic, many women cried openly.[27] Some regretted the loss of property; others mourned the severing of old relationships. Although slaveholders had used paternalism to bind slaves to their owners and to stifle independence or rebelliousness, the whites became victims of their own ethos. Self-interest and sentimentality, along with many other conflicting emotions, became hopelessly tangled as white women saw their world come crashing down around them. Many mistresses desperately tried to hold onto their slaves, alternatively pleading with, cajoling, and threatening them.

To somehow maintain the old sense of command, to appear imperturbable when a volcano was bubbling under one's feet, demanded more effort than disheartened Southerners could muster. "I did not miss the servants," Mary Rowe declared, "I rather felt relieved when I saw the last one close the yard gate." Perhaps so, but such remarks often lacked conviction, and few white women sincerely welcomed the end of slavery. To compensate for a sense of loss and betrayal, plantation mistresses tried to deny their emotions but could not hide their bitterness and anger. "The sooner that nest is broken up the better," the usually mild-mannered Mary Jones snapped. "My heart is pained and sickened with their vileness and falsehood in every way. I long to be delivered from the race."[28] This exasperation hardly meant turning one's back on the old order, and Mary Jones, like many other white women, still preferred black servants.

Whatever the wishes of their former owners, the freedmen wandered away from the farms and plantations and became more independent. All this caused much bewilderment and not a little resentment. After two of her kitchen servants had left, Mary Rowe fumed: "I feel like I could shoot them as soon as to look at them, the ungrateful imps." Outrage over the freed people's "disloyalty" revealed the depth of paternalistic self-deception. But women who could not pay their taxes, who watched their men scramble to earn a pittance, and who worked the land with little hope of making a living, readily blamed the Negroes for their woes. The course of Reconstruction also made the blacks natural scapegoats for white anger. By denouncing the freedmen (or their "Black Republican" friends), Southerners of both sexes could avoid responsibility for their own plight while at the same time holding onto their racial presuppositions. Emily Battey dreaded to see her nieces and nephews become " 'hewers of wood and drawers of water' . . . while a race of savages are placed actually politically *above* them."[29]

Of course many women themselves became "hewers of wood and drawers of water," and they surely must have wondered whether the curse of Ham had suddenly fallen upon them instead of on their hapless former slaves. For yeoman and planter alike, emancipation presaged a domestic world turned upside down. "People South will have to begin a new way of living," Sophia Witherspoon declared. "I always waited on myself as well as most people who had been raised with servants, & I miss mine very much." Claims of self-sufficiency followed by the inevitable admission of dependence on black labor typified the uneasy responses of slaveholding women to the sudden departure of their bondsmen. Wistfully recalling the servants in her father's house and frustrated by dealing with free Negroes, Margaret Gillis ruefully acknowledged that her "ignorance and inexperience" tried her husband's patience. She aptly described her new life: "I have my hands full certain, not knowing how to do any thing, it takes me long to do what I do." From ease and grace to sweat and drudgery, women marveled at the transformation. "I never even so much as washed out a pocket handkerchief with my own hands," a Louisiana plantation mistress confessed, "and now I have to do all my work."[30]

One of slavery's many ironies still haunted Southern households. White women had often bragged about pampering and petting their house servants, but emancipation showed who had really been pampered and petted. One girl could not comb her own hair; a matron cried at night because she had no one to wash her feet.[31] Although Northern travelers and white women themselves exaggerated this helplessness, pride of birth and class made some reluctant to soil their hands with honest work. In a society that had elevated pretense into an art form, keeping up appearances reflected a certain grim desperation.

Supposedly genteel women seldom fooled their neighbors or themselves. Few could afford to worry any longer about propriety or outmoded convention. Washtubs and cows marked the change. On washday, delicate hands grew chapped and blistered; every muscle ached in protest. And once that tiresome task was finished, the ironing awaited, though many families' depleted wardrobes mercifully reduced the labor. Novices approached these chores gingerly, first announcing their intention to undertake some unprecedented job, then slowly and often clumsily proceeding to work. Susan Bradford relied on a neighbor's generosity for milk because she would not approach a cow: "I am terribly afraid of Bossy. She looks like a dreadful monster to me." A braver housewife steeled herself for the ordeal but ended up squirting more milk in her hair and eyes than in the pail. As for the cow, she refused to stand still for such amateurish handling and angrily switched her tail across the woman's face.[32]

Of all the household tasks, cooking required the most careful and persistent attention. For women used to relying on slaves, preparing a meal became certainly an arduous, sometimes a humorous, and occasionally a dangerous undertaking. When Ella Thomas tried to make a cake, the batter stuck to her hands until a house servant finally extricated her from the mess. Cornelia McDonald awkwardly banged around the kitchen, badly burning her leg and foot with a hot teakettle. Menus became Spartan and monotonous. And even as women cleared the dishes from the table, the question of what to serve at the next meal loomed before them.[33]

However tentative these first efforts, plantation mistresses, farmwives, and their daughters slowly accommodated themselves to a new age. As during the war, successes in the kitchen and throughout the house produced a new pride of accomplishment. The labor seemed somehow less degrading when most other women could no longer avoid the drudgery. Susanna Waddell marveled at how easily she had grown accustomed to cooking dinner each day; Eugenia Carew boasted of her prowess in washing and sewing. Even when they hurt all over and the list of unfinished tasks seemed endless, many women thought they did a better job than black servants had ever done. Especially during the first months of freedom, plantation mistresses worked hard to show their former slaves that they could survive without help. But many could not quite bring it off and took to cursing the freedmen. "Plague take the lazy nigger," Mary Rowe declared after a long day of cooking, cleaning, and ironing. "I am independent of them."[34]

But such independence seldom came easily or brought much satisfaction. Often regretting the past, dreading the future, and deploring the present, plantation mistresses and farm women mechanically went about their work with increasingly less verve. The early pride of amateur housekeepers wore off quickly; weariness and despair took over. The daguerreotypes of the period often show pensive, grim-looking women obviously worn down and worn out by the demands of running large households. "I did the washing for six weeks," an exhausted Kate Foster wrote, "came near ruining myself for life as I was too delicately raised for such hard work." She may have overstated the challenge, but the physical and emotional demands forced some women to admit that their experiment in self-reliance had failed. Rising at six each morning, Emma Holmes swept the floors, washed clothes, cooked the meals and hated her new life. For all too many women, the days and years ahead promised little relief from soul-deadening toil.[35] Dramatic changes had soon given way to dull routine, and the domestic labor crisis remained a constant topic of conversation, speculation, and complaint in Southern homes. Especially among upper-class women, the conviction grew that running a proper household required black servants.

Although women in both the North and South had long grumbled about a shortage of reliable help, the withdrawal of many black women from the labor force after the war dismayed Southern housewives. Yet freedwomen had obviously imitated their former mistresses in showing a disdain for housework, especially housework performed in someone else's house, and in any case often ended up returning to domestic service. Despite some instability and uncertainty, there was an adequate supply of black servants. For white women, the problem came with having to pay wages and not being able to extract as much labor from the freedwomen as they had from female slaves.[36] Racial pride and the low status of domestic service prevented poor whites from taking up the slack. Experiments with Irish servants failed, and housewives admitted their preference for blacks.[37]

By often ignoring the distinction between slave and freedman and by still demanding unquestioning obedience from "their people," white women simply made their situation more difficult. Like anxious slaveholders who had sought reassurance in the supposed docility of their bondsmen, housewives still expected black people to act submissively. "My servants are just the same as before the war," Helen Sawyer announced hopefully. "They are attached to us and say they are willing always to live with us—freedom does not seem to affect them in the least." Oblivious to the contradiction, the same women who feared insurrections and the unsettling influence of Yankee soldiers declared blacks unchanged by emancipation. After descanting on the laziness and general worthlessness of free Negroes, a Virginian praised the fine service performed by several black women on her dairy farm.[38] Southerners had either to believe that ties of interest and even mutual affection still bound black to white or concede that their social system had always been held together by a rope of sand.

Convenient myths therefore brought important psychological benefits. For despite the bitterness and disillusionment of many former slaveholders, paternalistic ideology survived. Nearly a decade after emancipation, Elizabeth Oakes Smith rejoiced over the natural harmony between blacks and their former masters. From selecting Christmas presents for the servants to caring for the sick, some women still enjoyed presiding over their extended families.[39] Although poverty limited the more lavish displays of old-fashioned paternalism, the ideals of mutual obligation and protection somehow endured, at least among women who had once occupied comfortable positions in the Southern elite.

Despite the hollowness of many of these gestures, some whites and blacks knew their assigned roles in the traditional rituals of the ancien régime. In many instances, the funerals for elderly servants or their mistresses became the last rites of a dying social order. After the death of a family retainer, Myra Inman prayed she would see him again in heaven, where distinctions of "color or rank" did not matter. Both, of course, mattered a great deal on this earth despite white efforts to conceal arbitrary authority and an often irresponsible wielding of vast power. Perhaps to salve uneasy consciences but more likely to fulfill their own social ideals, some women made small bequests to their former slaves. A Texas mistress instructed her field hands and house servants to attend her funeral and even designated several black men as pall-bearers.[40] Although they faithfully carried out her wishes, such scenes became rarities—and for white women a sad reminder of a world they had lost.

For with a few notable exceptions the bonds between mistress and slave had to be broken.[41] Tearful partings, however romanticized in reminiscences and plantation fiction, softened the blow for both races. After all, love and mutual respect had occasionally grown in the inhospitable soil of exploitation and oppression. The exodus of "mammies" and other fixtures of the old order grieved white women already reeling from the twin blows of Confederate defeat and economic devastation. "Tonight Lulu came as usual to see me safe in bed," wrote Susan Bradford in describing a typical scene in this drama, "and when she had said 'goodnight' and she came back and leaning over me, she said, 'I'm always goin' to love my child,' then she was gone. It makes me feel queer; life has changed." But just as racism and condescension had corroded the old relationships, so also the departure of the freedmen sometimes exposed the shallowness of humanitarian pretensions. Eliza Andrews hated to see her former slaves acquire surnames and insist on being addressed as *Mr.* or *Mrs.* "All these changes are very sad to me despite their comic side," she confided to her diary. "There will be no more old mammies and daddies, no more old uncles and aunties. . . . The sweet ties that bound our old family servants to us will be broken and replaced with envy and ill-will."[42] Although she was determined that this would not happen in her home, the continuation of old racial customs either rested on brute force or the willingness of blacks to behave like grateful dependents for the benefit of their once mighty owners.

And the psychological shock of emancipation also produced for a time a new and phonier kind of paternalism. Annie Row remembered how her mistress, who had always freely used the whip, suddenly began saying good morning to her former slaves. As women wrestled with the question of how to treat—really how to manage—black servants, Cornelia Phillips Spencer offered the younger generation of housewives revealing advice on the subject. Hoping to preserve the more humane features of slavery, she urged women to take time for black religious instruction and to show an interest in their people's "little matters." As members of the superior race, white women should not expect too much of the freedmen and should tolerate their faults and occasional assertions of independence. Concluding a series of newspaper essays on the postwar servant problem, she urged her readers to assume the role of ladies bountiful stretching out their arms to uplift the members of an unfortunate and degraded race.[43] If slavery had been a school for civilization— as paternalistic mistresses had so often claimed—the obligation of white women to their black pupils survived both the war and emancipation.

Yet paternalism had always been a means of asserting authority, and white women continued to meddle in black people's private lives. Attempting to arrange marriages and offering stern lectures on chastity and monogamy, they sometimes kept the freedmen in a state of humiliating subservience. A Texas housewife allowed a black girl to eat with the family but treated her like a lap dog. In recalling those days, former slave Susan Smith admitted: "Dey mek monkey outer me at de table." White women often considered black children their responsibility, if not their property, and occasionally fought with the mothers for custody. In the eyes of their former mistresses, even black adults remained little more than amusing and exasperating children. After a favorite servant had fulsomely apologized for an insolent remark, Emma Holmes rejoiced to find her "once more the Nina of old, who had always petted us & whom we had always favored & indulged."[44] Maybe so, but in such cases appearances might be especially deceiving, and the complexity of black behavior during Reconstruction often defied easy categorization. Expressions of confidence in the old ways more often than not only set the stage for sobering disillusionment.

In the end, attempts to revive antebellum paternalism foundered; declarations of noble intent rang hollow; the shell remained, but the spirit had departed. "Just now we are passing a fine plantation," Mary Rives noted in her diary as she rode near the Red River in central Louisiana, "nearly all the cabins deserted. How differently it looks from what it was five years ago, then the slave was preparing for a long year of work, but his cabin was comfortable, his master attending to his wants. Now the 'Freedmen' are, many of them, wandering from place to place, with no abiding home." But however much they might worry about the fate of their former slaves, many white women felt their own emotional trauma more deeply. Mistresses shook their heads in wonder, and in sorrow, over how quickly their slaves had left, how little they had really cared for their owners, how little they had accepted the paternalistic ethos. "Many [slaves] I have raised from infancy, watched over their orphan childhood, and reared them to manhood," a confused and disheartened Nancy Robinson wrote. "Now regardless of my feelings for them, they seemed pleased with the change of going." Other blacks might feign loyalty so that they could still live off their white folks. At best, Grace Elmore concluded, the two races retained a "polite and gentle interest" toward each other, but more commonly "bitter feeling" and "sharp antagonism" characterized the relationship.[45] Bonds of affection, however strained and one sided they had often been, gave way to mutual suspicion if not open hostility.

Because white women now had to deal with blacks as free laborers rather than as slave workers or childlike dependents, economic considerations became paramount. Although more women took charge of farms and plantations after the war, they did so at an especially inopportune time. As economist Gavin Wright has perceptively argued, Southern "laborlords" suddenly became Southern "landlords" as emancipation stripped away their investment in human property. At the same time, land values plummeted, and once wealthy Southerners found that many of their assets had either disappeared or lost much of their worth. In the midst of all these difficulties, the labor situation remained unsettled for more than a decade after Appomattox. Experiments with wage labor soon gave way to more complex sharecropping arrangements, and white women joined white men in wrestling with the problems of this transition.[46]

For the first time, many women had to worry about both outdoor and indoor labor, and no longer could the servant problem be defined in strictly domestic terms. That the Negro would not work voluntarily had long been a white article of faith, and in the first few years after the war, housewives grumbled that the freedmen would rather live on government handouts or go hungry than earn an honest living.[47] Field hands appeared careless and sullen; house servants perfunctorily went about their tasks; the freedmen in general seemed aloof and required close supervision. Most labored only when the spirit moved, constantly testing the limits of freedom and their mistresses' patience by skillfully feigning various illnesses or injuries.[48] However reminiscent of slavery days, this familiar litany of complaints now also stemmed from the frustration of white women who found that the old methods of compulsion and cajolery no longer worked in a free labor society.

More even than their poor work habits, the freedmen's demeanor infuriated sensitive white women; the word *insolent* appeared often in postwar descriptions of black behavior. House servants suddenly refused to do tasks they had routinely performed as slaves, and their attitude outraged housewives used to a prompt response to any request. Plantation mistresses often confused assertiveness with impudence and interpreted any request for better wages or shorter hours as brash impertinence. Although these women might picture themselves as domestic martyrs, the long-suffering victims of surly and hard-to-please servants, Amelia Barr offered a more candid admission: "To be without them [black servants] is a misery and to have them is just as bad."[49] Like many others, she appeared caught between her need for help and her economic and racial prejudices. Expecting both efficiency and at least a modicum of the old subservience—white women might have seen it as the old intimacy—these former mistresses appeared doomed to disappointment on both counts.

To deal with blacks as autonomous human beings was nearly inconceivable, and few white women could tolerate challenges to their vaunted mastery in the household. Imperious housewives insisted that freedmen address them as mistress and act accordingly. Even women who had some basic understanding of black aspirations adjusted badly to the give and take of employer-employee relations. "It seems humiliating to be compelled to bargain and haggle with our servants about wages," Eliza Andrews wrote in exasperation.[50]

Yet bargain and haggle they did. With the encouragement of the Freedmen's Bureau, white women joined other farmers and planters in experimenting with annual labor contracts. In moments of candor, plantation mistresses praised Northern army officers for making the Negroes work and admitted the system operated far better than anyone could have expected.[51] Still, free labor conflicted with the habits of a lifetime. Even farm women and plantation mistresses who acted in good faith usually grew frustrated and angry, especially when black workers sought to change the terms of their contracts every few months.[52] Quaint notions about the proper relationship between mistress and servant seemed wildly irrelevant to the chaotic conditions of labor in the postwar South. But to view black people strictly as workers was also difficult for many white women.

Although a coldly economic calculus could never entirely supplant older, paternalistic attitudes, plantation mistresses talked more and more about profit and loss and less and less about loyalty and affection. Bristling at the slightest suggestion of bad faith on their part, they fumed over the mendacity of servants who seemed to do nothing but avoid work and complain about their wages. After two black drivers had brought Mary Jones before a Freedmen's Bureau officer to challenge the legality of a contract, she exploded in anger:

> I have told the people that in doubting my word they offered me the greatest insult I ever received in my life; that I had considered them friends and treated them as such, giving them gallons of clabber every day and syrup once a week, with rice and extra dinners; but that now they were only laborers under contract, and only the law would rule between us, and I would require every one of them to come up to the mark in their duty on the plantation. The effect has been decided, and I am not sorry for the position we hold mutually. They have relieved me of the constant desire and effort to do something to promote their comfort.[53]

Even if she exaggerated and in fact still worried about her black dependents, the trials of free labor often stretched the sinews of paternalism beyond the breaking point.

This new language of contractual obligation, which now competed with the traditional rhetoric about white and black families living together in an organic community, showed the severe strain placed on Southern households. Chronic poverty forced families to carefully consider every expenditure and exacerbated the racial tension on Southern farms and plantations. Managing black field hands made Clara Elizabeth Barrow "feel that I had taken up my abode in Pandemonium." After firing most of them, she angrily asked "what great crime . . . was sufficient to call down the terrible wrath of heaven upon my devoted head." Wild talk of shooting "saucy" blacks was heard occasionally among yeoman women. And if actions seldom followed such threats, the words themselves became more violent (and fantastic). "I wish the Yanks had the free negroes strung around their necks and all in the bottom of the arctic ocean covered with ice a hundred feet thick," Margaret Gillis fulminated.[54]

Venting their frustration in letters, diaries, and private conversations, white women were really searching for some way to control black labor.

Coercion became the desideratum for those who fondly recalled the advantages of forced labor. Hypersensitive about their eroding authority, some women harshly punished any black person bold enough to claim the prerogatives of freedom.[55] But even a stout stick or a powerful whip could not restore a world of domineering mistresses and submissive slaves. Instead of either cowing or patronizing black people, Southern women now feared them. Frightened housewives reported numerous robberies; rumors of idle freedmen rampaging through the countryside spread rapidly. When thefts occurred, the most loyal servants could not escape suspicion, and what little trust remained between the races was soon swallowed up by recrimination and anger.[56]

Tales of impending black insurrections—significantly embellished with lurid predictions of rape or forced marriages between black men and white women—steadily declined after the end of 1865, but strong racial feelings survived along with remnants of proslavery ideology.[57] Hoary biblical, biological, and cultural arguments for the inferiority of the Negro appeared in women's diaries and letters. Believing that God had ordained the institution of slavery in the best interests of both races, they predicted that the freedmen would soon revert to the barbaric condition of their African ancestors.[58] Emancipation seemed a nightmare to many white women, though they certainly fell victim to self-fulfilling prophecies. And even taking into account the obvious paranoia, a more virulent racism, shorn of its paternalistic trappings, appeared among women who had once proudly claimed to embody the ideals of the Christian slaveholder.

As usual in Southern history, caste proved stronger than class. Wives of tenant farmers would talk pleasantly with black neighbors so long as the Negroes remembered to call them Mrs. and tolerated being addressed by their first names. Yeoman women as well as plantation mistresses bristled at any hint of social equality. In July 1865 the Bradford family of Tallahassee, Florida, received a visit from Peggy, a former slave who appeared at their door "unkempt, unwashed, dirty and disgusting beyond description." Demanding to be treated like any other guest, she sauntered into the living room, sat down in a chair, and refused to leave. "De ladies what kums here sets in dese cheers an' I jis' as good as dey is," she declared.[59] Susan Bradford described the scene with more humor than outrage, but many of her neighbors would have suffered apoplexy.

Impoverished Southerners sought to preserve racial distinctions as the last barrier among themselves, the freedmen, and the horrors of amalgamation. Fanny Atkisson thought the "descendants of Ham" in Athens, Georgia, behaved the same as anywhere else, "a thievish, lying, impudent set" who spent most of their time in idleness. "I would not care if one half of them had been made food for the worms," she wrote in disgust.[60] Although such extreme statements may have reflected frustration more than hatred, a commitment to white hegemony failed to ease the depression and tension of postwar Southern life. Efforts to hold on to the customs of slavery days, desperate struggles to keep up appearances, flawed and often shallow attempts to preserve paternalism all failed. Racism helped sharpen social and economic distinctions and offered white women psychological reassurance, but the trials of free labor and racial fears inevitably compounded the difficulties of rebuilding household economies in an impoverished land. And if that was not enough, whether they lived on farms, in small towns, or even in the region's few cities, the white women of the Reconstruction South lived in a society and economy in which opportunities for their sex were shrinking. The powerful winds of postwar reaction swept away many of the loosely rooted changes of the war years and ushered in an era of diminishing expectations.

CHAPTER 13

The Janus-Faced Women of
the New South

O N A WARM AUGUST DAY IN 1861, Kate Sperry mused about what life
in the South would be like after the war: "The masculines will cook,
wash, and iron and the ladies attend to business—whew! Won't we have
fine times—voting, attending to patients—electioneering etc. We'll have
a little heaven below—husbands in blue cotton aprons with dishcloths
on their arms."[1] More whimsy than expectation, more fantasy than prob-
ability, this flight of imagination was not entirely unrealistic. Wars and
revolutions (and in some ways the Civil War was both) often produce
unintended and unexpected consequences. Although the status of women
had not been a central issue in the sectional conflict, the turmoil of the
1860s might well change traditional sex roles and alter the imbalance
of power.

Had the war made social life freer and easier? Surely peace would not
halt or reverse this trend. Might there be a roaring seventies coming in
the wake of disillusionment with the Confederate crusade? Certainly the
pressure on women to marry would lessen and the birth rate fall. Demographic change would in turn mean a better chance for women to get
a good education. Expanded schools would increase the demand for
female teachers. By the same token, teaching would be only one of many
professional fields with more opportunities for women. As the South
industrialized, as it unquestionably would, women would make up an
important part of the labor force. These dramatic changes would in turn
usher in an ideological transformation. Traditionalism would give way
to a new appreciation for women's contributions to Southern society,

more respect for women as autonomous human beings, and eventually equal rights for women, including the right to vote.

For a time it seemed that history would follow such a revolutionary course. The war had made some women less dependent and less willing to defer to the wishes of men. And as Confederate prospects dimmed, masculine authority seemed to be eroding. Harry Hammond, son of the imperious South Carolina patriarch James Henry Hammond, enjoyed having his wife fuss over household matters and could not understand why she had grown dissatisfied with the restrictions placed on her sex. Unaccustomed to any woman pushing against the limits of her sphere, he appealed to the classical formulas of feminine virtue. Believing that women helped their country by inspiring men and predicting they would rebuild and reform postwar society, Hammond surely *hoped* they would stop there.[2] In a world where intellectual, social, and economic assumptions had been shaken to their foundations, he could hardly be sure.

Inevitably the war had made women's lives less exclusively domestic. Distinctions between public and private had blurred, making faraway events suddenly seem vitally important. "Now for the first time in my life, no book can interest me," Mary Chesnut wrote excitedly in the summer of 1862. "But life is so real, so utterly earnest—fiction is so flat, comparatively. Nothing but what is going on in this distracted world of ours can arrest my attention for ten minutes at a time." With so many men away from home in the armies, women had taken on masculine jobs without worrying about propriety but without time to consider the implications. The often-frenzied scramble for survival produced more troubles than triumphs, more ennui than exhilaration. The intensity and anguish of these four years had at the same time made conservative ideals of womanhood seem more attractive as the upheaval deprived many Southern housewives of both their economic and psychological security. In extreme cases, shattering wartime experiences might create a temporary nihilism, described well by William Faulkner's Drusilla Sartoris:

> Why not stay awake now? Who wants to sleep now, with so much happening, so much to see? Living used to be dull, you see. Stupid. You lived in the same house your father was born in, and your father's sons and daughters had the sons and daughters of the same Negro slaves to nurse and coddle; and then you grew up and fell in love with your acceptable young man, and in time you would

marry him, in your mother's wedding gown, perhaps, and with the same silver for presents she had received; and then you settled down forevermore while you got children to feed and bathe and dress until they grew up too; and then you and your husband died quietly and were buried together maybe on a summer afternoon just before suppertime. Stupid, you see. But now you can see for yourself how it is; it's fine now; you don't have to worry about the house and the silver, because they got burned and carried away; and you don't have to worry about the Negroes because they tramp the roads all night waiting for a chance to drown in homemade Jordan; and you don't have to worry about getting children to bathe and feed and change because the young men can ride away and get killed in the fine battles; and you don't even have to sleep alone, you don't have to sleep at all; and so, all you have to do is show the stick to the dog now and then and say, 'Thank God for nothing.'[3]

Seldom of course did despair and cynicism run so deeply. Yet for most white women, as for Southerners generally, the promise of a "New South" remained unfulfilled. Social upheaval proved short lived and ephemeral when fashion and frivolity made an early return to the conquered South. Despite a temporary shortage of men, young women—with very few exceptions—were still expected to marry and have several children. Educational reform for women continued at the snaillike pace of the antebellum decades. Expanded teaching opportunities proved to be a decidedly mixed blessing, and most other professions remained closed to women. Industrialization advanced slowly, with yeoman and poor white women competing for a small number of jobs. An occasional example of progressive thinking and a modest expansion of female property rights could not forestall an ideological reaction. The rhetoric of progress might stir ambition, but dreams of achievement and mobility were usually frustrated, and reform, that glittering and dangerous Yankee notion, proved chimerical.

1

The most dramatic wartime social changes often masked the survival of traditional assumptions. Contemporaries exaggerated the importance of new customs and underestimated the potent influence of a deeply ingrained conservatism. Even if many women traveled without an escort for the first time or met young men without having a chaperon present, expectations concerning female roles and destiny remained largely un-affected.[4] Slight alterations in the Southern social landscape should not obscure the basic continuity of a class, racial, and sexual hierarchy.

Although older Southerners were sure that the war had made young people, especially young ladies, forget all sense of propriety, they should not have despaired so easily. Powerful inhibitions prevented women from conversing with a strange man or initiating an innocent corre-spondence. After demurely talking to a dashing officer on a train, refugee Malvina Waring had second thoughts: "Were we wrong in accepting the attention? . . . We have been thrust forth from the safe environment of our homes and cannot afford to take any risks." Such hesitancy and timidity stultified Southern social life and confined women to the safety of the home, where polite hypocrisy could cover up chronic frustration. In several novels but most notably in *Virginia*, Ellen Glasgow brilliantly recaptured the tension and uncertainty of young women coming of age in the postwar South: "To be feminine in the eyes of the period, was to be morally passive." No matter how impatiently, women still had to wait for men to take the initiative: "Never to be one's self—never to let one's soul or body relax from the attitude of expectancy into the attitude of achievement."[5] The war had destroyed so many things, but it had not destroyed women's sense of dependence and powerlessness. In the im-poverished South, the idea of female autonomy seemed as radical and unrealistic as ever. As the economic gap between rich and poor narrowed and when some of the once wealthy and privileged looked like tatter-demalions, old social prejudices—particularly the desire to maintain a certain social distance between the so-called respectable and the so-called ordinary people—acquired new importance.

Indeed much postwar social commentary has a timeless quality and is filled with familiar warnings about the dangers of violating genteel conventions. In a series of articles for a Presbyterian magazine, Cornelia Phillips Spencer counseled young girls to avoid the free and easy man-ners that had corrupted all classes during the war. Afraid that flirtation threatened "modesty and reserve," she advised her readers to value self-esteem over the flattery of smooth-talking men. Too many parents thoughtlessly encouraged coquetry and forgot that "the influence a young woman exerts is strongest where it is passive, where it radiates from her character."[6]

Such a definition of femininity may have sounded hopelessly outdated to young girls who had experienced the exhilaration of a freer social life during the war, but parents need not have worried that their daughters would go to the devil. Flirtation after all seemed no more widespread and still received a healthy share of criticism. "I do not allow caresses nor do I accept presents from young men," Susan Bradford declared. "Even if I am young I have learned one piece of wisdom, 'It is the unattainable that men sigh for.' "[7] The postwar debates between the more cautious and more daring young girls illustrated how little war had altered common social assumptions and practices.

Indeed the restoration of familiar social patterns occurred with startling speed. Though most parties seemed fairly sedate affairs and families had little money to spend on refreshments and entertainment, ambitious women still tried to ape their more prosperous neighbors, and by the late 1860s high society had revived. Even the hard pressed Ella Thomas attended a tournament, complete with knights in armor and ladies in fancy costumes.[8] Holding dress balls and other spectacles recalled a glorious past and a vanished splendor.

Such affairs caused heads to shake and tongues to wag as the old clashes between evangelical asceticism and elite hedonism intensified after the war. Given the economic hardships faced by most families, lavish social affairs appeared as obscene anomalies. Conspicuous consumption was bound to stir class resentment, not only among yeomen and poor whites, but also among women who had once been part of the upper crust. "In spite of national humiliation & grief & individual sorrow . . . Folly and Frivolity still reign supreme among a certain set, the same who danced before the sod was settled over the bloody graves of their kindred during the war," Emma Holmes complained.[9] Gentility and piety struggled for control of polite society, and the cultural debates within Southern homes raged fiercely.

Battle lines were drawn immediately on the fashion question. Although women still proudly wore calico dresses, the new designs from New York and other Northern cities beckoned those longing to replace their drab wartime attire. Only a year after the surrender, Paris ball gowns, velvet dresses, and elaborate headdresses appeared at elegant social affairs. In remote Sumter, South Carolina, women promenaded through the streets, bedecked in imported bonnets of every imaginable size, shape, and style. Squandering the remnants of fortunes on such displays or conforming to the latest fads seemed foolish and pathetic, but the social pressures were hard to resist. Prepared to spend five hundred dollars on new clothes, Eliza Smith resolved that her daughters should no longer wear the coarse stockings and dresses—the "slave" clothing—that had served so well during the war.[10] Her decision neatly encapsulates the persistent importance of social distinctions, especially those based on class and race.

But if such considerations widened the social distance between the poor, the precariously comfortable, and the quondam wealthy living in reduced circumstances, social excess also divided the upper class as one woman's necessity became another's extravagance. "Nothing is more contemptible than broken-down gentility trying to ape rich vulgarity," Eliza Andrews sniffed. Thrifty women refused to worship the golden calf of Northern fashion, and a faint echo of Confederate nationalism resounded in calls for distinctly Southern dress. All in vain. Mary Brown reported that too many so-called ladies had hiked their skirts far above their knees in the most brazen Yankee style. Even the debt-ridden went on occasional spending sprees. Warnings against acquiring a "fast" reputation failed to restrain exuberant young girls determined to enjoy buying new clothes after such a long period of doing without almost everything.[11]

After all, most Southern women well understood what society expected of their sex. Whether visiting a neighbor or attending a fancy party, whether wearing a torn calico dress or arrayed in a velvet gown, they remained part of a social order in which class differences and social performance still mattered. Poverty and practicality pulled women toward social restraint even as old habits and a desire for conformity drove them toward self-indulgence. However ragged and bedraggled, more often than not they clung to their faith in a social hierarchy.

2

Along with an old-fashioned social code, traditional definitions of woman's place also survived the war as female destiny remained closely tied to the domestic circle. The pressure to marry and raise a family remained powerful even though a shortage of men made the search for suitable husbands more difficult.[12] Because single women still had few alternatives to marriage, conventional thinking naturally prevailed. During the 1850s, Kate Foster had scorned marriage because it meant submission to male authority, but age and the betrothals of several friends changed her mind. By 1871 she dreaded the future: "An old maid's life presents no allurement to a woman who feels a woman's life is incomplete without man's sustaining influence, each needing the other to create that soul music which is the result of a happy union. A woman alone, in this cold world, how sad it is—no eye in which to see the reflection of her own love." Although women seldom described the problems of being single in a society where marriage defined the norm, hints of their suffering, struggles, and occasional triumphs appear in diaries and family correspondence.[13] With slim prospects for economic independence or mobility, women had to weigh the possibilities with a new realism. The last third of the nineteenth hardly seemed the right time in Southern history to challenge orthodox assumptions or to disturb long-established domestic habits. And though idealistic girls still tried to swim against the tide of cultural expectations or even briefly rebel against them, marriage remained for most women an unavoidable—and many would have thought a mostly desirable—fate.

Indeed the wartime matrimonial mania continued into the late 1860s as both men and women searched for affection, stability, and security in a time of upheaval and anxiety. Though most Southerners could barely afford the plainest wedding, the rush toward the altar proceeded apace. Old warnings about hasty and ill-considered matches went largely unheeded. Cordelia Scales decried small pox and matrimony as the "two dreadful epidemics" of postwar life.[14] But sarcastic remarks about marital bliss hardly deterred the unwary. The same women who condemned hasty nuptials often envied their married friends and feared being left alone.

At the same time, the trials faced by many of these couples in the postwar South—and again one can hardly exaggerate the effects of widespread poverty—raised unsettling questions. Too often a harsh reality clashed with hopes and expectations of domestic nirvana. Whether or not most men and women found connubial felicity, unhappy marriage became an important theme in advice literature and novels. Although a wife was still expected to obey her husband and ignore his shortcomings, signs of nagging discontent and sad resignation appeared. If forbearance remained the accepted standard of female behavior, forbearance now had limits. According to Cornelia Phillips Spencer, women had learned the lessons of tolerance all too well: "Let them not lose their own identity in the effort," she suggested with keen psychological insight, "nor for the sake of making others comfortable and happy, try to believe that a half is equal to a whole, or that after all there is very little difference between them." Wives had trouble living up to the ideal of what writer

Kate Chopin termed the "mother-women . . . who idolized their children, worshiped their husbands, and esteemed it a holy privilege to efface themselves as individuals and grow wings as ministering angels."[15] Both Spencer and Chopin worried that women might lose their individualism—the core of personality—but admitted that wives and mothers seldom questioned and rarely rebelled against their lot.

Simply getting by from day to day required most of their time and energy, and complaining seemed pointless. The demands of marriage and household chores blunted forceful expressions of discontent, and even more than the inevitable marital conflicts, frequent pregnancies, difficult deliveries, and the trials of child rearing wore women down. Although financial woes and general hopelessness may have reduced the number of births in some counties, the fertility rate for Southern women remained high compared to the northeastern and midwestern states. The common pattern of having a baby every two years produced a decided fatalism. "I hope before you receive this you will have passed over that rough road which every woman who is married and has children have to pass in their journey through life," Eliza Thompson wrote to a pregnant friend. Having one child after another strained household budgets, frayed nerves, and ruined the health of white women who often had to work much harder because of emancipation.[16] The popular image of an emaciated mother laconically caring for her glassy-eyed children was no mere figment of Northern newspaper reporters' fertile imaginations.

Although the Southern birth rate fell slowly after 1880, the drop was hardly noticeable to contemporaries. Sarah Morgan Dawson observed that bearing too many children had been women's curse since the Garden of Eden. "The simple minded culprit is well broken to the yoke," she wrote with biting irony, "that she had learned to regard her sentence as a badge of glory, and to walk to the stake like a whole band of Christian martyrs." That even sickly wives dutifully became pregnant proved to her the ultimate cruelty of an irrational and monstrous system.[17]

Such private reservations hardly ever received public expression; what passed for an official ideology seemed as rigidly conservative as ever. During the 1870 commencement ceremonies at Dunbar Female Institute in Winchester, Virginia, a physician read a poem extolling women's domestic virtues that could have been written in 1830 and would not have sounded out of place in the South of 1900 or even of 1920:

> Go to your homes, and of your mothers learn
> How to be women; *there* are earth's best schools
> ··
> Go catch from matrons by the sacred hearth
> The secret by whose might they rule the earth.
>
> The home is woman's throne; her sceptre love;
> Her crowning glory is a halo spread
> About her brow, reflected from above—
> From the soft glory round her Savior's head.

Whatever their literary shortcomings, these lines touched the important themes of female virtue and piety. Some of the graduates may have wondered whether the good doctor believed they had wasted their time gaining an education. But then even Cornelia Phillips Spencer, who held mildly progressive views on women's rights, encouraged young girls to develop domestic skills first. Despite criticizing the popular obsession with fashionable clothing, she accused any wife who failed to dress attractively of "sins against her marriage vows." For adolescents hoping to marry, she posed familiar questions: "Can you make a loaf of good bread? Can you broil a steak? Can you make good coffee? Do you know how to cook vegetables?" Describing these abilities as the "pivots on which wedded bliss turns," she admonished her young readers to cultivate practical talents.[18] On all levels of Southern society, orthodox notions of male and female spheres held sway, shaping women's lives but ironically recasting them at the same time.

For despite this apparent rigidity in defining sex roles, signs of uncertainty and change emerged. The war had revealed the absurdity of considering the "weaker sex" incapable of physical and mental exertion. "The barbaric idea that woman should occupy a subordinate and inferior position in the civilization of the world has long since exploded," Joel Chandler Harris declared twenty-five years after Appomattox, and he saw nothing wrong with women becoming writers, clerks, or even doctors and lawyers. Because Southern women had long since proved to be capable of caring for themselves, a former Confederate Colonel agreed, they should freely use all their talents.[19] Although these men stopped short of calling on women to enter the political arena and still referred to "ladies" with the usual condescension, their relatively advanced opinions showed how a conservative ideology could evolve in unexpected directions. As the postwar experience of Southern women suggested, the potential for limited change had always existed in what both contemporaries and historians have mistakenly considered a monolithic and static culture.

3

Of course these variations on conservatism opened more theoretical doors than real ones, and ideological flexibility should not be confused with meaningful social change. Nowhere was this ambivalent relationship between modest reform and the survival of conservative attitudes more apparent than in Southern schoolrooms. Most women still could not acquire the education needed to enter the professions, and even after the war, when thousands of widows had to support their families and young women had fewer chances to marry, private and public resistance to advanced training for females remained strong. Bright girls continued to sacrifice intellectual growth for marriage. As wives, they might read in their spare time or vicariously fulfill thwarted ambitions through the achievements of a son or daughter. Yet even highly motivated women faced imposing obstacles in a society where trite objections to female education passed for profound wisdom. An anonymous *Southern Review* writer baldly asserted that women were intellectually inferior to men because they preferred bonnets over books, read nothing more demanding than romantic novels, and could not comprehend complex subjects such as geometry. Concluding this article with some choice quotations from St. Paul on proper female roles, the author effectively appealed to the forces of intellectual and religious reaction.[20]

As during the antebellum decades, those seeking to reform female education had to tread cautiously. Attempting to disarm critics who worried about the dangers of domestic discontent and rebellion, they insisted that more schooling would make women better wives and mothers. As a Nashville teacher put it, young girls needed to become "dignified and refined in their manners remembering that dignity and discretion are the distinguishing marks which characterize the true woman from the counterfeit coin of her sex." Most promoters of female education spoke in similarly elevated tones intended to assuage conservative fears. Indeed, many of their arguments still appealed to class pride if not to class prejudice. Criticizing young girls for being slaves to fashion and indifferent to academic subjects, Cornelia Phillips Spencer suggested that mental development would have more lasting value than beauty, passion, or a strong will. At the same time, educated and refined women would use their intelligence and judgment to manage servants (and presumably engage in a host of charitable activities) rather than to compete with men outside the home.[21]

Yet even the most reactionary arguments for female education offered some benefits for women. Regardless of her belief in separate male and female spheres, Spencer denied the inferiority of the feminine sphere and upheld the intellectual equality of the sexes. More important, she questioned the assumption that all girls would one day marry and stoutly defended those who chose to remain single. From her perspective, education became intrinsically valuable to the woman herself rather than merely bait for potential husbands. Chastising adolescents for frivolity and their parents for encouraging flirtation, she claimed that women's intellectual development was a lifelong process whose importance rivaled spiritual growth.[22] Contending that schools should reinforce the values of an evangelical culture, she had nevertheless raised the possibility of female achievements outside the bounds of tradition.

Once the argument had proceeded this far, it might not stop at a "safe" place. Because society had failed to use the talents of half the population, Spencer believed that women must now study mathematics, chemistry, and other supposedly masculine subjects. Moreover, if female potential was to be tapped, education had to move beyond rote learning to the development of critical thinking. Predicting that women would one day work side by side with men in many fields—a radical notion in the South of the 1870s—Spencer concluded that women should obtain as much education as possible.[23]

But these advanced ideas seldom influenced popular attitudes or teaching practices, and the gap between the rhetoric of reform and the reality of the schools remained a yawning one. Belle Kearney sadly recalled how the brief and superficial education in a Canton, Mississippi, female academy had so frustrated her that she had become a religious skeptic and had later immersed herself in classical literature. After her father scotched her plans for becoming a lawyer, she felt depressed and abandoned her youthful dreams. Although few women expressed their disappointment so directly, they often looked back on years of thwarted ambition. Elizabeth Pringle admitted needing a "man's education," especially in mathematics, and regretted spending so much time on poetry and the Italian language—studies that had so little to do with running a plantation.[24]

The experiences of Belle Kearney and Elizabeth Pringle, in most ways all too typical of those who had the *best* opportunities, illustrated how women's education only marginally improved after the war. The academies and colleges offered the usual smattering of "ornamental" and academic subjects. On paper, many of these schools looked impressive, listing courses in mathematics, science, history, philosophy, literature, and classical languages.[25] Although the antebellum trend toward more advanced studies with less emphasis on music, art, and romance languages continued, many so-called colleges were little more than glorified academies, and most academies remained small, expensive, and pedagogically backward. Despite occasional evidence of scholastic rigor— for example, in the normal schools set up to train teachers—the Southern states badly lagged behind the North in women's education.[26]

Whatever progress took place still depended on the willingness of teachers to ignore convention and the ability of students to overcome the obstacles of a discouraging environment. A determination to take full advantage of limited opportunities propelled some women to remarkable achievement. "There is a refining power in the crucible of adversity," educator Milton Bacon remarked. "The girls now growing up are under different influences and are prompted by higher motives than those which activated their predecessors. They are more studious, more docile, more ambitious in pursuit of solid achievement." Letters to parents and friends showed more concern about grades and less about social conquests. Theresa Giles had an "insatiable thirst of learning" and eagerly pursued knowledge that she had once thought beyond her reach. Pleased with recitations for a professor at North Carolina's Trinity College, she hoped to take some of the same courses offered to the young men.[27] Enthusiastic and idealistic, she looked forward to expanding her intellectual horizons.

Such students, however, discovered all too soon the limits placed on their ambitions. The roadblocks were both financial and ideological. Despite much talk of expanded opportunity for women, few new female academies opened, and existing schools remained small, precariously financed operations. To most Southerners, coeducation still seemed a hazardous experiment that would destroy female delicacy and make young women dissatisfied with their lot. Even those who favored educating boys and girls together in the elementary grades argued only that girls added "refinement" to the classroom. For teacher and student alike, orthodox definitions of woman's place walled in their lives. Women learned how to be great ladies even though great ladies had become curious anachronisms. As late as 1890, Christine Franklin reported that most so-called women's colleges instilled more charm than knowledge. From a more traditional perspective, Wilbur Fisk Tillett, who thought women should cultivate their modesty rather than compete with men in business, maintained that improvements in female education were making young girls into fine conversationalists.[28]

The few women who made it through such a system generally embraced their elders' restrictive dogmas. Limited goals and aspirations— a circumscribed intellectual and social life—evolved naturally from an educational system short on both money and ideas. Signs of intellectual ferment were often deceiving, and for many graduates of the female academies and colleges, their highest ambition was either to marry or simply follow in their instructors' footsteps.

4

For clever schoolgirls who adored their teachers, the classroom seemed ideal, a safe stage on which to develop and display their talents. The expansion of the public schools during Reconstruction increased the demand for teachers, but not necessarily for female teachers. Although women from prominent families opened schools after the war, they by no means replaced men. In 1870, Virginia was the only Southern state with more than a thousand female teachers, and by the late 1880s, Southern schools still employed a much smaller percentage of women than did their Northern counterparts. Only as training became available—usually during the summers in the normal schools—and one or two state universities experimented with coeducation, did women begin to supplant men in the poorly paid elementary positions.[29] But a shrinking tax base eroded support for public schools, while academies and colleges seldom had openings even for the most highly qualified women.

For the fortunate few who managed to find a position, teaching appeared to provide an alternative to marriage and an opportunity for economic self-sufficiency. "I am glad poor girls don't die from love these times or feel they have to marry for a home," Maria Fleet commented, "for they can always study and prepare themselves to teach." Widows opened schools or held classes in their homes to avoid sponging off their relatives.[30] And even though many of these ventures failed, they show how intellectual ambition and a desire for community service might also lead to more personal autonomy.

Yet for every woman who eagerly sought mental, social, or emotional fulfillment, another entered the classroom more reluctantly. Either from laziness or an excessive sense of delicacy, young ladies accustomed to being waited on by solicitous slaves had trouble getting used to the idea of working for a living. When her mother proposed setting up a school, Elizabeth Pringle recoiled in horror. "Mamma, I cannot teach," she pleaded. "Don't ask me to do it. I just hate the thought. Besides, I don't know enough of any one thing to teach." But these excuses sounded lame and only made her feel guilty: "Am I really just a butterfly? Is my love of pleasure the strongest thing about me?" Even if personal reservations could be overcome, social snobbery and family opposition might discourage would-be teachers. A South Carolina father dreaded his daughter becoming "the slave of a haughty community" in an occupation that "commands no respect from the better classes."[31]

Social prejudice and personal preferences, however, could not feed children or support aging parents, and many women had to swallow their pride. By most standards teaching was a respectable vocation and, potentially at least, a profitable one. Genteel ladies offered classes in French, music, drawing, and etiquette; wives supplemented family income by tutoring students; widows opened schools in their homes.[32]

Poverty drove women into the classroom, but the classroom could not lift them out of poverty. Most teachers barely supported themselves, let alone their families. When Cornelia Phillips Spencer criticized delicate and refined teachers for working as waitresses in the summertime, she revealed her own blindness and insensitivity. Many of these women earned so little that they qualified for poor relief, and belonging to a respectable profession did not always put food on the table. For fifteen dollars a month plus room and board, Evaline Attaway readily agreed to teach black children on David Barrow's plantation in northeastern Georgia. "I am aware that the task is difficult," she admitted with obvious resignation, "but as a female can make scarcely any wages here and as I have nothing on which to depend for a support, except my industry and application to business, I have concluded to accept your offer."[33] Her highly formal and deferential tone also showed a sense of chastened realism that seemed far away from the attitudes of idealistic young girls dreaming about a rewarding life of service in the classroom. Scores of other women had to assume the same obsequious attitude and accept the lowest paid positions.

Bolder spirits might strike out on their own, but so many women started their own schools after the war that competition drove down tuition; hard pressed teachers spent much of their time scrambling for students or trying to collect money from equally strapped parents. In public schools, private academies, and female colleges, women seldom held the higher-paying administrative jobs and usually received lower salaries than their male colleagues. In 1873 female teachers in Memphis protested against such discrimination in angry letters to the school board. The board members replied that men had to be paid more or they would resign, that women made enough already, and that in any case female teachers seldom measured up physically or intellectually. When two of these women objected to such demeaning comments, they were fired. In 1878 the board decided to cut its budget by making the men's salaries equal to those of the women. Yet this backhanded equality failed to solve the more pressing problem of paying female teachers a living wage and had more to do with hard times than with fair treatment.[34] In the classroom, Southern women may have preserved their respectability, but they eked out a bare subsistence without significantly expanding opportunities for their sex.

The working conditions seldom made up for the low salaries and in many instances undermined pretensions to gentility. In Belle Kearney's school, the older boys spat tobacco juice on the floor and challenged her authority daily. After four years of disciplining and occasionally instructing these unlikely pupils, she felt physically and emotionally exhausted. Other conscientious teachers suffered bouts of temporary and often severe depression.[35] Little wonder they simply marked time waiting for the school term to end.

For teachers who chafed at their lowly status and at the same time wanted to do a respectable job, demoralization often set in early and in the end drove them from the profession. In Nashville, Abbie Brooks conducted a class full of "different grades of scholars, from Natural Philosophy down to cat," earning barely enough money to pay for board and clothing. In March 1865 she had only three students and wondered how long she could stay where people spent most of their time bickering over religious questions rather than appreciating her work. By April 3 she had eighteen pupils but still worried that the "star of my existence is set in inextinguishable night, that no sunshine is bright enough to penetrate the gloom which broods over me." Always the perfectionist, she tried to ignore those who envied her success in the classroom, and even during the gloomiest times she took pride in the awakening curiosity and developing mental discipline of her young charges. But such moments of satisfaction became increasingly rare. "The corroding cares of life annoy and worry me," she wrote despairingly, "and there seems to be no balm to cure or charm my troubles and trials from any of their bitterness." Parents fell behind in their tuition payments and seemed to think she taught their children for mere pleasure. She finally left both Nashville and teaching. Moving to Georgia, she traveled about hawking religious publications, Bible maps, and pictures of Robert E. Lee and Stonewall Jackson. Worn out by the hot weather and angered by rude treatment, she never found economic security or emotional contentment.[36]

For other women, the physical and psychological distress extended over many years. In February 1866, Fanny Atkisson complained that she had not bought any personal items except a bonnet and a pair of gloves since the end of the war. She had opened a school in Athens, Georgia, but so had several other women. Prostrated by an August heat wave, she well understood the spur of economic necessity ("I must do it, or starve") and hoped for more students by fall. Two years later, competing against thirty other schools in town, she had only seven pupils but considered herself fortunate. Determination carried her through the rest of the decade and into the next, but the financial panic of 1873 blighted her already slender prospects. Few parents could afford $12.00 a month for tuition. Forced to move her school, by 1876, Fanny Atkisson had reduced her fees for some students to as low as $1.50 a month.[37] After a decade in the classroom she had neither figured out how to make a decent living nor discovered intellectual and psychological fulfillment.

Aside from the spur of necessity, why did the Fanny Atkissons hang on so long given the low pay and frustrations? Dedication to the profession and love for the students explain part of their persistence, and of course teaching remained, despite abysmal salaries, the most respectable profession open to women. All in all, the classroom was not such a bad place in a spotty economy where few women could earn more than a modest living. In other fields, the pay might well be lower and working conditions even worse; the supposed benefits of teaching, however, became apparent only in comparison with the few available alternatives.

5

"What can I do to help support myself and help to get along," Carrie Hunter wrote plaintively. "Every one wants some kind of remunerative employment, and the avenues to such employment are few." Many other women must have asked this same question, but few found answers. In a stagnant economy with a persistently strong sense of sexual hierarchy, the barriers to female employment outside the home remained formidable. After viewing displays on women's work in the North and West at the Centennial Exposition in Philadelphia, Cornelia Phillips Spencer concluded that the South lacked the capital to fully develop native talent. And even when calling for expanded opportunities she couched her arguments in the most conservative terms. Women should become clerks in dry-goods stores, she maintained, not to advance the cause of their sex or even improve their own lot but because it was shameful that men sold female underwear.[38] Aside from Spencer's essays, which did not exactly sound a call for thoroughgoing change, Southern politicians, economists, and writers paid little attention to the question of female employment.

Nor did the wives and mothers who worked outside their homes to support their families see themselves as pioneers. Their jobs were seldom lucrative or fulfilling. When women sold pies and flowers on the streets, they hardly challenged conventional thinking about the feminine sphere. Having lost three sons and a brother in the war, Mary Wall tersely described the situation of countless others: "In all my troubles, I *had* to work." Although some Southerners later claimed that women had become more independent after the war, few working women would have agreed.[39]

Too often they merely traded one form of dependence for another; male bosses could be every bit as imperious and skeptical of their talents as the most insensitive fathers or husbands. Ignoring Confederate precedent, state and local governments seldom hired female civil servants. In seeking a position as a copyist, Mattie Dodson admitted that being a governess, teacher, seamstress, and writer of romantic fiction furnished "a most uncertain" support. "What are we ladies who have nothing but our own feeble efforts to make a support to do?" she asked Alabama Governor William H. Smith. "We are compelled to exist and woman's work brings but a poor support at best." To land the few available jobs, women had to show that they had no intention of usurping masculine authority. An applicant for a federal appointment wrote reassuringly that "I do not think woman has any business dabbling in politics; it completely unsexes her and hardens her heart." Even if playing up to male vanity succeeded, women still ran into resentment from their fellow workers. "Political government is bad enough! Petticoat government is worse!" an irate civil servant complained to a New Orleans newspaper. "But the two combined is a piling up of agony beyond endurance."[40] In government offices as well as private businesses, the door of opportunity might be slightly ajar but was more often closed if not locked.

Unable to enter most occupations, women saw their economic plight worsen. Supporting families while preserving a certain gentility became an often impossible task. Balancing such competing and contradictory goals only added poignancy to the struggle for survival. To look for what little work was available outside the home or to somehow get along by selling produce or doing a bit of sewing became a Hobson's choice. Few alternatives and low incomes put enormous economic and psychological pressure on Southern families, forcing many wives and mothers to sacrifice either their comfort or their social standing. Yeoman and upper-class women in particular scrambled to find their place in a strange new world. Ingenuity, determination, and luck might bring success, but for the most part Southern white women had to labor in the unprofitable backwaters of a destitute land.

Some tried to turn an avocation into a vocation. For moderately well-off housewives, writing for publication had long seemed an ideal diversion or part-time occupation. Being an author did not necessarily require training, experience, or separation from the family, and during the antebellum years a number of women had taken up their pens to entertain themselves, earn a little money, and perhaps improve their status. Many of these writers had labored desultorily, but the economic travail of the postwar South gave their efforts a new urgency. After she had lost her land and slaves, Augusta Evans began working on a book to obtain her "bread and butter." She offered Alabama politician and philanthropist J. L. M. Curry a touching picture of herself as a déclassé belle slinging soup and hash in a sweltering kitchen, but he need not have felt too sorry for her. Despite these distractions, her novel *St. Elmo* became one of the century's best sellers.[41]

Few other aspiring authors enjoyed such success. Instead they churned out never-to-be-published novels or stories and poems for obscure church publications and newspapers. Whatever their creative potential, most women barely had time to practice their craft. Margaret Junkin Preston found that household chores constantly pulled her away from writing. To fix dinner or put up catsup while revising a poem was hardly conducive to literary success. "Congratulate yourself," she advised poet Paul Hamilton Hayne, "that you are a *man*, and are thus free from the thousand petty housewifely distractions that fill up the life of a wife and mother!" Longing for an "al fresco life as would content itself with water from the spring, and fruit from the trees, and leave one free to devote one's energies to the getting up of intellectual dishes," yet she disdained Northern feminism. "I scorn to see a woman, who confesses even to very positive literary proclivities, turn with contempt from, or neglect the proper performance of a single woman's household duties," she wrote. "Let them [the woman's household duties] come first, by all her love for a husband and children; by all her self-respect; and if a margin of time is left, then she may scribble *that* over, to her heart's relief," she concluded in a typical paean to domesticity.[42] Yet how much frustration did this careful balancing of duties and desires cause? Did public acquiescence conceal private rebellion? Of course the harried housewife and struggling author could always labor in obscurity without royalties or public recognition. And like other women they always had to ask what else they could do.

For women seeking respectable employment as well as for those willing to accept more menial work, their choices were neither clear nor easy. With long odds against finding something profitable to do outside the home and little encouragement from male employers, resourceful women created their own jobs. Female peddlers suddenly appeared on the streets of Southern cities and towns, selling clothing, pies, and preserves. In unusual circumstances, women ran post offices, set type, or made shoes.[43] But these exceptional examples reveal little about general conditions because most opportunities remained in more traditional pursuits. In the countryside, women labored on farms; in towns and cities, they worked as laundresses or in other poorly paid jobs.[44]

Rather than leaving their houses and children to the care of others, many women still preferred sewing at home. So long as seamstress remained the most common female occupation, the shortcomings of Southern industrial development were all the more evident. Although the collapse of the cotton market and the rise of the textile industry are familiar themes in postwar economic history, these changes only gradually affected the lives of women who continued to work out of their homes well into the 1880s. Once comfortable plantation belles wielded needle and thread. "I've always considered seamstresses a dreadfully ill-paid class & always declared I would never take sewing as my means of livelihood, for it would soon kill me or at least make me feel like committing suicide," Emma Holmes confessed. But then women of her class had seldom worried about those who designed their fancy ball dresses. Now she strained her eyes, cramped her muscles, and ruined her posture sewing for fifty cents a day. Lack of experience limited her productivity, but even the most skilled women, including fancy dressmakers who had once prospered, found few customers in the impoverished South.[45]

Despite an abundance of "sewing women" willing to work at pinchpenny wages, technological innovation steadily depleted their ranks. Cornelia Phillips Spencer asserted that machines would never eliminate the demand for handmade linen and other fancy goods, but after the war few women put together and sold finished garments. Instead they did piece work at home or in a factory, and the Southern economy hovered in a temporary limbo between domestic manufacturing and factory production. The mechanization of sewing reduced demand for skilled workers, devalued female labor, and also threatened the health of young girls. "The average life of a woman who works daily on the sewing machine is three years," Milton Bacon warned his daughter.[46] Working conditions deteriorated as the need for seamstresses decreased and yeoman women were displaced by poor whites and blacks. In any case, most women could not afford to worry too much about potential hazards to their health. The combination of agricultural depression and the elimination of traditional sources of extra income further squeezed the already tight budgets of many families.

Former seamstresses might have found work in Southern textile mills, but the number of jobs increased too slowly to soak up the labor surplus. Employers often preferred to hire entire families and viewed women as a dependent and readily available source of cheap labor. With a combination of paternalist condescension and cold calculation, owners and managers eagerly sought adolescent girls to work in their expanding mills.[47] Low wages meant more jobs and helped spur the growth of the Southern textile industry, but they also made workers more dependent. Many women left Southern farms to escape poverty, only to find that the poverty had followed them from the countryside into town.

For women as well as men, New South industrialization always promised more than it delivered. In 1870, for example, Georgia had only 1,238 female "cotton-mill operatives," a modest figure that nevertheless led the Southern states.[48] Steady increases during the next several decades appeared substantial only because of the small base. By the 1880s, as the campaign to industrialize the South gathered momentum, managers justified their preference for women and children by adopting the progressive argument that the mills provided useful employment for people from rural areas who would otherwise be idle.[49]

And though such rhetoric was largely self-serving, it did contain a kernel of truth. The familiar accounts of poor white women coming down out of the hills to work in the factories tell only part of the story because yeoman women also competed for the available jobs. By 1885, spinners and weavers received an average of 65 to 75 cents a day with a few workers making $1.50 a day—high wages by Southern standards. In testimony before the United States Senate Committee on Education and Labor, several women glowingly described what they considered good-paying jobs in Southern mills.[50] For the time being, the dangers of long hours and hazardous conditions seemed less important than the opportunity to earn a decent living.

In the postwar Southern economy, women received a slightly larger piece of a shrunken pie. A few more professional and factory jobs and less resistance to women's working outside the home scarcely affected those living on farms and plantations. The often desperate battle to restore what might be termed the domestic status quo reinforced older views of proper sex roles and prevented most sisters, wives, and mothers from questioning the old household division of labor. Women who had beaten the odds to become teachers or writers or shopkeepers or factory workers were hardly the vanguard of social or economic reformation. They set no precedents, inspired few imitators, and unsettled few minds.

6

During an era of thwarted ambition, political turmoil, and social stagnation, most Southern women appeared unaffected by a growing feminist activism elsewhere in the country; Northern reform movements, especially the campaign for women's rights, seldom received a hearing in the South. Exhausted by struggles against poverty and demoralization, women clung ever more precariously to their religious faith. The churches remained bulwarks of theological, economic, social, and political orthodoxy, forcing female benevolence to flow in safely conservative channels. Raising money for disabled veterans, destitute widows, and ragged orphans dovetailed with old-fashioned poor relief.[51] When well-dressed society ladies paid the obligatory calls on their poor sisters, they simply strengthened old notions of social hierarchy.

As before the war, a modest flurry of activity outside the home had little effect on social attitudes or practices. Most public-spirited women remained suspicious of national reform movements—even those connected with Protestant churches. During the 1860s and 1870s, only the temperance crusade attracted much Southern support. Being an important part of the evangelical tradition, campaigning against demon rum also carried with it a distinctively domestic flavor, particularly in the emphasis on driving alcohol out of the home and making the family a center of virtue and piety. Yet despite its essential conservatism, temperance threatened to upset power relations in the household. Husbands, brothers, and fathers must have often wondered whether the antialcohol movement was directed against them. When Sally Chapin accused chivalric Southern men of failing to protect women from the effects of male drunkenness, she surely touched a raw nerve. But until the rise of the Woman's Christian Temperance Union in the 1880s, Southern women generally kept such thoughts to themselves and remained intellectually and politically isolated from more radical currents in the rest of the country.[52]

Even on questions directly affecting their welfare, Southern women usually held their tongues—a silence that reflected their relative powerlessness. For some, merely attending a meeting or listening to a speech seemed a bold departure from tradition. To speak publicly, to lobby for a bill, to petition for legislative favors, or to apply pressure on male politicians was almost unimaginable. The initiative for reform rested with men. When delegates to state constitutional conventions decided to expand female property rights, they did so for reasons politically attractive to their own sex. Helpless women (and their families) supposedly needed protection from fortune hunters, and financially strapped husbands needed relief from unscrupulous creditors eager to seize their wives' property. Yet Ella Thomas—who surely reacted out of her own experience with a financially irresponsible husband—bitingly observed that men only safeguarded women's property after the war had destroyed much of its value. In conventions, legislatures, and courts, where the rights of women seldom received serious consideration, men drafted, enacted, and interpreted laws to suit their own purposes. Therefore the same politicians who cautiously expanded women's property rights ridiculed and dismissed proposals for women's suffrage.[53]

Whether these men expressed their contempt out of arrogance or fear, the connections among temperance, property law reform, and voting rights that logically developed in the Northern states failed to appear in the South. Although a few women commented during the suffrage debates of the 1860s that white women deserved the franchise more than black men, such scattered remarks meant little. Even the pioneering speeches on women's suffrage delivered by Elizabeth Meriwether in Memphis seemed more a curiosity than a radical departure from Southern norms. She later recalled that city officials treated her as a "harmless 'freak' " when she tried to vote in a local election. Perhaps they could not imagine other women following her lead, but in any event they might have taken comfort in her cautious approach. In using racist arguments and explicitly appealing to the romantic spirit of the Lost Cause, Meriwether showed how conservatism could easily accommodate, if not co-opt, the voices of reform.[54]

And even if a few women indirectly challenged ingrained prejudices, many more remained bulwarks of the old order. Novelist Augusta Evans refused to deliver public speeches and idealized women's domestic role by blasting prohibition, divorce, and women's suffrage. At the conclusion of Evans's popular *St. Elmo*, a chastened Edna Earl writes a book extolling domesticity and criticizing women who aspired to become public orators, doctors, ministers, or politicians. Evans also inserted the conventional warnings about the dangers of women's losing their delicacy in a age of free and easy manners where the sexes mingled promiscuously. What little public discussion of women's rights that did occur after the war was still couched in the most conservative language. Using a classical ad horrendum argument, Louisiana newspaper editor Mary Bryan equated the agitation of Northern feminists with free love. Should Southern women follow this Yankee lead, they risked becoming "unsexed" or worse.[55]

But even in such a reactionary climate, ambiguity and contradictions appeared. As usual, Cornelia Phillips Spencer spoke for a cautiously progressive upper class. Believing that women must be "subordinate but not inferior" to men, she refused to place her sex in a reactionary straitjacket. Criticizing a county education association that had refused to admit women, she conceded that Northern "radicals" had opened doors in civil service, teaching, and church work but maintained that Southern women could take advantage of similar opportunities without becoming harridans or Amazons. Wishing to expand the feminine sphere without destroying the notion of separate spheres, she dismissed the suffrage question as irrelevant so long as women could slowly widen their horizons without acquiring the vote.[56] Despite her exaggeration of the potential for reform in the South, few other women would have dared go even this far.

Change without change. Women's roles and status in Southern society continued to evolve in new directions, creating a crazy-quilt pattern of modest and limited improvements in an atmosphere of ideological re-action. Southerners sometimes showed surprising flexibility without abandoning old definitions of feminine character, and women became both victims and beneficiaries of this complex process. Some adopted a mildly reformist rhetoric; others cringed at even the hint of change; still others seemed to have no clear ideas about their role and destiny in the world; and many acted—whether rationally or irrationally, whether with cool deliberation or warm emotion, whether with reluctance or eagerness—in ways that defy classification. The story of most women's lives in the postwar South was not especially ennobling or dramatic. They raised their families, tried to deal with their menfolk, and rarely broke loose from convention. In the midst of tragedy, failure, and despair, they found occasions to celebrate and many times to mourn, but above all else they survived. As important participants in the rebuilding of the Southern economy and culture, they remained loyal to their class and race, avoiding the risks of becoming involved in sexual politics. Although a few boldly looked to the future, and more nostalgically looked back to a glorious past, most lived from day to day, much as their mothers and grandmothers had done, praying for their families, perhaps hoping for better days, but seldom expecting miracles.

Notes

ABBREVIATIONS USED IN THE NOTES

ADAH	Alabama Department of Archives and History, Montgomery
AHS	Atlanta Historical Society
BTHC	Barker Texas History Center, University of Texas, Austin
CSW	Confederate Secretary of War
Duke	Duke University, William R. Perkins Library
Emory	Emory University, Robert W. Woodruff Library
GDAH	Georgia Department of Archives and History, Atlanta
LC	Library of Congress, Manuscript Division
LR	Letters Received
LSU	Louisiana State University, Department of Archives and Manuscripts
MDAH	Mississippi Department of Archives and History, Jackson
NA	National Archives
NCDAH	North Carolina Division of Archives and History, Raleigh
OR	*War of the Rebellion: Official Records of the Union and Confederate Armies.* 130 vols. Washington Government Printing Office, 1880–1901.
RG	Record Group
SCDAH	South Carolina Department of Archives and History, Columbia
SCHS	South Carolina Historical Society, Charleston

SCL   South Caroliniana Library, University of South Carolina, Columbia

SHC   Southern Historical Collection, University of North Carolina, Chapel Hill

SW   Secretary of War

Tulane   Howard Tilton Memorial Library, Tulane University

UGa   University of Georgia Library, Special Collections

UVa   Alderman Library, University of Virginia, Charlottesville

VSL   Virginia State Library, Richmond

CHAPTER I

1. Myrtie Long Candler, "Reminiscences of Life in Georgia during the 1850s and 1860s," *Georgia Historical Quarterly,* 33 (September 1949), 227.

2. Gerda Lerner has cleared up a host of problems with definitions in women's history. See her clear and cogent analysis in *The Creation of Patriarchy* (New York: Oxford University Press, 1986), 231–43.

3. On the relationship between women and a reactionary ideology, I have greatly benefited from Claudia Koonz's provocative analysis of German women during the nazi period. Although any simple analogy between the Weimar Republic and the nazi regime on the one hand and the antebellum and Confederate South on the other hand would be strained, to put it mildly, Koonz provides many insights on how and why German women would support an antifeminist political movement. Claudia Koonz, *Mothers in the Fatherland: Women, the Family, and Nazi Politics* (New York: St. Martin's Press, 1987), 3–7, 53–90.

4. Bonnie Smith has presented a most helpful analysis of how the inroads of capitalism and a shifting emphasis in the home from production to reproduction caused women to react against the ideals of liberalism, individualism, and even rationality. In the antebellum South, educated women and men expressed an aversion to these trends in thought even before they appeared in their own society. The slavery controversy and the seemingly endless sectional agitation of the 1840s and 1850s made them acutely sensitive to any social changes that might somehow disturb what they believed to be a fundamentally sound social and economic, and especially racial order. Bonnie G. Smith, *Ladies of the Leisure Class: The Bourgeoises of Northern France in the Nineteenth Century* (Princeton: Princeton University Press, 1981), 48–49.

5. November 16, 1848, Rebecca S. Pilsbury Diary, SHC.

6. *Southern Planter,* 1 (November 1841), 212; Daniel R. Hundley, *Social Relations in Our Southern States,* ed. by William J. Cooper, Jr. (Baton Rouge: Louisiana State University Press, 1979 [1860]), 72–74.

7. "The Condition of Woman," *Southern Quarterly Review,* 10 (July 1846), 148–

67; "The Rights of Woman," *Southern Literary Messenger,* 8 (August 1842), 530–35; ca. 1840s, Martha Lumpkin Diary, AHS; Virginia Cary, *Letters on Female Character* (Richmond: A. Works, 1830), ix.

8. [Louisa S. McCord], "Woman and Her Needs," *DeBow's Review,* 13 (September 1852), 267–91; D. Harland Hagler, "The Ideal Woman in the Antebellum South: Lady or Farmwife?" *Journal of Southern History,* 46 (August 1980), 405–19.

9. It is curious that many historians have followed the lead of Eugene Genovese and have made Fitzhugh, an erratic intellectual and atypical proslavery ideologue, into the chief theoretician of the Old South. But if Fitzhugh was the slaveholders' Marx, why did so many Southern politicians, newspaper editors, and planters reject his brilliant though eccentric attack on free society? How can Fitzhugh and his heterodox views on the Bible speak for a South permeated by evangelical religion? Nor did Fitzhugh apparently consider the subordination of women crucial to his defense of hierarchy. To be sure, he harshly criticized the women's-rights movement in the North for reducing woman to a "beast of burden." He also believed that women would be worshiped by men so long as they remained "nervous, fickle, capricious, delicate, diffident and dependent." Free society, he charged, "has thrown her into the arena of industrial war, robbed her of the softness of her own sex." By contrast, in a patriarchal order, "woman, like children, has but one right, and that is the right of protection." Yet such statements hardly make the oppression of women central to planter hegemony. After all, Fitzhugh devoted only a few pages to making these points, and other proslavery spokesmen ignored both his arguments and his imagery. George Fitzhugh, *Sociology for the South, Or the Failure of Free Society* (Richmond: A. Morris, 1854), 213–17. Cf. Eugene D. Genovese, *The World the Slaveholders Made* (New York: Random House, 1969), 118–224; Anne Firor Scott, "Women's Perspective on the Patriarchy of the 1850s," *Journal of American History,* 41 (June 1974), 52–55; Paul E. Conner, "Patriarchy: Old World and New World," *American Quarterly,* 17 (Spring 1965), 48–62; Catherine Clinton, *The Plantation Mistress: Woman's World in the Old South* (New York: Pantheon Books, 1982), 6, 13.

10. Even in Steven Hahn's meticulous mining of sources on Georgia yeomen, yeoman women seldom come alive. Although Hahn is sensitive to sexual roles, especially in economic life, most of his material on women deals with the Civil War period, when yeoman women were much more likely to write letters to both relatives and public officials. Perhaps the only way to attack the problem of treating the lives of yeoman women in the South is either through a strictly quantitative analysis based on census and tax records or through a painstaking examination of legal documents for a single county. Steven Hahn, *The Roots of Southern Populism: Yeoman Farmers and the Transformation of the Georgia Upcountry, 1850–1880* (New York: Oxford University Press, 1983), 30–31, 124–29.

11. Although one might also include here a discussion of middle-class South-

ern women, aside from a few relatively prosperous women living in towns and cities, this term, with its close ties to the rise of industrial capitalism, has little application to the Southern social structure. Likewise, *middling rank,* which appears in many seventeenth-and eighteenth-century documents, generally refers to yeomen but often cannot be used precisely enough to make much sense. Until a more thorough, and perhaps quantitative, analysis of the Southern class structure is made, the old tripartite division among planter, yeoman, and poor white will have to do for women as well as men.

12. Hundley, *Social Relations,* 98–100; Rosser H. Taylor, *Ante-Bellum South Carolina: A Social and Cultural History* (Chapel Hill: University of North Carolina Press, 1942), 12, 76. The question of numbers is a tricky one. Beyond saying that a majority of white women in the antebellum South belonged to the yeoman class, it is difficult to be more precise. Estimates of the number of poor whites have been revised upward, to perhaps one-fifth of the white population in the South Atlantic states. J. Wayne Flynt, *Dixie's Forgotten People: The South's Poor Whites* (Bloomington: Indiana University Press, 1979), 5.

13. Keith L. Bryant, "Role and Status of the Female Yeomanry in the Antebellum South: The Literary View," *Southern Quarterly,* 18 (Winter 1980), 77–81; August 27, 1850, Jane B. Beale Diary, UVa.

14. The best analysis of antebellum class tensions in a Southern state is in J. Mills Thornton, III, *Politics and Power in a Slave Society: Alabama, 1800–1860* (Baton Rouge: Louisiana State University Press, 1978), passim.

15. Catherine Piper to David C. Barrow, August 2, 1857, March 30, 1858, David Crenshaw Barrow Papers, UGa.

16. Hundley, *Social Relations,* 264–65; Fredricka Bremer, *The Homes of the New World: Impressions of America,* trans. by Mary Howitt, 2 vols. (New York: Harper and Brothers, 1854) 1:366; C. Vann Woodward, ed., *Mary Chesnut's Civil War* (New Haven: Yale University Press, 1981), 830–31; Edward King, *The Great South,* ed. by W. Magruder Drake and Robert R. Jones (Baton Rouge: Louisiana State University Press, 1972), 417; Frederick Law Olmsted, *The Cotton Kingdom: A Traveler's Observations on Cotton and Slavery in the American Slave States,* ed. by Arthur M. Schlesinger (New York: Alfred A. Knopf, 1953), 64, 281–83; Emily Burke, *Reminiscences of Georgia* (n.p.: James M. Fitch, 1850), 208–9.

17. June 30, 1862, Carrie Hunter Diary, in Cobb and Hunter Family Papers, SHC.

18. Robert C. Kenzer, "Family, Kinship, and Neighborhood in an Antebellum Southern Community," in William J. Cooper, Jr., et al., eds., *A Master's Due: Essays in Honor of David Herbert Donald* (Baton Rouge: Louisiana State University Press, 1985), 147–51.

19. Susan S. Arpad, ed., *Sam Curd's Diary: The Diary of a True Woman* (Athens: Ohio University Press, 1984), 84; June 13, 1855, Ella Gertrude Clanton Thomas Diary, Duke; Bremer, *Homes of the New World,* II, 464, 494; Carol K. Bleser, "The

Perrys of Greenville: A Nineteenth-Century Marriage," in Walter J. Fraser, Jr., et al., eds., *The Web of Southern Social Relations: Women, Family, and Education* (Athens: University of Georgia Press, 1985), 77; Allie Bayne Windham Webb, ed., *Mistress of Evergreen Plantation: Rachel O'Connor's Legacy of Letters, 1823–1845* (Albany: State University Press of New York, 1983), 32.

20. Martha Battey to Mary Halsey, June 6, 1858, Robert Battey Papers, Emory; Lizzie Clow to Mary A. Maverick, April 9, 1854, Alice Clow Papers, BTHC; Warren W. Hassler, ed., *The General to His Lady: The Civil War Letters of William Dorsey Pender* (Chapel Hill: University of North Carolina Press, 1965), 103, 114, 118, 202–3. Whether Southern couples used abortion as a means of limiting family size is impossible to determine. Beginning in the 1830s and continuing through Reconstruction, most states outlawed abortions performed after the quickening of the fetus and provided lesser penalties for those done earlier. The few contemporary references to abortion make it difficult to determine whether Southern legislatures were interfering with a commonly used means of birth control or reacting to a few sensational cases. James C. Mohr, *Abortion in America: The Origins and Evolution of National Policy* (New York: Oxford University Press, 1978), 40–41, 132, 139, 204–5, 223–24.

21. Olmsted, *Cotton Kingdom,* 304. For insightful discussions of work in the home, see Mary P. Ryan, *Cradle of the Middle Class: The Family in Oneida County, New York, 1790–1865* (Cambridge, Eng.: Cambridge University Press, 1981), 198–202; Carl N. Degler, *At Odds: Women and the Family in America from the Revolution to the Present* (New York: Oxford University Press, 1980), 52–55; and Suzanne D. Lebsock, *The Free Women of Petersburg: Status and Culture in a Southern Town, 1784–1860* (New York: W. W. Norton, 1984), 147–59.

22. September 3, 1850, Jane B. Beale Diary, UVa.; Robert Manson Myers, ed., *The Children of Pride: A True Story of Georgia and the Civil War* (New Haven: Yale University Press, 1972), 197–98; April 11, 1855, Ella Gertrude Clanton Thomas Diary, Duke. For seasonal variations in women's household chores, see Agnes B. Dozier to Julia Branche Munroe Kell, September 9, 1860, John McIntosh Kell Papers, Duke; August 21, 1861, Sarah Lois Wadley Diary, SHC; Susanna C. Clay to C. C. Clay, January 24, 1833, Clement Claiborne Clay Papers, Duke; Fanny J. Campbell to David Campbell, August 12, 1858, Campbell Family Papers, Duke; Orville Vernon Burton, *In My Father's House Are Many Mansions: Family and Community in Edgefield, South Carolina* (Chapel Hill: University of North Carolina Press, 1985), 124.

23. March 18, 1858, Susan Cornwall Book, SHC; July 16, 1859, Henrietta Embree Diary, BTHC; October 17, 1865, Abbie M. Brooks Diary, AHS.

24. For an interpretation that emphasizes the difficulty of obtaining divorces and ignores important legal changes in the latter antebellum period, see Bertram Wyatt-Brown, *Southern Honor: Ethics and Behavior in the Old South* (New York: Oxford University Press, 1982), 283–91. In dealing carefully with legal changes

in Virginia, Suzanne Lebsock found that more liberal divorce laws benefited men as much as women. Lebsock, *Free Women of Petersburg,* 67–72.

25. In general, my interpretation follows the excellent analysis in Jane Turner Censer, " 'Smiling Through Her Tears': Ante-Bellum Southern Women and Divorce," *American Journal of Legal History,* 25 (January 1981), 24–47 and Lawrence B. Goodheart, et al., "An Act for the Relief of Females . . . ?: Divorce and the Changing Legal Status of Women in Tennessee, 1796–1860, Parts I and II," *Tennessee Historical Quarterly,* 44 (Fall–Winter 1985), 318–39, 402–16. Goodheart and his colleagues also show that in Tennessee even legislative divorce did not necessarily favor men. In North Carolina, the legislature gradually eased its strictures against dissolving marriages, and divorces in Alabama also increased during the last two decades before the Civil War as both husbands and wives took advantage of a more liberal divorce law. Women also benefited from legal loopholes. Louisiana courts granted separations that could become final divorces after two years. Guion Griffis Johnson, *Ante-Bellum North Carolina: A Social History* (Chapel Hill: University of North Carolina Press, 1937), 217–23; Alabama Divorces, 1830–1863, ADAH; Wheelock S. Upton, "The Divorce Law of Louisiana," *Commerical Review,* 2 (September 1846), 155–64.

26. Beth G. Crabtree and James W. Patton, eds., *"Journal of a Secesh Lady": The Diary of Catherine Ann Devereux Edmondston, 1860–1866* (Raleigh: Division of Archives and History, 1979), 345.

27. November 15, 1857, January 16, 1858, March 29, 1858, Louisa Warren Patch Fletcher Diary, GDAH.

28. Charlotte L. McMurray to Louisa Hall, June 26, 1841, Bolling Hall Papers, ADAH; October 5, 1850, Jane B. Beale Diary, UVa; October 27, 1865, Abbie M. Brooks Diary, AHS.

29. July 3, 1862, Elizabeth Collier Diary, SHC; November 19, 1864, Sarah Lois Wadley Diary, SHC; Cary, *Letters on Female Character,* 19–26. For insightful general discussions on women and religion in nineteenth-century America, see Ann Douglas, *The Feminization of American Culture* (New York: Alfred A. Knopf, 1977), 44–60, and Barbara Welter, "The Feminization of American Religion, 1800–1860," in Barbara Welter, *Dimity Convictions: The American Woman in the Nineteenth Century* (Athens: Ohio University Press, 1976), 83–102.

30. Donald G. Mathews, *Religion in the Old South* (Chicago: University of Chicago Press, 1977), 313; Lebsock, *Free Women of Petersburg,* 215; Woodward, *Mary Chesnut's Civil War,* 313; Thomas R. Dew, "Dissertation on the Characteristic Differences Between the Sexes and on the Position and Influence of Women in Society," *Southern Literary Messenger,* 1 (May–August 1835), 621.

31. Joe L. Kincheloe, Jr., "Transcending Role Restrictions: Women at Camp Meetings and Political Rallies," *Tennessee Historical Quarterly,* 40 (Summer 1981), 158–69; Bryant, "Female Yeomanry in the Antebellum South," 73–88; May 30, 1855, Ella Gertrude Clanton Thomas Diary, Duke; Burton, *In My Father's House,*

131–32. For information on women in Northern revivals, see Ryan, *Cradle of the Middle Class,* 71–98.

32. Lebsock, *Free Women of Petersburg,* 215–25; Johnson, *Ante-Bellum North Carolina,* 424–26, 702–3; Carrie Shaffner to her husband, March 13, 1865, Fries and Shaffner Family Papers, SHC.

33. Lebsock, *Free Women of Petersburg,* 225–36.

34. Anne M. Boylan, "Evangelical Womanhood in the Nineteenth Century: The Role of Women in Sunday Schools," *Feminist Studies,* 4 (October 1978), 62–80; Jean E. Friedman, *The Enclosed Garden: Women and Community in the Evangelical South, 1830–1900* (Chapel Hill: University of North Carolina Press, 1985), 11–20; James C. Bonner, *Georgia's Last Frontier: The Development of Carroll County* (Athens: University of Georgia Press, 1971), 61. Jean Friedman's argument that women were systematically discriminated against in the evangelical churches oversimplifies the complexities of church governance. Her assertion that women tried to loosen the bonds of family and church through the manipulation of symbols in their dreams is provocative but psychologically questionable, based on extremely thin evidence, and mostly speculative. Friedman, *Enclosed Garden,* 39–53.

35. Barbara Bellows, "'My Children, Gentlemen, Are My Own': Poor Women, the Urban Elite and the Bonds of Obligation in Antebellum Charleston," in Fraser, et al., eds., *Web of Southern Social Relations,* 52–71. On the ambiguities of reform, see Mary P. Ryan, "The Power of Women's Networks: A Case Study of Female Moral Reform in Antebellum America," *Feminist Studies,* 5 (Spring 1979), 66–85. But see Carroll Smith-Rosenberg, "Beauty, the Beast, and the Militant Woman: A Case Study in Sex Roles and Social Stress in Jacksonian America," *American Quarterly,* 23 (October 1971), 562–84.

36. Virginia Gearhart Gray, "Activities of Southern Women, 1840–1860," *South Atlantic Quarterly,* 27 (July 1928), 266–68; "Causes of Aristocracy," *DeBow's Review,* 28 (May 1860), 565–66. For differing interpretations of the importance of women's reform activities in the South, see Clinton, *Plantation Mistress,* 11–14, and Lebsock, *Free Women of Petersburg,* 197–215.

37. Again for useful insights on why some women feared social change and sometimes embraced a reactionary and antifeminist world view, see Smith, *Ladies of the Leisure Class,* 1–17, 93–122, 214–17.

38. "The Condition of Woman," *Southern Quarterly Review,* 10 (July 1846), 167–73; James A. Norcom to Mary Harvey, May 25, 1848, James A. Norcom and Family Papers, NCDAH; Clement Eaton, *The Mind of the Old South,* rev. ed. (Baton Rouge: Louisiana State University Press, 1967), 32–33; "Woman's True Mission," *Southern Literary Messenger,* 19 (May 1853), 303–6; Stanford M. Lyman, ed., *Selected Writings of Henry Hughes: Antebellum Southerner, Slavocrat, Sociologist* (Jackson: University Press of Mississippi, 1985), 185–86. For the most careful and balanced discussion of the connection between organized benev-

olence and feminism, see the extended analysis in Lebsock, *Free Women of Petersburg,* 195–244 passim.

39. Arpad, *Sam Curd's Diary,* 44–45; [Louisa S. McCord], "Enfranchisement of Women," *Southern Quarterly Review,* 21 (April 1852), 322–41; [McCord], "Woman and Her Needs," 267–91.

40. John F. Marszalek, ed., *The Diary of Miss Emma Holmes, 1861–66* (Baton Rouge: Louisiana State University Press, 1979), 291; Mary D. Robertson, ed., *Lucy Breckinridge of Grove Hill: The Journal of a Virginia Girl, 1862–64* (Kent, Ohio: Kent State University Press, 1979), 21–22, 25.

41. Myers, *Children of Pride,* 340.

42. August 11, 1864, Sarah Lois Wadley Diary, SHC; November 14, 1848, Ella Gertrude Clanton Thomas Diary, Duke; Cary, *Letters on Female Character,* 167–75; Lucy, "Advice to Farmers' Daughters," *Southern Cultivator,* 1 (December 20, 1843), 204.

43. Myers, ed., *Children of Pride,* 443–44; Georgia King to Henry Lord Page King, May 12, 1861, Thomas Butler King Papers, SHC; Elisabeth Muhlenfeld, *Mary Boykin Chesnut: A Biography* (Baton Rouge: Louisiana State University Press, 1982), 51–53.

44. Margaret Jarman Hagood, *Mothers of the South: Portraiture of the White Tenant Farm Woman* (New York: W. W. Norton, 1977 [1939]), 69–71. Adult literacy rates were calculated from the raw figures in *Seventh Census of the United States, 1850* (Washington: Robert Armstrong, 1853), xli–xlii. Although their precision is doubtful, they do present a clear picture of regional differences.

45. October 18, 1860, Sarah Lois Wadley Diary, SHC; Nettie Alexander to her uncle, April 22, 1860, Iraminta Antoinette Alexander Papers, GDAH; Judith P. Rives, Autobiography, Rives Family Papers, UVa; Margaret H. Campbell to Virginia T. J. Campbell, March 17, 1839, Campbell Family Papers, Duke; Richard W. Griffin, "Wesleyan College: Its Genesis, 1835–1840," *Georgia Historical Quarterly,* 50 (March 1966), 62–63.

46. William Cain to Minerva Cain, February 22, 1837, Tod R. Caldwell Papers, SHC; Milton Bacon to Rosa Bacon, July 28, 1861, Southern Female College, Cox College Archives, UGa.

47. Walter Runnell, Jr., ed., " 'If Fortune Should Fail': Civil War Letters of Dr. Samuel D. Sanders," *South Carolina Historical Magazine,* 65 (July and October, 1964), 131–33, 140–44, 218–29.

48. James A. Norcom to Mary Matilda Norcom, August 18, 26, October 18, 1836, February 18, 1837, June 20, 1837, James A. Norcom and Family Papers, NCDAH. Daughters knew how to respond to fatherly admonition: with dutiful promises to do better. See, for example, Anna G. Barnsley to Godfrey Barnsley, July 31, 1848, Julia Barnsley to Godfrey Barnsley, April 6, 1852, Godfrey Barnsley Papers, Duke.

49. Dolly Sumner Lunt Burge to her daughter, June 3, 1858 (?), Burge Family

Papers, Emory; R. Acilie to "Dear Sir," February 16, 1863, South Carolina Female Collegiate Institute Records, SCL; Richard Trapier Brumby to A. E. Brumby, April 3, 1858, Ann Eliza Brumby Paper, SHC; Mary Kelley, *Private Woman, Public Stage: Literary Domesticity in Nineteenth-Century America* (New York: Oxford University Press, 1984), 93–99. For a perceptive discussion of how education reinforced family values—including the need to obtain parental consent for marriage— see Steven M. Stowe, "The Not-So-Cloistered Academy: Elite Women's Education and Family Feeling in the Old South," in Fraser, et al., eds., *Web of Southern Social Relations,* 90–106; Susan Dabney Smedes, *Memorials of a Southern Planter* (New York: Alfred A. Knopf, 1965 [1890]), 122. Only a rare father—Langdon Cheves was one—saw any need for female education beyond what was required to fashion a thoughtful, hardworking, and pious wife. Cheves encouraged his daughter Louisa to study mathematics, economics, and other supposedly masculine subjects. She became a skillful, and very conservative, polemicist, writing scathing reviews on political economy, feminism, and abolitionism for Southern magazines. Susan Phinney Conrad, *Perish the Thought: Intellectual Women in Romantic America, 1830–1860* (New York: Oxford University Press, 1976), 189– 95.

50. George F. Pierce, "Address on Female Education," *Southern Ladies' Book,* 1 (January 1840), 5–13; Letter of "Clara," August 7, 1840, "To the Gentlemen of Georgia," ibid., 2 (August 1840), 112–13; Letter of "Clara," September 16, 1840, "To the Gentlemen," ibid., 2 (September 1840), 147–49; "Editorial," *DeBow's Review,* 32 (January and February 1862), 164–65.

51. "On the Policy of Elevating the Standard of Female Education," *Southern Literary Messenger,* 1 (December 1834), 169–70; "Importance of Home Education," *Southern Ladies' Book,* 2 (July 1840), 1; "Female Education," *Southern Literary Journal and Magazine of the Arts,* 1 (December 1835), 277; L. Pierce, "On Female Education," *Southern Ladies' Book,* 1 (March 1840), 129–37; Edgar W. Knight, ed., *Documentary History of Education in the South Before 1860,* 5 vols. (Chapel Hill: University of North Carolina Press, 1949–53), 5:450. Educational reform in the North often had equally conservative objectives. See, for example, Nancy Green, "Female Education and School Competition, 1820–1850," *History of Education Quarterly,* 18 (Summer 1978), 129–42; Anne Firor Scott, "The Ever Widening Circle: The Diffusion of Feminist Values from the Troy Female Seminary, 1822–1872," ibid., 19 (Spring 1979), 3–26. For a more optimistic assessment of domestic ideology and women's education, see Glenda Gates Riley, "The Subtle Subversion: Changes in the Traditionalist Image of the American Woman," *Historian,* 32 (February 1970), 210–27.

52. Dew, "Dissertation on Differences Between the Sexes," 493–94; "Benefits of Knowledge on Morals," *Southern Literary Messenger,* 4 (December 1838), 771– 79; "Female Education," ibid, 6 (June 1840), 451–56.

53. "Lucy," *Southern Cultivator,* 2 (November 27, 1844), 185; Richard Cook,

An Address on the Education and Influence of Woman Delivered before the Sabbath School Union in the Lutheran Church, January 11, 1858 (Columbus, Tex.: Printed at Office of the Colorado Citizen, 1858), 4–6; Knight, *Documentary History of Education in the South,* 5:451; Alexander H. Sands, "Intellectual Culture of Woman," *Southern Literary Messenger,* 28 (May 1859), 324–25.

54. Dorothy Orr, *A History of Education in Georgia* (Chapel Hill: University of North Carolina Press, 1950), 351; Cook, *Education and Influence of Woman,* 6–12; *Southern Cultivator,* 1 (August 21, 1844), 133; James O. Andrew, *Family Government: A Treatise on Conjugal, Parental, and Filial Duties* (Charleston: B. Jenkins, 1847), 88–100; Jane Turner Censer, *North Carolina Planters and Their Children, 1800–1860* (Baton Rouge: Louisiana State University Press, 1984), 48–54.

55. Orr, *History of Education in Georgia,* 149–55. For a typical schedule of costs, see the 1859 circular in Spartanburg Female College Records, SCL.

56. "Proper Study for Ladies," *Southern Ladies' Book,* 1 (June 1840), 364; "Thoughts on Female Education," ibid., 1 (February 1840), 96–99; Censer, *North Carolina Planters,* 42–47. For the course of study earlier in the century, see Clinton, *Plantation Mistress,* 130–34.

57. These generalizations about curriculum are based on information gathered from sixty-two separate sources, including school catalogues and records, student letters, and scattered references in secondary works. For lists of courses for the 1840s and 1850s, see Elizabeth Barber Young, *A Study of the Curricula of Seven Selected Women's Colleges of the Southern States* (New York: Bureau of Publications of Teachers College, Columbia University, 1932), 14–15, 25–28, 31–32, 45–58; F. Garvin Davenport, *Cultural Life in Nashville on the Eve of the Civil War* (Chapel Hill: University of North Carolina Press, 1941), 41–45.

58. Eugenius A. Nisbet, "Views of Female Education and Character," *Southern Ladies' Book,* 1 (June 1840), 326–31; Mary Telfair to Mary Few, February 24, ca. 1830s, William Few Papers, GDAH; "Importance of Home Education," 1–7; "Education of Southern Women," *DeBow's Review,* 31 (October and November 1861), 381–90.

59. Barbara Leigh Smith Bodichon, *An American Diary, 1857–58,* ed. by Joseph K. Reed, Jr. (London: Routledge and Kegan Paul, 1972), 91; Rebecca Latimer Felton, *Country Life in Georgia in the Days of My Youth* (New York: Arno Press, 1980 [1919]), 72; Sarah Morgan Dawson, *A Confederate Girl's Diary,* ed. by James I. Robertson (Bloomington: Indiana University Press, 1960), 249–50.

60. Rev. L. Pierce, "The Education of the Poor," *Southern Ladies' Book,* 1 (April 1840), 222–29; Burke, *Reminiscences of Georgia,* 210; Clifford Dale Whitman, ed., "Private Journal of Mary Ann Owen Sims," *Arkansas Historical Quarterly,* 35 (Summer 1976), 183.

61. My analysis of women's property rights closely follows Wyatt-Brown,

Southern Honor, 254–72, but places more emphasis on change in both law and public attitudes.

62. Marylynn Salmon, "Women and Property in South Carolina: The Evidence from Marriage Settlements, 1730–1830," *William and Mary Quarterly,* 3rd. Ser., 39 (October 1982), 655–85; Lebsock, *Free Women of Petersburg,* 55–67, 72–86; George Douglass to Hannah Douglass, May 22, 1848, John T. McAfee Papers, SCL.

63. Ann Raney Thomas Coleman Reminiscences, p. 136, 162–64, 182, in Anne Raney Thomas Coleman Papers, BTHC. Louisa Warren Fletcher was so careful of her husband's financial prerogatives that she refused to purchase the smallest item on credit without his permission. October 30, 1857, Louisa Warren Patch Fletcher Diary, GDAH.

64. Anna Matilda King to James Hamilton Couper, March 3, 1842, William Audley Couper Papers, SHC. This evidence suggests that the transition from traditional to modern (or more companionate) marriages was much more complex and less clearcut than historians have suspected. Cf. Edward Shorter, *The Making of the Modern Family* (New York: Basic Books, 1975) and Lawrence Stone, *The Family, Sex, and Marriage in England, 1500–1800* (New York: Harper and Row, 1977).

65. Edwin A. Davis, ed., *Plantation Life in the Florida Parishes of Louisiana as Reflected in the Diary of Bennett H. Barrow* (New York: Columbia University Press, 1943), 270; March 15, 1861, Ada Bacot Diary in Ada Bacot Papers, SCL.

66. Daniel Blake Smith, *Inside the Great House: Planter Family Life in Eighteenth-Century Chesapeake Society* (Ithaca, N.Y.: Cornell University Press, 1980), 237–42; Lebsock, *Free Women of Petersburg,* 35–53; Burton, *In My Father's House,* 107; Censer, *North Carolina Planters,* 105–11.

67. Charles S. Sydnor, *The Development of Southern Sectionalism, 1819–1848* (Baton Rouge: Louisiana State University Press, 1948), 97–99; Sandra Moncrief, "The Mississippi Married Women's Property Act of 1839," *Journal of Mississippi History,* 47 (May 1985), 110–25; "Women Physiologically Considered," *Southern Quarterly Review,* 2 (October 1842), 305–11; "Right of Property of Married Women," *Southern Ladies' Book,* 1 (June 1840), 363–64; William L. Yancey, speech, "Rights and Wrongs of Women," n.d., William L. Yancey Papers, ADAH.

68. See the excellent analyses in Lebsock, *Free Women of Petersburg,* 112–33 and Wyatt-Brown, *Southern Honor,* 236–42. I think Wyatt-Brown overstates the case in describing spinsterhood as a "form of social death."

69. After making a name index for the female heads of households for the ten counties in tables 1 and 2, I was able to trace only sixty-one of them between the 1850 census and the 1860 census. Obviously many of the women in the 1850 group had married, left the county, moved in with another family, or died by 1860. Others were simply not counted in one census or the other. Because of

the small number who could be located in both census schedules, the conclusions about mobility are tentative at best. Men and women also underreported their assets to the census taker for fear their answers would be used by local officials for tax purposes. Property tax records are even more unreliable on this score. With these caveats in mind, however, it appears that few single women in the South could afford to remain unmarried for long.

70. Wyatt-Brown, *Southern Honor*, 214–17; Julia Davidson to John Mitchell Davidson, January 8, 1861, John Mitchell Davidson Papers, Emory.

71. Harriet E. Amos, "City Belles: Images and Realities of Lives of White Women in Antebellum Mobile," *Alabama Review*, 34 (January 1981), 11–12; Lebsock, *Free Women of Petersburg*, 176–94; Burton, *In My Father's House*, 51, 115, 125; R. Ingraham to Susan Fisher, January 5, 26, 1840, July 11, 1841, Susan Fisher Papers, SHC; Elizabeth Carter to Thomas Powell, July 9, 1839, Powell Papers, NCDAH. See, for example, *Charleston Courier*, July 9, 1836, February 3, 1846.

72. See, for example, Louisa Warren Patch Fletcher Diary, *passim*, GDAH.

73. Lyle Koehler, *A Search for Power: The "Weaker" Sex in Seventeenth Century New England* (Urbana: University of Illinois Press, 1980), 108–35; Nancy F. Cott, *The Bonds of Womanhood: "Woman's Sphere" in New England, 1780–1835* (New Haven: Yale University Press, 1977), 19–62; Alice Kessler-Harris, *Out to Work: A History of Wage-Earning Women in the United States* (New York: Oxford University Press, 1982), 24–72; Susan Estabrook Kennedy, *If All We Did Was to Weep at Home: A History of White Working-Class Women in America* (Bloomington: Indiana University Press, 1979), 15–47.

74. Percentages calculated from *Manufactures of the United States in 1860; Compiled From the Original Returns of the Eighth Census* (Washington: Government Printing Office, 1865), 13–14, 21–22, 60, 80–82, 202–4, 293–94, 436–38, 558–59, 577–79, 592–94, 635–39.

75. David R. Goldfield, *Urban Growth in an Age of Sectionalism: Virginia, 1847–1861* (Baton Rouge: Louisiana State University Press, 1977), 125–26; Burton, *In My Father's House*, 125–26; Mary E. Davis, ed., *The Neglected Thread: A Journal from the Calhoun Community, 1836–1842* (Columbia: University of South Carolina Press, 1951), 178; Olmsted, *Cotton Kingdom*, 213, 383–84; Eleanor Wolf Thompson, *Education for Ladies, 1830–1860: Ideas on Education in Magazines for Women* (Morningside Heights, N.Y.: King's Crown Press, 1947), 106–7.

76. Katherine Elizabeth Ozburn to Nat Mangum, September 11, 1860, Katherine Elizabeth Ozburn Papers, GDAH.

77. Lebsock, *Free Women of Petersburg*, 172–76; M. C. S. Noble, *A History of the Public Schools of North Carolina* (Chapel Hill: University of North Carolina Press, 1930), 166–67; Burton, *In My Father's House*, 124–25; Catherine Heriot to Louisa Heriot, January 28, 1862, Mackenzie Family Papers, SCL.

78. March 21, 1848, Martha Foster Crawford Diary, Duke; Myers, *Children of Pride*, 647; James A. Norcom to John Norcom, April 15, 1840, James A. Norcom

and Family Papers, NCDAH; Thomas Dyer, ed., *To Raise Myself a Little: Diary and Letters of Jennie A. Lines, Georgia Teacher, 1851–1886* (Athens: University of Georgia Press, 1981), 65, 67.

79. Dyer, *To Raise Myself a Little,* 83–84, 100, 113; Joseph Holt Ingraham, *The Sunny South* (Philadelphia: G. Evans, 1860), 267–29. For a rare description of the joys of teaching, see Nannie Rayburn to Susy Rayburn, October 27, 1861, Samuel King Rayburn Papers, ADAH.

CHAPTER 2

1. Koonz, *Mothers of the Fatherland,* 3–7.

2. For representative examples of the case for white women's hostility to slavery see Anne Firor Scott, *The Southern Lady: From Pedestal to Politics, 1830–1930* (Chicago: University of Chicago Press, 1970), 46–54; Clinton, *Plantation Mistress,* 181–98; Anne Goodwyn Jones, *Tomorrow is Another Day: The Woman Writer in the South, 1859–1936* (Baton Rouge: Louisiana State University Press, 1981), 29–31. For a more balanced treatment, which nevertheless puts much emphasis on white women's doubts about slavery, see Sudie Duncan Sides, "Women and Slaves: An Interpretation Based on the Writings of Southern Women," (Ph.D. dissertation, University of North Carolina, Chapel Hill, 1969), 30–94, 248–65.

3. C. Vann Woodward and Elisabeth Muhlenfeld, eds., *The Private Mary Chesnut: The Unpublished Civil War Diaries* (New York: Oxford University Press, 1984), 21, 43; Woodward, *Mary Chesnut's Civil War,* 168, 246. Most important, action seldom followed words. Suzanne Lebsock has argued that women were more likely than men to emancipate slaves in their wills, but her sample is too small and the differences between men and women not large enough to be statistically significant. Despite her imaginative use of legal documents, Lebsock's argument that women in Petersburg, Virginia, had a subversive influence on slavery is not persuasive. Lebsock, *Free Women of Petersburg,* 137–41.

4. Eugene D. Genovese, *Roll, Jordan, Roll: The World the Slaves Made* (New York: Pantheon Books, 1974), 344–47. For representative comments about white women being controlled by their slaves, see Smedes, *Memorials of a Southern Planter,* 179–80; Caroline Merrick, *Old Times in Dixie Land* (New York: Grafton Press, 1901), 17–19; Mrs. R. H. Marshall to John E. and Charles D. Marshall, April 19, 1852, Marshall Family Papers, Duke.

5. See, for example, the series of letters from Phoebe Elliott to William Elliott in the 1840s and 1850s, Elliott and Gonzales Family Papers, SHC.

6. James Oakes, *The Ruling Race: A History of American Slaveholders* (New York: Alfred A. Knopf, 1982), 50, 248–49; Dolly Sumner Lunt to a daughter, December 7, 1860, Burge Family Papers, Emory; Webb, ed., *Mistress of Evergreen Plantation,* 242.

7. Kate Cox to her slaves, April 11, 1852, Thomas Mulrup Logan Papers, SHC; Woodward and Muhlenfeld, *Private Mary Chesnut,* 47; Webb, *Mistress of Ever-*

green Plantation, 204; George P. Rawick, ed., *The American Slave: A Composite Autobiography,* 41 vols. (Westport, Conn.: Greenwood Press, 1972–1979), vol 2, pt. 1, p. 66.

8. Rawick, *American Slave,* supp., ser. 1, 10:2191, 2364–65, ser. 2, 4:1351–52, 9:3573; Charles L. Perdue, Jr. et al., *Weevils in the Wheat: Interviews with Virginia Ex-Slaves* (Charlottesville: University of Virginia Press, 1976), 40. Attempts to assess the treatment of slaves by counting the references to good and bad mistresses in the memoirs and interviews of former slaves have not been successful. Compare the simple analysis in Clinton, *Plantation Mistress,* 187–89, to the more restrained and sounder conclusions in Paul D. Escott, *Slavery Remembered: A Record of Twentieth-Century Slave Narratives* (Chapel Hill: University of North Carolina Press, 1979), 58–59. Too much of this "primary" evidence comes from people who had experienced slavery only as children—the group most likely to remember the positive qualities of masters and mistresses. Quantifying such testimony is statistically naive, but the interviews contain invaluable evidence about particular slaveholders and slaves.

9. Letitia Burwell, *A Girl's Life in Virginia Before the War* (New York: Frederick A. Stokes, 1895), 6; Rawick, *American Slave,* supp., ser. 2, 8:3222. Even children's games could be unintentionally cruel. Mary Peabody and her friends dressed up in carnival costumes and rode through the Virginia countryside, frightening slaves and threatening to have them whipped. This seemed like harmless fun, but then these girls never had to worry about feeling the lash. Mary Peabody to Elizabeth Peabody, March 4, 1835, Peabody Family Papers, UVa.

10. Perdue et al., *Weevils in the Wheat,* 63.

11. For instances of women protecting slaves, see Rawick, *American Slave,* vol. 2, pt. 1, p. 172, vol. 6 (Alabama), 58–59, 120, 150, vol. 11, pt. 7, pp. 99–100, vol. 12, pt. 1, pp. 74–75; August 26, 27, 1861, Priscilla Munnikhuysen Bond Diary, LSU. Women may have opposed harsh treatment of slaves because, as Suzanne Lebsock has argued, they viewed them more as persons than as property. But for every piece of evidence that supports this hypothesis, there is an equally compelling example that rebuts it. That white men and women differed essentially in their attitudes and actions toward the slaves remains unproven. Lebsock, *Free Women of Petersburg,* 137–41. For examples of women who freely used the whip, see Rawick, *American Slave,* vol. 2, pt. 1, p. 11, pt. 2, p. 209; supp., ser. 2, 4:963, 1055–56.

12. Rawick, *American Slave,* vol. 8, pt. 2, pp. 189–90, vol. 11, pt. 7, pp. 202–3, supp., ser. 2, 2:310, 408–9, 7:2643–44.

13. Ibid., vol. 6 (Alabama), 130, vol. 7 (Oklahoma), 135, 165–67; Perdue, et al., *Weevils in the Wheat,* 190–91.

14. November n.d., 1857, Ella Gertrude Clanton Thomas Diary, Duke; Ruth Smith to Mary C. Baber, October 2, 1836, Baber and Blackshear Papers, UGa.; Celeste Clay to Virginia Clay, July 19, 1861, Clement Claiborne Clay Papers, Duke.

15. On miscegenation in general, see Joel Williamson, *New People: Miscegenation and Mulattoes in the United States* (New York: Free Press, 1980), 56, 63–71. For the statistical debate, see Robert W. Fogel and Stanley L. Engerman, *Time on the Cross: The Economics of American Negro Slavery,* 2 vols. (Boston: Little, Brown, 1974), 1:131–33, 2:101–13, and Herbert Gutman, "Victorians All? The Sexual Mores and Conduct of Slaves and Their Masters," in Paul David et al., *Reckoning with Slavery: A Critical Study in the Quantitative History of American Negro Slavery* (New York: Oxford University Press, 1976), 148–53. For three accounts that overstate the importance of miscegenation, see W. J. Cash, *The Mind of the South* (New York: Alfred A. Knopf, 1941), 87–89, Anne Firor Scott, "Women's Perspective on the Patriarchy in the 1850s," *Journal of American History,* 61 (June 1974), 58–64, and Clinton, *Plantation Mistress,* 199–222. White women saw black women as either dangerously promiscuous or as obsequiously faithful, either as disloyal ingrates or virtuous mammies. Few could understand their slaves, either male or female, as complex human beings. See the detailed discussion in Minrose C. Gwin, *Black and White Women of the Old South: The Peculiar Sisterhood in American Literature* (Knoxville: University of Tennessee Press, 1985), 78–109.

16. January 2, 1858, Ella Gertrude Clanton Thomas Diary, Duke; Woodward and Muhlenfeld, *Private Mary Chesnut,* 42–43. Divorce petitions presented to the Virginia legislature often mentioned miscegenation; see James Hugo Johnston, *Race Relations in Virginia and Miscegenation in the South, 1776–1860* (Amherst: University of Massachusetts Press, 1970), 238–50. For the devastating effects of miscegenation on one Southern family, see Drew Gilpin Faust, *James Henry Hammond and the Old South: A Design for Mastery* (Baton Rouge: Louisiana State University Press, 1982), 313–17.

17. Rawick, *American Slave,* vol. 2, pt. 1, p. 150, 17:186; Perdue et al., eds., *Weevils in the Wheat,* 257; Webb, *Mistress of Evergreen Plantation,* 140; William Alexander Percy, *Lanterns on the Levee: Recollections of a Planter's Son* (New York: Alfred A. Knopf, 1941), 8–9.

18. Perdue et al., *Weevils in the Wheat,* 190, 330; Rawick, *American Slave,* vol. 13, pt. 3, p. 230, 15:98.

19. Catharine Kenan Holmes to Elizabeth J. Blanks, October 13, 1835, Elizabeth J. Blanks Papers, Duke; Anne Davis to Wilbur Davis, January 5, 1857, Beale and Davis Family Papers, SHC; Olmsted, *Cotton Kingdom,* 302–4; December 25, 1858, Ella Gertrude Clanton Thomas Diary, Duke; Mary Ann Cobb to Howell Cobb, n.d., 1837, Cobb, Erwin, and Lamar Papers, UGa; Martha Battey to Mary Halsey, December 17, 1856, December 10, 1860, Robert Battey Papers, Emory.

20. Louisa M. Davis to Alice W. Saunders, n.d., 1861, Irvine-Saunders Papers, UVa.; Martha Battey to Mary Halsey, November 7, 1855–56?, Robert Battey Papers, Emory; Ann Fripp Hampton, ed., *A Divided Heart: Letters of Sally Baxter Hampton, 1853–1862* (Spartanburg, S.C.: Reprint Co., 1980), 22.

21. A Lady of Georgia, "Southern Slavery and Its Assailants," *DeBow's Review*, 16 (January 1854), 46–61; January 31, February 22, 1861, Susan Cornwall Book, SHC. Of all the proslavery writers, only George Fitzhugh explicitly connected the status of women to the defense of the peculiar institution. Maintaining that paternalism safeguarded slaves, women, and children from despotic rule, he warned that female delicacy and health would inevitably decline amidst the ruthless competition of free society. Yet Fitzhugh saw little danger that Southern women would become abolitionists even though nervous men wondered about Southern women's soundness on slavery. Fitzhugh, *Sociology for the South*, 23–24, 105–6; Sands, "Intellectual Culture of Women," 330–31.

22. Margaret Ferrand Thorp, *Female Persuasion: Six Strong-Minded Women* (New Haven, Conn.: Yale University Press, 1949), 179–214.

23. Women novelists obliquely defended slavery, and some even directly responded to *Uncle Tom's Cabin*. For a provocative but ultimately strained and unconvincing attempt to uncover feminist themes in Mary H. Eastman's proslavery novel *Aunt Phillis's Cabin*, see Gwin, *Black and White Women*, 36–43.

24. [McCord], "Carey on the Slave Trade," *Southern Quarterly Review*, 9 (January 1854), 167–79; [McCord], "Charity Which Does Not Begin at Home," *Southern Literary Messenger*, 19 (April 1853), 193–95. For the use of cultural and racial arguments, see McCord, "Negro-Mania," *DeBow's Review*, 12 (May 1852), 507–24.

25. McCord, "Diversity of the Races; Its Bearing on Negro Slavery," *Southern Quarterly Review*, 6 (April 1851), 392–419; McCord, "British Philanthropy and American Slavery," *DeBow's Review*, 14 (March 1853), 258–80; McCord, "Negro and White Slavery—Wherein Do They Differ?" *Southern Quarterly Review*, 6 (July 1851), 118–32.

26. McCord, "Uncle Tom's Cabin," *Southern Quarterly Review*, 8 (January 1853), 81–120; [McCord], "Stowe's Key to Uncle Tom's Cabin," ibid., 8 (July 1853), 214–54.

27. [McCord], "Enfranchisement of Women," 331–41; "Women Physiologically Considered," 282–98; Myers, *Children of Pride*, 259.

28. [Dew], "On the Characteristic Differences Between the Sexes," 679–85. For useful suggestions on describing the political status of women in various cultures, see Sheila Ryan Johannsen, " 'Herstory' as History: A New Field or Another Fad?" in Berenice Carroll, ed., *Liberating Women's History: Theoretical and Critical Essays* (Urbana: University of Illinois Press, 1976), 407.

29. Elizabeth Bestor to Frances J. Bestor, November 30, 1844, Lida Bestor Robertson Papers, ADAH; Rachel McNeill to "Cousin Molly," August 30, 1855, Cronly Family Papers, Duke.

30. Mary Ann Cobb to Howell Cobb, December 21, 1856, Cobb, Erwin, and Lamar Papers, UGa.; Virginia Clay to a cousin, October 10, 1856, Clement Claiborne Clay Papers, Duke; Laura Bryan to Guy M. Bryan, February 18, April 3,

1858, Guy M. Bryan Papers, BTHC; Hudson Strode, ed., *Jefferson Davis: Private Letters, 1823–1889* (New York: Harcourt, Brace and World, 1966), 64.

31. Elizabeth F. Perry to Benjamin F. Perry, December 6, 1841, July 24, 1846, December 6, 1847, December 10, 1847, Benjamin Franklin Perry Papers, SCL. See the perceptive comments on the Perrys' political relationship in Bleser, "Perrys of Greenville," 79–84.

32. Eleanor M. Boatwright, "The Political Status of Women in Georgia, 1783–1860," *Georgia Historical Quarterly,* 25 (March 1941), 301–3; Virginia T. J. Campbell to William Campbell, June 26, 1840, Campbell Family Papers, Duke; Leroy P. Graf et al., eds., *The Papers of Andrew Johnson,* 6 vols. to date (Knoxville: University of Tennessee Press, 1967—), 3:408; James T. McIntosh et al., eds., *The Papers of Jefferson Davis,* 4 vols. to date (Baton Rouge: Louisiana State University Press, 1971—), 2:173.

33. Elizabeth G. Perry to Benjamin F. Perry, April 27, 1852, Benjamin Franklin Perry Papers, SCL; Myers, *Children of Pride,* 26; J. H. Easterby, ed., *The South Carolina Rice Plantation As Revealed in the Papers of Robert F. W. Allston* (Chicago: University of Chicago Press, 1945), 101.

34. Jane Caroline Pettigrew to Charles Pettigrew, October 30, 1859, Pettigrew Family Papers, SHC; Susan Eppes, *Through Some Eventful Years* (Gainesville: University of Florida Press, 1968), 119, 121–22; November 26, December 2, 1859, Sarah Rodgers Espy Diary in Sarah Rodgers Espy Papers, ADAH.

35. Frances Kirby Smith to Edmund Kirby Smith, November 3, 1860, Edmund Kirby Smith Papers, SHC; Crabtree and Patton, *Edmondston Journal,* 4, 10; October 26, 1860, Sarah Lois Wadley Diary, SHC; November 7, 1860, Grace B. Elmore Diary, SCL; H. J. Wayne to Mary Ann Harden, December 3, 1860, Edward Harden Papers, Duke; March 4, 1861, Anne Darden Diary in Anne Darden Papers, NCDAH.

36. November 13, 1860, Grace B. Elmore Diary, SCL; June 8, 1861, Mary Ezell Diary in Edward Conigland Papers, SHC; Easterby, *South Carolina Rice Plantation,* 175–76; Crabtree and Patton, *Edmondston Journal,* 37.

37. January 4, 31, February 4, 12, 1861, Susan Cornwall Book, SHC.

38. Samuel Proctor, ed., "The Call to Arms: Secession from a Feminine Point of View," *Florida Historical Quarterly,* 35 (January 1957), 266–70. Of course some women refused to be carried away by fire-eating speeches. Yet as historians have recognized, the divisions between immediate secessionists and cooperationists were more tactical than strategic. Cooperationist women denounced the Black Republicans with as much fervor as their more radical sisters. Myers, *Children of Pride,* 627–28; Martha Battey to Mary Halsey, December 10, 1860, Robert Battey Papers, Emory. A quantitative analysis of female attitudes on secession is of course impossible, and even a guess on the extent of Unionist sentiment is difficult. Because secessionists of both sexes put enormous social and political pressure on dissenters, unconditional Unionists usually held their tongues. Maria Hamblen fled North Carolina, but in Richmond, a Southern-rights

man called her a "damn Yankee" and spit tobacco juice down the back of her gray silk poplin dress. Louise ? to Caroline North Pettigrew, March 12, 1861, Pettigrew Family Papers, SHC; H. E. Sterkx, *Partners in Rebellion: Alabama Women During the Civil War* (Rutherford, N. J.: Fairleigh Dickinson University Press, 1970), 32; George W. Cable, ed., "The War Diary of a Union Woman in the South," *Century Magazine*, 38 (October 1889), 931; Maria Florilla Hamblen Reminiscences, p. 5, SHC.

39. Crabtree and Patton, *Edmondston Journal*, 11, 17, 34–36, 38–39, 54.

40. Eppes, *Through Some Eventful Years*, 86–87; Louise Wigfall to Halsey Wigfall, October 31, 1860, Louis T. Wigfall Papers, LC; G. Glenn Clift, ed., *The Private War of Lizzie Hardin: A Kentucky Confederate Girl's Diary of the Civil War in Kentucky, Virginia, Tennessee, Alabama, and Georgia* (Frankfort: Kentucky Historical Society, 1963), 3–4; Mrs. Thomas Taylor et al., eds., *South Carolina Women in the Confederacy*, 2 vols. (Columbia, S.C.: State Co., 1903–1907), 1:168–69.

41. John K. Bettersworth, *Confederate Mississippi: The People and Policies of a Cotton State in Wartime* (Baton Rouge: Louisiana State University Press, 1942), 7; Francis W. Dawson, ed., *Our Women in the War: The Lives They Lived; The Deaths They Died* (Charleston, S.C.: News and Courier Co., 1885), 169; J. B. Jones, *A Rebel War Clerk's Diary at the Confederate States Capital*, 2 vols. (Philadelphia: J. B. Lippincott, 1866), 1:19.

42. For the range of opinion, see Jane Caroline Pettigrew to Caroline North Pettigrew, December 20, 1860, Pettigrew Family Papers, SHC; January 5, 1861, Ann Hardeman Diary in Oscar J. E. Stuart Papers, MDAH; H. J. Wayne to Mary Ann Harden, December 3, 1860, Edward Harden Papers, Duke; Caroline H. Glover to Caroline Gilman, January 11, 1861, Caroline Gilman Letters, SCHS; Louisa Cunningham to William L. Yancey, January 18, 1861 (misdated 1860), Benjamin C. Yancey Papers, SHC; Myers, *Children of Pride*, 642–43.

43. Crabtree and Patton, *Edmondston Journal*, 32; Woodward, *Mary Chesnut's Civil War*, 43–44; October 1860, Grace B. Elmore Diary, SCL.

44. Sarah Frances Williams to her parents, April 28, 1861, Sarah Frances Williams Letters, SHC; July 16, 1861, Ella Gertrude Clanton Thomas Diary, Duke; John Q. Anderson, ed., *Brokenburn: The Journal of Kate Stone, 1861–1868* (Baton Rouge: Louisiana State University Press, 1955), 19.

45. Betsey Fleet and John D. P. Fuller, eds., *Green Mount: A Virginia Plantation During the Civil War* (Lexington: University of Kentucky Press, 1962), 52–53; Emma Sue Gordon to Addie Simpson, May 15, 1861, Allen and Simpson Family Papers, SHC; [Judith White Brockenbrough McGuire], *Diary of a Southern Refugee During the War*, 2d. ed. (New York: E. J. Hale and Son, 1867), 16.

46. Louis A. Bringier to Stella Bringier, January 28, 1862, Louis A. Bringier Papers, LSU; Eppes, *Through Some Eventful Years*, 151.

47. Bell Irvin Wiley, *The Life of Johnny Reb: The Common Soldier of the Confederacy* (Indianapolis: Bobbs-Merrill, 1943), 22; Marszalek, *Diary of Emma Holmes,* 43.

48. *Petersburg Express,* n.d., in *Richmond Enquirer,* March 26, 1861; *New Orleans Daily Delta,* February 23, 1861. Where women made brief remarks at flag presentation ceremonies, sentimentality reigned. Young girls swore fealty to the Confederate cause in sentences dripping with bathos, pathos, and too many modifiers. Sterkx, *Partners in Rebellion,* 39–41; Speech of Caroline Elizabeth Hunter, March 20, 1861, Cobb and Hunter Family Papers, SHC; Michael B. Dougan, *Confederate Arkansas: The People and Policies of a Frontier State in Wartime* (University, Ala.: University of Alabama Press, 1976), 71–72.

49. Mrs. Roger A. Pryor, *Reminiscences of Peace and War* (New York: Macmillan, 1908), 134–35; January 8, 1862, Mahala Roach Diary in Roach and Eggleston Family Papers, SHC; Dawson, *Our Women in the War,* 382; Wiley, *Life of Johnny Reb,* 174.

50. June 3, 1861, Betty Herndon Maury Diary, LC; Margaret A. Morgan? to her mother, April 18, 1861, Flora McCabe Collection, LC; Clift, *Private War of Lizzie Hardin,* 20–22; M. M. Jennings, "A Little Girl in the War," *Confederate Veteran,* 30 (October 1922), 375.

CHAPTER 3

1. May 11, 1862, Ann Hardeman Diary in Oscar J. E. Stuart Papers, MDAH. Romantic descriptions of Confederate womanhood also dominate the secondary literature. See, for example, Francis Butler Simkins and James Welch Patton, *The Women of the Confederacy* (Richmond, Va.: Garrett and Massie, 1936), 14–18; Mary Elizabeth Massey, *Bonnet Brigades: American Women and the Civil War* (New York: Alfred A. Knopf, 1966), 30; Sterkx, *Partners in Rebellion,* 41–45.

2. For the place of women in antebellum ideas of honor, see Wyatt-Brown, *Southern Honor,* 134–48, 199–253.

3. Mittie Williams to Miss S. E. Scarborough, September 8, 1863, Scarborough to Williams, January 30, 1864, Scarborough Family Papers, Duke; Bell Irvin Wiley, *The Plain People of the Confederacy* (Baton Rouge: Louisiana State University Press, 1943), 59–61; Annie Jeter to William G. Jeter, September 25, 1861, Annie Jeter Carmouche Papers, LSU; Woodward, *Mary Chesnut's Civil War,* 588–89.

4. Elodie Todd to Nathaniel Henry Rhodes Dawson, May 9, 1861, Nathaniel Henry Rhodes Dawson Papers, SHC; Sterkx, *Partners in Rebellion,* 149–52; "Matrimony," *Southern Illustrated News,* 1 (November 23, 1862), 3; LaSalle Corbell Pickett, *The Heart of a Soldier as Revealed in the Intimate Letters of Genl. George E. Pickett, C.S.A.* (New York: Seth Moyle, 1913), 73–76.

5. July 12, 1864, Ella Gertrude Clanton Thomas Diary, Duke; Henrietta ? to Ann Hardeman, January 9, 1864, John Bull Smith Dimitry Papers, Duke; Kate

Corbin to Sallie Munford, July 3, 1861, October 20, 1863, Munford-Ellis Family Papers, Duke.

6. Robertson, *Lucy Breckinridge,* 22, 31, 51.

7. Ibid, 33–34, 83, 86.

8. Ibid, 123–24, 134, 167, 170, 180.

9. Lizzie Pitts to Thomas Henry Pitts, May 5, 1863, Thomas Henry Pitts Papers, Emory; October 12, 1861, Betty Herndon Maury Diary, LC; Woodward, *Mary Chesnut's Civil War,* 436.

10. P. S. DeHay to Elizabeth N. DeHay, August 22, 1861, Elizabeth N. DeHay Papers, MDAH; Robert Harley Mackintosh, Jr., ed., *"Dear Martha": The Confederate War Letters of a South Carolina Soldier, Alexander Faulkner Fewell* (Columbia, S.C.: R. L. Bryan, 1976), 5–6; Sarah Myers Rivers Trotter to Cynthia Carter, March 1, 1862, Pope-Carter Family Papers, Duke; Mary Wilkinson to Micajah Wilkinson, August 1, 1862, Micajah Wilkinson and Family Papers, LSU. A proud Richmond woman who had three sons in service refused to apply to the local quartermaster for cheap cloth to make a suit for her husband. "He ain't never done nothing for the country as yet," she snapped. Her fifty-four-year-old spouse was in no condition to march, but she thought he could at least drive a supply wagon. McGuire, *Diary of a Southern Refugee,* 99–101.

11. L. Minor Blackford, ed., "The Great John B. Minor and His Cousin Mary Face the War: Correspondence between the Professor of Law and the Lynchburg Blackfords, 1860–1864," *Virginia Magazine of History and Biography,* 61 (October 1953), 447–48; October 7, 1862, Lizzie Hatcher Simons Diary, BTHC.

12. February 14, April 13, 1862, Betty Herndon Maury Diary, LC; January 7, 1861, Sue McDowell Journal in Sue McDowell Papers, SCL.

13. *War Days in Fayetteville, North Carolina* (Fayetteville, N.C.: Judge Printing Co., 1910), 30; Florence King Carteret to Henry Lord Page King, August 5, 1861, Thomas Butler King Papers, SHC; Anderson, ed., *Journal of Kate Stone,* 255–56. Lower Southern literacy rates may have lessened the importance of mail in sustaining family ties, while also leaving some families "completely" separated for the duration of the war. Educated women wrote and read letters for illiterate wives and mothers. George Peddy Cuttino, ed., *Saddle Bag and Spinning Wheel: Being the Civil War Letters of George W. Peddy and Kate Featherston Peddy* (Macon, Ga.: Mercer University Press, 1981), 30.

14. Samuel R. Latta to Mary Latta, June 11, 1861, Samuel R. Latta Papers, LSU. For typical examples of women describing their love for their husbands in the army, see Sarah Hamilton Yancey to Benjamin C. Yancey, August 27, 1861, Benjamin C. Yancey Papers, SHC; Dora Harper Couper to J. Maxwell Couper, June 22, 1862, Couper Family Papers, SHC.

15. G. Minerva Bone to Robert D. Bone, December 19, 1861, Robert Donell Bone Papers, Emory; Lou Wharton to Edward C. Wharton, November 18, 1861,

Edward Clifton Wharton and Family Papers, LSU; Elvie Eagleton Skipper and Ruth Gove, eds., "'Stray Thoughts': The Civil War Diary of Ethie M. Foute Eagleton," *East Tennessee Historical Society's Publications,* 41 (1969), 124; Alpha Edge to Andrew J. Edge, December 12, 1863, Andrew J. Edge Papers, Emory; Julia ? to J. Higgins, November 25, 1863, ms, Fredericksburg National Military Park. I am grateful to National Park Service historian A. Wilson Greene for calling this unusual letter to my attention.

16. Cuttino, *Saddle Bag and Spinning Wheel,* 12, 49–50, 72.

17. Mackintosh, *"Dear Martha,"* 52; Susan Dantzler to Absalom Dantzler, June 22, 1862, Absalom Dantzler Papers, Duke; Sarah Hamilton Yancey to Benjamin C. Yancey, November 24, 1861, Benjamin C. Yancey Papers, SHC.

18. Martha Fort to Tomlinson Fort, Jr., June 13, 1861, Fort Family Papers, SHC; Ann L. Hardeman to Edward Stuart, November 4, 1862, John Bull Smith Dimitry Papers, Duke; L. Minor Blackford, *Mine Eyes Have Seen the Glory* (Cambridge, Mass: Harvard University Press, 1954), 179; Daniel E. Huger Smith et al., *Mason Smith Family Letters, 1860–1868* (Chapel Hill: University of North Carolina Press, 1950), 9.

19. December 13, 1864, Lucy Williamson Cocke Diary in Lucy Williamson Cocke Collection, UVa; Charlotte L. Branch to John L. Branch, March 30, 1861, Margaret Branch Sexton Papers, UGa; Aubrey Lee Brooks and Hugh Talmage Leffler, eds., *The Papers of Walter Clark,* 2 vols. (Chapel Hill: University of North Carolina Press, 1948), 1:101–2. Men could also display a certain naiveté (or disingenuousness) about camp life. See, for example, J. Maxwell Couper to Dora Harper Couper, December 15, 1861, Couper Family Papers, SHC.

20. Julia Davidson to John M. Davidson, September 19, 1862, John Mitchell Davidson Papers, Emory; Mary Ann Cobb to John A. Cobb, August 18, 1861, Cobb, Erwin, and Lamar Papers, UGa; Margaret Houston to Sam Houston, Jr., November 24, 1863, Margaret Moffette Houston Papers, BTHC.

21. Addie Simpson to James Simpson, July 28, 1863, Allan and Simpson Family Papers, SHC; Elsie Bragg to Braxton Bragg, September 17, 1863, Braxton Bragg Letters, BTHC; Lila Chunn to Willie Chunn, January 17, 1862, Willie Chunn Papers, Duke; Florence King to Henry Lord Page King, May 11, 1861, Thomas Butler King Papers, SHC.

22. See, for example, Fleet and Fuller, *Green Mount,* 80; Mary J. Minor to W. B. Minor, December 31, 1863, Mary J. Minor Papers, BTHC.

23. Katherine M. Jones, ed., *Heroines of Dixie: Confederate Women Tell Their Story of the War* (Indianapolis: Bobbs-Merrill, 1955), 153–54; Ada Rucker to her husband, April 27, 1863, Ada Rucker Letter, LSU; April 28, 1862, Ella Gertrude Clanton Thomas Diary, Duke; Georgia King to Henry Lord Page King, April 11, 1861, Thomas Butler King Papers, SHC; Nancy Diamond to Euclidus Marlivet and Rebecca Diamond Marlivet, November 13, 1863, Civil War Miscellany, GDAH.

24. Crabtree and Patton, *Edmondston Journal,* 249; Celeste Clay to Virginia Clay, March 18, 1862, Clement Claiborne Clay Papers, Duke; Susan Leigh Colston Blackford, *Memoirs of Life In and Out of the Army in Virginia During the War Between the States,* 2 vols. (Lynchburg, Va.: J. P. Bell, 1894–96), 1:27.

25. Mary Eliza Calloway to Morgan Calloway, October 6, 1862, Morgan Calloway Papers, Emory; Sarah Hamilton Yancey to Benjamin C. Yancey, September 6, 1861, Benjamin C. Yancey Papers, SHC; Rosa H. Delony to William G. Delony, December 31, 1861, William Gaston Delony Papers, UGa.

26. Mary Latta to Samuel R. Latta, August 19, 1861, Samuel R. Latta Papers, LSU; Fleet and Fuller, *Green Mount,* 107; May 22, 1862, Mrs. Hill Diary, UVa.

27. James Simpson to Addie Simpson, April 22, 1863, Allen and Simpson Family Papers, SHC.

28. Addie Simpson to James M. Simpson, July 29, 1861, Allen and Simpson Family Papers, SHC; William M. Cash and Lucy Somerville Howorth, eds., *My Dear Nellie: The Civil War Letters of William L. to Eleanor Smith Nugent* (Jackson: University Press of Mississippi, 1977), 90–91, 168–70, 194–95; Ellen E. Hodges and Stephen Kerber, eds., "Children of Honor: Letters of Winston and Octavia Stephens, 1861–1862," *Florida Historical Quarterly,* 56 (July 1977), 65.

29. Hassler, *General to His Lady,* 31–32, 43–45. Whether women at home also faced such temptations became a hotly debated issue. As one of Mary Chesnut's friends wryly observed, men had more liberty (not to mention opportunity) to commit adultery. Besides the restraints of the double standard, most wives would have found it difficult to conduct a love affair discreetly. Closely knit rural communities had few secrets; word of a woman's infidelity would soon reach her husband in camp. As in all wars, soldiers seduced and then abandoned civilian women or else became bigamists, leaving behind a trail of deserted wives, illegitimate children, and vile gossip. Even ministers reportedly took advantage of absent husbands by triffling with their female parishioners. Woodward, *Mary Chesnut's Civil War,* 470; Julia Davidson to John M. Davidson, May 1, 1862, John Mitchell Davidson Papers, Emory; Wiley, *Life of Johnny Reb,* 209; Marszalek, *Diary of Emma Holmes,* 194.

30. Wiley, *Life of Johnny Reb,* 209; August 19, 1862, Mary Louisa Williamson Diary, ADAH; Fannie Gordon to John Brown Gordon, October 16, 1864, Fannie Gordon Papers, GDAH; Harriet Perry to Mary Person, October 22, 1862, Harriet Perry to Theophilus Perry, October 30, 1862, Presley Carter Person Papers, Duke.

31. Eppes, *Through Some Eventful Years,* 178; Lou Wharton to Edward C. Wharton, October 30, 1861, Edward Clifton Wharton and Family Papers, LSU; Hester Reeve to Edward Payson Reeve, December 22, 1862, Edward Payson Reeve Papers, SHC; Mary J. Minor to W. B. Minor, December 27, 1863, Mary J. Minor Papers, BTHC.

32. Harriet Perry to Theophilus Perry, August 3, September 5, 1862, January 6, December 16, 1863, Presley Carter Person Papers, Duke. Jean Friedman has

argued that the bonds of community reduced the stress on Southern families during the war, but her coolly demographic analysis ignores some important qualitative evidence as well as the breakdown of certain community services. Friedman, *Enclosed Garden,* 92–94.

33. Woodward, *Mary Chesnut's Civil War,* 238; Hassler, *General to His Lady,* 65; James A. L. Fremantle, *Three Months in the Southern States* (New York: John Bradburn, 1864), 102.

34. For typical letters, see, Mrs. P. M. Nelson to Jefferson Davis, February 11, 1862, LR, CSW, RG 109, NA, M437, roll 27; Mary F. Fitzhugh to Davis, April 9, 1862, ibid., roll 46; Sue Carter to Henry Wise, April 19, 1861, Eliza Perkins to John Letcher, May 21, 1861, Jane McPherson to Letcher, November 21, 1861, Lucy Clayton Mathews to Letcher, June 6, 1861, John Letcher Papers, VSL.

35. Alice Baldwin to Alexander H. Stephens, March 6, 1862, Alexander H. Stephens Papers, LC; Mrs. E. G. Rosser to Jefferson Davis, n.d., 1861, LR, CSW, RG 109, NA, M437, roll 1; Mattie Hubbard to Zebulon Vance, July 10, 1863, Zebulon Baird Vance Papers, NCDAH.

36. Rosa Delony to William G. Delony, January 4, 1863, William Gaston Delony Papers, UGa.; Elsie Bragg to Braxton Bragg, n.d., 1861, Braxton Bragg Papers in William P. Palmer Collection, WRHS; E. P. Garland to Jefferson Davis, June 2, 1863, LR, CSW, RG 109, NA, M437, roll 93; Lizzie Person Bullock to Zebulon Vance, February 19, 1864, Zebulon Baird Vance Papers, NCDAH; Crabtree and Patton, *Edmondston Journal,* 52.

37. Blackford, *Memoirs,* 1:42; Marszalek, *Diary of Emma Holmes,* 287; September 4, 1862, Mrs. Hill Diary, UVa.

38. June 8–10, 1862, Frances Jane Bestor Robertson Diary in Lida Bestor Robertson Papers, ADAH. Her relief was short lived because her brother was killed in battle less than two weeks after she received this telegram. Illiterate women had someone read the newspapers to them and were often surprised when such bulky publications contained nothing about their relatives. David Dodge [pseud.], "Domestic Economy in the Confederacy," *Atlantic Monthly,* 58 (August 1886), 236.

39. Betty C. Saunders to Fleming Saunders, July 24, 1863, Irvine-Saunders Papers, UVa; Anderson, *Journal of Kate Stone,* 133; Ann Scott to SW, July 30, 1863, LR, CSW, RG 109, NA, M437, roll 112.

40. Mary Randolph to Robert M. T. Hunter, December 10, 1864, Robert M. T. Hunter Papers, UVa.; Mary M. Smith to John J. Pettus, June 30, 1863, John J. Pettus Papers, MDAH; Mary L. Taliaferro to Jefferson Davis, July 15, 1861, LR, CSW, RG 109, NA, M437, roll 5; Mrs. L. L. Whitefield to George W. Randolph, May 18, 1862, ibid., roll 77; Sarah W. Turner to Randolph, September 24, 1862, ibid., roll 75.

41. Elizabeth Harding to William Giles Harding, April 27, May 26, June 8, August 29, 1862, Harding and Jackson Family Papers, SHC.

42. Lizzie M. Critcher to James A. Seddon, November 20, 1863, LR, CSW, RG 109, NA, M437, roll 88; Sarah Pumphrey to Seddon, August 19, 1863, ibid., roll 108; Mary E. Norman to J. A. Campbell, October 7, 1864, ibid., roll 137; Mary Ann Harris Gay, *Life in Dixie During the War* (Atlanta: Charles P. Byrd, 1897), 48–49; Woodward, *Mary Chesnut's Civil War,* 591.

43. Woodward, *Mary Chesnut's Civil War,* 420–21; Louisa S. Thompson to Alexander H. Stephens, November 9, 1863, Alexander H. Stephens Papers, LC; Mary Salter to SW, December 4, 1862, LR, CSW, RG 109, NA, M437, roll 73.

44. McGuire, *Diary of a Southern Refugee,* 231; Kate Cumming, *Kate: The Journal of a Confederate Nurse,* ed. by Richard Barksdale Harwell (Baton Rouge: Louisiana State University Press, 1959), 17; Hannah Lide Coker, *A Story of the Late War* (n.p.: n.p., n.d.), 5–9.

45. Mackintosh, *"Dear Martha,"* 77; Hassler, *General to His Lady,* 129–30.

46. Sara A. Dorsey, *Recollections of Henry Watkins Allen, Brigadier General Confederate States Army, Ex-Governor of Louisiana* (New York: M. Doolady, 1866), 420; Woodward, *Mary Chesnut's Civil War,* 371.

47. T. Conn Bryan, ed., "A Georgia Woman's Civil War Diary: The Journal of Minerva Leah Rowles McClatchey, 1864–65," *Georgia Historical Quarterly,* 51 (June 1967), 208; Eliza C. Waddell to Christopher G. Memminger, September 20, 1863, LR, CSW, RG 109, NA, M437, roll 117.

48. Nancy A. E. Williams to SW, February 11, 1862, LR, CSW, RG 109, NA, M437, roll 28; Harriet Barnhill to ?, January 24, 1863, ibid., roll 81; Mary Forbes to James A. Seddon, March 4, 1863, ibid., roll 91; Victoria Cone Daniel to Alexander H. Stephens, May 16, 1862, Alexander H. Stephens Papers, LC; Mrs. S. E. D. Smith, *The Soldier's Friend* (Memphis, Tenn.: Bulletin Publishing Co., 1867), 276–77; H. C. Wiltse to Jane Brady, October 23, 1865, April 6, 1866, Thomas Charles Brady Family Papers, BTHC.

49. William Wyndham Malet, *An Errand to the South in the Summer of 1862* (London: Richard Bentley, 1863), 107; Myrta Lockett Avary, ed., *A Virginia Girl in the Civil War* (New York: D. Appleton, 1903), 46–47.

50. Robertson, *Lucy Breckinridge,* 80–81; September 20, 1863, Anonymous Diary, MDAH; Kate Virginia Cox Logan, *My Confederate Girlhood,* ed. by Lily Logan Morrill (Richmond: Garrett and Massie, 1932), 42; May 19, 1862, Jane B. Beale Diary, UVa.

51. May 5, 1864, Sue Richardson Diary, Emory; Lula Hansell Oglethorpe to Charlotte L. Branch, July 6, 1863, July 21, 1866, Margaret Branch Sexton Papers, UGa.

52. November 15, 1863, Anonymous Diary, MDAH; Woodward, *Mary Chesnut's Civil War,* 406; Elizabeth Preston Allan, *The Life and Letters of Margaret Junkin Preston* (Boston: Houghton Mifflin, 1903), 142.

53. Fremantle, *Three Months,* 147.

54. Cumming, *Journal,* 9, 22–23; Spencer Bidwell King, ed., *Ebb Tide As Seen Through the Diary of Josephine Gray Habersham, 1863* (Athens: University of Georgia Press, 1958), 92–93; George Cary Eggleston, *A Rebel's Recollections* (Bloomington: Indiana University Press, 1959), 91.

55. Fannie J. Robertson to "Dear Afflicted Daniel," July 10, 1862, copy in Frances Jane Bestor Robertson Diary in Lida Bestor Robertson Papers, ADAH; Anderson, *Journal of Kate Stone,* 262; Woodward, *Mary Chesnut's Civil War,* 702; Isabella Middleton Leland, ed., "Middleton Correspondence, 1861–1865," *South Carolina Historical Magazine,* 65 (January 1964), 34.

56. L. G. North to her sister, July 21, 1863, Pettigrew Family Papers, SHC.

57. Robertson, *Lucy Breckinridge,* 28–29; Cable, "Diary of a Union Woman," 934–35; McGuire, *Diary of a Southern Refugee,* 211; May 13, 1862, Jane B. Beale Diary, UVa; May ? to Betty Stuart, June 6, 1863, John Bull Smith Dimitry Papers, Duke.

CHAPTER 4

1. Affidavits of Marcella League and Ruth M. Nicholson, July 15, 1861, LR, CSW, RG 109, NA, M437, roll 5. Unless otherwise indicated, all correspondence and petitions used in this chapter come from this extensive group of War Department records and will be cited by roll number for the sake of brevity. This collection contains letters and other documents from women of all economic and social classes. As a source for the study of family life and civilian problems, it has no equal.

2. Mary L. Scales to SW, September 8, 1862, roll 72.

3. Virginia A. Thornton to Jefferson Davis, October 22, 1862, roll 151; Fannie Baptist to Davis, March 10, 1863, roll 82; Mrs. L. W. Nicholson to John J. Pettus, December 17, 1862, John J. Pettus Papers, MDAH.

4. M. A. Howell to Mary Y. Harth, June 23, 1864, Mary Y. Harth Papers, SCL; Margaret E. Thompson to Joseph E. Brown, August 27, 1864, Governors' Papers, GDAH; Ann M. Hines to Jefferson Davis, December 10, 1862, roll 54.

5. E. J. Samuel to James A. Seddon, April 29, 1863, roll 111; Virginia Atkinson to ?, March 8, 1864, roll 118; Mrs. J. M. McKee to SW, July 27, 1862, roll 62; Woodward, *Mary Chesnut's Civil War,* 495.

6. Eliza Prosser to Joseph E. Brown, December 8, 1861, Governors' Papers, GDAH; Mary Hall to Leroy P. Walker, January 28, 1862, roll 24; Mary Holden to Judah P. Benjamin, February 1, 1862, roll 26; Mrs. A. S. Walker to Benjamin, February 5, 1862, roll 26; Annetta Goodman to "General Jones," March 12, 1863, roll 93; Affidavit of Catherine Flannegan, January 29, 1862, roll 25. In the War Department records and the Virginia, North Carolina, South Carolina, Georgia, Alabama, and Mississippi governors' correspondence, I found 536 discharge

requests written by women. Of these letters and petitions, 137 concern the enlistment of minors. Here is the breakdown of letters citing an age:

Age of soldier	Number of complaints
18	5
17	49
16	43
15	13
14	2
13	1
12	0
11	0
10	1

7. Mrs. M. C. Williams to Jefferson Davis, February 3, 1862, roll 26; Martha Goodwin to Davis, October 2, 1861, and endorsements, roll 11; endorsements attached to the following documents: Mrs. A. M. F. Crawford to George W. Randolph, September 1862, roll 40; Affidavit of Mrs. M. Baldwin, April 16, 1863, roll 82; Sarah Amanda Guerry to Jefferson Davis, May 23, 1863, roll 93; Affidavit of Mrs. C. Andrews, June 8, 1863, roll 80; M. A. Holden to SW, January 11, 1863, roll 94.

8. Mrs. Lewis Betts to SW, September 1, 1862, roll 35; Mary A. Tribble to William Smith, August 29, 1864, William Smith Papers, VSL; Mary A. Windsor to Zebulon Vance, February 1, 1865, Zebulon Baird Vance Papers, NCDAH. From the petitions in the War Department records and the files of the state governors, it appears that most of the *overage* recruits were in their late thirties and early forties. This material also points to a curious, premodern characteristic of some yeoman families: women sometimes did not know their husbands' birth dates or even their ages. Georgian Mary Bennett could only estimate her spouse's age at between fifty and sixty; North Carolinian Sarah Smith claimed her husband was nearly fifty when his actual age was forty-two. Mary Bennett to Joseph E. Brown, October 13, 1864, Governors' Papers, GDAH; Frontis Johnston, ed., *The Papers of Zebulon Baird Vance* (Raleigh: State Department of Archives and History, 1963), 424–25.

9. Nora Hayes to George W. Randolph, August 1862, roll 52; Maria A. Jones to Jefferson Davis, February 11, 1862, roll 27; E. Louise Carter to Judah P. Benjamin, February 24, 1862, roll 37; Mary Thomas to Joseph E. Brown, June 12, 1864, Martha Thompson to Joseph E. Brown, March 20, 1865, Governors' Papers, GDAH. Epilepsy was popularly viewed as evidence of insanity, but not by Confederate officials. Even after Sarah Bramman's husband dislocated his shoulder during a seizure, the field officers in his regiment refused to recommend a discharge. Sarah A. Bramman to George W. Randolph, October 14, 1862, roll 35. The army also accepted men with serious mental disorders. Mrs. A. E. Johnson

to Jefferson Davis, October 17, 1862, roll 55; Annie L. Aldren to Joseph E. Brown, November 2, 1864, Governors' Papers, GDAH.

10. Harriet F. Wright to James A. Seddon, May 8, 1863, roll 116; Martha Bole to Jefferson Davis, November 18, 1864, roll 146; Rebecca O. Neal to Davis, October 16, 1862, roll 64; Margaret W. Toone to John Letcher, August 28, 1861, roll 7; Rosetta Lewis to ?, January 21, 1863, roll 99; Juliana Hayes to George W. Randolph, September 8, 1862, roll 52; Mrs. J. F. King to Joseph E. Brown, February 28, 1862, Governors' Papers, GDAH; Ellen Oliver to Jefferson Davis, April 7, 1863, roll 106; Frances B. Tillery to Joseph E. Brown, July 26, 1864, Mrs. S. E. Cook to Brown, August 16, 1864, Governors' Papers, GDAH.

11. Elizar Ballard to Joseph E. Brown, January 17, 1863, Governors' Papers, GDAH; Johnston, *Vance Papers,* 380–81; Sarah F. Alsobrook to James A. Seddon, June 10, 1863, roll 80; Mary Howell to SW, March 6, 1863, roll 95; Mrs. John A. Garrett to Jefferson Davis, February 12, 1864, roll 131; Mrs. L. Hemington to Seddon, January 21, 1863, roll 94. Of course, not all claims for medical exemptions were legitimate. With a few well-turned phrases, an imaginative wife could easily make a healthy husband seem a physical wreck. See, for example, the endorsements on Mrs. S. H. Shepherd to Jefferson Davis, November 2, 1863, roll 113.

12. Mrs. M. J. Porter to Joseph E. Brown, July 22, 1864, Governors' Papers, GDAH; Mattie Millard to Jefferson Davis, May 10, 1864, roll 136; Nancy Staley to James A. Seddon, May 1, 1863, roll 111.

13. Barthena Busbee to Joseph E. Brown, September 3, 1864, Governors' Papers, GDAH; Cordelia S. Adams to John Letcher, December 8, 1861, John Letcher Papers, VSL; Bettie Williams to Jefferson Davis, June 13, 1862, roll 77; Indiana L. Kemp to "Dear Friend," September 7, 1862, roll 56; Elizabeth Gilliam to SW, June 28, 1862, roll 48; Mrs. E. M. Baber to SW, April 13, 1862, roll 32.

14. Ann Kidd to John Letcher, September 7, 1861, John Letcher Papers, VSL. For other descriptions of the travail of large families, see Susan Griggs to "Captain Kane," August 30, 1864, roll 128 and the letters sent to Governor Brown during 1863 and 1864 in Governors' Papers, GDAH.

15. M. M. Taylor to Joseph E. Brown, May 26, 1863, Catherine McDonald to Brown, October 12, 1864, Governors' Papers, GDAH; Lucy Williams to George W. Randolph, May 12, 1862, roll 77.

16. Frances Bolton to Joseph E. Brown, July 22, 1864, Governors' Papers, GDAH; Mrs. W. H. C. Lane to to John J. Pettus, June 15, 1861, Elizabeth C. Haley to Pettus, July 15, 1862, John J. Pettus Papers, MDAH; Fanny M. Le Doyen to Leroy P. Walker, September 16, 1861, roll 10.

17. For representative examples, see Eliza Davis et al. to Jefferson Davis, November n.d., 1862, roll 30; Mary Earnest to SW, March 3, 1862, roll 44; Eliza Sibley to SW, March 16, 1864, roll 140.

18. Elizabeth King to George W. Randolph, July 24, 1862, roll 56; Jennette H. Thompson to Randolph, May 1862, roll 74.

19. Sarah Driggers to John Gill Shorter, June 18, 1862, John Gill Shorter Papers,

ADAH; Bettie A. Bayliss to SW, December 12, 1862, roll 146; Anna Jones to Davis, January 20, 1862, roll 23; Mrs. J. M. Aiken to Davis, July 25, 1864, roll 118; Mrs. Thomas G. Hood to ?, October 14, 1862, roll 78; Mary Ann Atkins to Judah P. Benjamin, January 19, 1862, roll 22; Polly Tillery to Joseph E. Brown, July 27, 1864, Governors' Papers, GDAH; Lucretia Curtis to John J. Pettus, March 31, 1863, John J. Pettus Papers, MDAH.

20. In reading the letters and petitions sent by women to Confederate officials, one is struck by the magnitude of the problems confronted by yeoman families. A sick husband, three sons in the army, illness at home, and no one to harvest the crop was a typical list of troubles. In addition, few families could live on a soldier's salary, even if they received it. Martha Tyler's husband had been in service since January 1864, but in October she still had not drawn any money. Unable to feed or clothe their five children, she had little choice but to ask for his discharge. Tyler to Joseph E. Brown, October 11, 1864, Governors' Papers, GDAH.

21. Mrs. M. E. Houston to Joseph E. Brown, March 27, 1863, Governors' Papers, GDAH; Sarah D. Cook to Jefferson Davis, September 3, 1861, roll 8; Henrietta F. Ford to SW, August 24, 1861, roll 8; Margaret E. Adams to SW, June 10, 1862, roll 29.

22. Hannah B. Moore to John Letcher, May 30, 1861, John Letcher Papers, VSL; Darthula K. Fulcher to ?, January 25, 1864, roll 126; Narcis Nagle to SW, September 21, 1862, roll 64.

23. Selina S. Poe to Alexander H. Stephens, November 14, 1861, Alexander H. Stephens Papers, LC; Nannie Ellison to SW, March 31, 1863, roll 90; Mrs. S. E. P. Ball to Jefferson Davis, September 15, 1862, roll 35; Frances Williams to Davis, December 16, 1861, roll 19; Susan R. Lewis to James A. Seddon, January 2, 1862, roll 99.

24. Caroline Foster to SW, February 7, 1864, roll 126; Virginia M. King to Judah P. Benjamin, October 29, 1861, roll 16.

25. Carrie Bowie to Zebulon Vance, May 25, 1863, Zebulon Baird Vance Papers, NCDAH.

26. Mrs. C. Shaw to ?, April 12, 1863, roll 111; Eliza Thacker to George W. Randolph, November 8, 1862, roll 75; Mrs. Mary Grayson to James A. Seddon, April 30, 1863, roll 93.

27. For details on the conditions of these families, see the following letters: Elvinra Holt to James A. Seddon, April 25, 1863, roll 95; Nancy Daker to SW, November 28, 1862, roll 44; Mrs. C. A. Richards to George W. Randolph, October 29, 1862, roll 69; Alice B. Springler to John Letcher, May 11, 1861, John Letcher Papers, VSL; Julia Spencer to John J. Pettus, August 15, 1862, John J. Pettus Papers, MDAH.

28. Mrs. J. J. Plant to SW, January 22, 1862, roll 23; Elizabeth L. Cabell to SW, January 22, 1862; Eliza Jencks to "Dear Cousin," April 29, 1863, roll 98; Martha C. Hopkins to John Letcher, May 17, 1861, John Letcher Papers, VSL.

29. Mrs. L. A. Reedick to SW, September 20, 1862, roll 69; Louisa E. Alexander to Jefferson Davis, November 1, 1862, roll 30; Mary D. Cone to SW, December 7, 1862, roll 41; Mary Kirby to Jefferson Davis, June 24, 1863, roll 99; Susan A. Shields to Jefferson Davis, December 23, 1861, roll 19; Mary Garris to SW, November 17, 1862, roll 49; Sarah Peebles to ?, September 26, 1864, roll 138; Nancy R. Moon to SW, March 22, 1863, roll 102.

30. Mary McCrary to John M. McCrary, June 22, 1862, John Mathew McCrary Papers, AHS; Nancy Baggarly to Tilmon F. Baggarly, January 17, 1864, Tilmon F. Baggarly Papers, Duke; Margaret McCarthy to Thomas McCarthy, July 23, 1862, roll 62; Ida Wilkom to Judah P. Benjamin, February 7, 1862, roll 27.

31. Clifford Anderson to Annie Anderson, July 18, 1862, Anderson Papers, SHC; *OR,* ser. 4, vol. 2, p. 693; Anna E. Booker to Jefferson Davis, July 11, 1864, roll 121; September 16, 1864, Grace B. Elmore Diary, SCL.

32. Albert B. Moore, *Conscription and Conflict in the Confederacy* (New York: Hilary House, 1963 [1924]), 27–51.

33. November 6, 1862, Sarah Lois Wadley Diary, SHC; Lizzie Pitts to Thomas Henry Pitts, April 4, 1863, Thomas Henry Pitts Papers, Emory; Elizabeth Wood to James A. Seddon, July 31, 1863, roll 116; September n.d., 1862, Ella Gertrude Clanton Thomas Diary, Duke.

34. See Moore, *Conscription and Conflict,* 70–72, and E. Merton Coulter, *The Confederate States of America, 1861–1865* (Baton Rouge: Louisiana State University Press, 1950), 319–20.

35. Martha Moncrief to Jefferson Davis, December 15, 1862, roll 150.

36. Mrs. Bat Smith to "Mr. Fitzpatrick," May 15, 1862, roll 46; Petition of Nancy Fowler, November 17, 1862, roll 47; Mary V. Busnitt to George W. Randolph, September 31 [*sic*], 1862, roll 35; Petition of Mrs. N. N. Jones, October 17, 1862, roll 28; Lucy Allen to Randolph, October 1, 1862, roll 30; Mrs. G. W. Fisher to Jefferson Davis, December 6, 1862, roll 91; Sarah L. Stower to John J. Pettus, June 2, 1862, John J. Pettus Papers, MDAH.

37. Julia M. Porter to John Gill Shorter, August 30, 1862, John Gill Shorter Papers, ADAH; Mrs. R. A. Lawrence to John J. Pettus, February 17, 1863, John J. Pettus Papers, MDAH; Certificate of Martha L. Chumney, November 11, 1862, roll 36; Hattie Motley to James A. Seddon, May 25, 1863, roll 103.

38. Bell Irvin Wiley, *Southern Negroes, 1861–1865* (New Haven: Yale University Press, 1938), 50; Mary C. C. Archer to Jefferson Davis, October 21, 1862, roll 80.

39. Sue Rose Walker to George W. Randolph, October 11, 1862, roll 78.

40. Petition of Cynthia Collins, December 9, 1862, roll 41; Anna Daniel Brunswick to Judah P. Benjamin, January 3, 1863, roll 89; Addie Harris to George W. Randolph, October 29, 1862, roll 53. These conclusions are based on 230 requests from women for the exemption of planters or overseers. The documents are in the records of the Confederate War Department and the papers of state governors.

41. Moore, *Conscription and Conflict,* 74; Eliza Burch et al. to John Gill Shorter,

n.d., 1863, Shorter Papers, ADAH; Mrs. M. A. Hunter to Jefferson Davis, December 16, 1862, roll 54; Martha A. R. Anthony to George W. Randolph, November 7, 1862, roll 30; Mrs. Elizabeth R. Preston to Davis, September 30, 1863, roll 107; Mary W. Walls to James A. Seddon, May 15, 1863, roll 116.

42. Mrs. Sydney B. Anderson to SW, April 9, 1862, roll 32; Nancy F. Dillard to George W. Randolph, April 10, 1862, roll 42; Petition of Ann Swan, February 12, 1863, roll 94; Nancy Williams to Randolph, November n.d., 1862, roll 117; Mary A. Christian to Charles Clark, September 1864, Charles Clark Papers, MDAH.

43. Annette Fauntleroy to R. L. Maintaige, January 6, 1864, roll 126; Fannie G. Moss to George W. Randolph, October 1, 1862, roll 62; Johnston, *Vance Papers,* 374–75.

44. Mary F. Barr to George W. Randolph, October 4, 1862, roll 34; Mrs. Argent Rowland to Joseph E. Brown, March 5, 1864, Governors' Papers, GDAH; Julia Davidson to John M. Davidson, May 1, 1862, John Mitchell Davidson Papers, Emory.

45. Nannie Williams to James P. Williams, December 28, 1863, James Peter Williams Papers, UVa; Sallie M. Bradley to John Letcher, July 15, 1861, John Letcher Papers, VSL; Mrs. S. M. Jackson to Joseph E. Brown, May 31, 1864, Governors' Papers, GDAH; July 31, 1862, Mrs. Hill Diary, UVa; Harriet A. Strother to Jefferson Davis, February 20, 1864, roll 140.

46. Ann Dierson to SW, January 5, 1863, roll 89; Lucinda Powell to SW, July 14, 1862, roll 66; Mrs. S. D. Roper to Joseph E. Brown, May 9, 1864, Governors' Papers, GDAH; Mrs. C. A. O'Daniel to Jefferson Davis, January 25, 1864, roll 137; Elvira E. Magill to James L. Orr, March 1, 1863, roll 102; F. E. Metz to Jefferson Davis, June n.d., 1864, roll 136; Mildred Hutton to Davis, October 27, 1864, roll 130; Catherine R. Stanton to Davis, April 12, 1864, roll 141; Mrs. J. L. Reed to SW, June 7, 1863, roll 109.

47. January 1, 1863, Meta Morris Grimball Diary, SHC; Catherine Carson to Zebulon Vance, July 8, 1864, Kate E. L. Virdin to Vance, February 23, 1865, Zebulon Baird Vance Papers, NCDAH; Julia Jones to Alexander Jones, March 19, 1865, Jones Family Papers, SHC.

48. David Dodge [O. W. Blacknall], "Cave Dwellers of the Confederacy," *Atlantic Monthly,* 58 (October 1891), 518–19; *OR,* ser. 1, vol. 32, pt. 3, p. 633.

49. *OR,* ser. 1, vol. 53, pp. 350, 352; Thomas Settle to Zebulon Vance, October 4, 1864, Zebulon Baird Vance Papers, NCDAH.

50. *OR,* ser. 4, vol. 2, pp. 247, 856–57; Ella Harper to George W. F. Harper, November 5, 1862, George Washington Finley Harper Papers, SHC; Augusta J. Evans to J. L. M. Curry, December 20, 1862, Jabez Lamar Monroe Curry Papers, LC. For additional evidence on the primary importance of civilian hardship in causing desertion, see Ella Lonn, *Desertion During the Civil War* (New York: Century Co., 1928), 12–13; Bessie Martin, *Desertion of Alabama Troops from the Confederate Army* (New York: AMS Press, 1966 [1932]), 144–55.

51. Mrs. R. J. Causey to R. J. Causey, October 14, 1863, R. J. Causey Correspondence, LSU; Mrs. M. N. Humphries to M. N. Humphries, October 4, 1864, Civil War Miscellany, GDAH; John E. Johns, *Florida During the Civil War* (Gainesville: University of Florida Press, 1963), 160.

52. Crabtree and Patton, *Edmondston Journal*, 71; Simkins and Patton, *Women of the Confederacy*, 30; Jones, *Rebel War Clerk's Diary*, 2:100–101; John W. Bell to Nancy Bell, June 15, 1862, John W. Bell Letters, LSU.

53. Rosa H. Delony to William G. Delony, August 2, 1863, William Gaston Delony Papers, UGa.; *OR*, ser. 1, vol. 23, pt. 2, p. 951; Wiley, *Plain People*, 68; Cuttino, *Saddle Bag and Spinning Wheel*, 300.

54. Cumming, *Journal*, 296; Jefferson Davis, *The Rise and Fall of the Confederate Government*, 2 vols. (New York: D. Appleton and Co., 1881), 1:iii; *OR*, ser. 4, vol. 2, p. 687.

CHAPTER 5

1. McGuire, *Diary of a Southern Refugee*, 30; November 22, 1864, Grace B. Elmore Diary, SCL.

2. Cable, "Diary of a Union Woman," 937–38.

3. Dyer, *To Raise Myself a Little*, 201; October 29, 1863, Kate S. Sperry Diary, VSL; May 23, 1864, Sidney Harding Diary, LSU; Dwight Franklin Henderson, ed., *The Private Journal of Georgiana Walker, 1862–1865, with Selections from the Post-War Years, 1865–1876* (Tuscaloosa, Ala.: Confederate Publishing Co., 1963), 36.

4. Leland, "Middleton Correspondence," 35; Matilda Champion to Sydney S. Champion, April 21, 1863, Sydney S. Champion Papers, Duke; Harriet Perry to Theophilus Perry, January 27, 1864, Presley Carter Person Papers, Duke.

5. Mary Jane Lucas to Anne Ashley, December 25, 1862, Lucas-Ashley Family Papers, Duke.

6. Jones, *Children of Pride*, 1134; "Civil War Days in Huntsville; A Diary by Mrs. W. D. Chadick," *Alabama Historical Quarterly*, 9 (Summer 1947), 281.

7. Anderson, *Journal of Kate Stone*, 109–10; Eliza Frances Andrews, *The War-Time Journal of a Georgia Girl*, ed. by Spencer Bidwell King, Jr. (Macon, Ga.: Ardivan Press, 1960), 110–11.

8. Earl Schenck Miers, ed., *When the World Ended: The Diary of Emma LeConte* (New York: Oxford University Press, 1957), 16–17; Anderson, *Journal of Kate Stone*, 204, 291.

9. H. E. Sterkx, ed., "A Patriotic Confederate Woman's Diary, 1862–1863," *Alabama Historical Quarterly*, 20 (Winter 1955), 614; Anna Harden to Mary Ann Harden, May 14, 1864, Edward Harden Papers, Duke; Anderson, *Journal of Kate Stone*, 24–26, 206–7, 252.

10. King, *Diary of Josephine Habersham*, 103; February 29, 1864, Ann Shannon

Martin Diary, MDAH; Anderson, *Journal of Kate Stone,* 267; Crabtree and Patton, *Edmondston Journal,* 673.

11. Prices compiled from the following sources: Allan, *Margaret Junkin Preston,* 146–47, 167; McGuire, *Diary of a Southern Refugee,* 201, 235; Virginia ? to Lelia Willis, December 19, 1862, Larkin Willis Papers, Duke; Eliza Teague to Mary Scarborough, July 27, 1863, Scarborough Family Papers, Duke.

12. August 15, September 1, 1863, April 25, 1864, Priscilla Munnikhuysen Bond Diary, LSU; James I. Robertson, *The Diary of Dolly Lunt Burge* (Athens: University of Georgia Press, 1962), 88; November 21, 1864, Letitia Roane Diary, Duke. Sewing's other requisites became equally scarce and costly. At the end of the war a spool of thread could run as high as ten dollars. Buttons disappeared, though leather and persimmon seeds made adequate substitutes. But the shortage of pins and needles caused the most trouble. Seamstresses hoarded these precious items like gold because a book or paper of pins often cost five dollars. May 15, 1864, Meta Morris Grimball Diary, SHC; Bell Irvin Wiley, ed., *Letters of Warren Akin, Confederate Congressman* (Athens: University of Georgia Press, 1959), 127–28; Mary Love Edwards Fleming, "Dale County and Its People During the Civil War," *Alabama Historical Quarterly,* 19 (Spring 1957), 98; Mary Elizabeth Massey, *Ersatz in the Confederacy* (Columbia: University of South Carolina Press, 1952), 151–52; Dawson, *Our Women in the War,* 356–57.

13. Sterkx, "Patriotic Confederate Woman's Diary," 613–14; Fleming, "Dale County During the War," 72–76; Parthenia Hague, *A Blockaded Family: Life in Southern Alabama During the Civil War* (Boston: Riverside Press, 1888), 80–88.

14. Evangeline Shannon Crutcher to Levina Morris Shannon, February 1, 1863, Crutcher-Shannon Papers, MDAH; Cumming, *Journal,* 64, 193; Adeline Graves to Henry Graves, February 14, 1862, Graves Family Papers, SHC.

15. "The Southern Girl With the Home-Spun Dress" (Confederate Imprint No. 3208).

16. Eppes, *Through Some Eventful Years,* 181; Cumming, *Journal,* 189, 248–49.

17. Jones, *Rebel War Clerk's Diary,* 2:16; Massey, *Ersatz in the Confederacy,* 91–94.

18. Woodward, *Mary Chesnut's Civil War,* 464; Dawson, *A Confederate Girl's Diary,* 36–37; McGuire, *Diary of a Southern Refugee,* 251–52; Pryor, *Reminiscences of Peace and War,* 316–17; Massey, *Ersatz in the Confederacy,* 80–85; Eppes, *Through Some Eventful Years,* 238.

19. For fuller details on these makeshifts, see Massey, *Ersatz in the Confederacy,* passim.

20. Dodge, "Domestic Economy in the Confederacy," 234–35; Allan, *Margaret Junkin Preston,* 178; McGuire, *Diary of a Southern Refugee,* 257–58; Cumming, *Journal,* 248.

21. Dawson, *Confederate Girl's Diary,* 212–13.

22. I have taken these prices from hundreds of references in women's diaries and letters as well as a few price lists in secondary sources. For the most part, I have used prices actually paid because reported prices often exaggerated an admittedly bad situation. I have also been wary of prices that were much higher than other prices cited from the same area.

23. January 6, 1864, Julia Fisher Diary, SHC; March 8, May 1, 1864, Sidney Harding Diary, LSU; Cumming, *Journal,* 264–65; Miers, *Diary of Emma LeConte,* 83.

24. June 1, July 3, 1864, Lucy Muse Fletcher Diary, Duke; Fleming, "Dale County During the War," 94–95; April 15, 1864, Julia Fisher Diary, SHC.

25. Leland, "Middleton Correspondence," 102; Anderson, *Journal of Kate Stone,* 109, 258–59; Marszalek, *Diary of Emma Holmes,* 352.

26. Taylor et al., eds., *South Carolina Women in the Confederacy,* 1:207–8; Leland, "Middleton Correspondence," 40.

27. Dawson, *Confederate Girl's Diary,* 233; McGuire, *Diary of a Southern Refugee,* 247; Mary L. Smithie to Bennette M. Bagby, March 21, 1863, Bagby Papers, Duke. For the first time, wives and mothers in large numbers went into the fields. The sight of women plowing symbolized a world turned upside down, and for some Southerners a dangerous blurring of sex roles. With most of the young men in the army, females threshed wheat and performed other traditionally male tasks. J. M. Lucey et al., eds., *Confederate Women of Arkansas in the Civil War* (Little Rock, Ark.: H. J. Pugh, 1907), 155; Clarence Poe, ed., *True Tales of the South at War: How Soldiers Fought and Families Lived, 1861–65* (Chapel Hill: University of North Carolina Press, 1961), 59–60; Hague, *Blockaded Family,* 22–24.

28. Harriet Perry to Theophilus Perry, April 5, 1863, Presley Carter Person Papers, Duke; July 2, 1862, Ann Wilkinson Penrose Diary, LSU; April 23, 1862, Mary Greenhow Lee Diary, LC; Mary Bryson to Margaret Butler, January 16, 1862, Margaret Butler Papers, LSU; Cumming, *Journal,* 248.

29. Anne Laurie Harris Broidrick Recollections, p. 14, SHC.

30. Mary Elizabeth Massey, *Refugee Life in the Confederacy* (Baton Rouge: Louisiana State University Press, 1964), 278; Mamie Lloyd to Jefferson Davis, September 25, 1864, LR, CSW, RG 109, NA, M437, roll 133; Rives Lang Beaty, ed., "Recollections of Harriet DuBose Kershaw Lang," *South Carolina Historical Magazine,* 59 (July 1958), 164.

31. April 29, 1864, Sally Lyons Taliaferro Diary, VSL; Sarah Scarborough to Mittie L. Williams, May 10, 1863, Susan McLeod to Mary Scarborough, May 15, 1862, Scarborough Family Papers, Duke.

32. Harriet Perry to Theophilus Perry, February 8, 1863, Presley Carter Person Papers, Duke; January 11, 1864, Cora E. Watson Journal, LSU.

33. Elizabeth Collins, *Memories of the Southern States* (Taunton, Eng.: Bar-

nicott Printer, 1865), 33; Dougan, *Confederate Arkansas,* 105; T. J. Smith to John C. Breckinridge, February 28, 1865, LR, CSW, RG 109, NA, M437, roll 146; January 3, 1864, Julia Fisher Diary, SHC.

34. December 24, 1863, Priscilla Munnikhuysen Bond Diary, LSU; December 25, 1862, Carrie Hunter Diary in Cobb and Hunter Family Papers, SHC; December 30, 1863, Sarah Lois Wadley Diary, SHC; Dawson, *Confederate Girl's Diary,* 307.

35. Woodward, *Mary Chesnut's Civil War,* 515; Marszalek, *Diary of Emma Holmes,* 389; Mrs. Burton Harrison, *Recollections Grave and Gay* (New York: Charles Scribner's Sons, 1911), 169–70; December 25, 1864, Priscilla Munnikhuysen Bond Diary, LSU; January 2, 1865, Kate Garland Diary in Kate Garland Papers, LSU; January 6, 1864, Julia Fisher Diary, SHC.

36. December 25, 1864, Sarah Rodgers Espy Diary, ADAH; William P. Buck, ed., *Sad Earth, Sweet Heaven: The Diary of Lucy Rebecca Buck . . . 1861–1865* (Birmingham, Ala.: Cornerstone, 1973), 240; December 25, 1862, Ann Wilkinson Penrose Diary, LSU; Crabtree and Patton, *Edmondston Journal,* 648; Sally A. Putnam, *Richmond During the War; Four Years of Personal Observation* (New York: G. W. Carleton, 1867), 89, 201–2.

37. March 15, 1864, Ann Shannon Martin Diary, MDAH; Susanna C. Clay to C. C. Clay, Jr., July 25, 1863, Clement Claiborne Clay Papers, Duke; Dawson, *Confederate Girl's Diary,* 224; January 1, March 20, 1864, Julia Fisher Diary, SHC.

38. Crabtree and Patton, *Edmondston Journal,* 220; Lucy Irion to James Irion, August 26, 1862, Irion-Neilson Family Papers, MDAH.

39. Marszalek, *Diary of Emma Holmes,* 42–43, 166; July 2, 1861, Mary Ezell Diary in Edward Conigland Papers, SHC; January 1, 1862, Margaret Gillis Diary, ADAH; Mary Clark to Edward L'Engle, February 19, 1862, Edward L'Engle Papers, SHC; July 21, 1861, Ella Gertrude Clanton Thomas Diary, Duke; November 13, 1861, Sarah Rodgers Espy Diary, ADAH. Privately owned ships and naval vessels ran the blockade but within a few months, it was obvious that the Confederacy would never approach prewar Southern trade levels. The government discouraged and eventually prohibited the importation of luxury goods, but demand was too incessant and profits too large to shut off this traffic. For the most recent—and unpersuasive—attempt to downplay the importance of the blockade, see Richard E. Beringer, et al., *Why the South Lost the Civil War* (Athens: University of Georgia Press, 1986), 53–63.

40. Marszalek, *Diary of Emma Holmes,* 287; King, *Diary of Josephine Habersham,* 61; Hague, *Blockaded Family,* 89–100; Mrs. Felix G. de Fontaine, "Old Confederate Days," *Confederate Veteran,* 4 (1896), 301; Pryor, *Reminiscences of Peace and War,* 226–27; December 29, 1864, Robert A. Tyson Diary, LSU; August 14, 1861, Betty Herndon Maury Diary, LC; Mary P. Fletcher, ed., "An Arkansas Lady in the Civil War: Reminiscences of Susan Fletcher," *Arkansas Historical Quarterly,* 2 (December 1943), 370–71.

41. Richard Cecil Todd, *Confederate Finance* (Athens: University of Georgia

Press, 1954), 57–58; Cash and Howorth, *My Dear Nellie,* 137; Mrs. James K. Polk to General James R. Chalmers, December 20, 1863, LR, CSW, RG 109, NA, M437, roll 137; Donna E. Otey to "Colonel Henry," January 21, 1864, ibid., roll 137; Martha Cragin to Charles Clark, November 28, 1863, Clark to Cragin, December 6, 1863, Clark Papers, MDAH. Sarah Polk apparently received permission to sell her cotton to the enemy. Jones, *Rebel War Clerk's Diary,* 2:131.

42. Carrie R. Copes to Flora Garrett, December 22, 1861, Flora McCabe Collection, LC; Anderson, *Journal of Kate Stone,* 128; July 11, 1862, Jane B. Beale Diary, UVa.

43. August 31, 1861, April 6, 1862, Betty Herndon Maury Diary, LC; Amelia N. Pinkind to Isabella Woodruff, June 30, 1861, Isabella Woodruff Papers, Duke; Julia Davidson to John Davidson, May 1, 1862, John Mitchell Davidson Papers, Emory; February 23, 1864, Ann Shannon Martin Diary, MDAH; April 20, 1864, Margaret Gillis Diary, ADAH. Although Congress never declared the Treasury notes legal tender, they circulated as currency so long as people would accept them.

44. Eugene M. Lerner, "Inflation in the Confederacy, 1861–65," in Milton Friedman, ed., *Studies in the Quantity Theory of Money* (Chicago: University of Chicago Press, 1956), 163–75; November 6, 1863, Priscilla Munnikhuysen Bond Diary, LSU.

45. Paul W. Gates, *Agriculture and the Civil War* (New York: Alfred A. Knopf, 1965), 42–43; December 1, 1864, Louisa Warren Patch Fletcher Diary, GDAH; Gay, *Life in Dixie During the War,* 245–56.

46. A. Marie Brownson to Joseph E. Brown, August 3, 1863, Governors' Papers, GDAH; Woodward, *Mary Chesnut's Civil War,* 749; Andrews, *Journal of a Georgia Girl,* 116.

47. Kate C. Jones to Leroy P. Walker, July 19, 1861, LR, CSW, RG 109, NA, M437, roll 8; Mrs. Mar E. Acree to "Mr. Cooper," March 20, 1862, ibid., roll 29; Bettie A. R. L. Myrtie to Jefferson Davis, September 1, 1864, ibid., roll 136; Mahalay Hyatte to Joseph E. Brown, January 22, 1862, Governors' Papers, GDAH; Lucreesy Simmons to John Gill Shorter, July 17, 1862, John Gill Shorter Papers, ADAH; Elizabeth Wood to "Major Devereux," October 5, 1864, Quartermaster Department Correspondence, Civil War Collection, NCDAH.

48. William Porcher Miles to George W. Randolph, September 19, 1862, LR, CSW, RG 109, NA, M437, roll 63; Florence J. Duke to James A. Seddon, October 21, 1864, ibid., roll 125; Mary H. Davis to ?, December 18, 1864, ibid., roll 126; Martha Haisop to Davis, April 17, 1864, ibid., roll 129. Paul D. Escott has argued persuasively that the welfare problem is critical for understanding Confederate social and economic history. *After Secession: Jefferson Davis and the Failure of Confederate Nationalism* (Baton Rouge: Louisiana State University Press, 1978), 140–44, and Escott, "'The Cry of the Sufferers': The Problem of Welfare in the Confederacy," *Civil War History,* 23 (September 1977), 228–40.

49. Charles William Ramsdell, *Behind the Lines in the Southern Confederacy* (Baton Rouge: Louisiana State University Press, 1944), 61–68; Mary Spencer Ringold, *The Role of the State Legislatures in the Confederacy* (Athens: University of Georgia Press, 1966), 77–80; Jefferson Davis Bragg, *Louisiana in the Confederacy* (Baton Rouge: Louisiana State University Press, 1941), 237–40; Sterkx, *Partners in Rebellion,* 144–47. Some supplies did not reach the people. In North Carolina, for example, the Confederate army impressed corn originally purchased by the legislature for distribution to the poor. *OR,* ser. 4, vol. 2, p. 413.

50. Jane Boykin to John J. Pettus, July 10, 1862, Pettus Papers, MDAH; Ella Lonn, *Salt as a Factor in the Confederacy* (New York: Century Co., 1933), 112; Families Supplied with Salt, 1862–1864, "Salt Book," Office of the Commissary General, GDAH; Addie Harris to John Gill Shorter, October 16, 1862, John Gill Shorter Papers, ADAH; Buck, *Diary of Lucy Buck,* 253. Georgia and North Carolina sold cotton cards, which then went for as much as one hundred dollars, to soldiers' wives and widows for only ten dollars a piece. Lizzie C. Bachelder to Joseph E. Brown, November 22, 1863, Emma Cullens to Brown, November 18, 1863, Governors' Papers, GDAH; Cornelia Phillips Spencer to Zebulon Baird Vance, August 22, 1864, Zebulon Baird Vance Papers, NCDAH; Frances E. Huske to Vance, March 9, 1864, Quartermaster Department Correspondence, Civil War Collection, NCDAH.

51. Martin, *Desertion of Alabama Troops,* 174–78; Clyde Olin Fisher, "Relief of Soldiers' Families in North Carolina During the Civil War," *South Atlantic Quarterly,* 16 (January 1917), 60–72; William F. Zornow, "State Aid for the Indigent Soldiers and Their Families in Louisiana, 1861–1865," *Louisiana Historical Quarterly,* 39 (July 1956), 375–80 and "Aid for the Indigent Families of Soldiers in Virginia," *Virginia Magazine of History and Biography,* 66 (October 1958), 454–59.

52. Mrs. L. M. Corley to John Gill Shorter, August 18, 1862, John Gill Shorter Papers, ADAH; Petition of Nancy Owens, February 11, 1865, Andrew W. Magrath Papers, SCDAH; Mrs. Mary A. C. Loyd to Jefferson Davis, January 13, 1864, LR, CSW, RG 109, NA, M437, roll 132; Elvira Holmes to John Letcher, October 23, 1861, John Letcher Papers, VSL; Wiley, *Plain People,* 43.

53. Johnston, *Vance Papers,* 308; Martin, *Desertion of Alabama Troops,* 126–38. Averages computed from the following sources: William Diffee Standard, *Columbus Georgia in the Confederacy* (New York: William Frederick Press, 1954), 49–50; Kenneth Coleman, *Confederate Athens* (Athens: University of Georgia Press, 1967), 53–54; John D. Winters, *The Civil War in Louisiana* (Baton Rouge: Louisiana State University Press, 1963), 37–38; Statements of Committee for Meadow District, Johnston County, North Carolina, March 3, June 27, 1862, September 26, 1863, John C. Hood Papers, Duke; Money Paid the wives and widows of soldiers by I. Jarratt, 1864–1865, Jarratt-Puryear Family Papers, Duke.

54. Emily M. Farrar to David C. Barrow, February 21, 1865, David Crenshaw

Barrow Papers, UGa; November 28, 1862, Meta Morris Grimball Diary, SHC; Eugenia Jenson to Isabella Woodruff, December 14, 1863, Woodruff Papers, Duke. In addition to general contributions to charity, some women also tried to deal with their poor neighbors individually. Feeling guilty for complaining about minor problems when others went hungry and had no place to live. Ella Thomas salved her conscience with a basket of berries bought from a poor woman and her little boy or with five dollars given to a distraught refugee to buy Christmas presents for her children. July 12, December 27, 1864, Ella Gertrude Clanton Thomas Diary, Duke.

55. *Report of the Committee of the Free Market of New Orleans* (New Orleans: Bulletin Book and Job Office, 1862, Confederate Imprint No. 4961), iii–66; Peter F. Walker, *Vicksburg, a People at War: 1861–1865* (Chapel Hill: University of North Carolina Press, 1960), 60–61; Martin, *Desertion of Alabama Troops,* 164–69; *Report of the Board for the Relief of Families of Soldiers in the Parishes of St. Philip and St. Michael* (Charleston, S.C.: Steam Power Press of Evans and Cogswell, 1863, Confederate Imprint No. 4953), 5–10.

56. Mrs. A. P. Acors to Jefferson Davis, March 23, 1862, LR, CSW, RG 109, NA, M437, roll 29; Kate Mason Rowland and Mrs. Morris L. Croxall, eds., *The Journal of Julia LeGrand, New Orleans, 1862–1863* (Richmond: Everett Waddey, 1911), 37. For a good general description of class conflict in the Confederacy, see Escott, *After Secession,* 94–134.

57. Mary McCrary to John McCrary, May 17, 1863, John Mathew McCrary Papers, AHS; Margaret Hudlow to Joseph E. Brown, September n.d., 1864, Governors' Papers, GDAH; Cumming, *Journal,* 79; Mary Stead et al. to Brown, March 27, 1862, Governors' Papers, GDAH; Elsie Bragg to Braxton Bragg, March 7, 1862, Braxton Bragg Papers in William P. Palmer Collection, WRHS; Mrs. S. D. Bagley to SW, November 2, 1864, LR, CSW, RG 109, NA, M437, roll 122. Whether true or not, a widely circulated story told of a Richmond storekeeper trying to sell a barrel of flour to a poor woman for seventy dollars. Claiming she could not afford such prices and pointing to her starving offspring, she asked, "What shall I do?" In a reply worthy of Jonathan Swift, he coolly answered, "I don't know, madam, unless you eat your children." Jones, *Rebel War Clerk's Diary,* 2:78.

58. Mary P. Davis to Ben Davis, July 28, 1863, Mary P. Davis Papers, Duke; Henry L. Ingram, ed., *Civil War Letters of George W. and Martha P. Ingram, 1861–1865* (College Station: Texas A&M University Library, 1973), 45; Julia Davidson to John M. Davidson, July 17, 1863, John Mitchell Davidson Papers, Emory.

59. Martin, *Desertion of Alabama Troops,* 161–63; Sarah S. Wright to Joseph E. Brown, May 27, 1861, Governors' Papers, GDAH; Mary C. McKinley, "A Daughter of Georgia," to the *Macon Telegraph,* July 4, 1862, Cobb, Erwin, and Lamar Papers, UGa; Louisa Stone to Jefferson Davis, August 15, 1864, LR, CSW, RG 109, NA, M437, roll 141; Mrs. L. E. Davis to Jefferson Davis, August 22, 1864, ibid., roll 125.

60. Mary L. Cummings to SW, August 19, 1864, LR, CSW, RG 109, NA, M437, roll 124; August 14, 1862, Ella Gertrude Clanton Thomas Diary, Duke; "The Home-Spun Dress," *Southern Illustrated News,* 1 (November 2, 1862), 3; Smith, et al., *Mason Smith Family Letters,* 82–83.

61. December 18, 1863, Sarah Rodgers Espy Diary, ADAH; Coleman, "Mary Ann Cobb," 368.

62. Mrs. Dr. Welborn to Joseph E. Brown, November 16, 1862, Governors' Papers, GDAH.

63. Unless otherwise noted, I have drawn my account of the Richmond bread riot from Michael B. Chesson's excellent article "Harlots or Heroines? A New Look at the Richmond Bread Riot," *Virginia Magazine of History and Biography,* 92 (April 1984), 131–75. Although Chesson unjustifiably downplays the importance of class hostility in causing the riot, his careful sifting of the evidence supersedes previous accounts.

64. Pryor, *Reminiscences of Peace and War,* 237–39.

65. F. N. Boney, *John Letcher of Virginia* (University, Ala.: University of Alabama Press, 1966), 190.

66. Some useful but not always reliable detail is in Jones, *Rebel War Clerk's Diary,* 1:285.

67. For differing versions of Davis's words and actions, see Jones, *Rebel War Clerk's Diary,* 1:285–86; Varina Howell Davis, *Jefferson Davis, Ex-President of the Confederacy; A Memoir by His Wife,* 2 vols. (New York: Belford Co., 1890), 373–76.

68. See notation "Discharged for being in the riot" under the names of Ann Donovan and Sarah Brooks, in Timebook, January 1863–April 1865, Richmond Arsenal, ch. 4, vol. 99, Ordnance Department, War Department Records, RG 109, NA.

69. See the account of an eyewitness in Huldah A. Fain to M. C. Briant, April 14, 1863, Huldah Annie Fain Briant Papers, Duke.

70. *OR,* ser. 1, vol. 18, p. 958.

71. For typical comments, see, in addition to the sources cited in the notes above, Putnam, *Richmond During the War,* 208–11; Frank Vandiver, ed., *The Civil War Diary of General Josiah Gorgas* (University, Ala.: University of Alabama Press, 1947), 28–29; McGuire, *Diary of a Southern Refugee,* 202–4.

72. *American Annual Cyclopedia and Register of Important Events of the Year 1863* (New York: D. Appleton, 1864), 818. See the perceptive comments on yeoman discontent and violence in Paul D. Escott, *Many Excellent People: Power and Privilege in North Carolina, 1850–1890* (Chapel Hill: University of North Carolina Press, 1985), 65–67.

73. *American Annual Cyclopedia, 1863,* 6; Coulter, *Confederate States,* 423–24.

74. July 29, 1864, Sarah Rodgers Espy Diary, ADAH; Sarah Blackwell Gober

Temple, *The First Hundred Years: A Short History of Cobb County, in Georgia* (Atlanta: Walter W. Brown Publishing Co., 1935), 258.

75. Dawson, *Our Women in the War,* 276.

CHAPTER 6

1. Kate Burruss to Edward McGehee Burruss, February 18, 1864, John C. Burruss and Family Papers, LSU; Woodward and Muhlenfeld, *Private Mary Chesnut,* 145.

2. Because the Southern states were so heavily rural and agrarian, few women would leave their homes for factory work. And as historians of World War II have pointed out, the movement of women into defense plants, and into offices, and even the professions did not necessarily destroy old ideas about woman's place. Although William Chafe has come under attack for exaggerating wartime gains for women, both he and his critics correctly note how little basic attitudes were affected by the new but temporary opportunities that opened up for women. By the same token, no one at the time expected the Civil War to revolutionize sex roles, and there was certainly much less potential for dramatic changes in the Confederate South than in the United States of the 1940s. Cf. William H. Chafe, *The American Woman: Her Changing Social, Economic, and Political Roles* (New York: Oxford University Press, 1972), 135–73, and Susan M. Hartmann, *The Home Front and Beyond: American Women in the 1940s* (Boston: Twayne Publishers, 1982), 53–70, 209–16.

3. Elsie Bragg to Braxton Bragg, July 5, 1861, Braxton Bragg Papers, WRHS; Mrs. M. E. Fisher to John J. Pettus, n.d., John J. Pettus Papers, MDAH; Sarah Hamilton Yancey to Benjamin C. Yancey, December 8, 1861, Benjamin C. Yancey Papers, SHC.

4. James L. Roark, *Masters Without Slaves: Southern Planters in the Civil War and Reconstruction* (New York: W. W. Norton, 1977), 49; undated entry, Lizzie Hatcher Simons Diary, BTHC.

5. Elsie Bragg to Braxton Bragg, April 7, 1862, Braxton Bragg Papers, WRHS; Jones, *Children of Pride,* 1066–67. Mary Jones kept these plantations going for nearly five years before retiring in 1868 to New Orleans where she died the following year.

6. Amelia S. Montgomery to Joseph A. Montgomery, October 18, November 1, November 13, 1861, Joseph Addison Montgomery and Family Papers, LSU. In running their farms and plantations, white women may also have become more dependent on male slaves. Clarence Mohr has made the best case for this argument, but he tries too hard to force farmwives and plantation mistresses into a single mold and ignores the wide range of individual experience. Clarence L. Mohr, *On the Threshold of Freedom: Masters and Slaves in Civil War Georgia* (Athens: University of Georgia Press, 1986), 221–32.

7. Eliza Terry Prince to William Berry Prince, December 22, 1864, William

Terry and Family Papers, LSU. For similar examples during the American Revolution, see Mary Beth Norton, *Liberty's Daughters: The Revolutionary Experience of American Women, 1750–1800* (Boston: Little, Brown, 1980), 216–24.

8. Mary W. Pugh to Richard L. Pugh, November 9, December 15, 18, 1862, Richard L. Pugh to Mary W. Pugh, December 16, 1862, Richard L. Pugh Papers, LSU.

9. Crabtree and Patton, *Edmondston Journal,* 186–87; Sterkx, "Patriotic Confederate Woman's Diary," 616; January 4, 1862, Priscilla Munnikhuysen Bond Diary, LSU.

10. Smith, et al., *Mason Smith Family Letters,* 161–62; Frances Fearn, *Diary of a Refugee* (New York: Moffatt, Yard and Co., 1910), 1–8.

11. Sterkx, "Patriotic Confederate Woman's Diary," 615; Fearn, *Diary of a Refugee,* 8–9; Marszalek, *Diary of Emma Holmes,* 428. Blinded by their own class interests, mistresses tried to scare their slaves into remaining faithful by telling them frightening tales of Yankee cruelty. Clever slaves had every reason to play along, and even those who would later welcome the invaders, acted as if they feared being deserted by their owners. Despite the common belief that Negroes were natural dissemblers who could never be fully trusted, mistresses still wanted to believe these professions of loyalty. December 30, 1861, Priscilla Munnikhuysen Bond Diary, LSU; Bettie Alexander to her sister, August 24, 1861, Alexander Papers, Duke; Crabtree and Patton, *Edmondston Journal,* 74, 115; Fearn, *Diary of a Refugee,* 10–11.

12. Myers, *Children of Pride,* 1003; Rawick, *American Slave,* supplement, ser. 2, vol. 1, p. 5, vol. 5, pp. 1526–27, 1603–4; February 21, 1864, Grace B. Elmore Diary, SCL; Eppes, *Through Some Eventful Years,* 183.

13. Woodward, *Mary Chesnut's Civil War,* 48, 60, 464.

14. Dorsey, *Recollections of Allen,* 414–15; September 25, 1862, May 6, 1863, Ann Wilkinson Penrose Diary, LSU; Louticia Jackson to Asbury Jackson, August 23, 1863, Edward Harden Papers, Duke; May 1864, Lucy Muse Fletcher Diary, Duke.

15. Wiley, *Confederate Women,* 148; Susanna Clay to C. C. Clay, Jr., March 24, May 21, September 5, 1863, Clement Claiborne Clay Papers, Duke; Wiley, *Southern Negroes,* 75–76.

16. Myers, *Children of Pride,* 1241–42; McGuire, *Diary of a Southern Refugee,* 128; Rowland and Croxall, *Journal of Julia LeGrand,* 261–64; April 22–23, 1862, Mary Cary Ambler Stribling Diary, VSL.

17. Despite all their problems with the slaves during the war, few Southern women questioned the institution itself. For exceptions, see September 17, 23, 1864, Ella Gertrude Clanton Thomas Diary, Duke; Robertson, *Diary of Dolly Burge,* 98.

18. July 30, 1863, Kate D. Foster Diary, Duke; Dawson, *Our Women in the War,* 217; Cornelia McDonald, *A Diary with Reminiscences of the War and Refugee*

Life in the Shenandoah Valley (Nashville, Tenn.: Cullom and Ghertner, 1934), 169; Anderson, *Journal of Kate Stone,* 173.

19. July 25, 1863, Kate D. Foster Diary, Duke; Dorsey, *Recollections of Allen,* 418; Miers, *Diary of Emma LeConte,* 54; Dawson, *Confederate Girl's Diary,* 62.

20. If anything, Confederate women tended to still romanticize traditional Southern home life and usually seemed more than anxious to simply become wives and mothers once the war ended and the men came home. Again compare the reaction of Nazi women with the expansion of economic and political opportunities during Weimar period. Koonz, *Mothers in the Fatherland,* 21–49.

21. August 3, 1864, Carrie Berry Diary, AHS.

22. March 4, 1865, Grace B. Elmore Diary, SCL.

23. Crabtree and Patton, *Edmondston Journal,* 130–31, 287, 654; May 14, 1862, Jane B. Beale Diary, UVa; Myers, *Children of Pride,* 1244. For a good discussion of how Southerners and Northerners interpreted the lessons of emancipation in the British Empire and the Caribbean generally, see Eric Foner, *Nothing But Freedom: Emancipation and its Legacy* (Baton Rouge: Louisiana State University Press, 1983), 40–43.

24. November 21, 1863, Harriet Ellen Moore Diary, SHC; Rowland and Croxall, *Journal of Julia LeGrand,* 100–101; Crabtree and Patton, *Edmondston Journal,* 552; October 4, 1863, Kate Mason Rowland Diary in Kate Mason Rowland Papers, Confederate Museum.

25. Sallie Munford to Charles Ellis Munford, September 25, 1861, Munford–Ellis Family Papers, Duke; Fleet and Fuller, *Green Mount,* 72; Pryor, *Reminiscences of Peace and War,* 170–71.

26. October 10, 1862, Meta Morris Grimball Diary, SHC; Cumming, *Journal,* 45; Sallie A. Swope to Thomas Hill Watts, December 1863–January 1864, Thomas Hill Watts Papers, ADAH; Louise L. Price to John Gill Shorter, September 12, 1862, John Gill Shorter Papers, ADAH; Miss C. C. Godfrey to James A. Seddon, April 21, 1864, LR, CSW, RG 109, NA, M437, roll 127; Mart Rutledge Fogg to Jefferson Davis, September 16, 1861, ibid., roll 10.

27. Gay, *Life in Dixie During the War,* 97–101; Jorantha Semmes to Benedict Joseph Semmes, June 13, 1863, Benedict Joseph Semmes Papers, SHC; Phoebe Yates Pember, *A Southern Woman's Story,* ed. by Bell Irvin Wiley (Jackson, Tenn.: McCowat-Mercer Press, 1959), 123; Jonathan A. Leavy to Mrs. Eggleston, June 15, 1863, Eggleston-Roach Papers, LSU; McGuire, *Diary of a Southern Refugee,* 163; Broadside for Lynchburg Hospital Association, n.d., 1862, Irvine-Saunders Papers, UVa. In some cases, the hospital associations operated with impressive efficiency. Fourteen ladies from each church in Raleigh, North Carolina, called daily at the hospital, often finding little to do. Few other facilities, however had such a surfeit of volunteers. Adelaide Worth to William Henry Bagley, June 29, 1864, Bagley Family Papers, SHC.

28. Cumming, *Journal,* 93; Pember, *Southern Woman's Story,* 91–96; Fannie

A. Beers, *Memories: A Record of Personal Experience and Adventure During Four Years of War* (Philadelphia: J. B. Lippincott, 1888), 94–95, 204–6; May 23, 1862, Ada Bacot Diary in Ada Bacot Papers, SCL; John Connell to Cornelia Stewart, September 15, 1864, Albert A. Batchelor Papers, LSU.

29. Massey, *Bonnet Brigades,* 52; Monimia Fairfax Cary to Mrs. A. F. Hopkins, September 10, 1861, Monimia Fairfax Cary Papers, Duke; Frances E. Ballard to John Gill Shorter, August 30, 1862, John Gill Shorter Papers, ADAH; Madeline L'Engle to Edward L'Engle, August 10, 1862, Edward L'Engle Papers, SHC; Dawson, *Our Women in the War,* 147.

30. September 23, 1862, Kate Mason Rowland Diary in Kate Mason Rowland Papers, Confederate Museum; *OR,* ser. 4, vol. 2, pp. 199–200.

31. Cumming, *Journal,* 16, 40; David B. Sabine, "Captain Sally Tomkins," *Civil War Times Illustrated,* 4 (November 1965), 36–38; C. J. Clark to Juliet Opie Hopkins, December 10, 1862, Juliet Opie Hopkins Papers, ADAH; "A Paroled Prisoner" to John Hunt Morgan, March 23, 1864, John Hunt Morgan Papers, SHC.

32. Ellen E. Kehr to ?, February 1863, LR, CSW, RG 109, NA, M437, roll 132; Pember, *Southern Woman's Story,* 24, 173; Cumming, *Journal,* 92, 99–100. For similar conflicts during the American Revolution, see Linda K. Kerber, *Women of the Republic: Intellect and Ideology in Revolutionary America* (Chapel Hill: University of North Carolina Press, 1980), 58–61.

33. October 27, November 10, 1861, Ada Bacot Diary in Ada Bacot Papers, SCL; Cumming, *Journal,* 65–66, 99.

34. Constance Cary Harrison, "Richmond Scenes in '62," in Robert Underwood Johnson and Clarence Clough Buel, eds., *Battles and Leaders of the Civil War,* 4 vols. (New York: Castle Books, 1956 [1884]), 2:445; Putnam, *Richmond During the War,* 316.

35. Woodward, *Mary Chesnut's Civil War,* 149, 368, 414; Putnam, *Richmond During the War,* 71–74; Cumming, *Journal,* 26;

36. Sterkx, *Partners in Rebellion,* 124–26; March 19, 1862, Mahala Roach Diary in Roach and Eggleston Family Papers, SHC; Woodward, *Mary Chesnut's Civil War,* 667–68; February 14, 1862, Ada Bacot Diary in Ada Bacot Papers, SCL.

37. Beer, *Memories,* 113–52; Pember, *Southern Woman's Story,* 156; Cumming, *Journal,* 19–20, 35, 72, 91; January 28, 1862, Ada Bacot Diary in Ada Bacot Papers, SCL.

38. Lucy Barrow Cobb to John A. Cobb, August 25, 1864, Howell Cobb Papers, UGa; Cumming, *Journal,* 67; Pember, *Southern Woman's Story,* 83–86; Lucille Griffith, "Mrs. Juliet Opie Hopkins and Alabama Military Hospitals," *Alabama Review,* 6 (April 1953), 107–8. In obtaining supplies for the hospitals, nurses also had to deal with the inevitable alcohol question. Sick and wounded soldiers could tolerate short rations and torn bed sheets, but they insisted on having liquor to relieve pain and tedium. By taking control of the whiskey barrel from officers who too readily handed out drinks to their friends, matrons boldly

stepped on male prerogatives. At one point, Phoebe Pember held off an angry group of men with a pistol. Ultimately, she and other determined women fought a losing battle. Surgeons, nurses, laundresses, and cooks also dipped into the liquor supply, and some staggered drunkenly through the wards. Pember, *Southern Woman's Story,* 36, 39–40, 47–53, 72–81, 139–40.

39. Eppes, *Through Some Eventful Years,* 253–54; Cumming, *Journal,* 68, 77–78, 216–17; Anna Heyes Saunders to Samuel Preston Moore, October 31, 1864, Surgeon Hines to Saunders, November 26, 1864, Romulus Saunders Papers, Duke; Mary J. Blackford to Mrs. Judge Saunders, August 3, 1862, Irvine-Saunders Papers, UVa; Beers, *Memories,* 160–70.

40. Pember, *Southern Woman's Story,* 25–26; Cumming, *Journal,* 12–13, 38–39, 120, 124, 135; Smith, *Soldier's Friend,* 69.

41. Cumming, *Journal,* 65, 135, 178–79; Pember, *Southern Woman's Story,* 25; J. Fraise Richard, *The Florence Nightingale of the Southern Army: Experiences of Ella King Newsom* (New York: Broadway Publishing, 1914), 93–94; Woodward, *Mary Chesnut's Civil War,* 668.

42. Pryor, *Reminiscences of Peace and War,* 180–92; Cumming, *Journal,* 15, 25; April 10, 1864, Sidney Harding Diary, LSU; September 13, 1862, Ada Bacot Diary in Ada Bacot Papers, SCL; Lucy N. Bryan to ?, March 23, 1865, Scotch Hall Papers, SHC.

43. Griffith, "Hopkins," 110; Pember, *Southern Woman's Story,* 31, 146.

44. See, for example, July 28, 1864, Ella Gertrude Clanton Thomas Diary, Duke; Woodward, *Mary Chesnut's Civil War,* 641.

45. Mary H. Johnstone to Alexander H. Stephens, February 3, 1862, Stephens Papers, LC; Mrs. M. H. Abrahams to Jefferson Davis, June 1, 1864, LR, CSW, RG 109, NA, M437, roll 118; Blackford, *Memoirs,* 2:239–42.

46. Wyndham B. Blanton, *Medicine in Virginia in the Nineteenth Century* (Richmond, Va.: Garrett and Massie, 1933), 309–10; M. Ella Cooper to Alexander H. Stephens, n.d., 1862?, Alexander H. Stephens Papers, LC.

47. Griffith, "Hopkins," 105–11; *Report of the South Carolina Hospital Aid Association in Virginia, 1861–1862* (Richmond, Va.: MacFarlane and Ferguson, 1862; Confederate Imprint No. 4971), 8–19; 1st Cong., 2d sess., Proceedings, Senate, *Southern Historical Society Papers,* 46 (1928), 237.

48. Taylor et al., *South Carolina Women in the Confederacy,* 1:198; Peggy Cooper to SW, July 1863, LR, CSW, RG 109, NA, M437, roll 98; Florence Fleming Corley, *Confederate City, Augusta, Georgia, 1860–1865* (Columbia, S.C.: University of South Carolina Press, 1960), 41; Lucy et al., *Confederate Women of Arkansas,* 161. The revival of home manufacturing during the war also reinforced the traditional role of women in the Southern economy because many mothers still preferred staying with their children. After her husband's death, Cornelia McDonald considered working in an office and farming out her numerous brood to relatives but instead returned with them to Lexington, Virginia, to eke out a

living. Men often objected to their wives' leaving the domestic circle to become breadwinners, and many women shared these attitudes. Catherine Edmondston tried to dissuade her sister from opening a boardinghouse: "I can neither comprehend or have any patience with it—this pretense of Independence." McGuire, *Diary of a Southern Refugee,* 94–95; Winters, *Civil War in Louisiana,* 60; Betty C. Luckhard to SW, February n.d., 1862, LR, CSW, RG 109, NA, M437, roll 24; McDonald, *Diary of the War,* 241–47; Blackford, *Memoirs,* 2:160; Crabtree and Patton, *Edmondston Journal,* 272.

49. Taylor et al., *South Carolina Women in the Confederacy,* 2:84; Julia L. Main to Isabella Woodruff, May 20, 1861, Woodruff Papers, Duke; Noble, *Public Schools of North Carolina,* 242; May 4, 1861, Kate S. Carney Diary, SHC; "Civil War Days in Huntsville," 267.

50. George Ward Nichols, *The Story of the Great March; from the Diary of a Staff Officer* (New York: Harper and Brothers, 1865), 107; Dawson, *Confederate Girl's Diary,* 104–5.

51. Madeline L'Engle to Edward L'Engle, January 1, 1862, Edward L'Engle Papers, SHC; May 30, October 1, 1864, January 22, 1865, Margaret Gillis Diary, ADAH.

52. Ellen Cooper Johnson Reminiscences, p. 18 in Ellen Johnson Papers, Duke; Eugenia Holst to Isabella Woodruff, January 3, 1864, Anelia N. Pinkind to Woodruff, March 9, 1862, Isabella Woodruff Papers, Duke; Coleman, *Confederate Athens,* 153; Mrs. A. E. McNeill to Joseph E. Brown, November 9, 1864, Governors' Papers, GDAH; Sallie E. Caudell to Zebulon Vance, November 28, 1864, Zebulon Vance Papers, NCDAH. Some teachers applied for higher-paid government jobs. Anna E. Etter to Jefferson Davis, October 25, 1862, LR, CSW, RG 109, NA, M437, roll 126; Mrs. R. Jacobus to Alexander H. Stephens, August n.d., 1862, Alexander H. Stephens Papers, LC.

53. Catherine Cooper Hopley, *Life in the South,* 2 vols. (London: Chapman and Hall, 1863), 1:60–61, 2:103–4, 242, 244; Sarah Ridley Trimble, ed., "Behind the Lines in Middle Tennessee, 1863–1865: The Journal of Bettie Ridley Blackmore," *Tennessee Historical Quarterly,* 12 (March 1953), 66, 68, 70; Smith et al., *Mason Smith Family Letters,* 161.

54. Marszalek, *Diary of Emma Holmes,* 172, 176–77, 180, 185, 251, 315–17, 320, 325–26, 336–37, 340–41, 354, 378, 392, 397, 409–10, 417–20, 423–24.

55. Douglas Southall Freeman, ed., *A Calendar of Confederate Papers* (Richmond, Va.: Confederate Museum, 1908), 277; Hattie L. Davis to James A. Seddon, June 14, 1863, LR, CSW, RG 109, NA, M437, roll 89; Florence Clark to Jefferson Davis, February 4, 1864, ibid., roll 123; Louisa Boulware to Seddon, November 16, 1864, ibid., roll 122; Anne E. Bronaugh to Seddon, March 21, 1863, ibid., roll 81; Jones, *Rebel War Clerk's Diary,* 2:106.

56. McGuire, *Diary of a Southern Refugee,* 174; House and Senate, Proceedings, 1st Cong., 3d. sess., *Southern Historical Society Papers,* 49 (1943), 205, 261; Jones,

Rebel War Clerk's Diary, 1:276; Octavia P. Taylor to Jefferson Davis, February 3, 1863, LR, CSW, RG 109, NA, M437, roll 113.

57. Treasury-Note Division Payrolls, December 1862–January 1865, Records of the Confederate States Treasury Department, RG 365, NA; Senate, Proceedings, 1st Cong., 2d. sess., *Southern Historical Society Papers,* 47 (1940), 101; Senate, Proceedings, 1st Cong., 4th. sess., ibid., 50 (1953), 395; Wiley, *Letters of Akin,* 106; McGuire, *Diary of a Southern Refugee,* 252. Apparently the Treasury clerks received a final raise in September 1864 that pushed their salary to $3,750 a year, but this conclusion is based on calculations from fragmentary payroll records. In addition to low salaries, tedium took also took its toll on copyists and note signers. Belle Wilfong remembered signing 3,200 Confederate notes in five hours. This work required close attention because fines were levied for any blotted notes. McGuire, *Diary of a Southern Refugee,* 238–39, 244, 250–51, 258–59; Belle Wilfong, "Reminiscences of the Sixties," Miscellaneous Records, Civil War Collection, NCDAH.

58. Senate, Proceedings, 2d Cong., 2d sess., *Southern Historical Society Papers* 51 (1958), 369–70; ibid., 52 (1959), 117–20; W. S. Donner to Josiah Gorgas, March 27, 1862, LR, CSW, RG 109, NA, M437, roll 47; Mary F. Lutterloh to "Mr Devereux," February 25, 1863, Virginia Taylor to Devereux, October 10, 1861, Mrs. Kessler and Eliza Willeford to Captain P. A. Wilson, March 12, 1863, Quartermaster Department Correspondence, Civil War Collection, NCDAH; Marinda ? to Mary Newby, December 1863, Larkin Newby Papers, SHC.

59. Secretary of War, List of Persons to Be Paid, 1861–1865, chap. 9, vol. 98, Records of the Confederate States War Department, RG 109, NA; Record of Salaries in War Department, October-December 1864, Abstract of Disbursements by Alfred Chapman, Disbursing Clerk, War Department, Account of Incidental Expenses for War Department for quarter ending June 30, 1864, Miscellaneous Records, Records of the Confederate States Treasury Department, RG 365, NA.

60. Senate and House, Proceedings, 2d Cong., 2d sess., *Southern Historical Society Papers,* 52 (1959), 89–90, 117–20, 156–57, 286–87.

61. N. B. Burnett to Julia Blanche Munroe Kell, March 28, 1864, John McIntosh Kell Papers, Duke; Dawson, *Our Women in the War,* 315–16; Woodward, *Mary Chesnut's Civil War,* 631, 645, 691–92; Anonymous to SW, n.d., 1863, LR, CSW, RG 109, NA, M437, roll 80. For the similar problems of women working in Washington, see Bernice M. Deutrich, "Propriety and Pay," *Prologue,* 3 (Fall 1971), 67–72.

62. Vandiver, *Gorgas Diary,* 25–26; *Richmond Whig,* March 14, 16, 1862; Charles ? to "Dr. Lee," March 18, 1863, Dr. Lee Papers, Duke; J. W. Mallett, "Work of the Ordnance Bureau," *Southern Historical Society Papers,* 37 (1909), 15. Miraculously, Mary Ryan lived for four days after the explosion, long enough to explain what had happened.

63. Timebook, January 1863–April 1865, Richmond Arsenal, chap. 4, Vol. 99,

Ordnance Department, Records of the Confederate States War Department, RG 109, NA; William LeRoy Brown, "Confederate Ordnance During the War," *Southern Historical Society Papers,* 26 (1898), 373; Coulter, *Confederate States,* 236–37.

CHAPTER 7

1. McGuire, *Diary of a Southern Refugee,* 12–13.

2. "To a Company of Volunteers Receiving Their Banner at the Hands of the Ladies," *Southern Literary Messenger,* 33 (July 1861), 17.

3. *OR,* ser. 4, vol. 2, p. 790.

4. H. W. R. Jackson, *The Southern Women of the Second American Revolution* (Atlanta: Intelligencer Steam-Power Press, 1863), 34–38; Mrs. Isaac Winship to James A. Seddon, October 26, 1863, LR, CSW, RG 109, NA, M437, roll 92; Sisters of Charity to Major General Commanding, Military Department of Mobile, September 25, 1863, ibid., roll 112.

5. James B. Hall to Bolling Hall, August 9, 1862, Bolling Hall Papers, ADAH; Jones, *Rebel War Clerk's Diary,* 1:276. A little more than a month after these Texans marched through Richmond, the famous bread riot rocked the city.

6. Buck, *Diary of Lucy Buck,* 215; McGuire, *Diary of a Southern Refugee,* 102–3, 237; Crabtree and Patton, *Edmondston Journal,* 679.

7. Marszalek, *Diary of Emma Holmes,* 82; May 8, 1863, Amanda Worthington Diary in Worthington Family Papers, MDAH; Eppes, *Through Some Eventful Years,* 182–83.

8. Addie Simpson to James M. Simpson, August 23, 1861, Allen and Simpson Family Papers, SHC; Anderson, *Journal of Kate Stone,* 39; Robertson, *Lucy Breckinridge,* 66; Marszalek, *Diary of Emma Holmes,* 73–74, 101, 199.

9. *Richmond Enquirer,* April 23, 1861; Marszalek, *Diary of Emma Holmes,* 68, 222; July 14, 1861, Sarah Lois Wadley Diary, SHC; Dawson, *Our Women in the War,* 5.

10. For typical accounts, see McGuire, *Diary of a Southern Refugee,* 107–8; Sigmund Diamond, ed., *A Casual View of America: The Home Letters of Salomon de Rothschild, 1859–1861* (Stanford, Calif.: Stanford University Press, 1961), 122; Eppes, *Through Some Eventful Years,* 179; Taylor et al., *South Carolina Women in the Confederacy,* 1:11–21; Soldiers' Relief Association of Charleston, July 20, 1861, Mary Amarinthia Yates Snowden Papers, SCL.

11. Myers, *Children of Pride,* 688, 736; Taylor et al., *South Carolina Women in the Confederacy,* 1:21–26; List of Ladies' Aid Societies, January 1, 1862, John Gill Shorter Papers, ADAH; Undated Account of Soldiers' Aid Society, Tuskegee, Alabama, Cobb and Hunter Family Papers, SHC; *Raleigh State Journal,* May 1, 1861, typescript, Miscellaneous Records, Civil War Collection, NCDAH.

12. Mary Y. Harth to Mrs. F. H. Mayrant, December 9, 1861, Harth Papers, SCL; Lucy et al., *Confederate Women of Arkansas,* 46; Fleet and Fuller, *Green Mount,*

66; Woodward, *Mary Chesnut's Civil War,* 167; Mary Anna Jackson, *Memoirs of Stonewall Jackson, by His Widow* (Louisville, Ky: Prentice Press, 1895), 350; P. G. T. Beauregard to Mary A. Snowden, July 25, 1864, Mary Amarinthia Yates Snowden Papers, SCL.

13. Marszalek, *Diary of Emma Holmes,* 83–84; Virginia Dalton to SW, October 22, 1862, LR, CSW, RG 109, NA, M437, roll 44. For typical examples of requests for government cloth, see Almeria L. McGee to John J. Pettus, October 26, 1861, Susan E. Grisham to Pettus, September 13, 1861, Ladies' Aid Society, Palestine, Mississippi, to Pettus, September 7, 1861, John J. Pettus Papers, MDAH.

14. Dawson, *Our Women in the War,* 145; Johns, *Florida During the Civil War,* 170–71; Sterkx, *Partners in Rebellion,* 93–109.

15. Walker, *Vicksburg,* 54; Mrs. M. A. Buie to James Seddon, September 21, 1863, LR, CSW, RG 109, NA, M437, roll 83; B. J. Harrison to Leroy P. Walker, August 23, 1861, ibid., roll 8; Bettie Ridley to Mrs. Francis T. Ridley, April 24, 1864, Anna and Bettie Ridley Papers, SCL; *New Orleans Daily Delta,* June 1, 1861; Charles T. Kesse to Juliet Opie Hopkins, August 1, 1862, Juliet Opie Hopkins Papers, ADAH; Charles M. McGee, Jr. and Ernest M. Lander, Jr., eds., *A Rebel Came Home: The Diary of Floride Clemson* (Columbia: University of South Carolina Press, 1961), 77. In the larger cities, women also organized "ladies' gunboat societies." Newspapers promoted the work by publishing long lists of contributors even though the appearance of *women's* names in print shocked traditionalists. The treasurer of a Richmond group had ten thousand dollars in her coffers; South Carolina women raised thirty-thousand dollars to build a vessel christened *Palmetto State.* Hopley, *Life in the South,* 2:257; Coulter, *Confederate States,* 417–19; April 30, 1862, Betty Herndon Maury Diary, LC; Todd, *Confederate Finance,* 172; Marszalek, *Diary of Emma Holmes,* 147, 160.

16. September 19, 1862, Mrs. Hill Diary, UVa; Mrs. H. B. Ware to John Gill Shorter, October 10, 1862, John Gill Shorter Papers, ADAH; L. Blackmer to Judah P. Benjamin, November 12, 1861, LR, CSW, RG 109, NA, M437, roll 15; Winters, *Civil War in Louisiana,* 39–43.

17. Cable, "Diary of a Union Woman," 935; Diamond, *A Casual View of America,* 115; Miers, *Diary of Emma LeConte,* 12–13; *To the Friends of the Southern Cause at Home* (n.p.: n.p., n.d., Confederate Imprint No. 4969), 1–3.

18. For typical accounts, see Marszalek, *Diary of Emma Holmes,* 79; Buck, *Diary of Lucy Buck,* 244.

19. December 25, 1861, Priscilla Munnikhuysen Bond Diary, LSU; Percy L. Rainwater, ed., "The Civil War Letters of Cordelia Scales," *Journal of Mississippi History,* 1 (July 1939), 171–72; "Programme of the Tableaux-Vivants Sold for the Benefit of the Louisianian Soldiers," Natchitoches, Louisiana, January 1865, James Foster and Family Papers, LSU.

20. Dora Harper Couper to J. Maxwell Couper, October 30, 1862, Couper Family Papers, SHC; Anderson, *Journal of Kate Stone,* 329; Henry Watkins Allen to the

Ladies of Natchitoches, Louisiana, January 26, 1865, clipping in Fielding Yeager Doke Papers, LSU.

21. August 22, 1862, Carrie Hunter Diary in Cobb and Hunter Family Papers, SHC; Carrie Fries to J. F. Shaffner, October 11, 1861, Fries and Shaffner Family Papers, SHC.

22. Marszalek, *Diary of Emma Holmes,* 96; Robert H. Bremner, *The Public Good: Philanthropy and Welfare in the Civil War Era* (New York: Alfred A. Knopf, 1980), 47; April 14, 1864, Sidney Harding Diary, LSU; John Townsend Trowbridge, *The South: A Tour of Its Battlefields and Ruined Cities* (Hartford, Conn.: L. Stebbins, 1866), 189–90.

23. Nor was selfishness confined to the wealthy. Some soldiers and their families sold donated clothing on the black market, and some women used charitable contributions to secure special privileges for their relatives in the army. Emilie McDonald to John Gill Shorter, September 22, 1862, Rebecca Dennis to Shorter, May 25, June 28, 1862, Shorter Papers, ADAH; Marszalek, *Diary of Emma Holmes,* 103, 128.

24. The decline of charitable activities is best traced in the records of the relief associations. See Taylor et al., *South Carolina Women in the Confederacy,* 1:8–117; Greenville [South Carolina] Ladies' Association Minutes, 1861–1865, Duke; Ladies' Volunteer Aid Society of the Pine Hills [Chapel Hill, Louisiana], Minutes, 1861, Duke; Young Ladies' Hospital Association, Columbia, Records, 1861–1864, SCL; Kenneth Coleman, ed., "Ladies' Volunteer Aid Association of Saundersville, Washington County, Georgia, 1861–1862," *Georgia Historical Quarterly,* 52 (March 1968), 78–95.

25. *New Orleans Daily Delta,* April 27, 1861; Joseph Blyth Allston to Mary A. Snowden, February 14, 1865, Mary Amarinthia Yates Snowden Papers, SCL.

26. Mollie Colbert to John J. Pettus, September 6, 1861, John J. Pettus Papers, MDAH; January 5, 1863, Melinda Ray Diary, Civil War Collection, NCDAH.

27. Unlike the leaders of nazi women's groups who had expected an expansion of their public role but had capitulated to the demands of the party, few upper-class Southern women had such ambitions and only became restless as the war dragged on and the men appeared so powerless to end the fighting. Koonz, *Mothers in the Fatherland,* 127–34.

28. Mary Ann Webster Loughborough, *My Cave Life in Vicksburg* (New York: D. Appleton, 1864), 166.

29. August 22, 1861, Ada Bacot Diary in Ada Bacot Papers, SCL; Ada Sterling, ed., *A Belle of the Fifties: Memoirs of Mrs. Clay of Alabama, Covering Social and Political Life in Washington and the South, 1853–1866* (New York: Doubleday, Page, 1904), 194–95; Katharine M. Jones, ed., *Ladies of Richmond* (Indianapolis: Bobbs-Merrill, 1962), 267–68.

30. February 4, May 2, 1861, Susan Cornwall Book, SHC; McGuire, *Diary of a Southern Refugee,* 110; Crabtree and Patton, *Edmondston Journal,* 505–6; July

28, 1861, Sarah Lois Wadley Diary, SHC. Mary Elizabeth Massey has argued that women criticized Davis as freely as men, but this was true only in the last year of the war. Cf. Massey, *Bonnet Brigades,* 162–63.

31. March 12, 1862, Mary Ezell Diary in Edward Conigland Papers, SHC; Eppes, *Through Some Eventful Years,* 202; [Caroline Howard Gilman], "Letters of a Confederate Mother," *Atlantic Monthly,* 137 (April 1926), 507; Marszalek, *Diary of Emma Holmes,* 91, 407.

32. Marszalek, *Diary of Emma Holmes,* 125; McGuire, *Diary of a Southern Refugee,* 303–4; Fleet and Fuller, *Green Mount,* 108; Crabtree and Patton, *Edmondston Journal,* 492, 495.

33. Carl H. Moneyhon, ed., "Life in Confederate Arkansas: The Diary of Virginia Davis Gray, 1863–1865, Part II," *Arkansas Historical Quarterly,* 42 (Summer 1983), 137; M. W. H. to her husband, February 11, 1862, M. W. H. Papers, NCDAH; Smith et al., *Mason Smith Family Letters,* 54–55. In attacking the Davis administration for bungling in the western theater, women agreed with the generals in the so-called "western concentration bloc." Cf. Thomas Lawrence Connelly and Archer Jones, *The Politics of Command: Factions and Ideas in Confederate Strategy* (Baton Rouge: Louisiana State University Press, 1973).

34. Crabtree and Patton, *Edmondston Journal,* 516–17, 527–28; Woodward, *Mary Chesnut's Civil War,* 57, 330, 466.

35. Mary P. Davis to Ben Davis, August 9, 1863, Mary P. Davis Papers, Duke.

36. February 17, 1862, Mary Ezell Diary in Edward Conigland Papers, SHC; Anonymous to James A. Seddon, June 7, 1863, LR, CSW, RG 109, NA, M437, roll 80; Elsie Bragg to Braxton Bragg, August 13, 1862, Braxton Bragg Papers, WRHS; June 17, 1864, Elizabeth Collier Diary, SHC; McGuire, *Diary of a Southern Refugee,* 317–18; Cumming, *Journal,* 204.

37. Again see the useful analysis in Koonz, *Mothers in the Fatherland,* 100–110.

38. Augusta J. Evans to J. L. M. Curry, July 15, October 16, 1863, January 27, 1864, Jabez Lamar Monroe Curry Papers, LC.

39. Fleet and Fuller, *Green Mount,* 92; Emily Plympton Lovell to Mansfield Lovell, November 4, 1862, Mansfield Lovell Papers, Huntington Library.

40. Jackson, *Memoirs of Stonewall Jackson,* 336; McGuire, *Diary of a Southern Refugee,* 112; Woodward, *Mary Chesnut's Civil War,* 501.

41. Wiley, *Letters of Warren Akin,* 116–17; Hope Summerell Chamberlain, *Old Days in Chapel Hill* (Chapel Hill: University of North Carolina Press, 1926), 83.

42. June 26, 1861, Kate Mason Rowland Diary in Kate Mason Rowland Papers, Confederate Museum; Blackford, *Memoirs,* 2:94; Leland, "Middleton Correspondence," 102–3. A sharper tone suddenly appeared in women's comments. After fourteen generals attended church one Sunday, a Richmond woman tartly noted that they might have better spent their time drilling the troops. Woodward, *Mary Chesnut's Civil War,* 585.

338 | *Notes, pp. 149–50*

43. July 28, 1861, May 30, 1862, Betty Herndon Maury Diary, LC; Woodward, *Mary Chesnut's Civil War,* 361, 468; Crabtree and Patton, *Edmondston Journal,* 167–68.

44. Woodward, *Mary Chesnut's Civil War,* 468–69; Augusta J. Evans to J. L. M. Curry, July 15, 1863, Jabez Lamar Monroe Curry Papers, LC; Crabtree and Patton, *Edmondston Journal,* 427–28.

45. Elsie Bragg to Braxton Bragg, March 3, 1862, Braxton Bragg Letters, BTHC; Myers, *Children of Pride,* 1098–99; Woodward, *Mary Chesnut's Civil War,* 469; Crabtree and Patton, *Edmondston Journal,* 502.

46. Elsie Bragg to Braxton Bragg, March 26, April 7, 1862, Braxton Bragg Papers, WRHS; Annie Sehon to Bettie Kimberly, March 10, 1862, John Kimberly Papers, SHC; "A Daughter of Virginia" to ?, July 19, 1861, LR, CSW, RG 109, NA, M437, roll 5; "True Southern Woman" to SW, July 11, 1864, ibid., roll 118; Mrs. M. Johnson to Joseph E. Brown, March 27, 1862, Governors' Papers, GDAH; Georgia King Smith to Mrs. Burke, November 27, 1861, Thomas Butler King Papers, SHC. The one exception was the question of arming the slaves, which deeply divided white women. Because plantation mistresses and farmwives now had more intimate daily contract with their bondsmen than most men, they realized that blacks wanted freedom and feared that putting them in the Confederate army would bring on a general emancipation. When President Davis suggested freeing blacks who labored in the camps and on the fortifications, Catherine Edmondston lambasted the proposal as "folly too deep for me to fathom." Even Robert E. Lee's call for enrolling black troops did not lessen her outrage. "Our Country is ruined if we adopt his suggestions. We give up a principle when we offer emancipation as a boon or reward, for we have hitherto contended that slavery is Cuffee's normal condition . . . . No! freedom for whites, slavery for negroes, God has so ordained it." Converting the naturally skeptical to such a radical expedient proceeded slowly and painfully. Grace B. Elmore, who best exemplified the commitment of educated Southern women to proslavery ideology, preferred arming blacks to surrender but doubted that they would make good soldiers. The word *necessity* cropped up repeatedly in discussions of the question. Ella Thomas saw Confederate emancipation for a what it was: a sham. Why would blacks fight to gain their freedom, she wondered, if they could achieve the same result by fleeing to the Yankees? Crabtree and Patton, *Edmondston Journal,* 639, 651–53; March 12, 1865, Grace B. Elmore Diary, SCL; Robert F. Durden, *The Gray and the Black: The Confederate Debate on Emancipation* (Baton Rouge: Louisiana State University Press, 1972), 163–64: November 17, 1864, Ella Gertrude Clanton Thomas Diary, Duke.

47. Elsie Bragg to Braxton Bragg, October 15, 1862, Braxton Bragg Papers, WRHS; Annie M. Sehon to Bettie Kimberly, October 25, 1862, John Kimberly Papers, SHC; Lizzie Munford to Mrs. George W. Munford, June 13, 1862, Munford-Ellis Family Papers, Duke. Not all women, of course, disdained a defensive

strategy. Susan Blackford deprecated Lee's 1863 advance into Maryland because she did not think his army strong enough to fight in enemy territory. Blackford, *Memoirs,* 2:56.

48. Dawson, *Confederate Girl's Diary,* 390; Mary Latta to Samuel R. Latta, August 25, 1861, Samuel R. Latta Papers, LSU; November 22, 1861, Mary Ezell Diary in Edward Conigland Papers, SHC.

49. Note the similar reaction of women in wartime Germany who had grown up in the Nazi youth organizations and longed to serve the state directly in battle. Koonz, *Mothers in the Fatherland,* 194–95.

50. Louisa Campbell Sheppard Recollections, p. 11, SHC; Dawson, *Confederate Girl's Diary,* 174–76; William Perry Fidler, *Augusta Evans Wilson, 1835–1909* (Tuscaloosa: University of Alabama Press, 1951), 97; Meta Morris Grimball to John B. Grimball, July 9, 1863, John Berkeley Grimball Papers, Duke; Robertson, *Lucy Breckinridge,* 132–33.

51. Mary A. Bowen to John Letcher, May 10, 1861, Nannie G. Abbott to Letcher, July 7, 1861, Lucetta A. Clove to Letcher, June 15, 1861, John Letcher Papers, VSL.

52. November 15, 1860, Margaret Gillis Diary, ADAH; Emma Sue Gordon to Addie Simpson, May 15, 1861, Allen and Simpson Family Papers, SHC; Hopley, *Life in the South,* 1:285; Mrs. E. C. Kent, *Four Years in Secessia: A Narrative of a Residence at the South* (Buffalo, N.Y.: Franklin Printing House, 1865), 12–13; Cable, "Diary of a Union Woman," 932–33; Eppes, *Through Some Eventful Years,* 256.

53. Mrs. Forrest T. Morgan, "'Nancy Harts' of the Confederacy," *Confederate Veteran,* 30 (December 1922), 465; Coleman, *Confederate Athens,* 45; U. R. Brooks, ed., *Stories of the Confederacy* (Columbia, S. C.: State Co., 1912), 23; Bess Dell to Kate C. Encks, May 10, 1861, William R. Encks Papers, Confederate Miscellany, ser. 1e, Emory. An unknown number of women took the radical step of disguising themselves as men to enter the Confederate army. For a judicious assessment, see Massey, *Bonnet Brigades,* 81–84. For a compilation of widely scattered evidence, see Janet E. Kaufman, "'Under the Petticoat Flag': Women Soldiers in the Confederate Army," *Southern Studies,* 23 (Winter 1984), 363–75. Solid information on female spies is even harder to come by, but again, see Massey, *Bonnet Brigades,* 87–107.

CHAPTER 8

1. April 5, 1862, Mary Greenhow Lee Diary, LC; September 6, 1862, Mahala Roach Diary in Roach and Eggleston Family Papers, SHC; March 3, 1864, Myra Inman Diary, SHC; Maggie N. Tucker to Mrs. George B. Munford, May 18, 1862, Munford-Ellis Family Papers, Duke.

2. Andrews, *Journal of Georgia Girl,* 67; Benedict Joseph Semmes to Jorantha

Semmes, May 5, 1863, Benedict Joseph Semmes Papers, SHC; Nannie Cage to Cornelia Stewart, April 1864, Albert A. Batchelor Papers, LSU.

3. February 20, 1862, Amanda Worthington Diary in Worthington Family Papers, MDAH; Marszalek, *Diary of Emma Holmes*, 40; August 21, 1861, Melinda Ray Diary in Civil War Collection, NCDAH.

4. Pember, *Southern Woman's Story*, 168.

5. April 1, 1862, Kate S. Sperry Diary, VSL; December 12, 1862, Fannie Page Hume Diary, LC; Eggleston, *Rebel's Recollections*, 85–86.

6. Crabtree and Patton, *Edmondston Journal*, 159; Sterkx, "Patriotic Confederate Woman's Diary," 615; "Cousin Ella" to Jesse H. H. Person, December 16, 1861, Presley Carter Person Papers, Duke.

7. Hague, *Blockaded Family*, 145–55; May 7, 1863, Sarah Rodgers Espy Diary, ADAH; James C. Bonner, ed., *Journal of a Milledgeville Girl, 1861–1867* (Athens: University of Georgia Press, 1964), 51–52.

8. March 20, 1864, Emily Walker Diary in Whittington Collection, Tulane; Dawson, *Confederate Girl's Diary*, 82–83, 335–38; Cumming, *Journal*, 272.

9. Stella Bringier to Louis A. Bringier, July 28, 1862, Louis A. Bringier Papers, LSU; Adelaide Worth to William Henry Bagley, February 24, 1865, Bagley Family Papers, SHC; L. A. Syme to Richard E. Jacques, October 15, 1863, Richard E. Jacques Papers, Duke; Elsie Bragg to Braxton Bragg, April 29, 1862, Braxton Bragg Papers, WRHS. For the women who decided to leave their homes, see the account of refugee life in chapter 9.

10. Myers, *Children of Pride*, 1172–73; May 12, 1862, Priscilla Munnikhuysen Bond Diary, LSU; August 25, 1863, Sarah Lois Wadley Diary, SHC.

11. June 5, 1862, Kate S. Sperry Diary, VSL; Sarah Jane Sams to Robert R. Sams, February 3, 1865, Sarah Jane Sams Letter, SCL; Virginia K. Jones, ed., "The Journal of Sarah G. Follansbee," *Alabama Historical Quarterly*, 27 (Fall and Winter 1965), 229–34.

12. Maud Morrow Brown, "At Home in Lafayette County, Mississippi, 1860–1865," p. 88, MDAH; Taylor et al., *South Carolina Women in the Confederacy*, 2:322; Dawson, *Our Women in the War*, 64–65; Smedes, *Memorials of a Southern Planter*, 188–89.

13. Robertson, *Diary of Dolly Burge*, 91–92; Eppes, *Through Some Eventful Years*, 256; Belle Kearney, *A Slaveholder's Daughter* (New York: Abbey Press, 1900), 13–14; Perdue et al., *Weevils in the Wheat*, 188–89.

14. Jorantha Semmes to Benedict Joseph Semmes, May n.d., 1863, Benedict Joseph Semmes Papers, SHC; U.S. Senate, Committee on Education and Labor, *Testimony Relative to the Relations Between Labor and Capital*, 5 vols. (Washington: Government Printing Office, 1885), 4:334–35; Rosella Kenner Brent Recollections, LSU; Jones, "Journal of Sarah Follansbee," 245.

15. Dawson, *Confederate Girl's Diary*, 20; Jennings, "A Little Girl in the War,"

376; February 16, 1865, Grace B. Elmore Diary, SCL; Marszalek, *Diary of Emma Holmes,* 404; Anderson, *Journal of Kate Stone,* 179.

16. McGuire, *Diary of a Southern Refugee,* 21–22; April 23, 1863, Amanda Worthington Diary in Worthington Family Papers, MDAH.

17. Robertson, *Diary of Dolly Burge,* 105; Susanna C. Clay to C. C. Clay, Jr., June 24, 1863, Clement Claiborne Clay Papers, Duke; Kate Burruss to Edward McGehee Burruss, May 30, 1862, John C. Burruss and Family Papers, LSU; Mrs. M. A. Elliott, ed., *The Garden of Memories: Stories of the Civil War* (Camden, Ark.: H. L. Grimstead Chapter, U.D.C., n.d.), 29; Gay, *Life in Dixie During the War,* 196–214.

18. Anne Shannon to Evangeline Shannon, June–July 1863, Cruther-Shannon Papers, MDAH; Dawson, *Confederate Girl's Diary,* 191–93.

19. Octavia Hammond to Mrs. Adair, February 10, 1865, Augustus Dixon Adair Papers, AHS.

20. For a sampling of various types of treatment see June 26, 1864, Susanna Waddell Diary, SHC; Anderson, *Journal of Kate Stone,* 181; Cornelia Phillips Spencer, *The Last Ninety Days of the War in North Carolina* (New York: Watchman Publishing, 1866), 214–25; "Civil War Days in Huntsville," 302; Myers, *Children of Pride,* 1238–39; June 10, 1864, Alice Williamson Diary in Alice Williamson Papers, Duke; May 12, 1862, Priscilla Munnikhuysen Bond Diary, LSU.

21. Myers, *Children of Pride,* 1237; June 19, 1862, Mary Cary Ambler Stribling Diary, VSL; Sarah Ellen Phillips Reminiscence, pp. 2–5, SHC; Virginia Bedinger to Carrie Bedinger, April 21, 1862, Bedinger-Dandridge Family Papers, Duke.

22. Marszalek, *Diary of Emma Holmes,* 296; Reminiscences of Mrs. Eleanor McAffrey McGuire, p. 2 in Civil War Miscellany, GDAH; Rainwater, "Letters of Scales," 179; Lucy et al., *Confederate Women of Arkansas,* 31–33.

23. Rainwater, "Letters of Scales," 175; Sarah Ellen Phillips Reminiscence, p. 5, SHC.

24. Myers, *Children of Pride,* 1227–28; General Orders No. 20, May 8, 1864, vol. 61, entry 1167, pt. 2, RG 393, NA. National Park Service historian A. Wilson Greene kindly provided a copy of this court-martial order.

25. At least eighteen Union soldiers were executed for rape during the war, but this statistic says little about the prevalence of the crime. Bell Irvin Wiley, *The Life of Billy Yank: The Common Soldier of the Union* (Indianapolis: Bobbs-Merrill, 1952), 205; Joseph T. Glatthaar, *The March to the Sea and Beyond: Sherman's Troops in the Savannah and Carolinas Campaigns* (New York: New York University Press, 1985), 71–72.

26. "Vivid War Experiences at Ripley, Miss.," *Confederate Veteran,* 13 (June 1905), 262–65; Jackson, *Southern Women,* 13, 43–44; James G. Gibbes, *Who Burnt Columbia?* (Newberry, S.C.: Elbert H. Aull, 1902), 34.

27. Lucy London Anderson, *North Carolina Women of the Confederacy*

(Fayetteville, N.C.: North Carolina Division, United Daughters of the Confederacy, 1926), 54–55; Lucy et al., *Confederate Women of Arkansas,* 106; August 27, 1864, Belle Strickland Diary, MDAH.

28. Rainwater, "Letters of Scales," 178; Jane McCausland Chin Reminiscence, 1863, LSU; Sarah Myra Rivers Trotter to Cynthia Carter, April 2, 1862, Pope-Carter Family Papers, Duke.

29. December 28, 1863, Priscilla Munnikhuysen Bond Diary, LSU; Lucy et al., *Confederate Women of Arkansas,* 104; Dougan, *Confederate Arkansas,* 109.

30. Anderson, *North Carolina Women in the Confederacy,* 73–74; Edward A. Pollard, *Southern History of the War,* 2 vols. (New York: Fairfax Press, 1977 [1866]), 1:173–74; Clara B. Eno, "Activities of the Women of Arkansas During the War Between the States," *Arkansas Historical Quarterly,* 3 (Spring 1944), 18.

31. December 11, 1862, Jane B. Beale Diary, UVa; Dawson, *Confederate Girl's Diary,* 39–47, 51, 90–92.

32. Marszalek, *Diary of Emma Holmes,* 303.

33. Ibid., 283, 374; March 29, 1865, Mary D. Waring Diary, ADAH; Margaret Davis to Kate McGreachy, November 25, 1863, Catherine Jane Buie Papers, Duke.

34. See, for example, "Civil War Days in Huntsville," 201; Skipper and Gove, "Diary of Ethie Eagleton," 134–35.

35. May 11, 1862, Kate S. Carney Diary, SHC; James O. Hall, ed., " 'An Army of Devils': The Diary of Ella Washington," *Civil War Times Illustrated,* 16 (February 1978), 20.

36. Kate Corbin to Sallie Munford, November 19, 1862, Munford-Ellis Family Papers, Duke; September 20, 1863, Kate D. Foster Diary, Duke.

37. Hall, "Diary of Ella Washington," 21; "Civil War Days in Huntsville," 243–44, 299; Elliott, *Garden of Memories,* 29–30.

38. Mrs. E. L. Coleman to Andrew Johnson, January 4, 1865, Johnson Papers, LC; Elizabeth Avery Meriwether, *Recollections of Ninety-Two Years, 1824–1916* (Nashville: Tennessee Historical Commission, 1958), 66–76; "Civil War Days in Huntsville," 260–61.

39. "Diary of Miss Harriette Cary, Kept by Her from May 6, 1862, to July 24, 1862," *Tyler's Historical and Genealogical Magazine,* 9 (October 1927), 105; Rainwater, "Letters of Scales," 179; Myers, *Children of Pride,* 1228–29.

40. Ellen Wilkins Tompkins, ed., "The Colonel's Lady: Some Letters of Ellen Wilkins Tompkins, July-December, 1861, *Virginia Magazine of History and Biography,* 69 (October 1961), 401; McDonald, *Diary of the War,* 56–57.

41. Morgan, *Confederate Girl's Diary,* 30–31, 66–67, 69.

42. July 16, August 16, September 20, 1863, Kate D. Foster Diary, Duke. Ella Washington also badly wished that the dashing George Armstrong Custer had been attired in gray. Hall, "Diary of Ella Washington," 21.

43. June 9, 1862, Ada Bacot Diary in Ada Bacot Papers, SCL; "Civil War Days

in Huntsville," 203; April 20, 1863, Amanda Worthington Diary in Worthington Family Papers, MDAH; Sterkx, *Partners in Rebellion,* 173.

44. September 20, 1863, Kate D. Foster Diary, Duke; Lezinka? to Betty Stuart, August 15, 1863, John Bull Smith Dimitry Papers, Duke; Rowland and Croxall, *Journal of Julia LeGrand,* 61–63.

45. Merrick, *Old Times in Dixie Land,* 40; George Alfred Townsend, *Rustics in Rebellion: A Yankee Reporter on the Road to Richmond, 1861–65* (Chapel Hill: University of North Carolina Press, 1950), 197; Alice Shannon to Evangeline Shannon Crutcher, November 19, 1863, Crutcher-Shannon Papers, MDAH.

46. Benedict Joseph Semmes to Jorantha Semmes, November 19, 1863, Benedict Joseph Semmes Papers, SHC; Bettersworth, *Confederate Mississippi,* 281–82; Massey, *Bonnet Brigades,* 230–33; June 15, 1862, Kate S. Carney Diary, SHC; Anderson, *Journal of Kate Stone,* 181.

47. Anna Robinson Andrews to Mrs. Courtney Bird Jones, April 27, 1862, Charles Wesley Andrews Papers, Duke; January 14, 1864, Cora E. Watson Journal in T. Harry Williams Papers, LSU.

48. June 1, 1863, Journal of Mrs. W. W. Lord, LC; Loughborough, *Cave Life in Vicksburg,* 43–45.

49. George Washington Cable, ed., "Woman's Diary of the Siege of Vicksburg," *Century Magazine,* 30 (September, 1885), 771; Walker, *Vicksburg,* 173–74; William W. Lord, Jr., "A Child at the Siege of Vicksburg," *Harper's Monthly Magazine,* 118 (December 1908), 49.

50. Lida L. Reed, "A Woman's Experience During the Siege of Vicksburg," *Century Magazine,* 61 (April 1901), 922–23; Loughborough, *Cave Life in Vicksburg,* 63–64, 79–80; Sara Stevens, Reminiscences, Frederick M. Stevens Papers, Duke; Cable, "Woman's Diary of Siege of Vicksburg," 773.

51. Loughborough, *Cave Life in Vicksburg,* 16–17, 23–24; Walker, *Vicksburg,* 167–68, 170, 178, 182; Cable, "Woman's Diary of Siege of Vicksburg," 771. In January 1981, I witnessed similarly calm reactions to artillery bombardment by Palestinian families in Southern Lebanon. For the adjustment of women and children to shelling in Petersburg during the 1864–65 siege of that city, see Recollections of Mrs. Archibald Campbell Pryor Concerning Conditions in Petersburg, June 1864-April 1865, VSL; Carol Bleser, ed., *The Hammonds of Redcliffe* (New York: Oxford University Press, 1981), 122–23.

52. Reed, "Woman's Experiences in Vicksburg," 923–25; Lord, "Child at Siege of Vicksburg," 46; Loughborough, *Cave Life in Vicksburg,* 55–62, 97–98; Trowbridge, *The South,* 357.

53. June 28, 1863, Journal of Mrs. W. W. Lord, LC; Reed, "Woman's Experiences in Vicksburg," 925–26; Cable, "Woman's Diary of Siege of Vicksburg," 767; L. McRae Bell, "A Girl's Experience in the Siege of Vicksburg," *Harper's Weekly,* 56 (June 8, 1912), 12–13; Loughborough, *Cave Life in Vicksburg,* 72–74, 89–92.

54. Walker, *Vicksburg,* 137; Cable, "Woman's Diary of Siege of Vicksburg," 767–69, 771–72; Loughborough, *Cave Life in Vicksburg,* 71, 105–6, 137.

55. March 13, 15, April 3, 1862, Kate S. Sperry Diary, VSL; March 16, 21, 1862, Mary Greenhow Lee Diary, LC; April 26, 1862, Mary Cary Ambler Stribling Diary, VSL; Buck, *Diary of Lucy Buck,* 43.

56. December 15, 1862, Kate S. Sperry Diary, VSL; McDonald, *Diary of the War,* 119–21, 132; Buck, *Diary of Lucy Buck,* 165–69.

57. "Mrs. Henrietta E. Lee's Letter to General David Hunter on the Burning of Her House," *Southern Historical Society Papers,* 8 (1880), 215–16.

58. Robertson, *Lucy Breckinridge,* 185–86; May 8, 1864, Kate S. Sperry Diary, VSL.

59. Julia Davidson to John M. Davidson, July 19, 21, 26, 1864, John Mitchell Davidson Papers, Emory.

60. W. T. Sherman, *Memoirs of Gen. W. T. Sherman,* 4th ed., 2 vols. (New York: Charles L. Webster, 1891), 2:152, 174–76. Despite all the attention given Sherman's march by participants and historians, even the best works place far too much emphasis on the movement of the armies and local geography. Most accounts rely on official records and soldiers' letters, ignoring the reaction of Southern civilians. See, for example, Shelby Foote, *The Civil War: A Narrative,* 3 vols. (New York: Random House, 1958–74), 3:640–654. Even Joseph Glatthaar's solid new book on Sherman's march pays little attention to Southern civilians. Joseph T. Glatthaar, *The March to the Sea and Beyond: Sherman's Troops in the Savannah and Carolinas Campaigns* (New York: New York University Press, 1985).

61. November 22, 1864, Ella Gertrude Clanton Thomas Diary, Duke; Katharine M. Jones, ed., *When Sherman Came: Southern Women and the "Great March"* (Indianapolis: Bobbs-Merrill, 1964), 46–47; Candler, "Life in Georgia," 307–9; Myers, *Children of Pride,* 1218–19.

62. Mrs. A. Flournoy to Josiah Flournoy, March 2, 1865, Governors' Papers, GDAH; Jones, *When Sherman Came,* 20, 77–80; Peggy McDonough to Amanda and William Markham, December 14, 1864, Confederate Miscellany, ser. 1e, Emory.

63. Dawson, *Our Women in the War,* 130–39; Jones, *When Sherman Came,* 19; David P. Conyngham, *Sherman's March Through the South* (New York: Sheldon and Co., 1865), 79.

64. Bonner, *Journal of a Milledgeville Girl,* 63; Mary Buttrill's Experience in the War of the Sixties in Civil War Miscellany, GDAH; Thomas Conn Bryan, *Confederate Georgia* (Athens: University of Georgia Press, 1953), 183.

65. Myers, *Children of Pride,* 1242, 1227.

66. Jones, *When Sherman Came,* 23; Mrs. G. W. Anderson to "Dear Mary," January 1, 1865 [misdated 1864], Confederate Miscellany, ser. 1e, Emory; Myers, *Children of Pride,* 1228; Frances Thomas Howard, *In and Out of the Lines: An*

Accurate Account of the Incidents During the Occupation of Georgia by Federal Troops in 1864–65 (New York: Neale Publishing Co., 1905), 16–23; Jones, *When Sherman Came,* 20–21. As in other occupied areas, having an attractive daughter helped secure kindly attention and protection. Generals also took pity on down-and-out plantation mistresses. Caro Lamar to Charles Lamar, December 23, 1864, Charles Lamar Papers, GDAH; Jones, *When Sherman Came,* 17–18.

67. Conyngham, *Sherman's March,* 87–88, 127–28; Glatthaar, *March to the Sea,* 66–69; Mark A. DeWolfe Howe, ed., *Marching with Sherman: Passages from the Letters and Campaign Diaries of Henry Hitchcock* (New Haven, Conn.: Yale University Press, 1927), 61, 94, 103–4, 154–55.

68. Myers, *Children of Pride,* 1237, 1242.

69. Sherman, *Memoirs,* 2:254; Marszalek, *Diary of Emma Holmes,* 386; December 25, 1864, Grace B. Elmore Diary, SCL.

70. Katherine Theus Obear, *Through the Years in Old Winnsboro* (Columbia, S.C., R. L. Bryan, 1940), 66; Marszalek, *Diary of Emma Holmes,* 402.

71. Elizabeth W. Allston Pringle, *Chronicles of Chicora Wood* (Boston: Christopher Publishing House, 1940), 229–38; Dawson, *Our Women in the War,* 401.

72. Jones, *When Sherman Came,* 213–19.

73. Floride Cantey Reminiscences in Thomas J. Myers, Papers, NCDAH; Sallie Coles Heyward to her children, March 8, 1865, Mrs. Albert Rhett Heyward Papers, SCL; ?, Bennettsville, S.C., to ?, March 5, 1865, United Daughters of the Confederacy, South Carolina Division, Edgefield Chapter Papers, Duke; Easterby, *South Carolina Rice Plantation,* 208.

74. Jones, *When Sherman Came,* 213–16, 218.

75. Miers, *Diary of Emma LeConte,* 8, 13, 15; January 4, 1865, Grace B. Elmore Diary, SCL.

76. Miers, *Diary of Emma LeConte,* 29–31, 35; February 15, 1865, Grace B. Elmore Diary, SCL.

77. Sherman, *Memoirs,* 2:277; Dawson, *Our Women in the War,* 113–15, 253–56; Charles E. Thomas, ed., "The Diary of Anna Hasell Thomas (July 1864-May 1865)," *South Carolina Historical Magazine,* 74 (July 1973), 133–35; Miers, *Diary of Emma LeConte,* 44–49; August Conrad, *The Destruction of Columbia, South Carolina* (Roanoke, Va.: Stone Printing and Manufacturing Co., 1902), 17–18; Taylor et al., *South Carolina Women in the Confederacy,* 1:326; Logan, *My Confederate Girlhood,* 80–81; "A Southern Girl's Diary," *Confederate Veteran,* 40 (August 1932), 264–65.

78. Conyngham, *Sherman's March,* 333; Thomas, "Diary of Anna Hasell Thomas," 137; Dawson, *Our Women in the War,* 117–20; February 21, 1865, Grace B. Elmore Diary, SCL.

79. Miers, *Diary of Emma LeConte,* 49–51, 58–59, 66–67; March 6, 1865, Grace B. Elmore Diary, SCL.

80. Marszalek, *Diary of Emma Holmes,* 399; Grace Pearson Beard Reminis-

cences, pp. 5–12, SHC; Sue Thermutis Montgomery to Moultrie Reid Wilson, February 15, 1865, Moultrie Reid Wilson Papers, SCL; Woodward, *Mary Chesnut's Civil War*, 790.

81. *War Days in Fayetteville*, 50; Dawson, *Our Women in the War*, 147; Jones, *When Sherman Came*, 274–75; March 1865, Melinda Ray Diary in Civil War Collection, NCDAH; Janie Smith to ?, April 12, 1865, Miscellaneous Records, ibid.

82. Janie Smith to ?, April 12, 1865, Miscellaneous Records in Civil War Collection, NCDAH.

83. John G. Barrett, *Sherman's March Through the Carolinas* (Chapel Hill: University of North Carolina Press, 1956), 316.

CHAPTER 9

1. June 10, 1864, Louisa Warren Patch Fletcher Diary, GDAH; Rosa Postell to Mary Baber, March 13, 1863, Baber and Blackshear Papers, UGa; Madeline Saunders L'Engle to Edward L'Engle, March 18, 1862, Edward L'Engle Papers, SHC; Blackford, *Memoirs*, 1:160.

2. "Your affectionate mother" to Sarah Hamilton Yancey, September 18, 1864, Benjamin C. Yancey Papers, SHC; Easterby, *South Carolina Rice Plantation*, 206; McDonald, *Diary of the War*, 104.

3. Jorantha Semmes to Benedict Joseph Semmes, March 23, 1862, Benedict Joseph Semmes Papers, SHC; Burton N. Harrison to his sister, November 22, 1862, Burton N. Harrison Papers, LC; Clifton Paisley, ed., "How to Escape the Yankees: Major Scott's Letter to his Wife at Tallahassee, March 1864," *Florida Historical Quarterly*, 50 (July 1971), 55–61; Celeste Clay to Virginia Clay, April 11, 1864, Clement Claiborne Clay Papers, Duke; Emily Plimpton Lovell to Mansfield Lovell, October 29, 1861, Mansfield Lovell Papers, Huntington Library.

4. McGuire, *Diary of a Southern Refugee*, 9–11, 20–21; Massey, *Refugee Life*, 4–10; Francis Turner to James A. Seddon, February 12, 1864, LR, CSW, RG 109, NA, M437, roll 142; H. J. Wayne to Mary Ann Harden, December 6, 1861, Edward Harden Papers, Duke.

5. Massey, *Refugee Life*, 28–29; M. A. Hines to ?, February 2, 1863, Battle Family Papers, SHC; Mrs. D. Giraud Wright, *A Southern Girl in '61: The War-Time Memories of a Confederate Senator's Daughter* (New York: Doubleday, Page and Co., 1905), 228–29; N. E. ("Mae") Jett to Richard B. Jett, June 12, 1864, Richard B. Jett Papers, Emory. In trying to show that refugeeing did not disrupt traditional kinship networks, Jean Friedman has exaggerated the ability of families to maintain close ties during the war. For every example she cites of women and children moving in with relatives, there are many others of families cut adrift without financial or emotional support from kin, neighbors, or churches. Cf. Friedman, *Enclosed Garden*, 95–97.

6. For a solid discussion of refugee settlement patterns, see Massey, *Refugee Life,* 68–94.

7. Massey, *Refugee Life,* 50–68; Anderson, *Journal of Kate Stone,* 169; Unidentified school girl in Atlanta to Mary Lou Yancey, June 1, 1864, Benjamin C. Yancey Papers, SHC; Dawson, *Our Women in the War,* 85–87; H. J. Wayne to Mary Ann Harden, December 23, 1864, Edward Harden Papers, Duke.

8. McGuire, *Diary of a Southern Refugee,* 200–201; "Civil War Days in Huntsville," 234; Maria Adelaide Whaley, "Story of Maria Adelaide Whaley," p. 1, SCHS; Elvira Withrow to ?, n.d., 1864, Withrow Papers, Duke; Anderson, *Journal of Kate Stone,* 202–3.

9. September 22–October 15, 1863, Sarah Lois Wadley Diary, SHC; Dawson, *Our Women in the War,* 16–17; "Thomas R. R. Cobb: Extracts from Letters to His Wife, February 3, 1861-December 10, 1862," *Southern Historical Society Papers,* 28 (1900), 299.

10. Smith et al., *Mason Smith Family Letters,* 167–70; Louisa Campbell Sheppard Recollections, pp. 15–20, SHC; July 20, 1863, Sidney Harding Diary, LSU.

11. Woodward, *Mary Chesnut's Civil War,* 728; Wright, *Southern Girl in '61,* 178–81, 200–202; Andrews, *Journal of a Georgia Girl,* 21–56; Myers, *Children of Pride,* 1193.

12. "Last Days in a Confederate Home," Clara Minor Lynn Papers, Confederate Museum; August 8, 1863, Sidney Harding Diary, LSU; Dawson, *Confederate Girl's Diary,* 372; Mrs. A. M. Preston to Mrs. Alice W. Saunders, September 6, 1862, Irvine-Saunders Papers, UVa.

13. Anderson, *Journal of Kate Stone,* 190–94, 220–24, 226.

14. McGuire, *Diary of a Southern Refugee,* 238–41, 298–303, 307. For price quotations, see July 23, 1862, Meta Morris Grimball Diary, SHC; Marszalek, *Diary of Emma Holmes,* 186, 223; Georgia King Smith to Thomas Butler King, September 20, 1863, Thomas Butler King Papers, SHC; Mary Ann Whittle to Lewis Whittle, October 12, 1863, Louis Neale Whittle Papers, SHC; unidentified sister to Burton N. Harrison, March 20, 1864, Harrison Papers, LC.

15. McDonald, *Diary of the War,* 192–99; Pryor, *Reminiscences of Peace and War,* 251–52; Constance Cary Harrison, "Virginia Scenes in '61," in Johnson and Buel, *Battles and Leaders,* 1:162; McGuire, *Diary of a Southern Refugee,* 88–93, 172–73.

16. Massey, *Refugee Life,* 102–8; Dawson, *Our Women in the War,* 438; Fontaine, "Old Confederate Days," 302; February 17, 1863, Betty Herndon Maury Diary, LC; McGuire, *Diary of a Southern Refugee,* 237–38, 260.

17. Dawson, *Our Women in the War,* 212–14; Dawson, *Confederate Girl's Diary,* 203–6; Fearn, *Diary of a Refugee,* 14–20.

18. January 27, 1865, Abbie M. Brooks Diary, AHS; Ripley, *From Flag to Flag,* 67–70; Conyngham, *Sherman's March,* 96–98; George W. Guess to Mrs. S. H.

Cockrell, June 30, 1864, George W. Guess Letters, LSU; Annie Sehon to Bettie Kimberly, December 11, 1862, John Kimberly Papers, SHC. Unfortunately, few diaries, letters, or memoirs written by refugees from the yeoman class have survived.

19. June 20, 1861, Betty Herndon Maury Diary, LC; March 10, 1862, Mrs. Hill Diary, UVa; Myers, *Children of Pride*, 1079; Eliza Morgan to James Harris Morgan, October 11, 1863, Francis Warrington Dawson Papers, Duke; McGuire, *Diary of a Southern Refugee*, 152.

20. January 30, 1863, Betty Herndon Maury Diary, LC; Anderson, *North Carolina Women of the Confederacy*, 32; Dawson, *Our Women in the War*, 355–56, 469–70; May 16, 1863, Sarah Lois Wadley Diary, SHC.

21. Winters, *Civil War in Louisiana*, 211; Marsha Shorter to Alexander H. Stephens, May 10, 1863, Alexander H. Stephens Papers, LC; Massey, *Refugee Life*, 245–52; McGuire, *Diary of a Southern Refugee*, 252–54.

22. Taylor et al., *South Carolina Women of the Confederacy*, 1:174–75; Marszalek, *Diary of Emma Holmes*, 219–20, 225–27, 339–40; Leland, "Middleton Correspondence," 65–66. Even the poor tried to take advantage of refugees. Shortly before Mary Rawson fled Atlanta, several ragged-looking women came around looking for bargains, bluntly remarking that if she refused to sell anything they would take what they wanted after she left. September 15, 1864, Mary Rawson Diary in Mary Rawson Papers, AHS.

23. Woodward, *Mary Chesnut's Civil War*, 429; Anderson, *Journal of Kate Stone*, 238, 252; McDonald, *Diary of the War*, 93.

24. Trimble, "Journal of Bettie Blackmore," 66; July 7, 1861, August 27, 1862, Betty Herndon Maury Diary, LC; McGuire, *Diary of a Southern Refugee*, 32; Anderson, *Journal of Kate Stone*, 245; January 13, 14, May 11, 1864, Sidney Harding Diary, LSU.

25. Smith et al., *Mason Smith Family Letters*, 189; May 16, 1862, Meta Morris Grimball Diary, SHC.

26. L. A. Syme to Richard E. Jacques, October 15, 1863, Richard E. Jacques Papers, Duke; Woodward and Muhlenfeld, *Private Mary Chesnut*, 230–31.

27. Anderson, *Journal of Kate Stone*, 235; Louisa Campbell Sheppard Recollections, pp. 21–22, SHC; Annie Sehon to Bettie Kimberly, July 15, 1863, John Kimberly Papers, SHC.

28. Bettie A. Bylesam to George W. Randolph, October 21, 1862, LR, CSW, RG 109, NA, M437, roll 35; July 21, 1863, Elizabeth Collier Diary, SHC; Marszalek, *Diary of Emma Holmes*, 173–74, 197, 200–201, 225–27, 236, 251, 253–54.

29. March 7, 1864, Ann Shannon Martin Diary, MDAH; Dawson, *Confederate Girl's Diary*, 361–64; Anderson, *Journal of Kate Stone*, 223–25.

30. Fearn, *Diary of a Refugee*, 53; Cumming, *Journal*, 160, 261, 303; Anderson, *Journal of Kate Stone*, 204; Massey, *Refugee Life*, 143–44.

31. Dawson, *Our Women in the War,* 63; Elsie Bragg to Braxton Bragg, September 8, 1863, Braxton Bragg Letters, BTHC.

32. Marszalek, *Diary of Emma Holmes,* 56; Eppes, *Through Some Eventful Years,* 254–55; Crabtree and Patton, *Edmondston Journal,* 328–29. Schoolgirls especially became wrapped up in their own world. "The war is raging, but we, shut up here with our books, and our little school tragedies and comedies have remained very ignorant of all that is going on outside," Esther Allan perceptively remarked. Campaigns and battles seldom intruded on this blissful isolation. Sallie Fort, for example, paid more attention to a young mathematics teacher whom she suspected of teaching a "pretty black-eyed girl something else besides geometry with its angles and triangles!" Dawson, *Our Women in the War,* 354; Sallie Fort to Mary Y. Harth, August 22, 1861, Mary Y. Harth Papers, SCL.

33. Clift, *Private War of Lizzie Hardin,* 226–27; Anderson, *Journal of Kate Stone,* 292–93. The latest styles in clothing from the North and Europe remained an obsession in some quarters. Southern women scanned the fashion plates in *Godey's Lady's Book,* though Adelaide Worth patriotically suggested that Confederates ought to "originate our own fashions since we are separate from all the world." Some wealthy women admitted they still enjoyed fine clothes and believed there had to be limits to self-sacrifice. Marion Alexander Boggs, ed., *The Alexander Letters, 1787–1900* (Athens: University of Georgia Press, 1980), 272; "Parisian Fashions," *Southern Illustrated News,* 2 (August 15, 1863), 43; Adelaide Worth to William Henry Bagley, June 23, 1864, Bagley Family Papers, SHC; Refugitta, "A Blockade Correspondence," *Southern Illustrated News,* 2 (October 24, 1863), 125.

34. Louis A. Bringier to Stella Bringier, June 12, 1864, Louis A. Bringier Papers, LSU; Kate Burruss to Edward McGehee Burruss, February 19, 1863, John C. Burruss and Family Papers, LSU.

35. Marszalek, *Diary of Emma Holmes,* 52–53; Anderson, *Journal of Kate Stone,* 302; Kate Corbin to Sallie Munford, February 17, 1863, Munford-Ellis Family Papers, Duke; Fleet and Fuller, *Green Mount,* 301–2; Louise Wigfall to Charlotte Wigfall, May 19, 1862, Louis T. Wigfall Papers, LC; Gay, *Life in Dixie During the War,* 60–61.

36. Winters, *Civil War in Louisiana,* 27; Wright, *Southern Girl of '61,* 56; Alice West Allen, "Recollections of War in Virginia," *Confederate Veteran,* 23 (June 1915), 268; Elizabeth Allen Coxe, *Memories of a South Carolina Plantation During the War* (n.p.: privately printed, 1912), 7; Marszalek, *Diary of Emma Holmes,* 140–42; May 16, 1863, Sarah Lois Wadley Diary, SHC; Harrison, *Recollections Grave and Gay,* 47–48. When Hetty and Constance Cary, two attractive refugees from Baltimore, sang "Maryland, My Maryland," General P. G. T. Beauregard and his officers reportedly cried. Such sentimental effusions reinforced the role of women as lovely and delicate—if not frivolous—creatures who could inspire

men to great deeds through their example of pure devotion. Harrison, *Recollections Grave and Gay,* 57–58, 78; General P. G. T. Beauregard to ?, August 28, 1861, Burton N. Harrison Papers, LC.

37. Sterkx, *Partners in Rebellion,* 70–72; King, *Diary of Josephine Habersham,* 100.

38. Putnam, *Richmond During the War,* 41–42; Dawson, *Confederate Girl's Diary,* 279–80; Cumming, *Journal,* 46.

39. Anderson, *Journal of Kate Stone,* 213; Marszalek, *Diary of Emma Holmes,* 195.

40. Dougan, *Confederate Arkansas,* 111; Wiley, *Confederate Women,* 162; Bettersworth, *Confederate Mississippi,* 281; *New Orleans Daily Picayune,* May 9, 1862; Mrs. Jane Wright to Joseph E. Brown, April 18, 1864, and endorsement of Col. E. M. Galt, Governors' Papers, GDAH; Junius Henri Browne, *Four Years in Secessia: Adventures Within and Beyond the Union Lines* (Hartford: O. D. Case and Co., 1865), 133–34; Matilda Champion to Sydney Champion, June 11, 1864, Sydney S. Champion Papers, Duke.

41. Wiley, *Life of Johnny Reb,* 52–58; Bryan, *Confederate Georgia,* 187; *Richmond Daily Dispatch,* May 6, 1862; Emory M. Thomas, *The Confederate State of Richmond: A Biography of the Capital* (Austin: University of Texas Press, 1971), 39; *Richmond Enquirer,* November 6, 1863; Wiley, *Letters of Warren Akin,* 56. Unfortunately, none of this evidence comes from the prostitutes themselves.

42. Marszalek, *Diary of Emma Holmes,* 360; Mary W. Pugh to Richard L. Pugh, December 18, 1862, Richard L. Pugh Papers, LSU; McGuire, *Diary of a Southern Refugee,* 75–78.

43. With only nine thousand people and two dirty, insect-ridden hotels, Montgomery had never seemed a suitable capital for a new nation with grandiose ambitions. And from the beginning the quarrels and petty gossip that had plagued antebellum Washington continued there. Rumors of sexual infidelities and other scandals began circulating immediately. The prudish Kate Thompson, whose husband had been in President James Buchanan's cabinet, reported that Mary Chesnut and other married women had set tongues wagging by their persistent flirting but decided there were "*enough* righteous women to save the place [Montgomery] for many years at least." For contemporary descriptions of Montgomery society, see Woodward, *Mary Chesnut's Civil War,* 18, 27, 62, 73, 93–94; Woodward and Muhlenfeld, *Private Mary Chesnut,* 26–27, 35–36, 69; Thomas Cooper DeLeon, *Belles, Beaux and Brains of the 60's* (New York: G. W. Dillingham, 1907), 112–13; Ellen N. Jackson to Mary H. Noyes, February 19, 1861, Jefferson Franklin Jackson Papers, ADAH; Kate Thompson to Mary Ann Cobb, April 15, 1861, Cobb, Erwin, and Lamar Papers, UGa.

44. In her disappointingly dull biography of her husband, Varina Davis made only oblique references to the social cold war in Richmond. Davis, *Davis,* 2:202–3.

45. Woodward and Muhlenfeld, *Private Mary Chesnut,* 66, 85, 88, 90–91, 152–53. Chesnut's comments in her diary remain the best source of information on the Davises because she maintained good relations with both their friends and critics.

46. Strode, *Davis,* 124.

47. For assessments of Varina Davis by contemporaries, see McGuire, *Diary of a Southern Refugee,* 96; DeLeon, *Belles, Beaux and Brains of the 60's,* 66–67, 195–200; Woodward, *Mary Chesnut's Civil War,* 429; Putnam, *Richmond During the War,* 38–39; Harrison, *Recollections Grave and Gay,* 68–70; William Howard Russell, *My Diary North and South* (New York: Alfred A. Knopf, 1954 [1862]), 97–98. For a judicious historical analysis of Varina Davis as first lady, see Wiley, *Confederate Women,* 82–139.

48. Gilbert E. Govan and James W. Livingood, *A Different Valor: The Story of Joseph E. Johnston, C.S.A.* (Indianapolis: Bobbs-Merrill, 1956), 70–71, 162, 225, 228, 338; Lydia Johnston to Charlotte Wigfall, August 2, 1863, Louis T. Wigfall Papers, LC.

49. Charlotte Wigfall to Halsey Wigfall, April 29, 1861, Louis T. Wigfall Papers, LC; Woodward and Muhlenfeld, *Private Mary Chesnut,* 120; Woodward, *Mary Chesnut's Civil War,* 433; Edward Younger, ed., *Inside the Confederate Government: The Diary of Robert Garlick Hill Kean, Head of the Bureau of War* (New York: Oxford University Press, 1957), 89–90; Jones, *Rebel War Clerk's Diary,* 2:453; Easterby, *South Carolina Rice Plantation,* 178; Leland, "Middleton Correspondence," 30; Crabtree and Patton, *Edmondston Journal,* 176, 180.

50. Pember, *Southern Woman's Story,* 184–85; Addie Simms to Rufus K. Macomb, December 28, 1863, Addie J. Simms Letters, BTHC; Cuttino, *Saddle Bag and Spinning Wheel,* 214; L. A. Syme to Richard E. Jacques, September 22, 1863, Richard E. Jacques Papers, Duke; Anderson, *Journal of Kate Stone,* 203; Kate Corbin to Sallie Munford, February 13, 1862, Munford-Ellis Family Papers, Duke.

51. Extract from a letter, March 1863, Joseph E. Johnston Journal in Joseph Eggleston Johnston Papers, ADAH; Harrison, *Recollections Grave and Gay,* 150–52; Thomas Cooper DeLeon, *Four Years in Rebel Capitals* (Mobile, Ala.: Gossip Printing Company, 1892), 352–53; Putnam, *Richmond During the War,* 270; Woodward, *Mary Chesnut's Civil War,* 497.

52. DeLeon, *Four Years in Rebel Capitals,* 148–51; Harrison, *Recollections Grave and Gay,* 68, 172–77; Woodward, *Mary Chesnut's Civil War,* 432–33, 549–50, 554; Louise Wigfall to Halsey Wigfall, April 23, 1862, Louis T. Wigfall Papers, LC; Sterling, *Belle of the Fifties,* 168–69, 174–77; Pember, *Southern Woman's Story,* 161–62. Occasionally, however, reminders of wartime austerity appeared at elaborate social affairs. At a wedding reception held at the governor's mansion in Raleigh, North Carolina, Adelaide Worth thought that most of the guests came to eat, noting how the affair soon became a "snatch and grab" game. Worth to William Henry Bagley, April 12, 1864, Bagley Family Papers, SHC.

53. Woodward, *Mary Chesnut's Civil War,* 507–8, 528.

54. Marszalek, *Diary of Emma Holmes,* 264; Smith et al., *Mason Smith Family Letters,* 21–22; April 4, 1863, Metta Morris Grimball Diary, SHC; Leland, "Middleton Correspondence," 32, 34, 44, 158.

55. Woodward, *Mary Chesnut's Civil War,* 323, 434, 515, 548, 551. A fortunate few reveled in the profits of speculation. Because her merchant husband had made a killing from rising prices, in December 1864, Kate Robson held a dinner party for fifty in Albany, Georgia. While other women denounced the selfishness of speculators, her guests dined on roast pig, turkey, chicken sandwiches, pound cakes, fruitcakes, and a floating island. Kate Hester Robson Reminiscences, pp. 25, 27, AHS.

56. In making this point about culinary excesses, I have been careful to draw the examples from 1863 onward when many families were finding food scarce and prohibitively expensive. January 1, 1863, Meta Morris Grimball Diary, SHC; February 26, 1864, Ann Shannon Martin Diary, MDAH; Spencer, *Last Ninety Days of the War,* 29–30; Lucy N. Bryan to ?, March 3, 1865, Scotch Hall Papers, SHC; Anna M. Preston to Alice Saunders, April 15, 1864, Irvine-Saunders Papers, UVa; Sterling, *Belle of the Fifties,* 197–201; Logan, *My Confederate Girlhood,* 32.

57. Mobile *Advertiser and Register,* n.d., in *Southern Literary Messenger,* 38 (February 1864), 127; Leland, "Middleton Correspondence," 208; May 10, 1864, Virginia Clay Diary, Clement Claiborne Clay Papers, Duke; Woodward, *Mary Chesnut's Civil War,* 323, 528; Anderson, *Journal of Kate Stone,* 232.

58. "Glimpses of Army Life in 1864," *Southern Historical Society Papers,* 18 (1890), 411; Eugenia Holst to Isabella Woodruff, January 3, 1864, Woodruff Papers in Dalton Deposit, Duke.

59. Rembert W. Patrick, *The Fall of Richmond* (Baton Rouge: Louisiana State University Press, 1960), 9–10; Taylor et al., *South Carolina Women in the Confederacy,* 1:277–79; Vandiver, *Diary of Gorgas,* 163; Pember, *Southern Woman's Story,* 127; McGuire, *Diary of a Southern Refugee,* 328; Jones, *Ladies of Richmond,* 247–53; Pickett, *Heart of a Soldier,* 163–65; Sallie C. Bird to Sarah Hamilton Yancey, January 8, 1865, Benjamin C. Yancey Papers, SHC.

60. Extract from letter, August n.d., 1862, Joseph E. Johnston Journal in Joseph Eggleston Johnston Papers, ADAH; Woodward, *Mary Chesnut's Civil War,* 670.

CHAPTER 10

1. The only substantial study of Confederate morale is Bell Irvin Wiley's "The Waning of Southern Will," in his book *The Road to Appomattox* (Memphis, Tenn.: Memphis State College Press, 1956), 43–75. Unfortunately, Wiley does not distinguish between the morale of soldiers and civilians. He treats the question in a linear, almost organic fashion, as if public opinion had a life of its own. Although Wiley concedes that not all Southerners followed the pattern he so carefully delineates, his essay barely acknowledges the problem of diversity—a key con-

sideration for understanding the complex responses of women. See also Coulter, *Confederate States,* 69–83; Emory Thomas, *The Confederate Nation, 1861–1865* (New York: Harper and Row, 1979), 138–43, 284–85. James W. Silver has examined the role of organized religion in sustaining Confederate morale, but his study deals almost exclusively with the clergy. *Confederate Morale and Church Propaganda* (New York: W. W. Norton, 1967 [1957]).

2. Lucy D. Rodes to Alexander Brown, May 6, 1862, Brown Papers, Duke; August 17, 1861, Betty Herndon Maury Diary, LC; Lyon G. Tyler, *Letters and Times of the Tylers,* 3 vols. (Richmond, Va.: Whittet and Stephenson, 1884–86), 2:651; Amelia S. Montgomery to Joseph A. Montgomery, October 16, 1861, Joseph Addison Montgomery and Family Papers, LSU; Frances Kirby-Smith to Edmund Kirby-Smith, June 18, 1861, Kirby-Smith Papers, SHC. In analyzing how pious women interpreted the events of the war, I have benefited much from the provocative arguments in Beringer et al., *Why the South Lost the Civil War,* 82–102, 268–81, 351–67. The authors of this fine book have argued that Southerners at first proclaimed that God was on their side, then came to see defeats as punishment for sin, and finally had to wrestle with the problems of national guilt resulting from Confederate defeat. Despite their recognition of the complexity of this process, Beringer and his colleagues too often treat wartime religious faith as a simple evolution from confidence to defeatism. They effectively use the concept of cognitive dissonance to describe how Southerners dealt with the course of the war, but their assertion that many Southerners could accept—at least subconsciously—a Northern victory because of guilt over slavery is thinly documented. I have found little evidence, for example, that Southern women either felt guilty about slavery or attributed the death of the Confederate nation to the "sin" of slavery.

3. Ted R. Worley, ed., *At Home in Confederate Arkansas: Letters to and from Pulaski Countians* (Little Rock, Ark.: Pulaski County Historical Society, 1955), 6; Jane L. Petigru to Mary L. Baber, November 24, 1861, Baber and Blackshear Papers, UGa; Woodward and Muhlenfeld, *Private Mary Chesnut,* 82.

4. Crabtree and Patton, *Edmondston Journal,* 513; March 3, 1865, Lucy Irion Journal in Irion-Neilson Family Papers, MDAH.

5. July 23, 1861, Betty Herndon Maury Diary, LC; Emily Voss to Sallie Munford, July 24, 1861, Munford-Ellis Family Papers, Duke; July 23, 1861, Jane B. Beale Diary, UVa.

6. July 26, 1861, Annie Darden Diary in Annie Darden Papers, NCDAH; Rubie Browne to Margaret Browne, August 11, 1861, William Phineas Browne Papers, ADAH.

7. For representative examples of women's reactions to rumors during the war's first year, see June 12, 1861, Carrie Hunter Diary in Cobb and Hunter Family Papers, SHC; Celeste Clay to Virginia Clay, June n.d., 1861, Clement Claiborne Clay Papers, Duke; May 6, 1862, Clara E. Solomon Diary, LSU; July 17, 1862,

Priscilla Munnikhuysen Bond Diary, LSU; May 19, September 12, 1862, Ann Wilkinson Penrose Diary, LSU; Crabtree and Patton, *Edmondston Journal,* 171.

8. August 28, 1861, Elizabeth Collier Diary, SHC; Anderson, *Journal of Kate Stone,* 24, 87.

9. Crabtree and Patton, *Edmondston Journal,* 91–92; Hodges and Kerber, "Children of Honor," 65; Buck, *Diary of Lucy Buck,* 15–17; Robertson, *Diary of Dolly Burge,* 76; Anderson, *Journal of Kate Stone,* 85; November 14, 1861, Mary Ezell Diary in Edward Conigland Papers, SHC; L. G. North to Charles Pettigrew, November 30, 1861, Pettigrew Family Papers, SHC.

10. January 1, 1862, Ella Gertrude Clanton Thomas Diary, Duke; Dawson, *Confederate Girl's Diary,* 317; Crabtree and Patton, *Edmondston Journal,* 103; February 17, 1862, Susan Cornwall Book, SHC; McGuire, *Diary of a Southern Refugee,* 94.

11. Unfortunately, most of the literary evidence comes from upper class women. Yeomen and poor whites expressed their attitudes by encouraging men to join or desert the army. For more sensitive indicators of morale among these groups, see chapter 3.

12. February 12, 1862, Sarah Lowe Diary in Sarah Lowe Papers, ADAH; Annie Sehon to Bettie Kimberly, February 8, 1862, John Kimberly Papers, SHC; February 24, 1862, Fannie Page Hume Diary, LC; March 2, 1862, Sarah Lois Wadley Diary, SHC; Elsie Bragg to Braxton Bragg, n.d., 1862, Braxton Bragg Papers, WRHS; Evangeline Shannon Crutcher to William O. Crutcher, February 9, 1862, Crutcher-Shannon Papers, MDAH; Anderson, *Journal of Kate Stone,* 91; Myers, *Children of Pride,* 852.

13. Eugenia Phillips to Virginia Clay, April 23, 1862, Clement Claiborne Clay Papers, Duke; Cumming, *Journal,* 26.

14. Logan, *My Confederate Girlhood,* 119–20; Cely Nevins to Lou Wharton, March 2, 1862, Edward Clifton Wharton and Family Papers, LSU; Anderson, *Journal of Kate Stone,* 95, 97, 103; A. A. Hammett to Bettie Pérot, March 20, 1862, Lewis Texada and Family Papers, LSU; Almena Perkins Kilbourne to James G. Kilbourne, February 23, 1862, J. G. Kilbourne and Family Collection, LSU.

15. Myers, *Children of Pride,* 992, 1054; Buck, *Diary of Lucy Buck,* 175; December 28, 1862, Lizzie Hatcher Simons Diary, BTHC; Johns, *Florida During the Civil War,* 186; Kate Burruss to Edward Burruss, December 3, 1862, John C. Burruss and Family Papers, LSU; Eppes, *Through Some Eventful Years,* 241.

16. July 18, 1862, Sarah Lois Wadley Diary, SHC; Elizabeth Pinckney to "Dear Sir," May 13, 1862, Elizabeth Izard Pinckney Papers, SCL; Sophie Baylor to Lou Wharton, June 12, 1862, Edward C. Wharton Papers, LSU; J. G. de Roulhac Hamilton, ed., *Correspondence of Jonathan Worth,* 2 vols. (Raleigh: North Carolina Historical Commission, 1909), 1:163–64; April 2, 1862, Melinda Ray Diary in Civil War Collection, NCDAH.

17. February 27, 1862, Meta Morris Grimball Diary, SHC; McGuire, *Diary of a*

Southern Refugee, 155; Myers, *Children of Pride,* 1178; Dougan, *Confederate Arkansas,* 114; Woodward, *Mary Chesnut's Civil War,* 744.

18. April 11, 1862, Elizabeth Collier Diary, SHC; Martha Fort to Tomlinson Fort, April 14, 1862, Fort Family Papers, SHC; Cumming, *Journal,* 37; May 4, 1862, Mary Greenhow Lee Diary, LC.

19. McGuire, *Diary of a Southern Refugee,* 125–26; Crabtree and Patton, *Edmondston Journal,* 202–3; June 30, July 28, 1862, Carrie Hunter Diary in Cobb and Hunter Family Papers, SHC; Marszalek, *Diary of Emma Holmes,* 179–81; Woodward, *Mary Chesnut's Civil War,* 412; July 8, 1862, Jane B. Beale Diary, UVa.

20. McGuire, *Diary of a Southern Refugee,* 166; McDonald, *Diary of the War,* 112, 114–16.

21. Marszalek, *Diary of Emma Holmes,* 218; Cumming, *Journal,* 218; Martha Cheatham to Benjamin Franklin Cheatham, March 30, [1863], Benjamin Franklin Cheatham Papers, SHC; Carrie Fries to J. F. Shaffner, April 25, 1863, Fries and Shaffner Family Papers, SHC; Henderson, *Journal of Georgiana Walker,* 35–36; Rowland and Croxall, *Journal of Julia LeGrand,* 215.

22. Cumming, *Journal,* 82; McGuire, *Diary of a Southern Refugee,* 249–50; Marszalek, *Diary of Emma Holmes,* 231–32; April 26, 1863, Amanda Worthington Diary in Amanda Worthington Papers, SHC.

23. January 26, 1863, Melinda Ray Diary in Civil War Collection, NCDAH; March 8, 1863, Cornelia M. Noble Diary, BTHC; Candler, "Life in Georgia," 303–4.

24. November 21, 1864, Ella Gertrude Clanton Thomas Diary, Duke; Myers, *Children of Pride,* 807; "Diary of Harriette Cary," 106; Lila Chunn to Willie Chunn, May 19, 1863, Willie Chunn Papers, Duke.

25. Myers, *Children of Pride,* 677, 878, 1162–63; McGuire, *Diary of a Southern Refugee,* 41, 332–33; Crabtree and Patton, *Edmondston Journal,* 165, 650; Mary P. Gowan to Henry Graves, April 18, 1863, Graves Family Papers, SHC; May 3, 1862, Cornelia M. Noble Diary, BTHC.

26. Bonner, *Journal of a Milledgeville Girl,* 36; Carrie Fries to J. F. Shaffner, May 12, 1863, Fries and Shaffner Family Papers, SHC; Leland, "Middleton Correspondence," 97–98.

27. July 25, 1863, Amanda Worthington Diary in Worthington Family Papers, MDAH; Leland, "Middleton Correspondence," 161; July 19, 1863, Sarah Wadley Diary, SHC.

28. Carrie Fries to J. F. Shaffner July 16, 1863, Fries and Shaffner Family Papers, SHC; Crabtree and Patton, *Edmondston Journal,* 426–27; Anderson, *Journal of Kate Stone,* 229–30.

29. Wright, *Southern Girl in '61,* 141; King, *Diary of Josephine Habersham,* 57; Anderson, *Journal of Kate Stone,* 233.

30. Nannie Williams to James P. Williams, July 22, 1863, James Peter Williams Papers, UVa; July 15, 1863, Harriet Ellen Moore Diary, SHC; Meta Morris Grimball

to John Berkeley Grimball, July 29, 1863, Grimball Papers, Duke; Addie J. Simms to Rufus K. Macomb, August 16, 1863, Simms Letters, BTHC.

31. July 20, 1863, Carrie Hunter Diary in Cobb and Hunter Family Papers, SHC; McGuire, *Diary of a Southern Refugee,* 230–31, 234; Crabtree and Patton, *Edmondston Journal,* 434–35, 461.

32. July 23, 1863, Ann Wilkinson Penrose Diary, LSU; Hattie ? to Alexander H. Stephens, July 16, 1863, Stephens Papers, LC; McGee and Lander, *A Rebel Came Home,* 37; King, *Diary of Josephine Habersham,* 44–45; McGuire, *Diary of a Southern Refugee,* 229.

33. Logan, *My Confederate Girlhood,* 118; December 21, 1863, Sarah Lois Wadley Diary, SHC; Moneyhon, "Diary of Virginia Davis Gray," 60.

34. December 31, 1863, Cora E. Watson Journal in T. Harry Williams Papers, LSU; Crabtree and Patton, *Edmondston Journal,* 513; January 1, 1864, Sidney Harding Diary, LSU; Anderson, *Journal of Kate Stone,* 271; Robertson, *Diary of Dolly Burge,* 88; January 1, 1864, Carrie Hunter Diary in Cobb and Hunter Family Papers, SHC; January 1, 1864, Kate A. Garland Diary in Kate Garland Papers, LSU.

35. Woodward, *Mary Chesnut's Civil War,* 625; E. A. Cheny to Sarah A. Newell, February 3, 1864, Robert A. Newell Papers, LSU; Harriet Perry to Theophilus Perry, January 18, 1864, Presley Carter Person Papers, Duke; June 15, 1864, Belle Edmondson Diary, SHC; February 4, 1864, Carrie Hunter Diary in Cobb and Hunter Family Papers, SHC; Crabtree and Patton, *Edmondston Journal,* 566–67.

36. June 8, 1862, Carrie Hunter Diary in Cobb and Hunter Family Papers, SHC; Woodward, *Mary Chesnut's Civil War,* 730, 733.

37. October 31, 1863, Sue Richardson Diary, Emory; December 31, 1862, Cornelia M. Noble Diary, BTHC; McGuire, *Diary of a Southern Refugee,* 42–43. This vision of future reward had a particularly powerful effect on young women uncertain about their prospects and constrained by social conservatism. Robertson, *Lucy Breckinridge,* 57, 61.

38. Myers, *Children of Pride,* 839; Anderson, *Journal of Kate Stone,* 175; McDonald, *Diary of the War,* 90–91; July 17, 1863, Sarah Rodgers Espy Diary, ADAH; November 27, 1862, Meta Morris Grimball Diary, SHC. Historians dealing with religion during the Civil War have almost exclusively focused on the problems of church organization and revivalism. Even Drew Faust, who has most carefully described and analyzed the faith of the Confederate soldier, has emphasized how the men saw heaven as an escape from death or valued religious faith as a preserver of social solidarity. Her striking comparison of conversion to the battle fatigue of later wars and her argument that religion could reduce class conflict in the ranks still does not come to grips with the question of how Confederates used their religious faith to explain the course of the war, including the outcome of campaigns and battles. For soldiers as well as the women back home, a simple, folk theology provided not only comfort but a familiar prism

through which to interpret events. Drew Gilpin Faust, "Christian Soldiers: The Meaning of Revivalism in the Confederate Army," *Journal of Southern History,* 53 (February 1987), 82–90.

39. An exception was Fannie Gordon, wife of Confederate General John B. Gordon, who believed that Grant's tenacity combined with his superior numbers spelled trouble for Lee's bedraggled men. Fannie Gordon to John B. Gordon, May 15, 1864, Fannie Gordon Papers, GDAH.

40. Eppes, *Through Some Eventful Years,* 240; Phillips Russell, *The Woman Who Rang the Bell: The Story of Cornelia Phillips Spencer* (Chapel Hill: University of North Carolina Press, 1949), 49; Marszalek, *Diary of Emma Holmes,* 354.

41. For examples of continued hopefulness, see Robertson, *Lucy Breckinridge,* 192; McGuire, *Diary of a Southern Refugee,* 315–16; [Gilman], "Letters of a Confederate Mother," 510.

42. September 8, 1864, Grace B. Elmore Diary, SCL; Crabtree and Patton, *Edmondston Journal,* 639.

43. September 17, 1864, Ella Gertrude Clanton Thomas Diary, Duke; Marszalek, *Diary of Emma Holmes,* 375; Myers, *Children of Pride,* 1213.

44. Miers, *Diary of Emma LeConte,* 3–5; McGuire, *Diary of a Southern Refugee,* 325–26; January 15, 1865, Meta Morris Grimball Diary, SHC; January 1, 1865, Virginia Clay Diary in Clement Claiborne Clay Papers, Duke; Cumming, *Journal,* 246.

45. McGee and Lander, *A Rebel Came Home,* 76; "Civil War Days in Huntsville," 298; February 8, 1865, Abbie M. Brooks Diary, AHS.

46. Crabtree and Pattons, *Edmondston Journal,* 172; June 5, 1863, Sarah Lois Wadley Diary, SHC; Woodward and Muhlenfeld, *Private Mary Chesnut,* 161; Myers, *Children of Pride,* 1009.

47. March 27, 1864, Myra Inman Diary, SHC; March 10, 1862, Cornelia M. Noble Diary, BTHC; Cumming, *Journal,* 174.

48. Myers, *Children of Pride,* 1076, 1131, 1244; September 15, 1861, Sarah Lois Wadley Diary, SHC; October 21, 1862, Mrs. Hill Diary, UVa; Susan M. Kollock, ed., "Letters of the Kollock and Allies Families, 1826–1884," *Georgia Historical Quarterly,* 34 (December 1950), 313; July 30, 1863, Anonymous Diary, MDAH; April 8, 1865, Margaret B. Crozier Ramsey Diary in James Bettys McCready Ramsey Papers, SHC.

49. April 26, 1861, Sarah Lois Wadley Diary, SHC; June 16, 1861, Betty Herndon Maury Diary, LC; December 31, 1864, Sidney Harding Diary, LSU; Robertson, *Lucy Breckinridge,* 188–89.

50. Robertson, *Lucy Breckinridge,* 62; Clift, *Private War of Lizzie Hardin,* 233; Marszalek, *Diary of Emma Holmes,* 413; Blackford, "The Great John B. Minor and His Cousin Mary," 444; McDonald, *Diary of the War,* 247–48.

51. Woodward, *Mary Chesnut's Civil War,* 737, 768–69; Marszalek, *Diary of Emma Holmes,* 406; March 3, 1865, Grace B. Elmore Diary, SCL.

52. Jones, *Rebel War Clerk's Diary,* 2:418; McGuire, *Diary of a Southern Refugee,* 334; March 23, April 2, 1865, Mrs. William A. Simmons Diary, Confederate Museum.

53. April 2, 1865, Mrs. William A. Simmons Diary, Confederate Museum; Jones, *Ladies of Richmond,* 279–80; Pryor, *Reminiscences of Peace and War,* 354–57; Fannie Walker Miller, "The Fall of Richmond," *Confederate Veteran,* 13 (July 1905), 305; McGuire, *Diary of a Southern Refugee,* 343–49; Putnam, *Richmond During the War,* 366; April 2, 1865, Anita Dwyer Withers Diary, SHC; Jones, *Rebel War Clerk's Diary,* 2:467; Patrick, *Fall of Richmond,* 48–61; April 3, 1865, Kate Mason Rowland Diary in Kate Mason Rowland Papers, Confederate Museum. For a similar account of looting and mayhem in Mobile, Alabama, see April 12, 1865, Mary D. Waring Diary, ADAH.

54. Freeman, *Calendar of Confederate Papers,* 249–53; Pryor, *Reminiscences of Peace and War,* 361–71; Dawson, *Our Women in the War,* 99–108; Recollections of Mrs. Archibald Campbell Pryor concerning conditions in Petersburg, June 1864–April 1865, VSL; Mrs. W. S. Simpson to Annie ?, May 20, 1865, Mr. and Mrs. William S. Simpson Papers, VSL; Patrick, *Fall of Richmond,* 105, 116. After the Confederates evacuated Danville, Virginia, mothers, children, and discharged soldiers began looting the storehouses. One woman shouted, "Our children and we'uns are starving! The Confederacy is gone up! Let us help ourselves!" James I. Robertson, Jr., "Danville under Military Occupation, 1865," *Virginia Magazine of History and Biography,* 75 (July 1967), 331–32.

55. Skipper and Gove, "Diary of Ethie Eagleton," 117; Faulkner, *The Unvanquished,* 155; March 1, 1865, Grace B. Elmore Diary, SCL.

CHAPTER 11

1. For attempts at denial, see Fleet and Fuller, *Green Mount,* 361; Anderson, *Journal of Kate Stone,* 331; Cumming, *Journal,* 275; Clift, *Private War of Lizzie Hardin,* 223–24, 235.

2. Louis R. Wilson, ed., *Selected Papers of Cornelia Phillips Spencer* (Chapel Hill: University of North Carolina Press, 1953), 14–15; January 1, 1866, Lucy Williamson Cocke Diary in Lucy Williamson Cocke Collection, UVa; Miers, *Diary of Emma LeConte,* 21–22; Myers, *Children of Pride,* 1273; John Richard Dennett, *The South As It Is, 1865–1866,* ed. by Henry M. Christman (New York: Viking Press, 1965), 192–93; Marszalek, *Diary of Emma Holmes,* 437–38.

3. Eppes, *Through Some Eventful Years,* 270; Anderson, *Journal of Kate Stone,* 364; Buck, *Diary of Lucy Buck,* 297; May 13, 1865, Sarah Lois Wadley Diary, SHC; McGuire, *Diary of a Southern Refugee,* 352.

4. Allen W. Moger, "Letters to General Lee After the War," *Virginia Magazine of History and Biography,* 64 (January 1956), 41; June 7, 1865, Nancy McDougall Robinson Diary in Nancy McDougall Robinson Collection, MDAH; May 29, 1865, Abbie M. Brooks Diary, AHS; Chamberlain, *Old Days in Chapel Hill,* 83, 88.

5. See, for example, Lucy D. Rodes to Alexander Brown, December 16, 1862, Brown Papers, Duke; Marszalek, *Diary of Emma Holmes,* 191.

6. Crabtree and Patton, *Edmondston Journal,* 695–96; April 20, 1865, Sarah Lois Wadley Diary, SHC; Roark, *Masters Without Slaves,* 132.

7. May 10, 1865, Grace B. Elmore Diary, SCL; May 8, 1865, Myra Inman Diary, SHC; Robertson, *Diary of Dolly Burge,* 110–11; June 6, 1865, Kate A. Garland Diary in Kate Garland Papers, LSU. For an excellent analysis of how Southern clergymen attempted to explain Confederate defeat, see Charles Reagan Wilson, *Baptized in Blood: The Religion of the Lost Cause, 1865–1920* (Athens: University of Georgia Press, 1980), 58–78. Women embraced many features of postwar civil religion, but they did so with decidedly less certainty and a more pessimistic outlook than many men. For a brief but suggestive discussion of how several women dealt with the theological issues raised by Confederate defeat, see Richard M. Weaver, *The Southern Tradition at Bay* (New Rochelle, N.Y.: Arlington House, 1968), 270–73.

8. Marszalek, *Diary of Emma Holmes,* 438; May 22, 1865, Grace B. Elmore Diary, SCL; Pryor, *Reminiscences of Peace and War,* 374–75; May 29, 1866, Susan Cornwall Book, SHC; Fanny Atkisson to Marian Blackshear, May 6, 1866, Baber and Blackshear Papers, UGa.

9. For parallels, compare the statements quoted in the previous chapter with the following: Bryan, "Journal of Minerva McClatchey," 213–14; Annie Bryan Lawton to "Dear Asbury," May 24, 1865, Bryan, Willingham, and Lawton Families Papers, GDAH; April 27, 1865, Mary B. Crozier Ramsey Diary in James Bettys McCready Ramsey Papers, SHC; Bonner, *Journal of a Milledgeville Girl,* 73, 76–77; June 1865, Lucy Irion Journal in Irion-Nielson Family Papers, MDAH; May 2, 1865, Grace B. Elmore Diary, SCL; Cumming, *Journal,* 307.

10. Clift, *Private War of Lizzie Hardin,* 280–81.

11. Drew Faust has linked evangelism in the Confederate army with the everyday experiences of soldiers and especially with lost battles, lengthening casualty lists, and the need for greater discipline in the army. Yet pressure from home— the influence of wives and mothers—also played a part because many Confederate soldiers, for all their bluster and rough habits, remained sentimentalists. Homesickness and suffering also made them more amenable to the spiritual advice of their womenfolk. Faust briefly notes how some soldiers still thought it unmanly to acknowledge the need for a deeply emotional religious experience, but she might have given some attention to the relationship between the religion of the camps and increasingly female-dominated piety at home. Faust, "Christian Soldiers," 63–90.

12. Myers, *Children of Pride,* 1165; Coxe, *Memories of a South Carolina Plantation,* 23; Jorantha Semmes to Benedict Joseph Semmes, May 1863, Benedict Joseph Semmes Papers, SHC.

13. Frances B. Leigh, *Ten Years on a Georgia Plantation* (New York: Negro

Universities Press, 1969 [1883]), 12; "Southern Girl's Diary," 301–2; Andrews, *Journal of a Georgia Girl,* 225, 227.

14. For a useful comparative perspective, see Smith, *Ladies of the Leisure Class,* 93–122.

15. For typical accounts, see *Nation,* 2 (January 18, 1866), 79–80; Sidney Andrews, *The South Since the War* (New York: Houghton Mifflin, 1970 [1866]), 386.

16. Paul H. Buck, *The Road to Reunion, 1865–1900* (Boston: Little, Brown, 1937), 39–42; Andrews, *Journal of a Georgia Girl,* 171–72, 371.

17. Dawson, *Our Women in the War,* 28; Anderson, *North Carolina Women of the Confederacy,* 22; May 12, 1865, Mary Elizabeth Rives Diary, LSU; Crabtree and Patton, *Edmondston Journal,* 708–9; Miers, *Diary of Emma Holmes,* 90; Myron Adams to Eliza Button, April 18, 1865, Eliza Button Papers, Duke.

18. See the suggestive analysis in Gaines M. Foster, *Ghosts of the Confederacy: Defeat, the Lost Cause, and the Emergence of the New South, 1865–1913* (New York: Oxford University Press, 1987), 26–33. See also the interesting but not entirely persuasive treatment of male sexual anxiety in the South at the end of the nineteenth century in Joel Williamson, *The Crucible of Race: Black-White Relations in the American South Since Appomattox* (New York: Oxford University Press, 1984), 306–10.

19. July 9, 1865, Elizabeth Collier Diary, SHC; Woodward and Muhlenfeld, *Private Mary Chesnut,* 811; Julia ? to ?, November 10, 1865, David Weeks Papers, LSU.

20. I have constructed women's reasoning about Southern destiny from the following sources: April 25, 1865, Elizabeth Collier Diary, SHC; Cornelia Phillips Spencer to "My Dear Eliza," March 10, 1866, Spencer Papers, SHC; Andrews, *Journal of a Georgia Girl,* 254, 256; Miers, *Diary of Emma LeConte,* 103; Melissa Baker to Charlotte L. Branch, June 30, 1865, Margaret Branche Saxton Papers, UGa; May 18, 1865, Sarah Lois Wadley Diary, SHC; May 1, 1865, Ella Gertrude Clanton Thomas Diary, Duke; William Gilmore Simms, ed., *War Poetry of the South* (New York: Richardson and Co., 1866), 221–23; Anderson, *North Carolina Women of the Confederacy,* 136–37.

21. Clift, *Private War of Lizzie Hardin,* 243; July 31, 1865, Amanda Worthington Diary in Worthington Family Papers, MDAH; Mary P. Steger to Mrs. Robert M. T. Hunter, July 15, 1865, Hunter Papers, UVa; July 18, 1865, Anonymous Diary, MDAH; Augusta J. Evans to Mrs. J. H. Chrisman, February 3, 1866, Augusta Jane Evans Wilson Papers, ADAH; Ben W. Griffith, Jr., ed., "A Lady Novelist Views the Reconstruction: An Augusta Jane Evans Letter," *Georgia Historical Quarterly,* 43 (March 1959), 106.

22. Henry Deedes, *Sketches of the South and West; or, Ten Months' Residence in the United States* (Edinburgh, Scotland: William Blackwood and Sons, 1869), 87–88; Andrews, *Southern Since the War,* 10; Andrew Buni, ed., "Reconstruction

in Orange County, Virginia: A Letter from Hannah Garlick Rawlings to her Sister, Clarissa Lawrence Rawlings, August 9, 1865," *Virginia Magazine of History and Biography,* 75 (October 1967), 463–64; Andrews, *Journal of a Georgia Girl,* 305. In this world of defeat and military occupation, symbols of American nationalism also enraged female extremists. Some attacked the American flag as "a hateful old rag" while others deemed the Fourth of July seemed more an occasion for mourning than celebration. Andrews, *Journal of a Georgia Girl,* 219–20; 226; Chamberlain, *Old Days in Chapel Hill,* 132–33; July 4, 1865, Evelyn Harden Jackson Diary in Harden, Jackson, and Carithers Papers, UGa; July 4, 1865, Mary Elizabeth Rives Diary, LSU; July 4, 1865, Kate A. Garland Diary in Kate Garland Papers, LSU.

23. John Hammond Moore, ed., *The Juhl Letters to the Charleston Courier: A View of the South, 1865–1871* (Athens: University of Georgia Press, 1974), 25; F. N. Boney, ed., *A Union Soldier in the Land of the Vanquished: The Diary of Sergeant Mathew Woodruff, June-December, 1865* (University, Ala.: University of Alabama Press, 1969), 48–49; Amelia Barr to "Dear Jennie," October 25, 1866, Barr Letters, BTHC; March 11, 1866, Mary Ann Nolley Otey Diary in Mary Ann Nolley Otey Papers, MDAH.

24. Andrews, *South Since the War,* 9, 13–16, 320–21; March 12, 1866, Mary Ann Nolley Otey Diary in Mary Ann Nolley Otey Papers, MDAH; Eric L. McKitrick, *Andrew Johnson and Reconstruction* (Chicago: University of Chicago Press, 1960), 40.

25. See, for example, November 26, 1880, Ella Gertrude Clanton Thomas Diary, Duke.

26. Leigh, *Ten Years on a Georgia Plantation,* 12–13; Andrews, *Journal of a Georgia Girl,* 317–18; Augusta J. Evans to J. L. M. Curry, October 7, 1865, Jabez Lamar Monroe Curry Papers, LC; November 4, 1880, Ella Gertrude Clanton Thomas Diary, Duke. A notable exception to the general political lethargy among women in the postwar South was Rebecca Latimer Felton, who worked hard during her husband's campaigns, wrote articles for newspapers, and kept up a voluminous correspondence with Georgia Democrats before entering politics in her own right. She later joined Ella Thomas and a few other women in the campaign for women's suffrage. John Erwin Talmadge, *Rebecca Latimer Felton* (Athens: University of Georgia Press, 1960), 36–62.

27. Jeanie Chew Young to Louisa Wharton, January 16, 1866, Edward Cliffton Wharton and Family Papers, LSU.

28. Miers, *Diary of Emma LeConte,* 102; Smith et al., *Mason Smith Family Letters,* 181; Clift, *Private War of Lizzie Hardin,* 246; Andrews, *Journal of a Georgia Girl,* 259, 267, 306–7.

29. John Witherspoon DuBose, *Alabama's Tragic Decade: Ten Years of Alabama, 1865–1874,* ed. by James K. Green (Birmingham, Ala.: Webb Book Co., 1940), 3–6; Paula Stahls Jordan, *Women of Guilford County, North Carolina*

(Greensboro, N.C.: Greensboro Printing Co., 1979), 55–58; Loula Graves to ?, May 22, 1865, Graves Family Papers, SHC.

30. Andrews, *Journal of a Georgia Girl,* 329–30; Dennett, *South As It Is,* 278–79; Thomas North, *Five Years in Texas* (Cincinnati: Elm Street Printing Co., 1871), 188.

31. Bruce S. Greenawalt, ed., "Virginians Face Reconstruction: Correspondence from the James Dorman Davidson Papers, 1865–1880," *Virginia Magazine of History and Biography,* 78 (October 1970), 448–49; Joseph A. Waddell, *Annals of Augusta County, Virginia, From 1726–1871* (Bridgewater, Virginia: C. J. Carrier, 1958), 510; December 1, 1865, Cyrus B. Comstock Diary, LC.

32. July 4, 1865, Grace B. Elmore Diary, SCL.

33. For an example of an oath signed by a woman, see Mary M. Parr oath, September 21, 1865, Box 23, Civil War Miscellany, GDAH.

34. Crabtree and Patton, *Edmondston Journal,* 713; Myers, *Children of Pride,* 1329; Emma Inman Williams, ed., "Hettie Wisdom Tapp's Memoirs," *West Tennessee Historical Society Papers,* (1982), 119–20; New Orleans *Picayune,* July 20, 1862; Harry Willcox Pfanz, "Soldiering in the South during Reconstruction" (Ph.D. dissertation, Ohio State University, 1958), 79–80; Andrews, *Journal of a Georgia Girl,* 255–56; Avary, *Dixie After the War,* 124–27.

35. Annie Sehon to Bettie Kimberly, May 20, 1863, John Kimberly Papers, SHC; Reid, *After the War,* 156–57; Lucy Cunyus, *History of Bartow County, Formerly Cass* (Cassville, Ga.: Tribune Publishing Co., 1933), 245–46; Crabtree and Patton, *Edmondston Journal,* 716. A few wealthy women also had to apply for presidential pardons, though Cornelia Phillips Spencer described the requirement as "characteristic of the universal Yankee nation—a people utterly incapable of a noble or generous emotion." Smith et al., *Mason Smith Family Letters,* 249; Russell, *Woman Who Rang the Bell,* 75.

36. April 18, 1865, Carrie Hunter Diary in Cobb and Hunter Family Papers, SHC; Andrews, *Journal of a Georgia Girl,* 198; Bonner, *Journal of a Milledgeville Girl,* 74; Woodward and Muhlenfeld, *Private Mary Chesnut,* 247; Anderson, *Journal of Kate Stone,* 333–34; Anna R. Sherrard to "Sister Lizzie," April 7, 1866, Munford-Ellis Family Papers, Duke.

37. Marszalek, *Diary of Emma Holmes,* 436–37; Sarah Hine to Charlotte L. Branch, February 10, 1866, Margaret Branch Sexton Papers, UGa; Ella Cooper to Virginia Clay, July 1866?, Clement Claiborne Clay Papers, Duke.

38. Eppes, *Through Some Eventful Years,* 280; Cornelia Phillips Spencer to "My Dear Eliza," March 10, 1866, Cornelia Phillips Spencer Papers, SHC; October 22, 1868, Ella Gertrude Clanton Thomas Diary, Duke; Marszalek, *Diary of Emma Holmes,* 485–86.

39. Women had trouble looking upon Johnson as anything but a political turncoat or a "drunken ass," as Emma LeConte caustically labeled him. Those who had always disparaged Lincoln's lowly birth and vulgar habits found John-

son—the son of poor white parents, a runaway apprentice, and East Tennessee tailor—no improvement. "In the seething cauldron, the thickest scum ever rises to the surface," Catherine Edmondston commented sharply. But of all the words used to denounce the new president, *renegade traitor* appeared most often. Miers, *Diary of Emma LeConte*, 93; April 18, 1865, Sarah Leach Diary, UVa; Crabtree and Patton, *Edmondston Journal*, 702–3, 716.

40. Marszalek, *Diary of Emma Holmes*, 484–85; Russell, *Woman Who Rang the Bell*, 86; September 20, 1866, Ella Gertrude Clanton Thomas Diary, Duke.

41. Miers, *Diary of Emma LeConte*, 90–91; Chamberlain, *Old Days in Chapel Hill*, 118; October 6, 1865, Amanda Worthington Diary in Worthington Family Papers, MDAH.

42. Hudson Strode, *Jefferson Davis*, 3 vols. (New York: Harcourt, Brace and World, 1955–64), 3:303; Griffith, "A Lady Novelist Views the Reconstruction," 105; Myers, *Children of Pride*, 1379.

43. February 21, 1868, Mary Hort Journal, SCL; Sarah Catherine Himes to Adam Himes, November 8, 1867, Sarah Catherine Himes Letters, Duke; November 30, 1867, January 1, 1868, Sally Perry Diary in Sally Perry Papers, ADAH; Bonner, *Journal of a Milledgeville Girl*, 126. Mary Elizabeth Massey has argued that Southern women became more embittered during the 1870s than during the war, but her own evidence, like that presented above, comes from the 1860s. From 1868 on, political comments by women in diaries and family letters are rare. Cf. Massey, *Bonnet Brigades*, 321–29.

44. Mary Watkins to Franklin Brown, September 4, 1868, Joseph E. Elizabeth G. Brown Collection, UGa; Zuleika Haralson Cleveland Poem, 1874, SHC; September 8, 1870, Ella Gertrude Clanton Thomas Diary, Duke; Fanny Atkisson to Marian Blackshear, March 3, 1877, Baber and Blackshear Papers, UGa; Loula Ayres Rockwell Recollections, p. 1 in Rockwell Papers, SHC; Nancy R. Willard to Micajah Wilkinson, November 30, 1874, Micajah Wilkinson and Family Papers, LSU. No one has yet made a thorough study of either Unionist women or the wives of Southern Republicans. Widely scattered evidence suggests that these women faced social ostracism and some persecution. They also had to worry about terrorist attacks against their husbands and families. John William De Forest, *A Union Officer in the Reconstruction*, ed. by James H. Croushore and Davis Morris Potter (New Haven, Conn.: Yale University Press, 1948), 146–50, 167–70; *New Orleans Tribune*, July 28, 1865; *House Executive Documents*, No. 30, 40th Cong., 2d sess., 134–35; Mrs. John Cochran to Robert K. Scott, October 27, 1868, Scott Papers, SCDAH; "The Friend of all Loyal People" to Mrs. Albion W. Tourgée, October 16, 1866. Albion Winegar Tourgée Papers, SHC.

45. McGuire, *Diary of a Southern Refugee*, 360; *War Days in Fayetteville*. 59–60; Foster, *Ghosts of the Confederacy*, 173–74.

46. Wilson, *Baptized in Blood*, 28, 48; Bryan, *Confederate Georgia*, 185–86;

History of the Confederated Memorial Associations of the South (n.p.: Confederate Southern Memorial Association, 1904), 48.

47. *History of the Confederated Memorial Associations,* 66–67 et passim; Augusta J. Evans to J. L. M. Curry, April 15, 1866, Jabez Lamar Monroe Curry Papers, LC; Evans to Mayor, Board of Aldermen, and Common Council of Mobile, May 18, 1866, Augusta Jane Evans Wilson Papers, ADAH; Athens Ladies Memorial Association, Objects of Association, ca. 1867–68, UGa; Eppes, *Through Some Eventful Years,* 324–25; "Monument to General Robert E. Lee," *Southern Historical Society Papers,* 17 (1889), 188, 194–201.

48. McGee and Lander, *A Rebel Came Home,* 114–15; Kathryn Reinhart Schuler, "Women in Public Affairs in Louisiana During Reconstruction," *Louisiana Historical Quarterly,* 19 (July 1936), 689–90; Thomes Nelson Page, *Social Life in Old Virginia* (New York: Charles Scribner's Sons, 1897), 57–58; T. C. DeLeon, "Southern Women in the Civil War," *Southern Historical Society Papers,* 32 (1904), 146–50; Eggleston, *Rebel's Recollections,* 84–85.

49. "Address of Hon. John Lamb," *Southern Historical Society Papers,* 38 (1910), 307; Bishop Collins Denny, "Robert E. Lee, The Flower of the South," ibid., (1916), 6–7; "Monument to the Defenders of Vicksburg, Unveiling at Vicksburg, April 25, 1893," ibid., 21 (1893), 199–200; W. R. Aylett, "Women of the South," ibid., 22 (1894), 57.

50. [General M. C. Butler], "Southern Genius," *Southern Historical Society Papers,* 16 (1888), 290–91; "Address of General R. E. Colston Before the Ladies Memorial Association, Wilmington, N.C., May 10, 1870," ibid., 21 (1893), 41–43; William Faulkner, *Sartoris* (New York: Random House, 1929), 53–54.

51. Ruoff, "Southern Womanhood," 95–106; "The Confederate Dead of Mississippi," *Southern Historical Society Papers,* 18 (1890), 296–97; *History of the Confederated Memorial Associations,* 56. After World War II, many Americans believed that women should return to the home, a belief held in 1865 by Southern men and women. Whether this phenomenon is a general one, the desire to go back to more conservative sex roles seems common after a prolonged period of social stress and upheaval. And after the Civil War, Southern women faced the additional challenge (and expectation) of again creating havens of morality and security for the returning soldiers. As Bonnie Smith has perceptively noted, historians need to examine both the internal and external sources of reactionary social values. Chafe, *American Woman,* 174–95; Smith, *Ladies of the Leisure Class,* 1–17.

52. William Faulkner, *Absalom, Absalom!* (New York: Modern Library, 1936), 12.

CHAPTER 12

1. October 8, 1865, Amanda Worthington Diary in Worthington Family Papers, MDAH; July 5, 1865, Nannie K. Rayburn Diary in Samuel King Rayburn Papers, ADAH.

2. Reid, *After the War,* 222–24; Eppes, *Through Some Eventful Years,* 291; Kate McGreachy Buie to "Mr. Bradley," September 25, 1866, Catherine Jane Buie Papers, Duke; Mary N. Bostell to Mrs. Algernon Sullivan, April, 1867, Ellen D. Coleman to ?, April 8, 1867, Sallie Hamblet to J. J. Roosevelt, n.d., 1867, New York Southern Relief Association Papers, Confederate Museum. The collapse of the monetary system wrecked havoc during the summer of 1865. Left with worthless Confederates notes, women could not buy the necessities. Few people had managed to hoard any gold, greenbacks were scarce, and in many counties, little money of any kind circulated. Ordinary business transactions often stopped, and a barter economy prevailed in rural areas. Smith et al., *Mason Smith Family Letters,* 208; Mary Y. Harth to "Mrs. Watson," November 26, 1865, Harth Papers, SCL; Woodward, *Mary Chesnut's Civil War,* 830; Sarah P. Crump Brown to L. C. Alexander, February 4, 1867, New York Southern Relief Association Papers, Confederate Museum; Eugenia Carew to Harriet Frances Ronan, April 23, 1865, Harriet Frances Ronan Papers, Duke.

3. E. Marges to Mary W. Pugh, April 23, 1865, Richard L. Pugh Papers, LSU; Andrews, *Journal of a Georgia Girl,* 286; Cumming, *Journal,* 285; Mary G. H. Harley to Sarah V. K. Stark, December 5, 1865, Harley File, Civil War Miscellany, GDAH.

4. Russell H. Conwell, *Magnolia Journey: A Union Veteran Revisits the Former Confederates States,* ed. by Joseph C. Carter (University, Ala.: University of Alabama Press, 1974), 109; Leigh, *Ten Years on a Georgia Plantation,* 144–45; Smedes, *Memorials of a Southern Planter,* 232–33; Sarah Hughes to Mrs. Algernon Sullivan, March 25, 1867, New York Southern Relief Association Papers, Confederate Museum; Betsey Fleet, ed., *Green Mount After the War: The Correspondence of Maria Louisa Wacker Fleet and Her Family* (Charlottesville: University of Virginia Press, 1978), 98. See also Ellen Glasgow's description of a "great lady" struggling to maintain her dignity in the postwar South. Glasgow, *Virginia* (New York: Doubleday, Page, 1913), 38–39.

5. Wilbur Fisk Tillett, "Southern Womanhood as Affected by the War," *Century Magazine,* 43 (November 1891), 9–16; Anderson, *North Carolina Women of the Confederacy,* 63; Roark, *Masters Without Slaves,* 203. See the excellent analysis of the changing relationship between Virginia and Clement Clay, Jr. in Carol K. Bleser and Frederick M. Heath, "The Impact of the Civil War on a Southern Marriage: Clement and Virginia Tunstall Clay of Alabama," *Civil War History,* 30 (September 1984), 211–20.

6. July 31, 1863, October 9, 1865, November 29, December 4, 1868, Ella Gertrude Clanton Thomas Diary, Duke.

7. May 3, 14, June 19, 1869, ibid.

8. August 7, 1869, January 10, November 29, 30, December n.d., 12, 1870, February 3, 1880, ibid. Mary Elizabeth Massey suggested that the family's financial troubles spurred Ella Thomas's interest in writing and reform. But despite her

work for women's suffrage and advanced views on racial issues, she also joined conservative organizations such as the Woman's Christian Temperance Union and the United Daughters of the Confederacy. Massey, "The Making of a Feminist," *Journal of Southern History,* 39 (February 1973), 16–22.

9. Dennett, *South As It Is,* 104–5; Anna Cheatham to Benjamin Franklin Cheatham, March 30, April 30, August 15, December 16, 1866, Benjamin Franklin Cheatham Papers, SHC; Kate Hester Robson Reminiscences, p. 31, AHS; Eliza C. Rives to Susannah Willcox, March 24, 1867, James M. Willcox Papers, Duke; August 11, 1877, March 3, 1879, Emily Jane Winkler Bealer Diary, GDAH. In Edgefield County, South Carolina, about the same percentage of women operated farms in 1870 as in 1860. Burton, *In My Father's House,* 262–63. For a useful comparison of attitudes, see Hagood, *Mothers of the South,* 77–91.

10. February 26, 1867, September 1868, Margaret Gillis Diary, ADAH.

11. De Forest, *Union Officer in Reconstruction,* 49–52, 140–45; Anderson, *Journal of Kate Stone,* 359.

12. Andrews, *South Since the War,* 180–81; De Forest, *Union Officer in Reconstruction,* 135–40, 145–46.

13. *Relations Between Labor and Capital,* 4:340–41; Dennett, *South As It Is,* 96, 119–20, 146, 243–46.

14. Schuler, "Women in Public Affairs in Louisiana," 687–88; Mary A. Palmer to "Philanthropist of New York," January 30, 1867, Josephine M. Gadsden to Mrs. Algernon L. Sullivan, May 18, 1866, Susannah Perry to Arthur Leary, August 13, 1867, Caroline Breaux to Southern Relief Association, August 10, 1867, New York Southern Relief Association Papers, Confederate Museum; Burton, *In My Father's House,* 112.

15. Walter L. Fleming, ed., *Documentary History of Reconstruction,* 2 vols. (Cleveland: Arthur H. Clark Co., 1906–7), 1:20–21; *American Annual Cyclopedia, 1865,* 392–93; Caroline J. Greer to Mary Y. Harth, July 20, 1868, Mary Y. Harth Papers, SCL; Alan Conway, *The Reconstruction of Georgia* (Minneapolis: University of Minnesota Press, 1966), 102; Ann M. Davis to Arthur Leary, June 1867, Claudia M. Legare to Mrs. A. Sullivan, March 23, 1867, New York Southern Relief Association Papers, Confederate Museum.

16. Abbie Pope to David C. Barrow, May 10, 1865, David Crenshaw Barrow Papers, UGa; Sarah Youngblood to Mrs. Sullivan, October 21, 1867, New York Southern Relief Association Papers, Confederate Museum; Mrs. Thomas J. ("Stonewall") Jackson et al. to ?, March 17, 1875, Battle Family Papers, SHC; Wilson, *Selected Papers,* 20–22, 43–44.

17. Louisa C. Hughes to William H. Smith, November 24, 1868, William H. Smith Papers, ADAH; Georgia Warren to Mr. Wood, January 25, 1867, Caroline Ball to Mr. Leary, March 30, 1867, New York Southern Relief Association Papers, Confederate Museum; Eugenia Carew to Harriet Frances Ronan, April 19, 23, 1865, Harriet Frances Ronan Papers, Duke.

18. Pryor, *Reminiscences of Peace and War,* 383; Leigh, *Ten Years on a Georgia Plantation,* 16; [Gilman], "Letters of a Confederate Mother," 514–15.

19. Rawick, *American Slave,* supp., ser. 2, vol. 3, pp. 594–95: Recollections of Mrs. Gordon Pryor Rice, VSL; Sarah Hine to Charlotte L. Branch, February 10, 1866, Margaret Branch Sexton Papers, UGa.

20. For typical complaints, see Easterby, *Southern Carolina Rice Plantation,* 226; Anderson, *Journal of Kate Stone,* 368–69; Myers, *Children of Pride,* 1391.

21. Rawick, *American Slave,* supp., ser. 2, vol. 3, pp. 885–86; Smith et al., *Mason Smith Family Letters,* 246; Roxanna Worth to Jonathan Worth, August 22, 1865, Jonathan Worth Papers, SHC; Bleser, *Hammonds of Redcliffe,* 144–45; Meta Morris Grimball to John Berkley Grimball, December 6, 1865, Grimball Family Papers, SHC.

22. Clara Elizabeth Barrow to Clara Barrow, November 30, 1865, David Crenshaw Barrow Papers, UGa; Easterby, *South Carolina Rice Plantation,* 212–14; Myers, *Children of Pride,* 1308–9, 1374, 1407, 1409; Amelia S. Montgomery to Joseph A. Montgomery, April 9, 1866 et passim 1866, November 18, 1867, Joseph Addison Montgomery and Family Papers, LSU; Robertson, *Diary of Dolly Burge,* 117–18; Mary B. Hall to William B. Hall, December 31, 1866, William B. Hall Papers, ADAH; Mary A. Snowden to Pamela Cunningham, October 1, 1866, Mary Amarinthia Yates Snowden Papers, SCL; Ann Faulkner to her brother, June 12, 1865, Battle Family Papers, SHC.

23. Elizabeth Stanley Hoole to Evelina Gertrude Brown Wilson, June 8, 1869, Moultrie Reid Wilson Papers, SCL; Myers, *Children of Pride,* 1365, 1369; Woodward and Muhlenfeld, *Private Mary Chesnut,* 259; Fleet, *Green Mount After the War,* 104–5.

24. Anne Firor Scott has argued that the entrance of women into plantation management after the war undermined the Southern patriarchy, but women had run plantations before the war without challenging traditional notions about woman's place. The apparent quantitative change during Reconstruction meant less than it might have because women now managed estates the value of which had declined sharply or which had fallen into ruin. In a study of five Alabama black belt counties, Jonathan Wiener has pointed out that few women entered the planter elite after the war, but his focus on the top of the economic pyramid ignores the women who ran small to medium-size places. Wiener confines his attention to planters who owned real estate valued at ten thousand dollars or more in 1870, a figure that would have excluded virtually all the female heads of household from the ten counties included in table 5. Scott deals with individual examples, while Wiener measures "persistence" among the wealthiest planters. Because of frequent marriages and remarriages, tracing the histories of individual female planters through the manuscript census becomes nearly impossible. From the conflicting evidence and arguments presented by Scott and Wiener and the comments of female planters themselves, three conclusions emerge: more women

ran farms and plantations after the war; few of these women became part of the planter elite; few plantation mistresses saw their activities as either striking blows for female independence or as improving the status of women in the South. Scott, *Southern Lady,* 96–97, 106–7; Wiener, *Social Origins of the New South,* 17, 28–33.

25. Suzanne Sparks Keitt to William A. Carrigan, n.d., 1878, April 2, May 20, 22, October 29, November 20, December 15, 24, 1879, Suzanne Mandeville Sparks Keitt Papers, SCL.

26. Robertson, *Diary of Dolly Burge,* 112–13; Myrta Lockett Avary, *Dixie After the War* (New York: Doubleday, Page, 1906), 181; Mrs. W. S. Simpson to "Dear Annie," May 1865, Mr. and Mrs. William S. Simpson Papers, VSL; May 7, 8, 1865, Ella Gertrude Clanton Thomas Diary, Duke.

27. The best accounts of the diverse reactions of plantation mistresses to emancipation come from the WPA interviews with former slaves. Rawick, *American Slave* vol. 2, pt. 1, pp. 181, 292; vol. 7 (Oklahoma), p. 114; vol. 12, pt. 1, p. 78; vol. 18 (Unwritten History of Slavery), 62; supp., ser. 1, vol. 7, p. 426; vol. 8, pp. 846–47; supp., ser. 2, vol. 8, pp. 3233, 3329; Perdue et al., *Weevils in the Wheat,* 36–37.

28. "Southern Girl's Diary," 300–301; Kollock, "Letters of Kollock and Allied Families," 318; Myers, *Children of Pride,* 1313; May 24, 1865, Grace B. Elmore Diary, SCL.

29. Crabtree and Patton, *Edmondston Journal,* 717–18; "Letters of a Confederate Mother," 514; "Southern Girl's Diary," 301; May 30, 1865, Grace B. Elmore Diary, SCL; Andrews, *Journal of a Georgia Girl,* 344, 362–63; Bryan, "Journal of Minerva McClatchey," 215; Emily V. Battey to Mary Ann Halsey, June 30, 1867, Robert Battey Papers, Emory.

30. J. G. de Roulhac Hamilton and Max R. Williams, eds., *Papers of William A. Graham,* 6 vols., (Raleigh: North Carolina Division of Archives and History, 1957–76), 6:341; June 3, 1866, Margaret Gillis Diary, ADAH. For the quote from the Louisiana woman and a helpful discussion of how Southern white women responded to the challenge of running their households without slaves, see Leon F. Litwack, *Been in the Storm So Long* (New York: Alfred A. Knopf, 1979), 354–58.

31. Laura S. Haviland, *A Woman's Life Work: Labors and Experiences* (Chicago: Publishing Association of Friends, 1881), 421–23; Lucy Paxton Scarborough, "So It Was When Her Life Began: Reminiscences of a Louisiana Girlhood," *Louisiana Historical Quarterly,* 13 (July 1930), 434; July 14, 1865, Grace B. Elmore Diary, SCL; John D. Barnhart, ed., "Reconstruction on the Lower Mississippi," *Mississippi Valley Historical Review,* 21 (December 1934), 391–92.

32. Mrs. Irby Morgan, *How It Was; Four Years Among the Rebels* (Nashville, Tenn.: Publishing House of the Methodist Episcopal Church, South, 1892), 144; May 1865, Ella Gertrude Clanton Thomas Diary, Duke; Marszalek, *Diary of Emma*

Holmes, 456; Avary, *Dixie After the War,* 189; Eppes, *Through Some Eventful Years,* 310.

33. Ball, *Clarke County,* 299–300; March 29, 1865, Ella Gertrude Clanton Thomas Diary, Duke; McDonald, *Diary of the War,* 264–68; Eppes, *Through Some Eventful Years,* 310.

34. Andrews, *Journal of a Georgia Girl,* 374–75; August 7, 1865, Susanna Gordon Waddell Diary, SHC; Eugenia Carew to Harriet Frances Ronan, May 2, 1865, Ronan Papers, Duke; Marszalek, *Diary of Emma Holmes,* 444–45; M. C. Dalton to "Dear Cousin Lucy," March 17, 1866, William Dunlap Simpson Papers, Duke; "Southern Girl's Diary," 301.

35. November 15, 1863, Kate D. Foster Diary, Duke; Maria Adelaide Whaley, "Story of Maria Adelaide Whaley," p. 6, SCHS; Marjorie Stratford Mendenhall, "Southern Women of a 'Lost Generation,'" *South Atlantic Quarterly,* 33 (October 1934), 337–40; Celeste Clay to Virginia Clay, March 21, 1867, Clement Claiborne Clay Papers, Duke; Marszalek, *Diary of Emma Holmes,* 466–67; Eppes, *Through Some Eventful Years,* 310.

36. For the reaction of black women to the war, emancipation, and Reconstruction, see Jacqueline Jones, *Labor of Love, Labor of Sorrow: Black Women, Work, and the Family From Slavery to the Present* (New York: Basic Books, 1985), 44–78. See the brief but perceptive discussion of the partial withdrawal and reduction of black labor in Roger L. Ransom and Richard Sutch, *One Kind of Freedom: The Economic Consequences of Emancipation* (Cambridge, Eng.: Cambridge University Press, 1977), 44–47.

37. Daniel E. Sutherland, *Americans and Their Servants: Domestic Service in the United States from 1800 to 1920* (Baton Rouge: Louisiana State University Press, 1981), 57–58; Strode, *Davis,* 205; Henrietta Smith Meriwether to Marietta Smith Lovett, April 22, 1867, Robert Watkins Lovett Papers, Emory; Trowbridge, *The South,* 328; Mary Ann Nolley Otey to Frances Nolley, July 15, 1866, Otey Papers, MDAH; Myers, *Children of Pride,* 1287; Mrs. B. S. Holmes to Nickels J. Holmes, July 7, 1868, Nickels J. Holmes Papers, Duke. For a good analysis of the servant problem in the South that extends beyond the period treated here, see David M. Katzman, *Seven Days a Week: Women and Domestic Service in Industrializing America* (New York: Oxford University Press, 1978), 184–95.

38. Helen J. Sawyer to "Sallie," August 8, 1865, Helen J. Sawyer Daugherty Papers, Duke; Elizabeth M. Ross to Susan Ross, July 25, 1868, Elizabeth M. Ross Letters, MDAH; Woodward, *Mary Chesnut's Civil War,* 834; July 1, 1865, Grace B. Elmore Diary, SCL; Recollections of Mrs. Gordon Pryor Rice, VSL.

39. Elizabeth Oakes Smith to Mr. and Mrs. William J. Spence, June 30, 1874, Appleton Oaksmith Papers, SHC; Woodward and Muhlenfeld, *Private Mary Chesnut,* 254; Easterby, *South Carolina Rice Plantation,* 221; December 14, 1870, Ella Gertrude Clanton Thomas Diary, Duke.

40. December 22, 1865, Myra Inman Diary, SHC; Rawick, *American Slave,* vol. 7 (Oklahoma), p. 129, vol. 8, pt. 2, p. 166, vol. 9, pt. 4, p. 224.

41. For examples of blacks working "faithfully" for their former mistresses after the war, see Pringle, *Chronicles of Chicora Wood,* 283–84; Crabtree and Patton, *Edmondston Journal,* 722–23; Perdue et al., *Weevils in the Wheat,* 134; Rawick, *American Slave,* vol. 2, pt. 1, p. 181.

42. Eppes, *Through Some Eventful Years,* 272, 285; Andrews, *Journal of a Georgia Girl,* 347, 377.

43. Rawick, *American Slave,* supp., ser. 2, vol. 8, p. 3374; Wilson, *Selected Papers of Spencer,* 17–18, 28–30, 115–19.

44. September 16, 1866, Ella Gertrude Clanton Thomas Diary, Duke; Meriwether, *Recollections,* 174–75; Rawick, *American Slave,* supp., ser. 2, vol. 1, p. 151, vol. 8, pp. 2919, 3269, vol. 9, pp. 3606–7, 3667; Eppes, *Through Some Eventful Years,* 333–34; Marszalek, *Diary of Emma Holmes,* 459–60.

45. January 20, 1866, Mary Elizabeth Rives Diary, LSU; Avary, *Dixie After the War,* 188–90; August 14, 1865, Nancy McDougall Robinson Diary in Robinson Collection, MDAH; June 25, 1865, Grace B. Elmore Diary, SCL.

46. See the useful synthesis of a vast literature as well as an original analysis of changes in the postwar Southern economy in Gavin Wright, *Old South, New South: Revolutions in the Southern Economy Since the Civil War* (New York: Basic Books, 1986), 81–90.

47. For typical complaints on this score, see Sally Diamond to Eli Reamer, September 8, 1867, James Diamond Family Papers, UGa; Martha Battey to Mary Halsey, June 29, 1867, Robert Battey Papers, Emory. Although Reconstruction was an era of unstable labor relations, there was a large pool of black workers available for the rest of the nineteenth century. Katzman, *Seven Days a Week,* 58–59.

48. Smith et al., *Mason Smith Family Letters,* 223–24; Leigh, *Ten Years on a Georgia Plantation,* 24–25, 56–58, 127; May 27, 1865, Ella Gertrude Clanton Thomas Diary, Duke; Crabtree and Patton, *Edmondston Journal,* 712–13; August 4, 23, October 9, 1865, Mary Elizabeth Rives Diary, LSU; Katzman, *Seven Days a Week,* 167, 195–202.

49. Susan Bradford Eppes, *The Negro of the Old South: A Bit of Period History* (Chicago: John G. Branch Publishing Co., 1925), 117; Andrews, *Journal of a Georgia Girl,* 292–93; Amelia Montgomery to Joseph A. Montgomery, September 5, 1865, Joseph Addison Montgomery and Family Papers, LSU; Dennett, *South As It Is,* 182–83; Sarah Catherine Himes to Adam Himes, January 29, 1870, Sarah Catherine Himes Letters, Duke; Easterby, *South Carolina Rice Plantation,* 212; Myers, *Children of Pride,* 1405; Amelia Barr to "Dear Jenny," March 3, ca. 1867, Amelia Barr Letters, BTHC.

50. Roark, *Masters Without Slaves,* 143; Perdue et al., eds. *Weevils in the Wheat,* 285; Sarah Catherine Himes to Adam Himes, November 23, 1868, Sarah Catherine

Himes Letters, Duke; Barnhart, "Reconstruction on the Lower Mississippi," 393; Andrews, *Journal of a Georgia Girl,* 319.

51. Crabtree and Patton, *Edmondston Journal,* 709–10; Eppes, *Through Some Eventful Years,* 305; Ann Faulkner to "My Dear Brother," June 12, 1865, Battle Family Papers, SHC; Easterby, *South Carolina Rice Plantation,* 216.

52. Leigh, *Ten Years on a Georgia Plantation,* 87–91; June 28, 1865, Mary Elizabeth Rives Diary, LSU; Crabtree and Patton, *Edmondston Journal,* 718–19, 722–23; Smith et al., *Mason Smith Family Letters,* 225–26.

53. Mrs. Armand J. De Rosset to Louis J. De Rosset, January 12, 1868, De Rosset Family Papers, SHC; June 25, 1865, Grace B. Elmore Diary, SCL; Myers, *Children of Pride,* 1340–41.

54. Eliza G. Wilkins to John Berkley Grimball, September 10, 1865, Grimball Family Papers, SHC; Clara Elizabeth Barrow to Clara Barrow, November 30, 1865, July 8, 1866, David Crenshaw Barrow Papers, UGa; Amelia S. Montgomery to Joseph A. Montgomery, January 10, 1866, Joseph Addison Montgomery and Family Papers, LSU; Mary Caldwell to Minerva Cain, July 17, 1865, Tod R. Caldwell Papers, SHC; Dennett, *South As It Is,* 194; June 3, 1866, Margaret Gillis Diary, ADAH.

55. George C. Rogers, Jr., *History of Georgetown County, South Carolina* (Columbia: University of South Carolina Press, 1970), 433; Fleming, *Documentary History of Reconstruction,* 1:68; Rawick, *American Slave,* vol. 8, pt. 2, p. 128; supp., ser. 1, vol. 10, pp. 2168–69, supp., ser. 2, vol. 4, p. 1051, vol. 5, pp. 1857–58, vol. 9, pp. 3884–85; Perdue et al., *Weevils in the Wheat,* 16–17; *Augusta* (Ga.) *Loyal Georgian,* March 3, 1866.

56. Andrews, *Journal of a Georgia Girl,* 322–23; Nancy Willard to Micajah Wilkinson, March 18, 1868, Micajah Wilkinson and Family Papers, LSU; Eliza G. Thompson to Benjamin S. Hedrick, March 17, 1866, Benjamin Sherwood Hedrick Papers, Duke; Myers, *Children of Pride,* 1276, 1280, 1285; Sarah Catherine Himes to Dolly Himes, March 26, 1869, Sarah Catherine Himes Letters, Duke; Easterby, *South Carolina Rice Plantation,* 213.

57. Robertson, *Diary of Dolly Burge,* 114; October 1, 1865, Grace B. Elmore Diary, SHC; Ann Bridges to Charles E. Bridges, July 17, 1865, Charles E. Bridges Papers, Duke; Andrews, *Journal of a Georgia Girl,* 314–16; Strode, *Davis,* 199; Cash, *Mind of the South,* 117–19; Easterby, *South Carolina Rice Plantation,* 224–25; Rachel Susan Cheves to John Richardson Cheves, November 26, 1865, Rachel Susan Cheves Papers, Duke; Kate McKinley Taylor to Middleton Pope Barrow, August 29, 1865, David Crenshaw Barrow Papers, UGa.

58. Worley, *At Home in Confederate Arkansas,* 35; Leigh, *Ten Years on a Georgia Plantation,* 71, 147–48; Woodward, *Mary Chesnut's Civil War,* 828; January 27, May 7, 1869, Ella Gertrude Clanton Thomas Diary, Duke.

59. Recollections of Mrs. Gordon Pryor Rice, VSL; Eppes, *Through Some Eventful Years,* 294–95.

60. Fanny Atkisson to ?, February 25, 1866, Baber and Blackshear Papers, UGa.

CHAPTER 13

1. August 23, 1861, Kate S. Sperry Diary, VSL.

2. Woodward, *Mary Chesnut's Civil War,* 346; February 11, 1864, Grace B. Elmore Diary, SCL; Bleser, *Hammonds of Redcliffe,* 123–24. Historians have sharply disagreed over the impact of war on the status and roles of women. Anne Firor Scott made the classic case for the Civil War as a watershed that unleashed female energy and undermined the Southern patriarchy. But, as Suzanne Lebsock has perceptively observed, changes had occurred before the war even in the absence of organized (or, one might say, any other kind) of feminism. In her view the war helped a few women to find fulfillment outside the domestic sphere but on the whole was probably a setback for women. Jean Friedman has agreed that the slow modernization of the South after the war failed to alter sex roles substantially and that women's energies were still channeled in conservative directions. For the postwar period, both the literary and statistical evidence is thin, though local studies undoubtedly will uncover much important new information. Scott found dramatic change because she focused on members of the elite, while Lebsock and Friedman gave more attention to yeoman and lower-class women. Some historians have even tried to interpret the history of women in the postwar South as a series of small and unambiguous triumphs that laid the groundwork for larger victories in the twentieth century. [For a recent example of this largely reductionist approach, see Janie Synatzske Evins, "Arkansas Women: Their Contribution to Society, Politics, and Business, 1865–1900," *Arkansas Historical Quarterly,* 44 (Summer 1985), 118–33.] What follows in this chapter is an attempt to reconcile these interpretations by showing that a paradoxical mixture of change and continuity characterized the lives of women in the postwar South. Seemingly dramatic changes often added up to very little, and unexpected challenges to traditional ideas came from ostensibly conservative directions. Both persistence and change strengthened traditional social assumptions. Scott, *Southern Lady,* 81–102; Lebsock, *Free Women of Petersburg,* 240–49; Friedman, *Enclosed Garden,* 110–11.

3. Woodward, *Mary Chesnut's Civil War,* 359; September 22, 1864, Ella Gertrude Clanton Thomas Diary, Duke; Faulkner, *The Unvanquished,* 114–15.

4. Pember, *Southern Woman's Story,* 112; Crabtree and Patton, *Edmondston Journal,* 635; Avary, *Virginia Girl in the War,* 43; DeLeon, *Belles, Beaux and Brains of the 60's,* 136–45; February 21, 1869, Ella Gertrude Clanton Thomas Diary, Duke. When a black man was executed in Cherokee County, Alabama, in December 1866, Sarah Espy noted that "even ladies will attend." That such an event elicited comment suggests the snaillike pace of social change in the Reconstruction South. December 13, 1866, Sarah Rodgers Espy Diary, ADAH.

5. Nannie Rayburn to Susy Rayburn, October 27, 1861, Samuel King Rayburn Papers, ADAH; Kate ? to "Dear Fannie," April 9, 1863, Keen-Armisted Papers, Confederate Miscellany, ser. 1e, Emory; Marszalek, *Diary of Emma Holmes,* 118–19; L. H. Pugh to Thomas B. Pugh, February 12, 1871, Colonel W. W. Pugh and Family Papers, LSU; Taylor et al., *South Carolina Women in the Confederacy,* 1:278; Glasgow, *Virginia,* 148–49.

6. Wilson, *Selected Papers of Spencer,* 351–52, 378–80, 402–4.

7. Eppes, *Through Some Eventful Years,* 322; September 3, 1865, Carrie Hunter Diary in Cobb and Hunter Family Papers, SHC.

8. For descriptions, see McGee and Lander, *A Rebel Came Home,* 94; December 3, 1868, Ella Gertrude Clanton Thomas Diary, Duke; Mary Fort to Frank Brown, January 7, 1871, Joseph E. and Elizabeth G. Brown Papers, UGa; Lucy B. Cobb to "Dear Poole," March 24, 1870, David Crenshaw Barrow Papers, UGa.

9. Marszalek, *Diary of Emma Holmes,* 487.

10. Obear, *Through the Years in Old Winnsboro,* 116–17; Pringle, *Chronicles of Chicora Wood,* 286–88, 316–23; Strode, *Davis,* 236; Moore, *Juhl Letters,* 118–19; Smith et al., *Mason Smith Family Letters,* 220.

11. Andrews, *Journal of a Georgia Girl,* 380–81; E. Merton Coulter, *The South During Reconstruction, 1865–1877* (Baton Rouge: Louisiana State University Press, 1947), 308–11; Bertram Groene, ed., "A Letter from Occupied Tallahassee," *Florida Historical Quarterly,* 48 (July 1969), 73–74; Marszalek, *Diary of Emma Holmes,* 478; Wilson, *Selected Papers of Spencer,* 86–88, 415–16.

12. The available demographic evidence can be read several ways. Anne Firor Scott has argued that an unfavorable sex ratio forced women to seek fulfillment in careers and greater independence from patriarchal control. Yet at the same time Southerners strove to restore their families, build new ones, and reaffirm the values of kinship and community. Scott, *Southern Lady,* 106–9; Friedman, *Enclosed Garden,* 94–97. For useful statistics on the sex ratio for Southerners between the ages of twenty and twenty-nine, see Ruoff, "Southern Womanhood," 139.

13. December 7, 1871, Kate D. Foster Diary, Duke; Myers, *Children of Pride,* 1325; Bonner, *Journal of a Milledgeville Girl,* 116. I have found few examples in Southern sources to corroborate the more positive description of single women's lives in Lee Virginia Chambers-Schiller, *Liberty, a Better Husband: Single Women in America: The Generations of 1780–1840* (New Haven, Conn.: Yale University Press, 1984).

14. Moore, *Juhl Letters,* 68; Smith et al., *Mason Smith Family Letters,* 224; Marszalek, *Diary of Emma Holmes,* 463, 471, 483; Frances Polk to Frances Polk Shipwith, February n.d., 1866, Polk Family Papers, SHC; Wilson, *Selected Papers of Spencer,* 50–52; Rainwater, "Letters of Cordelia Scales," 181.

15. Wilson, *Selected Papers of Spencer,* 372–75; Kate Chopin, *The Awakening* (New York: W. W. Norton, 1976 [1899]), 10. The antebellum trend toward more

liberal divorce continued during the 1860s and the divorce rate rose slowly. With few exceptions, however, the divorce rate in the Southern states remained well below the national average. Southern judges were also more inclined than their Northern counterparts to grant divorces to men, especially on grounds of adultery. Department of Commerce and Labor, Bureau of the Census, *Marriage and Divorce, 1867–1906* (2 vols.; Washington: Government Printing Office, 1908–1909), I, 64–65, 72, 92–93, 95.

16. Chopin, *The Awakening,* 11, 109; Burton, *In My Father's House,* 265–68; Dudley Poston and Robert H. Weller, eds., *The Population of the South: Structure and Change in Social Demographic Context* (Austin: University of Texas Press, 1981), 26–27; Eliza J. Thompson to Ellen Hedrick, July 4, 1865, Benjamin Sherwood Hedrick Papers, Duke; Kearney, *Slaveholder's Daughter,* 22.

17. Sarah Morgan Dawson, "Comment on the Role of Women as Childbearers," ca. last quarter of nineteenth century, Francis Warrington Dawson Papers, Duke. Although her husband defended female intellectual equality and encouraged her to write newspaper articles on women's rights, Sarah Morgan Dawson confined her most subversive ideas to unpublished manuscripts. E. Culpepper Clark, *Francis Warrington Dawson and the Politics of Restoration* (University, Ala.: University of Alabama Press, 1980), 102–4. Of course the Civil War had caused what demographers call a "trough" in the national birth rate, bringing about a "deficit" of something over half a million births between 1862 and 1866. Ansley J. Coale and Melvin Zelnik, *New Estimates of Fertility and Population in the United States* (Princeton, N.J.: Princeton University Press, 1963), 24–25.

18. G. W. Archer, "Poem Read at the Commencement of the Dunbar Female Institute, Winchester, Va., June 30, 1870," *Southern Review,* 8 (October 1870), 445; Wilson, *Selected Papers of Spencer,* 376–78, 481.

19. Francis Butler Simkins and Robert Hilliard Woody, *South Carolina During Reconstruction* (Chapel Hill: University of North Carolina Press, 1932), 324–25; Joel Chandler Harris, "The Women of the South," *Southern Historical Society Papers,* 18 (1890), 280–81; Aylett, "Women of the South," 59–60.

20. September 18, 1866, January 17, 1868, Tennie Keys Embree Diary, BTHC; "The Education and Influence of Women," *Southern Review,* 8 (October 1870), 408.

21. March 17, 1865, Abbie M. Brooks Diary, AHS; Wilson, *Selected Papers of Spencer,* 167–69, 357–59.

22. Wilson, *Selected Papers of Spencer,* 218–21, 421–23.

23. Ibid., 267–70, 276–78, 286–89.

24. Kearney, *Slaveholder's Daughter,* 45–52; Pringle, *Chronicles of Chicora Wood,* 340–41. Postwar reformers also followed the antebellum pattern of criticizing the ornamental character of female education. "More money is spent in North Carolina to teach girls to sing (to yell like hyenas) and tear the piano to

pieces ... than would sustain ten first-class male schools," Cornelia Spencer commented sadly. Ruoff, "Southern Womanhood," 155–61; Russell, *Woman Who Rang the Bell,* 161.

25. For lists of courses, see Young, *Curricula of Women's Colleges,* 15–16, 30–37; North Texas Female College Catalog, 1877–78 North Texas Female College Records, BTHC; Clarence Herbert Bradshaw, *History of Prince Edward County, Virginia* (Richmond, Va.: Dietz Press, 1955), 480–81; Julia O'Keefe to Jamie Farrow, September 17, 1875, Henry Patillo Farrow Papers, UGa.; Kate Landing to Thomas M. Smith, February 10, 1872, Smith Papers, Duke.

26. A. D. Mayo, *Southern Women in the Recent Educational Movement in the South,* ed. by Dan T. Carter (Baton Rouge: Louisiana State University Press, 1978 [1892]), 56–70; Young, *Curricula of Women's Colleges,* 61–62. Some female academies and colleges had sustained wartime damage, and their administrators unsuccessfully sought compensation for property destroyed by Federal armies. As early as 1867 the Peabody Education Fund provided grants for Southern schools, but women's institutions received little of this philanthropy. To be dependent on tuition income meant atrophy or death for small schools because most families had trouble even paying for a daughter's elementary education. During the war, yeoman families had withdrawn girls from school to work in the fields and kitchens, a practice that continued for the rest of the century. Board of Trustees of the Demopolis Female Academy to Lewis E. Parsons, October 18, 1865, Parsons Papers, ADAH; "Letter of the Women of the South to Mr. Peabody," *DeBow's Review,* (After the War Series), 7 (January 1870), 200–201; Candler, "Life in Georgia," 14–15; Wiley, *Plain People of the Confederacy,* 54–55; Kearney, *Slaveholder's Daughter,* 33–42. For a typical list of expenses, see the statement for Kate Landing at Davenport Female College, July 1, 1871, Thomas M. Smith Papers, Duke.

27. Milton Bacon to ?, November 18, 1873, Southern Female College, Cox College Archives, UGa; Kate Landing to Thomas M. Smith, August 12, 1871, Smith to Landing, November 3, 1871, Thomas M. Smith Papers, Duke; Theresa Giles to A. J. Fordham, September 21, 1874, Mary Zilpha Giles Papers, Duke.

28. Wilson, *Selected Papers of Spencer,* 278–79, 288–91; "Boys," *DeBow's Review* (After the War Series), 2 (April 1866), 369–70; Christine Ladd Franklin, "The Education of Woman in the Southern States," in Annie Nathan Meyer, ed., *Woman's Work in America* (New York: Henry Holt and Co., 1891), 89–106; Wilbur Fisk Tillett, "Southern Womanhood as Affected by the War," *Century,* 43 (November 1891), 12.

29. Mrs. H. Parson to Lewis E. Parsons, August 9, 1865, Parsons Papers, ADAH; *Statistics of the United States . . . from the Original Returns of the Ninth Census,* 3 vols. (Washington: Government Printing Office, 1872), 1:688–89; Mayo, *Women in the Recent Educational Movement in the South,* 52, 124, 163–71; Coulter, *South*

During Reconstruction, 326; Wilson, *Selected Papers of Spencer,* 273–76; Mendenhall, "Southern Women of a 'Lost Generation,' " 342–46; Noble, *History of Public Schools of North Carolina,* 412–13.

30. Fleet, *Green Mount After the War,* 42; Kearney, *Slaveholder's Daughter,* 66–72; Frances Polk to Frances Polk Shipwith, June 6, 1866, Polk Family Papers, SHC.

31. Pringle, *Chronicles of Chicora Wood,* 289–90; November 26, 1865, Kate D. Foster Diary, Duke; Oze Robe to Margaret Caroline Broyles, March 17, 1866, Maverick and Van Wyck Families Papers, SCL.

32. Grace King, *Memories of a Southern Woman of Letters* (New York: Macmillan, 1932), 24; Margaret Isabella Weber Reminiscences, pp. 23–25, SHC; Macrae, *Americans at Home,* 246; Easterby, *South Carolina Rice Plantation,* 243–44.

33. Annie Bruce to Robert E. Bruce, November 18, 1869, Robert E. and Annie J. Bruce Papers, UGa; Fannie ? to Mary A. Lyndall, February 28, 1867, Mary A. Lyndall Papers, Duke; Sallie Caldwell to Mrs. Algernon L. Sullivan, April 4, 1867, New York Southern Relief Association Papers, Confederate Museum; Ann Thomas Coleman Reminiscences, pp. 276–332, BTHC; Evaline Attaway to David C. Barrow, November 12, 1866, David Crenshaw Barrow Papers, UGa.

34. Mrs. Walter A. Huske to Mrs. A. A. Low, February 12, 1867, Margaret L. Hunter to Mrs. Brooks, February 16, 1867, New York Southern Relief Association Papers, Confederate Museum; Julia E. Harn, "Old Canoochee-Ogeechee Chronicles; War Time and After," *Georgia Historical Quarterly,* 16 (December 1932), 310; Schuler, "Women in Public Affairs," 706–15; Kathleen Christine Berkeley, " 'The Ladies Want to Bring Reform to the Public Schools': Public Education and Women's Rights in the Post-Civil War South," *History of Education Quarterly,* 44 (Spring 1984), 45–58.

35. 1876 passim, Sarah Virginia Means Diary, GDAH; January 4, 1879, Ella Gertrude Clanton Thomas Diary, Duke; Kearney, *Slaveholder's Daughter,* 74–89; April 4, 1865, Abbie M. Brooks Diary, AHS.

36. February 27, March 7, 27, April 3, May 26, June 2, 7, 22, September 21, 1865, March 1870, Abbie M. Brooks Diary, AHS.

37. Fanny Atkisson to Marian Blackshear, February 25, August 19, 1866, February 3, 1868, March 1, 1874, February 20, 1876, Baber and Blackshear Papers, UGa.

38. September 3, 1865, Carrie Hunter Diary in Cobb and Hunter Family Papers, SHC; Wilson, *Selected Papers of Spencer,* 170–71, 192–94, 200–203. For a different interpretation that stresses the new opportunities for women after the war, see Scott, *Southern Lady,* 108–33. Much of Scott's evidence, however, deals with the period after 1880, and her focus on elite women naturally leads to a closer attention to exceptions than to more general patterns.

39. Mrs. James Legare, Jr. to Treasurer, Southern Relief Association, February

26, 1867, New York Southern Relief Association Papers, Confederate Museum; Merrick, *Old Times in Dixie Land,* 76; Mary S. Wall to Kate Burruss, November 7, 1866, John C. Burruss and Family Papers, LSU; Tillett, "Southern Womanhood," 12; Smedes, *Memorials of a Southern Planter,* 264–65.

40. Mattie A. Dodson to William H. Smith, March 8, 1869, Mrs. E. L. Dupree to Smith, July 16, 1868, Sallie Bachelder to Hugh McCullough, December 3, 1868, William H. Smith Papers, ADAH; *New Orleans Picayune,* March 21, 1869.

41. Augusta J. Evans to J. L. M. Curry, October 7, 1865, Jabez Lamar Monroe Curry Papers, LC; Fidler, *Wilson,* 128–44.

42. Schuler, "Women in Public Affairs in Louisiana," 673–74; Mrs. John L. Colbert to Mrs. Algernon L. Sullivan, February 26, 1867, New York Southern Relief Association Papers, Confederate Museum; Allan, *Margaret Junkin Preston,* 230–42, 246, 248–49. A few women became newspaper editors, though usually of country papers with small circulations. Scott, *Southern Lady,* 119–21.

43. Coulter, *South During Reconstruction,* 200–201; Schuler, "Women in Public Affairs in Louisiana," 672–73, 695–706; Laura Elizabeth Battle, *Forget-Me-Nots of the Civil War* (St. Louis: A. R. Fleming, 1909), 177–205; Nancy Bostick Desaussure, *Old Plantation Days* (New York: Duffield, 1902), 102.

44. *Statistics of the United States . . . Ninth Census,* 1:719, 721, 728–29, 736, 742, 751, 756–58, 761. Even in a growing city such as Atlanta, occupational patterns for women remained remarkably stable. Grigsby H. Wooten, Jr., "New City of the South: Atlanta, 1843–1873" (Ph.D. dissertation, Johns Hopkins University, 1973), 221.

45. Marszalek, *Diary of Emma Holmes,* 461–62, 469; Mrs. M. A. Mackay to Southern Relief Association, July 1867, Mrs. H. R. Biddlecome to Ladies Relief Association of New York, March 1, 1867, New York Southern Relief Association Papers, Confederate Museum.

46. Kessler-Harris, *Out to Work,* 78–107; Wilson, *Selected Papers of Spencer,* 348–51; Milton Bacon to Ella Bacon, October 26, 1873, Southern Female College, Cox College Archives, UGa.

47. Wright, *Old South, New South,* 138–46.

48. *Statistics of the United States . . . Ninth Census,* 1:690–91.

49. David L. Carlton, *Mill and Town in South Carolina, 1880–1920* (Baton Rouge: Louisiana State University Press, 1982), 76–77.

50. Clarence D. Long, *Wages and Earnings in the United States, 1860–1900* (Princeton, N.J.: Princeton University Press, 1960), 84, 88–89; *Relations Between Labor and Capital,* IV, 598–99. For other useful statistics and regional comparisons, see Scott, *Southern Lady,* 121–24. Scott overemphasizes the importance of the growing number of women employed in Southern factories, but she also cites evidence showing that yeoman women sought mill jobs because they either lacked other skills or hoped to avoid sewing at home.

51. Fearn, *Diary of a Refugee,* 145–48; Schuler, "Women in Public Affairs in

Louisiana," 671–72; Wilson, *Selected Papers of Spencer,* 367–72; Lee Ann Whites, "The Charitable and the Poor: The Emergence of Domestic Politics in Augusta, Georgia, 1860–1880," *Journal of Social History,* 17 (Summer 1984), 600–616.

52. *Relations Between Labor and Capital,* 4:831–47; Elizabeth Oakes Smith to Mr. and Mrs. William Spence, August 18, December 31, 1874, Appleton Oaksmith Papers, SHC. For a useful analysis of how temperance could both challenge and reinforce female subordination in the home, see Barbara Leslie Epstein, *The Politics of Domesticity: Women, Evangelism, and Temperance in Nineteenth-Century America* (Middletown, Conn.: Wesleyan University Press, 1981), 89–146. Rebecca Latimer Felton also blamed Southern white men for not protecting Southern white women from supposed black rapists. Williamson, *Crucible of Race,* 124–30.

53. Fleet, *Green Mount After the War,* 155; June 19, 1869, Ella Gertrude Clanton Thomas Diary, Duke. My interpretation of postwar legal reform follows the strikingly original and persuasive analysis in Suzanne D. Lebsock, "Radical Reconstruction and the Property Rights of Southern Women," *Journal of Southern History,* 43 (May 1977), 195–216.

54. Mayo, *Southern Women in the Recent Educational Movement in the South,* 54–55; Kearney, *Slaveholder's Daughter,* 107–24; November 2, 1868, Ella Gertrude Clanton Thomas Diary, Duke; Meriwether, *Recollections,* 217–26. For the link between feminism and conservative ideology, see the excellent treatment in Kathleen Christine Berkeley, "Elizabeth Avery Meriwether, 'An Advocate for Her Sex': Feminism and Conservatism in the Post-Civil War South," *Tennessee Historical Quarterly,* 43 (Winter 1984), 390–407. Anne Firor Scott described the growth of the women's suffrage movement in the South but also noted its conservative qualities and relative weakness. Scott, *Southern Lady,* 165–84.

55. Fidler, *Wilson,* 163–65, 169–70; Wilson, *St. Elmo,* 552–54; James S. Patty, "A Woman Journalist in Reconstruction Louisiana: Mrs. Mary E. Bryan," *Louisiana Studies,* 3 (Spring 1964), 94–95; *New Orleans Daily Picayune,* July 31, 1870. For examples of the continued importance of reactionary views on women's place in Southern intellectual life, see [George Fitzhugh], "What's To Be Done with the Negro?" *DeBow's Review* (After the War Series), 2 (June 1866), 579–80; Albert Taylor Bledsoe, "The Mission of Woman," *Southern Review,* 10 (October 1871), 923–42.

56. Wilson, *Selected Papers of Spencer,* 158–66.

Bibliography of Manuscript Collections

This section does not include collections consulted that contained no useful information on southern women during the Civil War era.

Alabama Department of Archives and History, Montgomery
    Alabama Divorces, 1830-1863
    William Phineas Browne Papers
    Elizabeth Ann Daniel Divorce
      Papers
    Sarah Rodgers Espy Diary
    Margaret Gillis Diary
    Bolling Hall Papers
    William B. Hall Papers
    Juliet Opie Hopkins Papers
    Jefferson Franklin Jackson Papers
    Joseph Eggleston Johnston Papers
    Sarah Lowe Papers
    Lewis E. Parsons Papers (Official)
    Sally Perry Papers
    Sarah Ellen Phillips, Reminiscences
      of War and Episodes of Wilson's
      Raid near Selma, Alabama,
      April 1865
    Samuel King Rayburn Papers
    Lida Bestor Robertson Papers
    John Gill Shorter Papers (Official)
    William H. Smith Papers (Official)
    Mary D. Waring Diary
    Thomas Hill Watts Papers (Official)
    Mary Louisa Williamson Diary
    Augusta Jane Evans Wilson Papers

    William L. Yancey Papers
Atlanta Historical Society
    Augustus Dixon Adair Papers
    Carrie Berry Diary
    Abbie M. Brooks Diary
    Sara Clayton Crane Papers
    Jane Louisa Killian Crew Papers
    Crumley Family Papers
    Martha Lumpkin Diary
    John Mathew McCrary Papers
    Mary Rawson Papers
    Kate Hester Robson Reminiscences
Barker Texas History Center, University of Texas, Austin
    Amelia Barr Letters
    Thomas Charles Brady Family
      Papers
    Braxton Bragg Letters
    Guy M. Bryan Papers
    Chenney Family Papers
    Alice Clow Papers
    Ann Raney Thomas Coleman
      Papers
    Davenport, Crittenden, and Harvey
      Families Papers
    Henrietta Embree Diary
    Tennie Keys Embree Diary
    W. W. Fontaine Papers

Margaret Moffette Houston Papers
Amanda Lindley Papers
Mary J. Minor Papers
L. S. Neblett Papers
Cornelia M. Noble Diary
North Texas Female College
    Records
Mary Rabb Papers
Addie J. Simms Letters
Lizzie Hatcher Simons Diary
Confederate Museum, Richmond
    Clara Minor Lynn Papers
    New York Southern Relief
        Association Papers
    Kate Mason Rowland Papers
    Mrs. William A. Simmons Diary
Duke University, William R. Perkins
    Library
        Frances Walker Yates Aglionby
            Papers
        Bettie Alexander Papers
        Charles Wesley Andrews Papers
        Bennette M. Bagby Papers
        Tilmon F. Baggarly Papers
        Godfrey Barnsley Papers
        Thomas Baxter Papers
        Bedinger-Dandridge Family Papers
        Henry Besancon Diary
        Elizabeth J. Blanks Papers
        Huldah Annie Fain Briant Papers
        Charles E. Bridges Papers
        Alexander Brown Papers
        Bettie R. Brown Papers
        Catherine Jane Buie Papers
        William H. Busbey Papers
        Eliza Button Papers
        Patrick H. Cain Papers
        Campbell Family Papers
        Monimia Fairfax Cary Papers
        Sydney S. Champion Papers
        Rachel Susan Cheves Papers
        Willie Chunn Papers
        Clement Claiborne Clay Papers
        Martha Foster Crawford Diary
        Cronly Family Papers
        Absalom Dantzler Papers
        Helen J. Sawyer Daugherty Papers
        Mary P. Davis Papers
        Francis Warrington Dawson Papers
        James H. DeVotie Papers

John Bull Smith Dimitry Papers
John B. Evans Papers
Lucy Muse Fletcher Papers
Kate D. Foster Diary
Mary Zilpha Giles Papers
Rose O'Neal Greenhow Papers
Greenville Ladies' Association
    Minutes
John Berkeley Grimball Papers
Edward Harden Papers
David Bullock Harris Papers
Henry St. George Harris Papers
Benjamin Sherwood Hedrick
    Papers
Sarah Catherine Himes Letters
William Woods Holden Papers
Nickels J. Holmes Papers
Theophilus Hunter Holmes Papers
John C. Hood Papers
Richard E. Jacques Papers
Jarratt-Puryear Family Papers
Ellen Johnson Papers
George Wesley Johnston Papers
John McIntosh Kell Papers
Ladies' Volunteer Aid Society of
    the Pine Hills Minutes
Dr. Lee Papers
James Longstreet Papers
Mathew N. Love Papers
Lucas-Ashley Family Papers
Mary A. Lyndall Papers
William McCutcheon Papers
Marshall Family Papers
Ann Eliza Miller Papers
Jacob Mordecai Papers
Munford-Ellis Family Papers
John Gibson Parkhurst Papers
Presley Carter Person Papers
Sarah Ellen Phillips Papers
Pope-Carter Family Papers
Letitia Landon Roane Diary
Harriet Fances Ronan Papers
John Rutherford Papers
Romulus Saunders Papers
Scarborough Family Papers
William Dunlap Simpson Papers
Thomas M. Smith Papers
Frederick M. Stevens Papers
Ella Gertrude Clanton Thomas
    Diary

United Daughters of the
Confederacy, South Carolina
Division, Edgefield Chapter
Papers
Elizabeth S. Wiggins Papers
Alice Williamson Papers
James M. Willcox Papers
Larkin Willis Papers
Elvira Withrow Papers
Isabella Woodruff Papers
Emory University, Robert W. Woodruff
Library
Robert Battey Papers
Robert Donnell Bone Papers
Burge Family Papers
Morgan Calloway Papers
James Osgood Clark Papers
Confederate Miscellany, Series 1e
John Mitchell Davidson Papers
John S. Dobbins Family Papers
Andrew J. Edge Papers
Richard B. Jett Papers
Robert Watkins Lovett Papers
Orr Family Papers
Thomas Henry Pitts Papers
Sue Richardson Diary
Kate Rowland Papers
Georgia Department of Archives and
History, Atlanta
Iraminta Antoinette Alexander
Papers
Emily Jane Winkler Bealer Diary
Bryan, Willingham, and Lawton
Families Papers
Civil War Miscellany
Families Supplied With Salt,
1862-1864
(Salt Book)
William Few Papers
Louisa Warren Patch Fletcher
Papers
Fannie Gordon Papers
Sarah Gordon Papers
Governors' Papers (Joseph E.
Brown)
Charles Lamar Papers
Sarah Virginia Means Papers
Katherine Elizabeth Ozburn Papers
Mary Wealthy Van Valkenburgh
Papers

University of Georgia Library, Special
Collections
Miss Abby Diary
Athens Ladies Memorial
Association, Objects of
Association
Baber and Blackshear Papers
David Crenshaw Barrow Papers
Barrow Family Papers, Addenda
Joseph E. and Elizabeth G. Brown
Papers
Robert E. and Annie J. Bruce
Papers
Howell Cobb Papers
Cobb, Erwin, and Lamar Papers
William Gaston Delony Papers
James Diamond Family Papers
Henry Patillo Farrow Papers
Rebecca Ann Latimer Felton
Papers
Harden, Jackson, and Carithers
Papers
Hattie Harmon Papers
Mary Kinsland Papers
Kollock Family Papers
Charles Augustus Lafayette Lamar
Papers
Joseph Henry Lumpkin Papers
Margaret Branch Sexton Papers
Southern Female College, Cox
College Archives
Zebulon, Georgia, Academy,
Trustees Records
Henry E. Huntington Library and Art
Galley, San Marino, California
Mansfield Lovell Papers
Library of Congress, Manuscripts Division
Douglas J. and Rufus W. Cater
Papers
Cyrus B. Comstock Diary
Jabez Lamar Munroe Curry Papers
Burton N. Harrison Papers
Fannie Page Hume Diary
Andrew Johnson Papers
Mary Greenhow Lee Diary
Journal of Mrs. W. W. Lord
Flora McCabe Collection
Betty Herndon Maury Diary
Alexander H. Stephens Papers
Louis T. Wigfall Papers

Louisiana State University, Department of Archives and Manuscripts
    Albert A. Batchelor Papers
    John W. Bell Letters
    Priscilla Munnikhuysen Bond Diary
    Rosella Kenner Brent Recollections
    Louis A. Bringier Papers
    John C. Burruss and Family Papers
    Margaret Butler Papers
    Thomas O. Butler and Family Papers
    Annie Jeter Carmouche Papers
    Samuel A. Cartwright Papers
    R. J. Causey Correspondence
    Jane McCausland Chinn Reminiscence
    Fielding Yeager Doke Papers
    Eggleston-Roach Papers
    James Foster and Family Papers
    Kate Garland Papers
    George W. Guess Letters
    Sidney Harding Diary
    G. T. Harrower Letters
    J. G. Kilbourne and Family Collection
    Josiah Knighton and Family Papers
    Samuel R. Latta Papers
    Joseph Addison Montgomery and Family Papers
    New Orleans Scrapbook
    Robert A. Newell Papers
    Ann Wilkinson Penrose Diary
    Richard L. Pugh Papers
    Colonel W. W. Pugh and Family Papers
    Mary Elizabeth Rives Diary
    Ada Rucker Letter
    Clara E. Solomon Diary
    Jefferson W. Stubbs Papers
    William Terry and Family Papers
    Lewis Texada and Family Papers
    Robert A. Tyson Diary
    Cora E. Watson Journal, T. Harry Williams Papers
    David Weeks Papers
    Edward Clifton Wharton and Family Papers
    Micajah Wilkinson and Family Papers
    Inez Smith Wilsford Reminiscence

Mississippi Department of Archives and History, Jackson
    Anonymous Diary
    Ida Trotter Barlow Papers
    Elizabeth Jane Beach Letter
    Calvin S. Brown Papers
    Maud Morrow Brown, "At Home in Lafayette County, Mississippi"
    Charles Clark Papers (Official)
    Crutcher-Shannon Papers
    Elizabeth N. DeHay Papers
    Mrs. H. B. DeLonne Reminiscence
    Lousiana Dunlevy Garret Papers
    Annie E. Harper Reminiscence
    Irion-Neilson Family Papers
    T. J. Koger Collection
    Maggie R. Lauderdale Papers
    Ann Shannon Martin Diary
    Mary Ann Nolley Otey Diary
    John J. Pettus Papers (Official)
    N. P. Porter and Family Papers
    Nancy McDougall Robinson Collection
    Mrs. Roy Rollins Papers
    Elizabeth M. Ross Letters
    Mary E. Wilkes Shell Papers
    Eunice J. Stockwell Papers
    Belle Strickland Diary
    Oscar J. E. Stuart Papers
    Worthington Family Papers
National Archives
    Records of the Confederate States Treasury Department, RG 365
    Records of the Confederate States War Department including Letters Received by the Confederate Secretary of War, RG 109
North Carolina Division of Archives and History, Raleigh
    Panthea Sharpe Allison Papers
    James B. Birkdell Papers
    W. Vane Brown Papers
    Civil War Collection
    Anne Darden Papers
    M. W. H. Papers
    Thomas J. Myers Papers
    James Norcom and Family Papers
    Powell Papers
    Thomas Settle Papers

Zebulon Baird Vance Papers
Jonathan Worth Papers
Samuel Wheeler Worthington
Papers
South Carolina Department of Archives
and History, Columbia
Andrew W. Magrath Papers
(Official)
Robert K. Scott Papers (Official)
South Carolina Historical Society,
Charleston
Caroline Gilman Letters
Robert Barnwell Rhett Papers
Maria Adelaide Whaley, "Story of
Maria Adelaide Whaley"
South Caroliniana Library, University of
South Carolina, Columbia
Mrs. W. K. Bachman Papers
Ada Bacot Papers
Edgefield Female Institute Records
Emily Caroline Ellis Papers
Grace B. Elmore Diary
Hammond, Bryan, and Cumming
Families Papers
Mary Y. Harth Papers
Mrs. Albert Rhett Heyward Papers
Mary Hort Papers
Janney and Leaphart Family Papers
Suzanne Mandeville Sparks Keitt
Papers
Maverick and Van Wyck Families
Papers
John T. McAfee Papers
Sue McDowell Papers
Mackenzie Family Papers
Benjamin Franklin Perry Papers
Phillips Family Papers
Elizabeth Izard Pinckney Papers
Elizabeth Pratt Papers
Anna and Bettie Ridley Papers
Sara Jane Sams Letter
Mary Amarinthia Yates Snowden
Papers
Sosnowski and Schaller Families
Papers
South Carolina Female Collegiate
Institute Records
Spartanburg Female College
Records
Moultrie Reid Wilson Papers

Young Ladies' Hospital
Association, Columbia Records
Southern Historical Collection, University
of North Carolina, Chapel Hill
Allen and Simpson Family Papers
Clifford Anderson Papers
Bagley Family Papers
Lucy Baldwin Papers
Battle Family Papers
Beale and Davis Family Papers
Grace Pierson Beard
Reminiscences
Anne Laurie Harris Broidrick
Recollections
Ann Eliza Brumby Paper
Tod R. Caldwell Papers
Kate S. Carney Diary
Benjamin Franklin Cheatham
Papers
Zuleika Haralson Cleveland Poem
Cobb and Hunter Family Papers
Elizabeth Collier Diary
Edward Conigland Papers
Susan Cornwall Book
William Audley Couper Papers
Couper Family Papers
Nathaniel Henry Rhodes Dawson
Papers
De Rosset Family Papers
Margaret Devereux Papers
Belle Edmondson Diary
Elliott and Gonzalez Family Papers
Julia Fisher Diary
Susan Fisher Papers
Eleonore Fleming Papers
Fort Family Papers
Fries and Shaffner Family Papers
Gordon and Hackett Family Papers
William P. Graham Papers
Graves Family Papers
Meta Morris Grimball Diary
Grimball Family Papers
Elizabeth Seawell Hairston Papers
Maria Florilla Hamblen
Reminiscences
Harding and Jackson Family Papers
George Washington Finley Harper
Papers
Maria Hawes Reminiscences
Maria L. Haynworth Letter

Ernest Haywood Collection
Rachel Lyons Huestis Papers
Mary T. Hunley Diary
Myra Inman Diary
Jones Family Papers
Julia Louisa Hentz Keyes
  Manuscript
John Kimberly Papers
Thomas Butler King Papers
Edmund Kirby Smith Papers
Edward L'Engle Papers
Thomas Mulrup Logan Papers
Augustus White Long Papers
Stephen R. Mallory Papers
Harriet Ellen Moore Diary
John Hunt Morgan Papers
Larkin Newby Papers
Appleton Oaksmith Papers
Pettigrew Family Papers
Sarah Ellen Phillips Reminiscence
Phillips and Myers Family Papers
Rebecca S. Pilsbury Diary
Leonidas Polk Papers
Polk, Brown, and Ewell Family
  Papers
Polk Family Papers
James Bettys McCready Ramsey
  Papers
Edward Payson Reeve Papers
Roach and Eggleston Family Papers
Loula Ayres Rockwell Papers
Scotch Hall Papers
Benedict Joseph Semmes Papers
Louisa Campbell Sheppard
  Recollections
Cornelia Phillips Spencer Papers
Springs Family Papers
Albion Winegar Tourgeé
Susanna Gordon Waddell Diary
Sarah Lois Wadley Diary
Margaret Isabella Weber
  Reminiscences
Lewis Neale Whittle Papers

Sarah Frances Williams Letters
Anita Dwyer Withers Diary
Jonathan Worth Papers
Amanda Worthington Papers
Benjamin C. Yancey Papers
Howard Tilton Memorial Library, Tulane
  University
  William Preston Johnston Papers
  Lise Mitchell Papers
  Emily Walker Diary, Whittington
    Collection
Alderman Library, University of Virginia,
  Charlottesville
  Jane B. Beale Diary
  Blackford Family Letters
  Blackford Family Papers
  Lucy Williamson Cocke Collection
  Mrs. Hill Diary
  Robert M. T. Hunter Papers
  Irvine-Saunders Papers
  Sarah Leach Diary
  Peabody Family Papers
  Rives Family Papers
  James Peter Williams Papers
Virginia State Library, Richmond
  John Letcher Papers (Official)
  Recollections of Mrs. Archibald
    Campbell Pryor
  Recollections of Mrs. Gordon Pryor
    Rice
  Mr. and Mrs. William S. Simpson
    Papers
  William Smith Papers (Official)
  Kate S. Sperry Diary
  Mary Cary Ambler Stribling Diary
  Sue Lyon Taliaferro Diary
  Martha Varnier Diary
  Weisiger Diary
Western Reserve Historical Society,
  Cleveland
  Braxton Bragg Papers,
    William P. Palmer
    Collection

Index

Note on the Author

George C. Rable is director of American studies at Anderson University. He is a graduate of Bluffton College and has master's and doctoral degrees from Louisiana State University. Rable is the author of *But There Was No Peace: The Role of Violence in the Politics of Reconstruction.*

10/02 ① 4/01
2|06 ③ 6|03
7/16 ⑮ 4/16